The
GLORY GAME

The New Edition of the British Football Classic

HUNTER DAVIES

When the first edition of *The Glory Game* was published in 1972, it was instantly hailed as the most accurate book about the life of a football team ever published. "His accuracy is sufficiently uncanny to be embarrassing," wrote Bob Wilson in the *New Statesman*. "Brilliant, vicious, unmerciful," wrote *The Sun*.

It caused great controversy at the time. Hunter Davies was the first writer to be allowed into the inner sanctums of a top football team, and his pen and his eyes spared nothing and no one. Now the main controversies have been forgotten. Or forgiven. Instead, his work has turned into a classic, probably the best book about football ever written.

MAINSTREAM
PUBLISHING·EDINBURGH

First published 1972
Second edition 1985
Third edition 1990
This edition published 1992 by
MAINSTREAM PUBLISHING COMPANY
(EDINBURGH) LTD
7 Albany Street
Edinburgh EH1 3UG

ISBN 1 85158 376 9

Cover design by James Hutcheson
Cover illustration by Janice Nicolson

Printed by Billings & Sons, Worcester

Contents

Illustrations

The 1971-72 season began with the ceremonial unveiling of Spurs record signing, Ralph Coates. He kneels modestly, despite his £190,000 fee.
Frank Herrmann

The photographers then capture for posterity the other stars, each hoping to shine in the new season ahead. *Frank Herrmann*

Straining, training: once a week every team's performance is public and glamorous, but every weekday in private they have their bodies and souls beaten into shape. *Frank Herrmann*

Basic skills in the ball court: Barry Daines bowls, Mullery strolls, Perryman lifts a dainty foot, Chivers collects, and Joe Kinnear kicks.
Frank Herrmann

Sunshine exercises in rural Cheshunt, at Spurs own training ground: Roger Morgan, one of that season's jokers, finds time to grin while Bill Nick bends.
Frank Herrmann

Travelling: in the 1971-72 season Spurs did 7,750 miles round England and 10,238 miles round Europe. Steve Perryman, the season's Boy Wonder, manages a smile. Gilzean, behind, has seen it all. *Frank Herrmann*

Our heroes put in the travelling hours, whether it's to Manchester or Milan, by playing cards. Left to right: Mullery, Gilzean, Kinnear.
Frank Herrmann

Away the lads. Johnny Wallis and Bill Nicholson, both still at Spurs today, exhort the troops.

The classic goal, the classic photo: Chivers and Neighbour cuddle, Peters and Gilzean rejoice.

Dressing room analysis: Martin Chivers, superstar — or Bill Nicholson's cross in life?

Meanwhile Pat Jennings listens to the thoughts of Eddie Baily, assistant manager.

Young boys who have seen a lot: Steve Perryman and John Pratt, two of the 1972 players, still at Spurs today.

More post-match words of wisdom from Bill Nicholson — but is Alan Gilzean by now too knackered to hear? *Frank Herrmann*

Teachers and pupils: Bill Nicholson keeps up the advice, but even Eddie Baily, right, is tiring, while Terry Naylor starts to dress.

Still life in the dressing room: Cyril Knowles, left (now Darlington manager), Martin Chivers, Mike England (now Wales manager) and Joe Kinnear.

Frank Herrmann

Victory in our time: a fitting climax to the pains and pleasures of the 1971-72 season. Spurs won the UEFA Cup for the first time.

Carleton

Garth Crooks: elegant striker, but suffered somewhat during the season.

Professional Sport

Steve Perryman: Captain Steve, the only player still performing for Spurs from the 1971-72 team. *Professional Sport*

Chris Hughton: overlapping full-back but carrying worries in an unsettled season.

Two present day England stars, Gary Stevens and Glenn Hoddle.

Tony Galvin: Spurs star with the BA in Russian Studies, a sign of the social and educational changes in football in the last decade. *Kicksports Foto*

Some emotions never change: Mark Falco, Clive Allen, Graham Roberts rejoice. *Professional Sport*

Clive Allen: cost £700,000, the present day most expensive Spurs player.

Professional Sport

John Chiedozie: one of four black players, now first team regulars. In 1972 there were none. *Professional Sport*

Ray Clemence: from Liverpool to Spurs, but still at the top.

Professional Sport

Glenn Hoddle: the most naturally talented player ever to grace the Spurs team . . . ?

Mike Hazard: midfield master, but so often in the shadow of the Blessed Hoddle. *Professional Sport*

Ossie Ardiles: Spurs import from Argentina — who DID go to Wembley.

Professional Sport

Mr O. Ardiles: law student, *Times* reader, chess player. Also plays a bit of football.

Cheers: salutes to each other from Hoddle, Falco and Perryman.

Professional Sport

Paul Miller: behind that dour, uncompromising exterior, today's dressing room joker. *Professional Sport*

Graham Roberts: iron man with greying hair, one of nine present Spurs players with England experience. *Professional Sport*

Introduction to the 1992 Edition

This is now getting out of hand. Yet another introduction to yet another edition, the fourth in all, how can anyone work out what is going on, where to start, is it just a book of introductions or a real book, and who are these players anyway. No football fan under the age of 25 can possibly have seen them playing, let alone recognise most of their names. So, sorry about that, I mean this, the latest introduction.

But, the publisher has insisted. The book has sold out yet again. A new edition means a new introduction. The public will expect it. Get cracking, Hunt.

It's 20 years since the book first appeared. Some of the changes in football during that time, and at Spurs, are recorded in the earlier introductions, which you will come to in a moment, unless you skip and go straight to the book itself. Very wise.

However, now that I am being forced to sit and think about the changes in the last two years, since the previous edition, I have to admit they have been rather dramatic. In fact, whole books are now being written about one particular recent interlude in the history of Tottenham Hotspur FC. For almost a year, the Spurs Saga was hardly off the front pages, the city pages and, of course, the back page. It all began one day in the autumn of 1990 with the news that Spurs was £18 million in debt and that the club might very soon go bankrupt. Gosh. Golly.

We learned that the Irving Scholar regime, after nine years, was about to collapse in much the same way as the

Sidney Wale era collapsed — and by a neat irony, each went out with the team winning the FA Cup. Back in 1981, the building of the West Stand had plunged the club into debt. In 1991, it was the new East Stand, and also the failure of their diversification into leisurewear and merchandising, which had caused such problems. (I moaned about this in my 1990 introduction, without knowing the real story.)

For a while, one of the saviours appeared to be Robert Maxwell — remember him? — who was on the point of taking control, for very little money, and probably not his own. Where would Spurs be now if that deal had come to pass? Sold to pay off his debts? That episode ended in tears and resignations; the Stock Exchange suspended dealings in Spurs shares. After various other saviour figures had been touted, the final solution was partly internal — Terry Venables, the manager, backed by Alan Sugar, the million-aire behind the Amstrad computer business, mounted their own successful bid. It was a complicated financial story, but one that is bound to happen again as other football clubs get themselves into similar problems.

From a purely football point of view, it was interesting to see an ex-footballer landing at the top of the pile. Terry Venables became Chief Executive and a director, a most unusual position for a mere ex-player. Will we see more of them in the future? It is now perfectly possible for a star player, who keeps fit and in form for at least ten years, and is also sensible with his money, to end up as a millionaire. I was talking recently to John Fashanu, the Wimbledon player, who is already a successful businessman. His ambition is not to be the first black manager, which is what many people predict for him, but to be the first player, black or white, to buy his own football club. Owning it and running it.

At Spurs, it is to be hoped we are in for a period of financial and board-room stability. On the pitch, who knows? As I write, our two star players, Gascoigne and Lineker, are due to leave — one to Italy, and possibly greater glory, or greater dramas, and the other to retirement, sorry, to Japan. The reign of Peter Shreeves, in his second spell as manager, looks none too secure. The present team seems only capa-ble of playing well against Arsenal or in Cup matches, not in the mundane work of the League. Will the Premier League make any difference to anything or anybody? We shall see. Meanwhile, something interesting has been happening to the players I wrote about all those years ago, the ones you are about to meet. If you skip for a moment to the appendices at the end, Appendix 11, page 321, you will see that I quizzed them about the possibility of staying in football. Out of 18 in the first-team pool that year, 11 said things like, 'Not bloody likely, I've seen Bill Nicholson [their manager] after a game, and I couldn't stand it, I'd end up in a loony bin.' Six said they'd like to coach, either amateurs or professionals, but that was all. Only one actively contemplated being a manager. That was Martin Peters. 'I love the game so much,' he said.

After training, most players, then and now, talk about cars, girls, clothes, holidays, money, clubs. Martin would watch the apprentices and point out things I'd missed, predict who would make it, and he was always right. He did become a manager, but alas not for long. Too soft, too remote, too cerebral? There is a theory that only failed or flawed players make it in management. If you have known only success as a player, it is hard to cope with failure as a manager. Martin Peters is now working in insurance.

But the strange thing is — eight of that group went on to become managers, despite what they said at the time. Alan Mullery, captain that year, seemed obvious management material, though at the time he denied it. He was the one fearing he'd end up in a loony bin. For a while, he did well as a manager, at Brighton and Fulham. Mike England, known as 'Brains' behind his back because they all thought he was slow, became a good manager of the Welsh national team. Still in management, at this moment, are Steve Perryman at Watford, Phil Holder at Brentford and Joe Kinnear at Wimbledon. Perhaps the most successful of all is Graeme Souness of Liverpool, a Spurs reserve at the time, though he did make the book. The eighth manager is the late and much lamented Cyril Knowles, who died in August 1991, aged 47, the first fatality amongst the players who appeared in *The Glory Game*.

On a personal note, I have spent my own time, these last

20 years, writing 20 or so books on completely different topics, from Wordsworth to Columbus, from travel to children's books. Now I have written my first novel about football, *Striker*. I have tried to keep it real, in that my hero plays for real teams, against real players, none of that Melchester Rovers stuff. Readers of this book might see similarities with life in ye olden tymes at a certain North London club. But don't tell anyone.

Hunter Davies
Loweswater, March 1992

Introduction to the 1990 Edition

WELCOME to the third edition of this book. And the third set of introductory words. If you feel confused already, don't worry. The book itself is very simple: it records the year in the life of an English First Division football club during the season 1971–72. Go straight to it if you like. Or pause a while and ponder.

What a long time ago that was. Almost another country, where they did things differently, at least on the outside. The clothes, the money, the characters have all changed. But inside any professional club I suspect that things are very much the same. The tensions, the terrors, the tedium of training, the dramas of the dressing-room, the problems of motivation, the clashing of personalities, are all very similar. That must be the reason this book continues to sell long after the players have retired.

You don't have to know those 1972 names, or even be a follower of Spurs today, to pick up the smell of the liniment, the roar of the crowd, the abuse of the coaches, and feel part of that special soccer club atmosphere I tried to capture all those years ago.

I have continued to follow Spurs every season since this book first came out. They are *my* team. Always will be. So it goes. That's the nature of the beast which lurks inside every football fan. And yet, and yet. A strange and rather sad thing happened to me during the season that I'm now looking back upon. I grew to hate them.

Many of the reasons were fairly trivial. I took a scunner to the Spurs programme: all those glossy photographs, the bland, uncritical prose and the appalling amount of space devoted to advertisements for their mail order sportswear – sometimes there were as many as 20 pages aimed at getting parents to buy the ever changing kit for their offspring. The whole accent on merchandising and sponsorship began to infuriate me. It seemed we were no longer a football club, just another branch of the leisure industry in which what mattered most were the interests of the wealthiest supporters and the most strident sponsors. (In the end I discovered, as a shareholder, that the sportswear side was not doing very good business anyway.)

I grew to hate the press box at White Hart lane. It is so low down you can hardly see the other half of the pitch. They obviously preferred to sell off the better, higher positions. The new board, when it arrived, did seem to have many good ideas, compared with the old-fashioned, totally out-of-date previous directors (i.e. the ones in this book) but I began to dislike them all, and their values. I got furious when the ticket office mucked up my tickets and I felt angry every time I saw the word 'Holsten' on the chests of the people I wanted to be my heroes.

If the team had been doing brilliantly, of course, none of these minor irritations would have mattered. We can accept almost anything if our lads are doing well. Look at the squalor and discomfort all football fans, everywhere, have put up with for decades, just for the privilege of following their teams.

I started going to Arsenal, not instead of Spurs, but on the Saturdays that Spurs were away. I went hoping to see them getting stuffed, of course, but I felt guilty all the time,just from the act of turning up at Highbury and paying my money. Then I thought, why not? Why should I not chop and change my loyalties? Who said you have to be totally blind to be a football fan? People change nationalities, religions, wives. Why not their football team? Why should we make ourselves suffer?

There were several Spurs games in mid-season when I wondered, what am I doing? Why am I here? I thought many a time of that devoted supporter Morris Keston (whom you will meet later in this book). He never watched the last 15 minutes of any Spurs game, even in the real glory days. It was all too unbearable. When they were winning, he knew it might well end in tears. His love for Spurs was agony.

The team seemed to fall apart when Chris Waddle left. I couldn't understand why on earth they let him go, our only true star. I had this out on a radio programme with the Spurs chairman who maintained that once an offer comes in for a star player, they can't keep him. A player becomes unsettled. He wants to go. All the same, I would have thought a money-mad, money-bags club like Spurs could have found ways to keep their biggest star.

Waddle had taken Hoddle's place in my affections, and was the only player I went early for, just to watch him knocking up before the match. In theory, we were left with two other stars, Lineker and Gascoigne. At first I thought Lineker's days were over, his speed gone, his determination blunted. As for Gazza, I hated the way the tabloids had turned him into a character, a cheeky chappie. And on the pitch I was not convinced. I screamed when he started messing around in his own half and lost the ball. I despised the way he dived in recklessly at the nearest opponent, after he himself had made some stupid mistake. He argued with the ref and was petty and childish. A talented player, I thought, but not good enough. He unbalanced the team if anything, subconsciously browbeating other players by his own innate and amazing confidence, making them give him the ball when often there was no need to.

The rest of the team seemed decidedly Second Division. And that was where they appeared to be heading in the first part of the 1989/90 season, despite the fact that Terry Venables had spent over £8 million assembling them. I felt the crowd becoming depressed and angry. Gates were low – almost half the Arsenal average at one time. There was a great resentment from many hard-core, loyal fans, still annoyed by the changes to the standing area known as the 'Shelf'. The arrival of a very good fanzine, *The Spur*, which regularly attacked Venables and mocked Paul Stewart, was a sign that the worms were turning, that many supporters felt like me: fed up, cheesed off, sick as an old cockerel.

Then something rather unexpected happened. The team hit a good run, just as it had done towards the end of the previous season. We ended up third in the League. Miles behind Liverpool and Aston Villa, but we were ahead of Arsenal if only just. What rapture. That did make up somewhat for a long, mainly annoying, mainly depressing season.

However, if I consider what happened carefully, then I know that the late, good run was against teams who didn't really care, whose position was in no danger. Lineker did get back to top form, for which many thanks, but deep down I finished the season still not convinced of Gazza's brilliance. His best games were against the poorest teams. I sensed Bobby Robson felt the same, but he did pick him for the World Cup in Italy. He improved all the time and turned out to be one of England's successes. Naturally, we were all shouting for him. He went as a Spurs player. Come on you Lillywhite.

That is the point. There is no changing of colours or favours. Once a Spurs fan, always a Spurs fan. Managers and players can move around, go to the highest bidder, but a supporter takes on a team for life. Once the love affair has begun, there is no going back. The surprise for me this season was the discovery that in this love affair, as in all love affairs, hatred can still creep in.

The club itself, as all clubs do, hates any hatred, can't stand any criticism, and when I made some of these observations out loud (in a weekly football column I was doing in *The Independent*) they got very upset and accused me of being destructive and disloyal. I maintain that being part of a family, which is what fans become when they take on a team, you are allowed to criticise our lads, while still cheering them on.

I know, without knowing it, that nothing I can say or the most abusive supporter shouting from the terraces can compare with the hatred a manager must feel when things are not going well. He knows the worst long before we do. He realises the mistakes he has made, the dummies he has bought. He sees loss of form weeks before we do, knows about injuries being hidden, weaknesses being carried. He hears about domestic daftness, drink problems, driving problems which players are striving to keep secret. He has to deal with the ones who can't be told, the ones too thick to learn, the ones too clever for their own good. He knows the cowards and the cheats.

I also know how the players suffer. They feel the agony and experience the pain far more than we do – and they have to live it, seven days a week. We can go home at five o'clock on a Saturday, kick the telly, switch on the wife, settle down with a Holsten Pils and feel sick. That gets it over with, for another week. The players, poor petals, cannot escape.

Should we have more pity on them? Do they not bleed when we attack them? Yes, but they chose to be up there.

No one forced them. And they do get well rewarded. In the last five years, wages and commercial benefits have increased enormously and there is now no reason why any First Division regular, who has had a normal span at the top, need afterwards ever work again purely for the money. He just has to be wise with his earnings and opportunities.

They should be prepared to be shot at, shat on, by fans who don't quite understand what is going wrong and why, by reporters who know only part of the story and by managers who know too much and appear at times nasty, brutish and short-memoried.

All the same, the players are human. They are not primarily in it for the money, whatever we might think when they float off to foreign parts. They do try hard, train hard and truly cannot understand loss of form, loss of confidence, or loss of loyalty from people they thought would always love them, or of the club they currently play for. This book is an attempt to take you into their world, to give an understanding of the pains and pleasures of being a professional footballer.

Hunter Davies
London, NW5
June 1990

Introduction to 1985 Edition

One of the disappointments which authors these days have to be prepared for, at least those who produce books regularly, is that very often their books are quickly remaindered. You might have struggled for two years or more on a project then the rotten publisher, sometimes after only six months in the bookshops, decides it's a flop and that he can't afford the warehouse space any more. The whole lot gets sold off to the bookseller's equivalent of the knacker's yard. So it goes. I almost cried a few years ago when a biography I'd done of George Stephenson, father of railways, was remaindered.

Yet now and again, if you keep at it, don't let the beggars get you down, something you have done in the past, long sold out, almost forgotten, acquires a new lease of life. The authorised biography of The Beatles, which I did in 1968, has new life breathed into it every few years and updated editions get reprinted, all over the world, but then you might expect that, with the pulling power which the Beatles have these days.

But who would have thought that a book about a North London football team, a subject only of obvious interest to those who happen to live in that particular area of North London, one that was written a long time ago, containing players who have disappeared, about conditions and wages and styles which are no longer the same, even about a club which has drastically changed, who would have expected such a book to be reprinted thirteen years after it first came out? Well here it is, folks. Keep it safe and clean. You never know. It could become valuable. The first edition of 1972 is already a collector's item.

I have been constantly asked for it over the years. Not just by local Spurs fans, but by bookshops, new and second hand, all over the world. I only have one copy of the original left. And that is very filthy because my son Jake, now aged eighteen, used to read and re-read it in bed every night. The whole book is full of very complicated red crosses and ticks. He gave each section and each player a star rating, then he'd change his mind, and his ratings systems.

I suppose the most correspondence I have had concerns the forty or so pages of Appendices I put at the end of the book, all about the players' football details, life styles and opinions. I'm a sucker for any sort of list, and I always bung in at the end of a book all the stuff in note form I haven't been able to work into the body of the book. I realised anyway that as I had such intimate access to a group of eighteen or so sportsmen, at the height of their career, I should take the opportunity to ask them all the cheeky questions I'd always wanted to ask. Getting each of them at home, on their own, not being ridiculed by their team mates, made it fairly easy to put personal questions, the sort an outsider would never dare ask otherwise.

I did ask an academic friend, Dr John Carrier of LSE, to help me phrase the questions, as he said I owed it to future research to get the thing done properly. At the time, I rather scoffed. But over the years, I should think not a month has gone by without some student somewhere writing to tell me that he or she is using my material in their own research thesis. What normally happens is that they put my findings against a present day group of sportsmen, not necessarily footballers, not necessarily in Britain. You can of course get degrees in sport these days, at various colleges and universities. Nice to think I've helped a few PhD's along the way.

I've also had of course the ordinary fan letters. Not long ago, I got a letter from Bryan Robson, the Manchester United and England captain, who was still a schoolboy when the book first came out. 'A friend of mine has told me your book *The Glory Game* is the best of its kind yet written. If at all possible, could you please let me have a copy?' Thanks, Bryan. But I wasn't able to help him. I just couldn't find a copy. Morris Keston, that ardent Spurs supporter who was interviewed in the book (see Chapter 18) has frequently wanted more copies to give as presents to his friends. Even he, with all his connections, has failed to get any. (Mr Keston, by the way, is now a real member of the Spurs family, despite being rather cold shouldered by the previous Spurs directors. His daughter is married to Paul Miller.)

All the same, vanity apart, and despite all this boasting, I never thought any publisher would ever want to bring it back into print. Then out of the blue this terribly good firm in Edinburgh, yes Edinburgh in Scotland, said they would like to reprint it, just as it was, but with a new introduction and some up to date details about the present first team. Why? Well, Cyril Connolly once said that any book which is reprinted over ten years after publication has become a classic. So I suppose this book must, in its modest little way, be considered some sort of classic. Of its kind.

All I was trying to do, back in 1972, was tell the story of an English football team, during the season 1971-72. We did hope at the time to suggest it was really about *any* first-class football team, in any city, even any country, but I'm not sure how well that message got across. I don't expect many Arsenal fans bought it, but then what do they read?

It sold out fairly quickly in its original hardback edition, and even reprinted, but Weidenfeld and Nicolson, the original publisher, in their wisdom, did not think it was worth reprinting again the next year. Who was interested they said, in a book about *last* season? The paperback edition, from Sphere, also sold out. The most surprising aspect of all was that we sold *foreign* editions. Now this is very unusual with such a book. It was published in Norway, as *Kong Football* and in Denmark as *Kong Fodbold*. The Scandinavian interest can be explained as they take our *Match of the Day* live, though they do have their own players and teams to follow. It was even published in the United States, by St Martin's Press, which was the biggest surprise of all, considering at the time that soccer was not being played much in America, and the names of the Spurs players were completely unknown across the Atlantic.

It was also serialised by two London newspapers, at the same time, which was a great help, *The Sunday Times* and *The People*. And that was where my problems began. It ended with me getting a threatening letter from a solicitor, the only one

I've had in thirty books, from no less a figure than Lord Goodman, our leading legal light of the day, at least it was from his firm, Goodman Derrick. The Spurs board, so the letter said, wanted the book withdrawn while changes were made.

During the first few months of doing the book, living with the team, both at the training ground and in the dressing room, I had always expected something to go wrong. This was a bit more than I had bargained for.

It all began when I approached the club, as a book writer not a sports journalist, saying I wanted to observe them over a season. I had been a Spurs fan ever since 1960 when I'd arrived in London, so naturally I wanted to devote my time to a team I had always enjoyed watching. But any other First Division team would have done. The experts I spoke to, sports writers like Brian Glanville, warned me off Spurs. Their board was known as being very stuffy and unfriendly and Bill Nicholson, the manager, could also be stiff and cool. I wouldn't be allowed in. No football reporter in Britain, then or now, is ever given entry to the dressing rooms.

Looking back, I'm not sure how I did it. I suppose *not* being a football correspondent was a help. They didn't know my name and therefore had nothing against me. I wrote to the chairman, the manager, the captain, explaining in detail what I had in mind. I then had various chats with them, promising that each person in the book would read the bits about themselves, and the manager and the chairman could read the whole lot before publication and correct any factual mistakes. I also agreed to share the profits, 50-50, with the first team pool. (This in the end drove my agent nearly demented. As small payments dribbled in, he had to divide them nineteen ways. I think he was quite pleased in the end when the book went out of print.)

Nobody at the club ever actually said no, I couldn't do the book, but at no time did I have a contract with any official. That was why I feared, for so long, that if my face did not fit, I would be straight out and all my work would have been wasted. I was willing to accept that. I was doing the book for my personal interest, because I wanted to get inside a dressing room, to see what life was really like at a professional club.

Very often I never had the proper tickets, and all football clubs are obsessed by passes and tickets, but after a few weeks I managed to walk around as if I was part of the club. Travelling away, both here and abroad, was the easiest, because I was presumed to be a reserve player. All the players were completely helpful and honest. I went to all of their homes, got invited to their parties, heard their worst fears, but I hope did not betray any real confidences. There was one senior player they all disliked behind his back, but he never knew this, so I felt it was unfair to point it up, though there are clues. Naturally, I kept references to girls in hotels to the minimum.

The most exciting part of all was being in the dressing room before and after a match. I always tried to hide, to get into a corner, because I felt sure that one day the manager, in some rage with the team, would suddenly catch sight of me out of the corner of his eye, and I would be out. The scene I remember most was in Nantes (Chapter 11) when Bill for once had a proper row with Chivers, the one which finished, by chance, with the broken glass on the floor. I knew then he was looking for someone to vent his rage on, but I managed to escape.

It was interesting to read Bill Nicholson's own book *Glory Glory*, published many years later (by Macmillan, 1984) in which he says that he was upset that I had been allowed 'to become virtually one of the players'. With hindsight, he would not have allowed it. After that Nantes match, so he writes, he found himself keeping quiet when he wanted to say a lot of things, just because I was there. 'Davies needed that sort of freedom to enable him to write such a revealing book. People in the game and our supporters enjoyed the book . . . but there were occasions when I deliberately held back because of his presence.'

I apologise, Bill, if I did inhibit you. But of course the real basis of his problems at that time, which he honestly admits in his very interesting book, was Chivers. I could see it in Bill's eyes all the time, yet he never let his real emotions come out, even when I wasn't there. (And though I got into the dressing rooms, he did bar me from team talks, in which players told me he was equally tight-lipped.) He could never find a way to motivate Chivers, a task beyond most managers, and would be driven into silent rages when Chivers, for all his gifts, would disappear completely in vital games.

At the training ground, however, Bill was always very helpful, making me a welcome visitor, allowing me to take part in the pre-season training, joining in all the exercises, wearing the normal strip, getting in the bath with them afterwards. That was a marvellous beginning to my season and gave me excellent material for the first chapter of the book.

When the book came out, several football reporters on the popular papers tried to stir things up by inferring I had been cruel to the players, making them out to be morons. This is untrue, as I hope you will see, though I did finish the season feeling rather sorry for modern footballers, their lives so regulated by those background coaches, missing out on so much of the normal growing up years, continually under tension, both physical and mental, and most of all, getting such little pleasure out of actually playing football.

The popular press also got Eddie Baily, the assistant manager, to say he was upset. If I did upset him, then I do regret it. There is this conspiracy in football that all books about the game, especially about individual clubs, must be utterly anodine, with no flesh and blood people, no real conversations or feelings, no emotions, just the usual ghosted banalities or dry statistics, and certainly no bad language. In the book, Eddie does shout and swear quite a bit, but then he's a coach. That's what coaches do. And in far stronger terms than anything I reported.

I like to think that it did give a glimpse of the real world of football. Not the whole truth, of course, but there were no lies, no public relations gloss or supporters club genuflections. The strangest thing of all is that no one has done a similar book since. Perhaps I ruined the pitch for everyone else. The word got round in football that I had done a hatchet job, been nasty about them, revealed things which they preferred to keep secret, so perhaps other clubs have been determined to keep nosey writers out of their dressing rooms. Whatever the reason, a similar book, with similar access, has not appeared.

The legal row, of course, gave people in football the idea that I had indeed been horrid. What caused the Spurs directors to instruct a solicitor was the way *The People* did their serialisation of the book. I'm not blaming them. They naturally gutted it very cleverly, stringing all the juiciest bits together. I honestly didn't think there were any, and still don't, but I suppose a superficial reader could see lots of references to, say, Gilzean having lots of empty bottles in front of him, and be led into thinking that the book must be full of footballers boozing. Tut tut. Footballers drinking? What an allegation.

I never got to the bottom of what happened, but apparently certain directors, who had not read the book, wanted it withdrawn while they went through and vetted it, taking out any disgusting stuff about drinks and girls. (They don't exist, of course, so if you're looking for that in the book, hard cheese.)

As I agreed with the players, they read the bits about themselves. Bill was given the whole manuscript, though I doubt if he ever read it properly. But I had proof that the chairman indeed read every word because he sent it back, with his handwritten comments on a lot of pages. I told the lawyers all this, and sent them evidence, and that was the end of the matter. I never heard another word.

In the chairman's defence, I'm sure he read the bits *not* about himself rather quickly, and probably did not recognise them when he saw them reproduced in *The People*. It is now all rather trivial, a very small storm in a half-time tea cup. But I suppose it did help to give the impression that the book might be hot stuff. Reading it now, such allegations are laughable. When you think what modern pop stars reveal about themselves in the public prints, and even many footballers, then this book reads like Enid Blyton.

Although I've been trying to persuade you that it is now a classic, it is in so many ways a period piece. In the first chapter, there are references to 'flairs', meaning flaired trousers. In 1971, the first team smoothies thought they were bang in fashion with their flairs, long-collared shirts and kipper ties, and felt rather superior to Ralph Coates, arriving fresh from the North in his old-fashioned tight trousers. And of course the references to money and house prices are now completely out of date.

The sort of World War Two language and metaphors which Eddie Baily used to exhort his troops, urging them over the top, were still typical of the times. Both he and Bill had been in the Army, had seen men act like men, not like these long-haired fairies. As with so many managers and coaches of the day, they were from another world, another generation. Their hatred of long hair was real. It did drive them mad, hence that time when Bill made the whole youth team have a new photograph taken, with shorter hair this time. Imagine that happening today.

The gulf between such managers and their players was enormous. They had grown up in the age of a maximum £20 wage, which meant that in their playing days footballers had earned little, with no nightclub life, no commercialisation, no TV, no agents, no groupies chasing them. People like Nicholson, and Bill Shankly, in many ways despised their players for being soft and cosseted. I once met a famous Liverpool player who said that when he had a broken leg, Shankly accused him of doing it deliberately. Oh, they were hard men, those old 1960s managers.

There are still hard men, like Brian Clough, Laurie McMenemy and Jock Wallace, who believe footballers have to be treated like children, disciplined and kept in their place, but they are dying out. The modern manager, someone like Terry Venables, has much more in common with the modern footballer. He too got a big wage as a player, and all the perks, and in turn he has a big wage as a manager. That is one of the main changes in the last ten years, the rise of the Manager as Star. Successful ones are courted by the media, have their own columns, dress like dandies with jewellery and long hair — as long as they can still get it to grow — and rival clubs, at home and abroad, offer them fortunes, enough to set them up for life, if it is thought they can save their team. I don't know what Bill Nicholson earned at Spurs, but I bet it was ridiculous. Kevin Keegan's gardener or Ron Atkinson's hairdresser probably made more.

The other big change, in the last ten years, is the arrival of black footballers. Spurs had none, at any level, when I did the book. Behind the scenes, there was clear antipathy and prejudice, though that again was conditioning, people brought up in a certain way at a certain time. That mentality has gone. As I write, Spurs often have four black players in the first team, with more coming through. Most English clubs (but not Scottish) have a similar proportion. Their arrival and ascendance would have been interesting to observe.

Spurs now have a university graduate, Tony Galvin, which would also have been fascinating. The huge wages in football, with the top players able to make themselves financially secure, will probably mean that more university and middle-class people will enter the profession. Even Arsenal have now a public schoolboy, Stewart Robson, in the first team.

There must be some very interesting social changes going on in football, in the way modern footballers lead their lives and in where they have come from, now that we have so many races and classes and nationalities represented. I often wonder how they view the future, once it becomes clear to the top ones that they need never work again. How does it affect their families and children? What part do the agents play behind the scenes? And apart from K. Keegan, how many have in fact become millionaires?

I leave all that to some future author, and hope he or she manages to talk some club into giving cooperation, but in the meantime I have kept in touch from a distance with Spurs, watching them from the terraces, keeping in touch with those players who remained from that 1972 team.

The arrival of the Argentinians has been the most dramatic Spurs story in the last thirteen years. I went to see Osvaldo Ardiles and Ricardo Villa play their first game for Spurs, up at Nottingham on August 19, 1978, reporting the match for *The Sunday Times*. We'd had a dreary and very unglamorous few years, we Spurs supporters, watching the team drop to the Second Division, oh ignominy, and even worse, having to suffer Arsenal's success, but Keith Burkinshaw had pulled a master stroke, spiriting away two Argentine World Cup players, though no one then knew how well they would do. On that occasion, Villa looked the likelier to succeed, as the Forest players found it almost impossible to knock him off the ball, but Ossie seemed a bit more frail and perhaps not up to our rough English styles. (It ended 1-1.)

At Cheshunt, the next day, almost 10,000 turned up at an open day, just to watch the new Argentinians go through a training session. That sort of thing happens in Italy and South

America, when a new signing arrives, but was unheard of in Britain. It heralded in the age of the foreign imports. Even old-fashioned, traditional British managers decided it was time to start scouting abroad, instead of the lower reaches of the Scottish divisions.

In the end, Ossie proved to be the better buy, and he has had some outstanding seasons, though at present I fear his injuries and age mean we have probably seen the best of him. Villa went home more quickly, and was never an automatic first team choice, yet he has left behind an image which will remain with all British football supporters, at least those who have been alive in the last four years and remember the Cup Final of 1981, the Centenary Final, in which Villa dribbled, as if in slow motion, as if he was never going to get there, right through a crowded penalty area and scored his extraordinary goal. I should think that image will be re-shown on television as long as we have television and as long as there is football.

The other two figures in these intervening years who captured the imagination of all Spurs fans have been Steve Archibald and Glenn Hoddle. Archibald took a while to get established when he arrived in 1980, from Aberdeen, and seemed hardly to concentrate in some matches, yet the crowd took to him from the beginning. The lads on the terraces, reviled though they are by some authorities, very often do get it right. It was Arch-ee-bald, Arch-ee-bald, Arch-ee-bald, from the first match, even when he didn't score, even when Crooks or someone else had played a better game. It was his speed and mental quickness that was exciting, rather than being flash on the ball, a bit like Gilzean in that respect, another Scot loved by the crowd.

It was a shame he fell out with the manager, a clash of personalities as much as anything else, which led in the end to his move to Barcelona, where he quickly became Spain's leading scorer, and I suspect it was part of the reason why Burkinshaw felt in the end he had had enough of Spurs.

As for Hoddle, he has probably infuriated Spurs managers even more than Chivers ever did. Of all the Spurs players I have watched, including the Double Team, he is the single most gifted player. Whether he has fulfilled his promise, which those Double Team players certainly did, is a matter for argument.

In the end, managers want fulfilment and performance, or their jobs are in jeopardy. On the terraces, I like to think that we ordinary supporters also hope for flair and entertainment. Every time, in the last ten years, when I have known that Hoddle was *definitely* going to play, which alas was far from ever certain, I arrived half an hour earlier than usual, just to see him in the knock-up. I'd pay to watch him put on his boots.

So why hasn't he fulfilled his promise? Ah, if we could explain that, we would all be managers. I used to think it was lack of physical strength. Then not enough mental strength. He has improved in both capacities, but still he is rarely consistent, seldom able to dominate the way he should. Perhaps he is over-gifted, born with too much silver on his spoon. Players like Bryan Robson and Kevin Keegan always knew their weaknesses and realised very quickly that they would have to work hard in life to get to the top. So they did.

The only person left from the 1971-72 Spurs team, still alive and well and playing for Spurs, is Steve Perryman, the captain. John Pratt is still with Spurs, but on the coaching side, as assistant first team coach. Pat Jennings, in 1984-85, was still playing in the First Division, but with Arsenal, another North London club, though he too was about to retire.

Graeme Souness, who was in the original book as a young reserve player, is still a top player, playing with Sampdoria in Italy. Looking back I suppose Souness turned out to be the most *successful* of all those players mentioned in *The Glory Game*. Martin Peters' best years were behind him, for West Ham and England's World Cup team, whereas Graeme's best years were yet to come.

In many ways, Steve Perryman's career has been the most remarkable. He was such an established player for Spurs, even in 1971, despite his tender years, taken for granted as a vital member, sensible and dependable. Now, fourteen years later, he is even wiser and more sensible. He played his 600th first team League game for Spurs in 1984, which means he has now had more games for Spurs than any other player in their history.

He was unmarried, in 1972, but today he has his own family, the perfect footballer's unit, a girl and boy. Loren who is ten and Glenn, named after guess who, is seven. His single sports shop has blossomed into a veritable chain and he now has four. — Three are in London and one, recently opened, is in another town. Any guesses? It's a question I ask all football supporters — and no one so far has guessed correctly. The answer is Bergen.

'I now go to Norway a lot to look after the shop and people always tell me the same thing — that they've read *The Glory Game*. You must have had good sales in Scandinavia . . .'

Over the fourteen years since the book was written, which in Steve's case means looking back at almost his whole career, he thinks the tensions for every player are just as bad as they were, if not worse. Being near the top of the League, as they were in early 1985, made little difference.

'We had two defeats on the run early in the season, against Sunderland and Sheffield Wednesday, and before our next match a reporter from a national paper rang me and said "Is it a crisis, Steve?" I couldn't believe it. We went out and beat QPR 5-0 and went top of the league. Yet only 90 minutes earlier, people were talking about a "crisis".

'What happens now in football is that a lot of people try to take away your enjoyment. It is so serious, when you play for money. You have to put up with so much criticism from the crowd and the media.

'Personally, I think I enjoy it more than I did in 1972. I make the best of it now. I've learned my lessons. I can listen to criticism, work it out in my mind what to do for the best, then try to get on with it. When I was eighteen, and I got some stick, it used to slaughter me.

'I was the youngest in those days and the others would pull me along. Now I have to pull other people along.'

The changes at his own club have been enormous, perhaps more than at any other British club in the last decade, thanks firstly to the building of the new stand, then the arrival of a new board with completely new ideas, turning Spurs into a public company with a large staff, a vast income and expenditure, and a passion for all the latest ideas in commercialisation, electronics, sponsorship and management methods. By comparison, the 1972 club and the directors were practically Victorian.

In February, 1982, the new West Stand was opened, the

most modern in Europe, at a cost of £5½ million. It has 5,700 seats, banqueting rooms, conference halls, lounges, new offices, but is perhaps best known for its 72 executive boxes. The idea of having specially enclosed, luxury boxes, where the toffs can watch in comfort, was not new. Several other British clubs have introduced them in the previous ten years, notably Manchester United, Coventry, Nottingham Forest, Aston Villa, West Brom, QPR and even comparatively humble clubs like Fulham and Orient. But Spurs, in building a brand new, super modern stadium, had equipped their boxes with everything a lazy supporter might possibly wish — armchairs, fridge, kitchen, cocktail cabinet, personal uniformed hostesses and a TV on which you can either watch the racing, if the football outside is too boring, or see the best bits from the current match. Spurs installed their own video cameras and now film every match, but only for the benefit of those in the executive boxes. At half-time, should they so wish, they can watch the goals all over again.

The price in 1982, for one of these boxes, was £30,000. Gulp, gulp. You do get a box big enough to hold eight people, and it is yours for three years. All were sold within a year. I noticed, when I was prying round one day, that at least half are owned by companies, such as Barclays, Beechams, Mecca, Tesco, National Giro, who presumably use their box to treat themselves or favoured customers.

I have a friend who has one, privately owned, and I have been invited into his box several times. It is terribly comfortable, like sitting in a suite at the Hilton. You do feel spoiled and cosseted. It is especially nice to be able to arrive at a football stadium in a civilised manner, with carpets on the floor, soft furnishings, warmth, clean lavatories, proper refreshments available. In an ideal world, all supporters should have most of these things. Goodness knows, we do deserve it, when you think of the squalor we have put up with for decades.

Yet I have stopped accepting my friend's invitation. I grew to dislike watching through that thick glass window, being stuck in a goldfish bowl, cut off from all the atmosphere. There is a knob you can turn, so you can hear all the shouting and roars outside, piped into your little hermetically sealed space, but it is not the same as the real thing. I'm now back to the cold and starkness of the neolithic North Stand, where I take my twelve-year-old daughter, and my eighteen-year-old son if he's kind to me, and we put up with the graffiti and the horrible lavatories and the inedible food and the enormous queues for everything.

I like *looking* at the new stand and admire its design. I approve of the concept, its facilities and its ambitions, I even agree with the huge expense, which is what brought about the second dramatic change in Spurs since I wrote the original book.

As with several other clubs, such as Chelsea, who catapulted themselves into the twentieth century with a brave new stand, Spurs took on debts and bank charges which their income could simply not accommodate. Less than a year after the new stand was opened, by Sir Stanley Rous, we all woke up one day, all we Spurs supporters, to find that 'our' club had been bought over by a group of young, thrusting, businessmen, mostly based in the property fields, with names we didn't recognise. One of them, at the time, did not even live in London but was based in Europe.

Their arrival was long overdue. Even in 1971, I could see that the old gang, most of whom had inherited their shares, were not exactly thrusting or dynamic, living in another age, trying their level best to preserve the image of the old Spurs and keep the vulgar commerical world at bay as long as possible.

The new directors immediately set about reconstituting the board to increase the equity base of the club, and thereby reduce its dependence on bank borrowings, promising not just to turn Spurs into a modern football club, but into a public company, securely based in the leisure and entertainments industry. With this in mind, 3,800,000 ordinary 25p shares in Tottenham Hotspur PLC were offered at 100p a share. I bought 100, for £100, the minimum you were allowed to buy, out of loyalty and also out of faith in the new gang.

I have my share certificate on my bathroom wall, along with my 1920s Spurs team photographs, my 1930s programmes, my photographs of the winning Double Team, a drawing by Wally Fawkes of Danny Blanchflower, my signed letter from Jimmy Greaves, which says "Thank God I wasn't at Spurs when you were there", team autographs from the 1950s and 1960s, plus all the tickets and memorabilia from the year I travelled with them, 1971-72. One of these days I might charge an entrance fee to my bathroom.

The present chairman is Irving Scholar, aged only thirty-seven, a property developer who was living in Monaco at the time of the takeover. According to the latest figures, he owns 29% of the shares of the new company. Paul Bobroff, aged thirty-four, also from the property world, owns 15%. They are the two major shareholders.

Back in 1972, the club's annual income from all sources came to £500,000. In 1979 it was £1,413,000. In 1985 it had jumped to almost £5 million. The new executive boxes, on their own, bring in over £500,000 a year. Around £1 million comes from sponsorship, lotteries, advertising and other promotional devices.

The latest annual report shows that in the year ended May 31, 1984, it cost £3,857,000 to run the club, around half of that going in wages. Their total income was £4,759,000, which left a profit on the year of £902,000 — or £410,000 after transfer fees had been included. The declared dividend per share came to 2.3p. For my £100 investment, I received £2.30. I won't get rich investing in Spurs, but think of the pleasure and pride in being part of that brave new stand and that brave new public club.

In 1972, there were forty players on the staff, which is more than today. Now they have 31 professionals, plus five apprentices. All British clubs have cut down on their playing staffs to save wages. But the background staff at Spurs has almost doubled. There were 30 full-time administrative people in 1972. Now there are 54, plus another 250 temporary staff on match days.

Spurs was rather a homely club in 1972, with some ramshackle, old-fashioned offices clustered round an old car park. Everybody knew everybody else. All the players used to go into Mrs Wallace's office as soon as they arrived, for a match or for training, have some tea and chat, pick up their post, swap stories. Now the old offices have gone and everything is streamlined and somehow remote.

'It is less personal,' says Steve Perryman. 'It was a family club in those days. You could bring your kids in and they could hang around and be quite happy with people keeping a vague eye on them. Now it's all spread out. It's become big business. The organisation, the methods, the computers, it's all red hot. Sad in a way, I suppose, but it had to happen. I haven't quite got used to it. The security is incredible. I was told yesterday we have 12 full-time security men. In the old days we had none at all.'

On the management side, Keith Burkinshaw took over from Bill Nicholson in 1976. He brought in a more relaxed, calmer atmosphere in the dressing room. Under him, Spurs won the FA cup twice, in 1981 and 1982, and then the UEFA cup in 1984. He did not appear to be as happy after the new board arrived, then there were differences with players such as Archibald, and he retired gracefully at the end of the season. His assistant, Peter Shreeves, became manager in his place, in 1984, and appears to be continuing the same style of management.

Spurs now have their own psychologist, John Syer, introduced by Keith Burkinshaw, which provided a lot of fun cartoonists. It is basically all commonsense, helping players individually who might be worried about keeping up their concentration, or not fighting hard enough. In team talks in the old days, especially after a match, it was the manager and coach, followed by a few senior players, who dominated the post mortems. The younger ones might have their say at the end, if at all, by which time they were usually struck dumb, or just agreed with what had already been said. Now, everybody is encouraged to give their opinion, especially the younger ones, to try to explain and work out what went wrong. The young ones are usually allowed to talk first, and not be inhibited.

The club now has a proper dietician, which was long overdue. I was astounded, in 1972, when they were worried about Jimmy Neighbour being overweight and running out of energy, yet he was taking something like three teaspoonfuls of sugar in every cup of tea. Nobody could see the connection. Apart from diet, they now have a lot more medical tests and special medical programmes worked out for each player.

'Bill Nick had very few management aids in his day,' says Steve. 'He and Eddie were on their own. Everything was done from their own knowledge of the game. And that was how Bill liked to do it. He didn't go in for giving other people responsibilities. That's all changed, as we've grown into a much bigger club. But in the end, it is the manager who has to make up his own mind.'

Amongst the players, life in the dressing room sounds very much the same, even if the names have changed. Senior players now live in £100,000 houses and can earn £40,000 a year just from football, but the jokes and the characters remain, as with any group of sportsmen, amateur or professional, who work together, week after week.

In 1972, Cyril Knowles was the joker in the pack, teasing new people, playing tricks. It is interesting to note that despite what he said in 1972, about a career in management ('Seeing Bill after a match puts you off about staying in football'), he is now a manager, with Third Division Darlington. Mike England was often considered a bit slow, and behind his back other players called him 'Brains', but he has since gone on to have a distinguished career in management with Wales.

Today, Paul Miller, from all accounts, is the main funny man in the dressing room. Tony Galvin is the intellectual, naturally enough, as he's the one with a degree, a BA in Russian. He's also the token Lefty, which is still not hard to be, as most footballers are rather right-wing in their views. The quiet one in the dressing room is John Chiedozie. The one known for his flash clothes, and footballers are still as obsessed by their appearance as ever they were, is Garth Crooks.

If you can forget all those physical changes which have taken place, such as the new stand with its plush boxes, and appreciate that turning the club into a modern public company in the leisure field was bound to happen some time, and if you keep realising that inflation has rather altered money values and that all fashions date very quickly, just as do the names of our football heroes, then you might find, I hope, that *The Glory Game* is still understandable today.

Some things don't change. The hopes and fears of footballers as they start a new season, their aspirations and ambitions, the accidents and ill luck which befall them, the pressures and the pains, the pleasures and the praise, all of them shared by the supporters and club officials, just as much as the star performers, these things go on for ever, even when the old faces fade away. This then was a year in the life of one club, a year in the life of football.

Hunter Davies
London NW5
1985

Introduction to 1972 Edition

Tottenham is a district of North London and as a district of London it hasn't got very much to commend it.

Robert the Bruce had his home in Tottenham – Bruce Castle still stands – and Izaak Walton walked through rural Tottenham when he was going fishing, but Tottenham today is not exactly a district which tourists flock to, not like Chelsea. In the minds of the British public Tottenham stands for only one thing – Tottenham Hotspur Football Club.

Spurs, as the club is called, was founded in 1882. The name is thought to have come from Shakespeare's Hotspur – Harry Hotspur, son of the Duke of Northumberland – because they played their early games on Northumberland Park. In 1899 they moved to their present ground, White Hart Lane, buying the site from Charringtons the brewers. (In the deal they guaranteed that attendances would be at least one thousand, thereby benefiting Charrington's public house next door, the White Hart.)

Spurs today is one of the top six football clubs in Britain. Their status, reputation and facilities are unsurpassed. They're considered the richest club in the country. They own all their own premises, which not all clubs do, and a lot more besides. White Hart Lane still appears in the annual reports at its 1906 valuation of £500,000. They see no point in bringing it up to date. Football is a game in which millions of pounds are spent, especially by a club like Spurs. But the object of a football club is very simple: to win football matches.

In their long and distinguished career Spurs have won many matches but perhaps their finest hour so far was in 1961. That was when they won the English First Division title and the FA Cup, the first club this century to win the two major trophies in the same season. This double team, as it was called, went on to win the FA Cup again the next year and following that they won the European Cup Winners' Cup, becoming the first British club to win a major European championship.

That's all history now, a matter for the football freaks and their record books, but even a decade later the legend of that double team lives on, hanging over the present team. The fans still sing Glory Glory Hallelujah, the Spurs song which arose in the double days. And the manager is the same, Bill Nicholson.

This book revolves round a season with the present team. I haven't attempted to describe all the matches. Accounts of matches are very boring, even for the most committed, compared with actually being there. Football as a game is beyond words anyway – at least that's what people inside the game are always saying. Words can't make a team play better nor can they properly describe what happened on the park. Managers of football teams are notorious for wasting little time on things like words.

Little attempt either has been made to explain the techniques of football. It's been more a matter of trying to illuminate the lives of the people taking part; what led up to the matches, rather than the matches themselves. I've been concerned with the background human story of the season, trying to view the club from the inside, as the players and staff go about their work, and at home in their social setting.

The first team are the stars but the lives of the reserve players, waiting in the wings as in every club and in every walk of life, can be just as interesting. There's also the youth players, cleaning out the dressing-rooms, the chairman and his directors, the manager and his training staff. It takes a large efficient organisation to make every big club function. Then there's the fans, the rich ones in their flash cars down to the skinheads on the terraces. It's the story of a year in all their lives and how they were affected by Spurs.

It happens to be Spurs because I happen to be a fan and I happen to live near, but all clubs have the same sort of hopes and fears and most top players have the same problems and pressures. Fans have their favourites but for the majority it's football they like best, even if they're just one of the millions who watch it on the small screen and never go near a ground.

Football today is the world's biggest sport. Whether you're interested in it or not, its growth has been phenomenal and its stars have become contemporary heroes. This is the story about one year in the life of one club.

Dramatis Personae

First team players Alan Mullery (captain), Martin Peters, Martin Chivers, Pat Jennings, Alan Gilzean, Mike England, Cyril Knowles, Philip Beal, Joe Kinnear, Steve Perryman, Roger Morgan, Jimmy Pearce and Ralph Coates.
Leading reserves Tony Want, John Pratt, Terry Naylor, Peter Collins, Ray Evans, Jimmy Neighbour, Barry Daines and Phil Holder.

Manager Bill Nicholson
Assistant manager Eddie Baily
Trainers Johnny Wallis and Cecil Poynton
Youth team manager Pat Welton
Club doctor Brian Curtin

Directors Sidney Wale (Chairman), Charles Cox (Vice-Chairman), Arthur Richardson, Godfrey Groves, Geoffrey Richardson
Club secretary Geoffrey Jones
Assistant secretary Bill Stevens

1

The First Day

Summer had been very late acomin' in and June had been all rain but now we'd had over a week of sweltering sun with temperatures over eighty and everyone was convinced that summer summer had at last arrived. It was Thursday, 15 July and Wimbledon had just finished. Miss Goolagong was still in everyone's minds but cricket was now dominating the sports pages. The school holidays had yet to begin. Most of the population were thinking about their summer holidays. Very few were thinking about football. It wasn't the weather, it wasn't the season, it wasn't the time for football.

Tottenham High Road, up in the anonymous terraced wilds of North London, looked almost pleasant. It was nearing ten o'clock and the morning rush hour was over for another day. The first of the early shoppers were appearing, rolling up their summer dress sleeves.

The home of Tottenham Hotspur Football Club is at 748 High Road, N17. You could easily miss it, if you were rushing down the High Road with your head down. It's set slightly back from the road with the main entrance down a little lane beside a pub, the White Hart. But once you've stepped back and taken it all in, it's hard to believe that anyone could miss it. The stadium lurks behind the High Road like a vast battleship with its floodlights towering over the rooftops for miles around. The stands were empty. There was just one car in the large car park, stranded in a far corner like a left-over from one of last season's forgotten dramas. As far as Spurs were concerned, 15 July was the start of a new season. For any professional club, the four weeks of full-time pre-season training are four of the most vital of the year.

An empty coach swung into the car park and reversed, backing up towards a door in the corner of the stadium. Inside the boot room were ten boys, in sparkling clean shirts and well pressed hipster trousers. Three of them were sixteen and the others were only fifteen. One was reading out bits from the *Melody Maker* while the others jeered. When they heard the coach, they stopped and opened the door of the boot room and allowed the sun to stream in.

For seven of the boys, all newly signed apprentice professionals, it was the first day of their lives as full-time footballers. The other three were apprentices who'd been at it for up to a whole season already. They told the others to put the boots in the skips and then push the skips out and put them in the boot of the coach.

Johnny Wallis, the trainer, was sorting out the strips. Above him were rows and rows of boxes, all labelled with their contents. 'White tops for black feet' said a box behind his head. He supervised the boys as they loaded the skips, the balls and finally a large weighing machine onto the coach. Then the boys got on the coach themselves and sat on their own at the back, waiting. Johnny sat at the front with the driver.

Two of the older boys had their arms round each other's shoulders, almost abstractedly, as if for comfort, looking out of the windows towards the offices, waiting for Pat Welton, the youth team manager. The fifteen-year-olds seemed nervous. They looked too young for the battles ahead, too innocent for the world they were entering. They appeared unaware that in almost every way they'd voluntarily given up living a normal life.

In many ways, they'd taken the major step years ago. At least one of the ten had been first approached by Spurs when he was only twelve and a half years old. From that moment, he'd lost interest in school work or any desire for a trade apprenticeship. All of them had known for at least a year they were going to Spurs. All of them had been passionately desired, coaxed and coached, encouraged in almost every

way, except financially, to sign on the dotted line and
become a Spurs' apprentice.

Of the ten hopefuls in the back of the bus, sitting so
eagerly and so patiently, probably only one would reach the
top and finally make the Spurs first eleven. Three or four
more might make it to full professional status and play for
the reserves, then leave to play in other teams, lower down
the Leagues. The rest, well, they could end up at eighteen
without a job in football and unqualified for anything else.

Two of the sixteen-year-olds said yes, they knew the
problems. They knew the chances were against them. But
having once got to Spurs, you could always go somewhere
else. If you started at a lower club and failed, that was it.

A dark haired boy from Belfast, ex-captain of the
Northern Ireland schoolboys team, said he had chosen Spurs
from a total of twelve professional clubs who had
approached him. If he failed at Spurs, he'd be too disappointed to carry on. He'd go straight back to Belfast and get
an ordinary job. The boy beside him, who came from Oxford, said he'd play for anyone, in any League, if Spurs
chucked him out. He'd manage somehow.

At the front of the bus, the driver was peeping his horn.
Johnny Wallis, sitting beside him, said that Pat must be in
Bill Nicholson's office. They'd have to wait.

'Oh Gawd,' said the driver, 'I hope it's not like this every
day.'

'Don't worry,' said Johnny.

'I've done some miles since last season,' said the driver,
making conversation.

'Oh yes,' said Johnny, not listening. 'I was in Japan. You
should have seen the turf. It was like coconut matting.'

The boys at the back strained to hear any of the Japan
gossip. It had been the first team's close season tour, not of
course for the youth or reserve players. Two and a half weeks
at luxury hotels, all expenses paid, plus pockey money.
They'd only got back on 11 June, tanned and affluent
looking, loaded down with cheap dolls, transistors and cas-
settes.

At one time, just a few years ago, all footballers got three
months off in the summer, taking other jobs to supplement

3

their wages. These days, with wages up to £200 a week, they don't need other jobs, but they do need time off. Apart from those ten boys on the coach, every full professional making his way to Cheshunt that day felt that the new season had arrived too quickly. They thought of the four weeks of training ahead as a long hard drag.

At last a message came that the coach could go. Pat was going by car. As they drove out of the ground, past the White Hart pub and right up the Tottenham High Road, a very fit looking middle-aged lady in a short summer dress was going past on a bicycle. She waved at the coach and Johnny Wallis waved back. The boys took no notice. It was Darky, wife of Bill Nicholson, Spurs' manager. Their house is only a few minutes from the ground. She always says he would like to be even nearer, perhaps have a flat in the stand, so that he need never leave.

It was almost a rural sight, the trainer waving to the manager's wife as she cycled past to do her shopping, as if Spurs were a village football team. It all comes down to scale, when the car park is empty and fifty thousand people aren't thronging the High Road.

The coach was heading for the club's training ground at Cheshunt, nine miles up the Cambridge Road. Football clubs never practise on their own pitch – the turf is too valuable. The sixteen-year-olds were talking about the training sessions they'd done at Cheshunt last season, being men of the world, having seen it all before. The younger ones took it all in, apprehensively. The Oxford boy said he'd hurt his back right at the beginning, with all the exercises, and had felt rotten for half of the season.

'I didn't know whether I was coming or going,' he said.

'It was being told not to hold the ball,' said another. 'That's what I didn't like. I thought they'd let me show a bit of individual skill, but that was the last thing they wanted. No one can show off. You must get rid of the ball at once.'

On the back row was a deaf and dumb boy, Bobby Scarth, the son of a former Spurs professional, looking out of the window. He'd shown such natural ability in evening trials while still at school the previous year that the club had decided to sign him on as an apprentice for one year. The

4

other boys had already got used to him, and he to them. He was to be treated like everyone else and no fuss made of him. It was hoped by the club that the Press would be unaware of him for as long as possible.

There are three pitches at Cheshunt, one with a miniature stadium, plus extensive dressing-rooms, showers and a large dining-room. In all, about nine acres of lush lawns in the best part of suburban Hertfordshire. They bought it twenty years ago for about £35,000. Today it must be worth around a quarter of a million. They own it freehold, just as they own their ground in Tottenham. Many clubs lease their stadium and their training ground, if they have one.

A few of the first team were just arriving. Alan Gilzean was getting out of his Jaguar. Joe Kinnear was signing autographs by his new MGB GT. Mike England arrived in his new Capri, a surprise present from his wife (even footballers' wives have money these days). A group of about half a dozen teenage girls screamed and ran towards him, then stopped, hesitant. Girls who run after pop stars keep running, desperate to grab hold of everything, half-convinced he's their property anyway. They buy his records and feel they own him. But girls, and boys, who hang around football stars are much more respectable. They keep their distance, cowed when they reach the presence. The girls held each other, nudging and whispering, and then giggling they shyly asked for his autograph.

The apprentices got off the coach and Johnny told them to help with the balls and the gear. All apprentices have work to do as well as training. While the professionals go home after training is over for the day, the boys have to clean boots, wash out the dressing-rooms. Although this was the first day of the club's pre-season training, the boys had had to report three days earlier, on the Monday. They'd been set to work right away, doing painting jobs, cleaning and whitening the lines on the practice pitches.

The first team stood around on the lawns like nature's stars talking to each other in their own confident group. Even if you didn't know any of their faces you could have told immediately they were the sixth form. They looked so adult and famous compared with the thin, half-developed apprentices. In another group stood the reserves, looking like reserves, lacking the first team's Mediterranean tan or their natural superiority. They were equally stocky, but somehow rougher and tougher with the right length long hair but unkempt and all ends.

The first team were saying hello and how are you and how's it going to Ralph Coates. Everybody stood back to eye him. From the first team down to the apprentices, everybody wanted to have a look at Ralph Coates. It was his very first day at Spurs, the beginning of a new life, new friends, new rituals, new traditions. He had narrow trousers, compared with the first team's obvious flares, and shoes which looked remarkably pointed. Surely even up in darkest Burnley they weren't still wearing Italian shoes.

Bill Nicholson had signed Ralph Coates during the summer for £190,000. It was the highest amount of cash which had ever been paid for a British player. A record which no doubt would soon go, just like other records which Spurs have created in the transfer world over the years. But Coates wasn't the most expensive player in the country that day – Martin Peters held that particular record, though his price of £200,000 had been made up of cash and a player in exchange. Martin Peters, of course, also plays for Spurs.

Coates looked nervous as he shook hands all round, very politely. He'd been the star player in a team which had failed and been demoted. Would he be a star player in a team full of stars? How long would it take for him to settle in? Who's place would he take? Any new player, any new person, in any new group causes question marks.

The new season would find Coates' true worth, whatever that might be. The new season, like every other season, would also result in a new find. One of those young reserves would be bound to come through and join the sixth form and immediately start looking like a star. And if that happened, which star would fall? Apart from players maturing and finding form, or losing it, the season would also bring injuries. By the law of averages, there was bound to be at least one serious injury, putting a player's whole career in jeopardy. It had happened last season. It would happen again.

6

Martin Peters arrived, bringing the total of Jaguars to three. Pat Jennings had slipped in quietly, without saying much, and was standing at the back of the first group. Goalkeepers don't say much.

Peters went across and said hello to Coates, asking him curtly if he'd got a house, then he went in to the dressing-rooms to change. Martin Peters hates hanging around, doesn't go in for chat and is never happier than when he's sitting stripped and ready, all tense, with half an hour to go to kick-off.

Peters, like Alan Mullery and Martin Chivers, already knew Coates. All three, being full England internationals, had played with him in the England team. The arrival of Coates now brought Spurs' total of current England internationals to four, a greater number than any other club in London would have for the start of that season.

The first team went into the first team's dressing-room and hung up their coloured long collared shirts. Cyril Knowles, the left full back, admired Coates' old fashioned shirt. Coates said thanks, very sincerely. 'You're only allowed the same clothes two days running,' said Cyril, nodding to Philip Beal for confirmation. Philip said yes. 'That's the rule, Ralph.' Coates looked suddenly very worried. They all laughed.

Bill Nicholson, their manager, was changing with them, putting on his training shoes and shorts. For fifty-two, his body was hard and sturdy. He could almost have been mistaken for a player. Only his hair gave away his real age. It's so closely cropped he looks as if he's been sentenced.

They went out and stood in front of the rose garden, waiting for Bill to say something. Each year, on the first day of the pre-season training, he usually gives a little pep talk, welcoming everybody briefly with a homily about the good name of the club and how it mustn't be spoiled by things like long hair. Like most football managers, he has a phobia about long hair. But he said nothing. When he was ready, he simply led the way out of the room, across the lawns to the pitches.

It was already seventy degrees and not quite ten thirty. The sun was blazing down as forty footballers in brilliant red, blue, yellow and green training sweaters appeared and started spanning out across the pitches. Behind them came Johnny Wallis and two other members of the coaching staff, dragging behind them forty brand new sparkling white footballs.

The sweater colours had been decided by Bill Nicholson. Inside in the dressing-rooms he'd pinned up lists of four teams of ten, each a different colour. It was all very democratic. Each group had first, reserves and youth players, equally mixed. For the next four weeks, every new fifteen-year-old on £10 a week would be treated the same as an experienced £200 a week man, twice his age.

'We've got wonderful facilities here,' says Nicholson. 'Every player, from apprentice to first team, has the same opportunities to use them. That's our promise when they join and we live up to it. They have to take turns of course, but no one says bugger off, this is the first team's ball court. It's everyone's.

'We try to make it varied and interesting. I've never heard our players complain about the training. Obviously no player likes practising a skill in the rain so we go indoors to the ball court. Footballers don't like endless running round the track. They prefer to run with a ball at their feet, but you've got to practise both.'

He strode out across the pitches and stood in the middle of one pitch, surrounded by his players. He shouted to them that he wanted everyone to get a ball each and do some juggling, keeping it up six times, and then six times heading it, just to get the feel of it. After five minutes, he moved on to passing movements, telling them to split into pairs. Then they moved onto fives, with one in the middle, giving wall passes to the others in turn.

For an hour he took them through a succession of ball exercises, each one getting more complicated. He blew a whistle when each was over, bellowing from the middle the directions for the next.

Alan Mullery, captain of Spurs, was in the same group as the deaf and dumb boy. He bent down in front of him and went over any complicated instructions so that the boy could read his lips and understand his gestures.

Ralph Coates looked more worried than the deaf and

dumb boy. He was in a far group and finding it impossible to hear what Bill was saying. The old hands, like Mullery, had been through most of the exercises before. But to Coates, Nicholson's was a strange voice with new tones, new phrases, new likes and dislikes to be mastered.

During all the exercises, Nicholson kept up insistent criticism or encouragement. 'Cyril Knowles, I was watching you there!'

'You bloody would be,' muttered Knowles, well out of earshot.

'And I saw that, Gilly,' barked Nicholson.

Alan Gilzean had yawned, quickly turning his back to Nicholson when he'd felt it creeping out, but not quick enough.

After an hour, they moved to another pitch where Bill Watson, an ex-Olympic weight lifting champion, took over. Twice a week throughout the season he takes Spurs for weight training and other exercises. He lined them up in rows and soon the sweat was pouring off them. The mid-day temperature was seventy-seven degrees. As he demonstrated each new exercise he breathed out heavily, giving a roar which echoed round the ground like a London bus putting on its air brakes.

By this time there were about fifty spectators at the end of the pitch, kept at bay behind a rope, many of them girls, some families with kids, some working men just off night shift. They laughed at Bill Watson as he shouted and then oohed with sympathy as the forty players bent and desperately tried to keep up with him.

Two press photographers were watching the training, the only two allowed on the ground that day. One was an agency man, to get the picture every London newspaper had asked for – Coates shaking hands with Mullery.

The other was a local Cheshunt photographer, one used by the club for official pictures such as the club handbook and programmes. One of the jobs he'd had at the end of last season was to do the Spurs youth team because they'd won the Youth Cup. The club wanted a colour photograph of the team which would be sent as a present to each proud parent. 'Terrible, terrible,' Bill Nicholson had told the photographer when he brought in the print. The photographer was about to defend his work when Nicholson pointed at the haircuts. He wanted the photograph taken again – *after* they'd all had their hair cut.

At eleven thirty, Bill Nicholson called a break. The groundsman brought tea and they all rushed to grab a plastic cup each, then threw themselves on the ground for a ten minute rest. 'We didn't get no tea at Burnley,' so Coates told his group. Nor did they touch a ball for the first week of training. It was all road runs at Burnley. 'That's this afternoon,' someone told him, groaning.

After tea, they returned to ball games, doing intricate five-man passing movements, heading games, hand ball matches, all with complicated sounding rules, some so new that even the older players couldn't follow them.

'Get your hair cut, Chivers, then you'd hear me,' shouted Nicholson.

Eddie Baily, the assistant manager, arrived. He'd been with his wife to hospital. He joined in, shouting loudly for greater effort. Eddie, like Bill Nicholson, is an ex-Spurs and England player. But whereas Bill keeps his thoughts and his tensions to himself, very rarely losing his temper, Eddie is more on the surface, shouting aloud his thoughts, even his prejudices, managing to work himself into a rage on apparently very little. But today he was relatively subdued, because of his wife. A few of the more senior players asked how she was. He said not very good. They hadn't operated after all.

They finished with some practice games, firstly five-a-side, and then two full-scale matches, with all four teams playing on the same pitch. Forty players playing two games at once. They all looked in amazement. It was the first time Bill had told them to do such an exercise. It was surprisingly interesting. There was a constant series of attacks with the two goalkeepers in each goal constantly diving to save shots. Given TV exposure, it could catch on.

Then they broke for lunch. While they showered, their sweaty clothes were put back in the skips and into the coaches and sent back to Spurs to be dried. A new set of training clothes, forty shirts, undershirts, shorts, socks and training shoes, all clean, were already laid out for the after-noon training. Every article of clothing is dried immediately after use by the two full-time laundry ladies, back in Spurs' own laundry.

In the dining-room, the first team sat together. Coates was again being asked about his house and was he liking it. It was the only thing they could think of to ask him. The conversation then left him behind as it ranged round Japan, parties, cars, investments and girls.

It was chicken soup, roast beef, tinned fruit and custard. During the season, their daily training always finishes by one thirty. But for the four weeks of the pre-season, Cheshunt becomes a camp, where they spend each entire day, training and eating together. Meals by Mecca, a nice concession they've had for some years. At two thirty, Bill Nicholson, who'd had lunch in the dining-room at his own table with Eddie Baily and the rest of the coaching staff, said they were going on a run. He was already in shorts and a training shirt and red training shoes. When everyone else was ready, he set off out of the ground, his legs going like pistons, and turned left up a country lane. Everyone followed behind, most of them running to keep up.

It's known as Bill's road run, although it's really a very fast walk. The leaders, who kept carefully abreast of Bill and never ahead, were flaying themselves like professional walkers to match his incredible stride. Even at his age it was obvious that he could equal any of them at road walking and was better than most.

We spread out in a long line. From about the middle onwards, they were doing a fast jog to keep up. Eddie Baily was bringing up the rear on a bicycle, screaming at everyone to keep at it. Pat Welton, the youth team manager, was running in the line, dressed in a track suit.

I was wearing the normal training outfit, number 22, the number vacated by one of the reserves who'd moved to Torquay during the summer. Every professional on joining the club is given a number which is printed on each item of clothing. The numbers go from 1 up to 40. You get it at random, depending on which are vacant when you arrive. Joe Kinnear, for example, is number 8, the same number which Danny Blanchflower had when he was at the club. Way back in the thirties, before they were all born, Bill Nicholson had number 8 when he too played for Spurs.

It was by now well over eighty degrees and the road was running in tar which splatted as we went along. I felt myself falling further back and ended up with the slackers at the end, led by Roger Morgan, Cyril Knowles and Jimmy Neighbour.

We went up a hill and the sweat was dripping from everyone. Eddie Baily was labouring heavily on his bicycle. Roger and Cyril were gently holding the back of his seat, unbeknown to Eddie.

'Come on you lot. Keep running. I'm surprised at you, Jimmy Neighbour. You know that Roger Morgan is a bad influence on you.'

They were puffing and panting, too tired to comment till they got up the hill. Roger and Jimmy are two of Spurs' wingers. Their future in the first team looked pretty gloomy, now that Ralph Coates had arrived.

Roger Morgan, bought for £100,000 two seasons ago, had been out through injury much of last season. Jimmy Neighbour, a former Spurs apprentice and now still only 20, had managed to make his first team debut while Roger was injured. He'd been hailed as a new boy wonder by many papers. Jimmy, being younger and more innocent, tends to take a lead from the cocky, more experienced, rather flash Roger Morgan.

'You've got nowhere, Jimmy Neighbour,' shouted Eddie. 'And you'll get nowhere, not with him.'

'Thanks Ed,' said Roger, laughing directly at him.

'I mean it,' said Eddie. 'The object of a football team is to win trophies . . .'

'Jimmy's got a few,' said Roger. 'You should see the notches on his cock.'

'That's the sort of remark I mean,' said Eddie. He shook his head in heavy disapproval.

Eddie cycled on to shout at another group who were wandering off the pavement and into the road and looked in danger of being run over. When he went ahead, a bottle of orange juice appeared from someone's shirt and was passed round, then thrown in a hedge. We passed a school and all the kids in the playground stopped to cheer and wave. One or two shouted 'Arsenal, Arsenal'.

Eddie screamed at everyone to take care and go into single file as we came to some workmen mending the road. A coloured labourer looked out of a hole and gave us a cheer. 'Man, you've got it easy,' he said to Eddie, jeering at him because he was on a bicycle.

'Don't force me,' said Eddie, very quietly, cycling on, saving his reply till he was out of earshot. 'Why don't you go back to the jungle and eat bananas.'

'Ignorant twat, that's what you are,' said Cyril Knowles, running beside Eddie.

'I call you a white bastard, so what's wrong with that?' said Eddie. 'I tell you to get back to your igloo, don't I? You're the one who's ignorant.'

Cyril comes from the far North, Yorkshire. He's usually first when it comes to the cheeky remarks, baiting Eddie. His accent sounded funny. Almost everyone else at Spurs speaks broad London. About eighty per cent of the professionals come from the London area, which is unusual for a London club. At Arsenal and Chelsea a much larger proportion come from the North or from Scotland. Ralph Coates had been amazed that morning to be told he was the only Geordie in the Spurs camp. At Burnley there had been so many Geordies they'd often played Geordies against the rest in practice matches. Geordieland of course produces professional footballers out of all proportion to its size.

'Christ, I could go a cold lager,' said Alan Gilzean, the only Scotsman in the Spurs first team. He was jogging with difficulty, the sweat covering his ample forehead. He hates road walking. He thinks footballers aren't meant to walk.

Eddie moved along the long line again and Roger and the others got back to more serious topics. For several miles they discussed investments, houses and furnishings. They were trying to get Jimmy Neighbour, who is unmarried, to move out of his mum's house and buy a little flat, which of course they would help him to use. They shouted to Joe Kinnear, who'd become a director of a furnishing company during the summer, asking what discount he could get for them.

13

At the front, Bill was silently pounding on, with Martin Chivers and Peter Collins at his elbows and a trio of eager apprentices just behind. There was no talking at the front. At the back, it was all talking and jokes and oaths.

We ran through a council estate and Roger gave a run down on the trade-in price of every car outside every door.

'Heh, there's some new council houses going up,' shouted Cyril. 'You wanna get your name down, Ralph.'

The road run finished about four. We covered about six miles. Not much, for a group of athletes, but arduous enough on the first day back in training, especially after a whole morning of other more gruelling physical exercises. Most of them made a great show of groaning and complaining, making out it was worse than it was, like a lot of schoolboys, all for Eddie's benefit. No one moaned in Bill Nicholson's presence.

'I've always been good at road walks,' said Bill Nicholson afterwards in the communal plunge bath, lying down with his players, soaking himself. Roger Morgan had got a shampoo from somewhere and was doing his hair. Martin Chivers was in the shower, waiting for one of us to get out of the plunge so he could get in.

'Road work is very good for footballers,' continued Bill. 'It gets all the muscles going without too much strain. I always take the first couple of days fairly easily. I like a short easy start, which is why I always start the new season on a Thursday. They have the weekend to get any stiffness out. We get down to hard training next week.'

Roger Morgan was telling a long story about someone who'd been trying to sell some players some stolen furniture. Everyone laughed when he'd finished, including Bill.

Martin Peters was the last out of the bath. Bill and Eddie were out and getting dried, watching him.

'Can you manage or do you want a hand, Martin,' asked Eddie.

'I hope you'll soon be fit, Martin,' said Bill, all smiles. The two managers were laying it on heavy, smiling, but serious like most of their jokes. Martin Peters had cried off from the Japan summer tour at the last minute, saying he had gas-tro-enteritis. Most players suspected he'd just done it because

14

his wife wanted him to stay at home. Martin gave a lop-sided grin, his ears sticking out even more than usual with his short wet hair pushed back. Martin Peter's hair, clothes and life style and his attitude to training have Mr Nicholson's full approval, which can't be said for all his players.

'Come on, Mart,' said Eddie. 'I'll give you a hand. You must still be weak.'

Martin still didn't reply.

'I hope you will be fit Martin,' said Eddie. '*If* you're in the team, that is.'

'Yes, just because you play for England, doesn't mean you'll play for Spurs,' said Bill.

'We knew Alf before you, you know,' said Eddie.

'That's right,' said Bill, smiling. Sir Alf Ramsey, England's team manager, played for Spurs alongside both Bill Nicholson and Eddie Baily.

It was the sort of gentle if rather heavy teasing, meant affectionately, which Bill now and again goes in for, if things are going well or at the beginning of a virgin season when nothing has gone wrong, so far. All the players take it, quite proud to be picked on. One or two of the flash ones, like Roger Morgan, might make faces behind Bill's back when he's doing it, but they never answer back in case they ruin it all.

'On you go, Martin,' said Bill, smiling, the incident over.

Martin went to get dressed and Bill and Eddie followed him. The groundsman, Don, an ex-Spurs apprentice, but one who never made it, brought in a tray set with tea for two, for the two managers. Eddie had a folder marked 'Pre-season training' and he chatted to Bill for some time about the next day's training programme. Some years ago, Bill Nicholson used to write out exact details of every minute of the training schedule. After fifteen years as Spurs coach and then manager, he knows what exercise he is going to use, although he is always adding to them. Eddie is the one who now keeps any notes, under Bill's direction, and writes out the training schedules.

They drank their tea alone. Outside stood five very worried looking young professionals, all around eighteen, all with just one season as a professional behind them. Everyone

15

else had gone home, roaring away in their fast sports cars or in the case of the reserves, their secondhand Fords.

One of the youngsters, Joe Peck, had a nasty feeling that Bill had asked them to wait because they were going to be told they were getting a free – a free transfer. A few players had got them at the end of the last season. Joe had stayed at school, Holloway Comprehensive, until he was seventeen, which is unusual. He'd played for Spurs youth team as an amateur until he'd signed professional forms a year ago. He has five O levels and one A level, which puts him in the intellectual class as far as footballers go. He at least would have some qualifications if he was now rejected.

Mr Nicholson eventually came out. He looked serious and dour, his normal expression. It was impossible to tell what he was going to say to them. The jokes in the bath had been forgotten.

He told them briefly and to the point that all five of them were to be given another £5 a fortnight. They bounded away, as soon as he'd finished, most of them piling into an old Anglia belonging to Graeme Souness. Not long ago, when he'd still been an apprentice, Graeme had run away from Tottenham, leaving his club digs and going home to Edinburgh, because he felt homesick. This is one of the problems many young players of fifteen have to face when they arrive in a big alien city and nobody can understand their funny accent. It happened to George Best of Manchester United. He returned to Belfast after only a few weeks because he found Manchester so strange.

Bill got into his white Rover 2000 and drove away. The coach was being loaded up with the afternoon's dirty washing, forty sets of sweaty, sodden training strips. Then the ten apprentices, the ones who'd come in the coach that morning, got into the coach and settled down for the journey back to Tottenham. Their first day of training was over.

All the boys looked tired and exhausted but they were noisily discussing whether they'd be stiff tomorrow and what they thought of Ralph Coates. They wondered if he'd feel as stiff tomorrow as they knew they were going to feel. Most boys agreed Coates looked a bit out of things, which wasn't surprising. One boy said he thought he'd looked clumsy, compared with someone like Martin Peters. 'Well, Martin Peters now, he's a bit special, isn't he,' said another boy thoughtfully. They all nodded.

There was a groan of pain from a boy at the back, John Margerison, ex-Hertfordshire Boys and an England Boys trialist. He suddenly jerked his body forward and was violently sick. His action had ruined his shirt, a brand new one he'd got specially for the first day, but at least he missed the boys beside him. They all helped him to clean himself up.

It hadn't been a hard day. It was probably just that Margerison had drunk too much saline water, provided by the club after training to put back salt in the body lost through sweating. He'd also had some tea, which couldn't have helped his stomach. As Bill Nicholson had said, he'd only been breaking them in gently, as it was the first day. The hard days were ahead.

2

Ralph Coates

Ralph Coates went straight home from the first day's training to the flat which the club had provided for him till he found a house of his own. He and his wife Sandra, along with their two-year-old daughter Lisa, had arrived in London only four days previously, on the Monday. So far, they'd disliked everything about London.

It was an anonymous upstairs flat in Green Lanes, Palmers Green, one of the busiest throughfares in North London. The traffic noise, night and day, was inescapable. Each evening so far they'd sat alone, feeling lost and abandoned, with nothing to do and nobody to speak to. They couldn't go out and leave the baby alone and they didn't know how to get a babysitter. There was no phone, no radio and no television. Spurs were refusing to give their address to any friends from Burnley who were ringing up, trying to find where they were. Spurs never gives home addresses. He was beginning to feel he didn't exist.

In Burnley, he'd been the idol of the town. They mobbed him in the streets and when it was announced he was going they were crying on his doorstep. At Burnley they put his name on the programme even when he'd been injured all week. They'd push him on, strapped up and full of cortisone. They feared half the crowd wouldn't turn up if Ralph Coates wasn't playing.

In Burnley, he'd had a secluded luxury bungalow, with fields all around. On their first night in London they'd had to sleep under raincoats. They'd been told the flat would have everything they needed, but none of the beds had blankets.

18

It was the lack of telephone which was the worst of all. They couldn't even ring estate agents to start looking for houses, not that they had any idea which area of London they wanted to live in. They'd been told the terrible prices they would have to pay for a house and were valiantly prepared to go up to £15,000, though they knew that would be three times the price of a comparable house in Burnley. They'd had trouble selling their Burnley house, with that part of Lancashire being a depressed area, and had to bring the price down, just to get shot of it.

'Monday was terrible,' said Ralph. 'We'd driven all the way down from Burnley and we couldn't even get in because there was no key. We had to wait outside till somebody came. Then when we saw the bare flat with no blankets or phone or nothing, Sandra said I don't like it, I want to go home. I thought hell, what a start. I said come on lass, we'll give it a try for a few days. But I said if she still didn't like it, I'd go and see Bill and tell him we were going back home. If he wouldn't let me out of my contract, then I'd leave football, that's all there would be to it. If ever Sandra was unhappy with me being a footballer, I'd pack it in at once. I don't know what I'd do. I'd be a dustman, anything.'

In repose, Coates normally looks worried. He's a bit like Bobby Charlton, with the same fair hair, receding on top, and the same rather intense furrowed brows. Sandra is small with long dark hair, pretty and lively. 'She's the brains,' he says. 'I wouldn't have done nearly as much without her.'

Unlike most footballers' wives, she has far greater educational qualifications than her husband – she did O and A levels and then went to college in Liverpool for three years to become a state registered occupational therapist. Unlike many footballers' wives, she actively encourages him to go on overseas tours, if she thinks it will help his career. Three times she pushed him abroad with the England party as substitute when each time he wanted to cry off and get his club to pretend he was injured as he was so fed up travelling with the team and never playing, convinced he was never going to make it. In the end, she was proved right. He'd recently become a full member of the squad.

Sandra is a football fan, which again is rare for a footballer's wife. She followed Burnley from the age of twelve. She even came down to London with her father when they played in the Cup Final in 1962, being beaten by Spurs, 3-1. 'Spurs have never been my favourite team, until now.'

I said that a few of the players had been saying that day that they thought Ralph looked a bit tired. Sandra replied that he'd been ill. He'd caught a mysterious allergy complaint and had rung Mr Nicholson at one point to say he would miss the pre-season training completely.

Ten days before, apparently, at home in Burnley, he'd wakened in the middle of the night covered in giant lumps. The doctor couldn't diagnose it. Most friends thought that it must be psychological, with worrying about coming to Spurs.

Whatever the cause, it had led to its own worries and he'd been on sleeping pills all the previous week. But it had now gone, just as suddenly, without the cause being discovered.

Coates is twenty-five, though like all footballers, he looks older. He was born in Hetton le Hole, a mining village in County Durham. His father, who died when Ralph was eleven, was a coal miner. It was expected that Ralph would go down the pit, though his ambition was always to be a footballer. At fifteen he joined Burnley straight from school.

According to all the football writers, he'd been expected to leave Burnley for the last three years. It seemed obvious that an England player wouldn't stay in a small town with a small club, struggling every year to stay in the First Division. Burnley's average gate last season was sixteen thousand, the smallest in the First Division – less than half that of Spurs.

'When it was obvious we were going to finish bottom, I knew I would have to leave. I decided that if the club refused to transfer me, at the end of the season I would have to ask. I always expected I'd go to Manchester or Liverpool or Leeds. Those are the places I fancied. I wanted to stay in the North. Both of us preferred the North.

'On the last Wednesday of the season, Jimmy Adamson, the manager, rang me at home and asked where I was training. Burnley's season was over but I was training for England's home international in the local park. He said why didn't I come up to the Turf, Burnley's ground, to train. He said we'll put you a bath on. I said I was OK. But he was

20

insistent that I came to the ground, so I said OK then, I'd come.

'After lunch I didn't feel like going into town. I never thought for one minute they'd had a transfer offer. The local papers were full of denials that Burnley were thinking of selling me. There had been so many letters that the club had had to say it officially.

'I went shopping and then came home and was just about to get going on the lawns when I heard this voice in a sort of hoarse whisper over the garden wall. It was Dave, our chief scout. He said "Quick, into the house, I can't talk outside." He said the papers had spies everywhere. Even in the house, he said he couldn't say much, just that Tottenham had made a bid. There was to be a secret meeting somewhere on the M6. I hadn't to tell anyone. I picked up the phone to ring Sandra and he grabbed it from me saying you never knew who was listening. So I left a message for Sandra to come home, with no explanations. Then Dave made a phone call to his wife, telling her to pass on a message: "I've made contact. I'll be three quarters of an hour late for the rendezvous." I thought the whole thing was ridiculous and said so, but he said it had to be dead secret. I needn't laugh.'

'I was sure Ralph had had an accident,' said Sandra. 'Or perhaps it was Lisa. I rushed home and got changed out of my uniform and Dave put both of us in his car. At least it wasn't his car. To cover his tracks, because he was convinced the Press were after him, he'd driven his own car into one entrance of a garage and driven a new one, on a test drive, out the other end. It was like a James Bond film.'

The M6 rendezvous was at the Post Horn, a public house near Keele, a place where the Burnley Football Club, and many others, often stop for lunch on the way to and from away matches.

'I knew the manager very well and he recognised me as soon as I stepped in, which rather spoiled all their secrecy. It was very crowded. We couldn't see the Spurs chairman or Bill Nicholson. When they did arrive, they said it would all have to be done outside as there were too many people around.

'Jimmy took me aside first of all and put his arm round

21

me and said he didn't want me to leave but he had no option. Then I went into the back seat of Bill Nicholson's car and he explained to me the terms he was offering. I didn't know what transfer fee they were paying for me, but he said my five per cent signing on fee would be £9,500. He hoped I wouldn't waste it. I worked it out later that the transfer fee was £190,000. We chatted for about half an hour, then I signed the forms, there and then.'

If Spurs hadn't come when they did, he would have asked for a transfer fee and therefore lost his £9,500, according to the rules of football.

'When I first played for the England Under 23 team Bill Nicholson was the team manager. I told Sandra at the time what a great bloke he was. Not too strict, but everyone toed the line. I like that. It was a major factor in agreeing to come here, because of Bill.'

It's hard to see in some ways why Burnley were quite so fanatical about keeping it secret. It was to Spurs advantage, of course, to keep it quiet, so that no other club could hear what was happening and make a higher offer. There's no doubt there could have been an auction, with the price escalating up to perhaps a quarter of a million. But apparently Burnley had made a promise years ago that Spurs would have first offer. That was why they wanted it done quickly and quietly. Arsenal would certainly have made a high offer, but it's thought that the Burnley directors hadn't got on with Arsenal and were determined not to let their prize possession go there. Relations between Spurs and Burnley have always been good.

Looking back at Burnley, there were a lot of things he obviously enjoyed. 'When I ran out and the crowd shouted my name I felt great. It didn't matter there were only twelve thousand. It was fabulous. I felt I couldn't do a thing wrong with them on my side. People would stop you in the street to shake your hand. "Can you do it for us, Ralph? Can you beat this London lot?" And I'd say of course. We'll hammer them. It was a great feeling, though you knew the London lot already had twice as many points as we were ever likely to get.'

But mentally he suffered a lot. The worry and responsibility began to keep him awake at night till at length he was on sleeping pills.

'The manager himself even asked me what I thought, which front runners I'd pick. But it was always the same sort of decision, an experienced player or a young lad. I never gave him any answers. I honestly didn't know. It wasn't my job. Jimmy was the manager. But I didn't envy him the task.

'I played with Jimmy when I first went there as a youngster. I've never seen such a cool player on the pitch. When he became coach he was still very cool. But as manager, I've never seen anyone change so much. He seemed to be on tenterhooks all the time. He went grey in one year. Harry Potts, the previous manager, had been just the same. He used to wash his face *before* a match because the sweat was so bad. He'd shake all over, bury his head in his hands and be purple in the face by the end of the match. But when Harry became general manager, he was a changed man. It was good morning lads, how's the wife. None of this slamming the door and not talking when things are going bad. I'd hate to be a manager. If you're with a team like Burnley the pressures are unbearable.'

'Ralph is very loyal,' said Sandra. 'He felt the closeness and the loyalty of Burnley very much, but I always told him he'd have to move in the end. What's loyalty, when you get to the end of your days? Ralph's not the sort of player they'll give an easy coaching job to, not when he can be sold for a fee.

'I'm ambitious for Ralph's sake. I know I'll never achieve anything myself, but I might achieve it through Ralph. It's nice for him to be somebody instead of anybody.

'Ralph does want to be a success, but unlike me, he can't bear to be an unsuccess. He'll give up very quickly if he can't do it right away, like mending something in the house. He hates it when he can't do it at once. He took up cine films, but was furious when he couldn't manage the splicing. He's always taking up things and dropping them. He wasn't brilliant first time at golf, so he dropped it at once, having bought all the gear.

'He's terrible on Saturdays. He hates it when people come to the house or anything happens to spoil his routine. He's like a prima donna. If there's any noise or disturbance he says, that's it, now you've spoiled everything, and I have to calm him down very gently.

'The psychology of being a footballer is very difficult. Ralph really is completely confident in his football ability. He has to be, otherwise he'd never go out there. Even at Burnley, when they were a goal down, he'd try even harder, convinced they could still do it. But the drawback about being a footballer is that logically, you can do nothing else. Because you have to be convinced you are going to make it, you never have any interest in anything else. You end up being unable to *do* anything else. You *know* you're going to be a footballer, so everything else is pointless.'

Ralph finds it hard to express what he feels. He appears trapped by himself, in some ways, and by his own abilities. It's sad to consider that to the outside world last season he'd been apparently one of football's success stories, picked for England, a super-fit, highly paid athlete of only twenty-five – yet unable to sleep and reduced to sleeping pills because of worrying.

'There is never any relief when the team is doing badly. They don't know what it's like at Spurs.

'But I don't regret having spent all those years at Burnley. If I was fifteen, I'd do the same again. But I know that at fifteen I enjoyed my football much more than I have done these last seven years.'

He was unwilling to predict his future at Spurs or what the coming season might bring. Just the thought of being with a team bred on success rather than failure was enough to look forward to.

'They seem a good set of lads. Very friendly, even the ones I was a bit worried about, the ones I might replace, Gilly, Jimmy Pearce and Jimmy Neighbour. They all came up and said hello and hoped I'd get on well, which was nice. I know the crowd will give me some stick if I don't do well, but I'll settle down.

'Chivers and Peters were both saying this morning that they had a hard time when they arrived. They said I might find the same. It doesn't worry me. It'll be my problem, no one else's. It'll either be because I'm not training right or I'm

24

not living right. I'll find out the cause and put it right on my own.'

Last season Spurs had finished third in the league. To Bill Nicholson, that was failure. At Burnley it would have meant dancing in the streets. Spurs *had* to be top. Otherwise, bodies would topple and the cheque book would come out. Ralph smiled and said it didn't worry him. He would keep his place, as long as people didn't expect miracles.

'On the road walk this afternoon, they were all saying that everyone was convinced this was going to be Spurs' season, that we'd do great and win something really big. I've heard it myself from lots of people since I arrived in London. The Press are saying it. We're being tipped by everybody.

'As they were all talking about it, Alan Mullery turned to me and said "Yes, and it's all up to you, Ralph." I know it was a joke. I think it was. But it's a bit worrying, if it's me everyone is depending on for the season ahead.'

3

Pre-season Training

On the second week at Cheshunt it became a ritual every morning for all the players to stand around in the shade in the dining-room, waiting for the day's work to begin. They stood chatting in groups, according to status. But there was another way of telling the stars. They were the ones opening letters.

During the season, the players pick up their mail at the club, usually from Mrs Wallace's office, the lady who looks after the general office. But during the four weeks of pre-season training they don't go to the club. It's all brought to Cheshunt. So first thing, there were always great shouts and laughs and jeers as players read out their fan letters to each other, taking the mickey out of yet another football magazine or comic which wanted them to put their name to some daft article.

The reserves, of course, and the youth players, not being names, don't get any letters or offers. They tended to talk even louder in their little groups, pretending they didn't care, keeping half an ear open, hoping to hear about the latest free money which was being thrown at the big stars, who already, God knows, got so much money for nothing just by putting their name on the dotted line.

One morning Alan Mullery had about fifty letters. They must have included a backlog, accumulated during the summer months. As captain of the team and an England star he'd be expected to get most. He opened a few. They seemed to be mostly from schoolboys, wanting his photograph. He stuffed the rest in his pocket, to open at home. He intended to answer them, he said. He always did. He looked upon it as his duty.

Martin Peters had a questionnaire from a magazine called

Shoot! asking him his favourite TV programme and other important things, for a fee of course. Chivers had something from a TV rental company asking him if he'd like a free colour TV set.

Cyril Knowles gave a great shout. He had an invitation from a girl asking him to her party. When he turned over the page he found out she was aged eight. Six of the players had the same letter. Joe Kinnear had a postcard from a girl which read 'I am seventeen and very pretty and I would like you to take me out.' But there was no address. He held the card up to the light for any secret messages.

When Bill Nicholson arrived, he'd also had a letter. Someone was getting up a petition to stop the Government taking over a local sports centre. He got the players together and told them about it. 'The Government wants to turn it into a centre for drop-outs, hippies and other wasters,' he said, making it very clear what he thought of such awful people.

'For Roger Morgan,' said a voice at the back, and everyone laughed. Bill Nicholson paused for a minute, realising perhaps that everyone didn't share his attitude.

'Any views?' he said, stopping and pausing when the laughter died down. Nobody answered. 'Right then, I hope you'll sign the petition. I'll leave it here.' Then they began the day's work.

Since the first couple of fairly gentle breaking-in days, they'd got down to some very hard work. The road walks gave way to runs, either on the road, round the pitches or up and down a nearby canal. One of Bill's favourites was a fast sprint for seven hundred yards along a canal bank, followed by a fast walk round the houses, then a sprint back down the canal bank.

In the second week, Bill Watson moved on from straight-forward physical exercises to weight training. He keeps it up every Tuesday and Thursday during the season itself. He arranged his weights on the lawn in front of the dressing-room in twelve little piles, like the twelve stations of the cross. Some bars had to be lifted high in the air, others across the shoulders, or backwards, lifting them behind the legs. Each player had to do four sets of ten press-ups on each

27

station, doing each to the whistle, and then moving on to the next station, completing all the stations in twenty-five minutes. Bill Nicholson went round each station, urging on each person, making sure nobody cheated. A few did, like Roger Morgan, doing only three press-ups instead of ten, if he thought Bill wasn't looking.

When it was the youngsters' turn they did the same exercises as the big lads like Chivers and England had done. No allowances were made for their tender age or their strength.

Ralph Coates had never done exercises like these at Burnley, not for ten years when, by a coincidence, the same Bill Watson had travelled up to Burnley for a spell to train their players. Coates struggled manfully with the weights, having forgotten the technique. 'I thought you did them ten years ago,' said Bill Nicholson. 'Yes, when I was about twelve,' said Coates. 'You've got a birth certificate like Gilly,' said Nicholson. Alan Gilzean is the oldest Spurs player, but looks even older than he is because of his lack of hair. The club keeps his date of birth very quiet.

'Now this is called the Hack lift,' bellowed Bill Watson. 'Named after George Hack, who died last year at ninety-three.'

Bill Watson always puts a lot of show into his exercises, laying on a big performance with lots of grunts and loud breathing. He's very proud of all the teams he's coached over the years and the new ideas he's thought up. He also takes West Ham two days a week for weight training, giving them similar exercises to Spurs.

Most of Bill Watson's successes are printed so large on the top of his headed notepaper that there's hardly any room for his address. 'First Middle Weight in British weight lifting history to clean and jerk more than 312 pounds over-head,' so his notepaper announces in heavy large blue type at the top. 'Originator of the Dumb Bell Agility fitness system for football'. His house is called Olympus.

'Never call it weight lifting,' he said. 'It's weight *training*. What footballers need is agility, flexibility and strength. We want explosive power. Weight *lifting* would give the wrong sort of hefty muscles. We want athletes' muscles.'

His exercises are worked out progressively, starting at the beginning of the season with about fifty sit-ups at a time. By Christmas they would be at their peak with each player being able to manage two hundred sit-ups. He's written two books and sends leaflets on agility and fitness for footballers to thirty-two League clubs, in Britain and in Germany.

'I suppose Chivers is the best of this bunch. He can lift those hand weights like peanuts. But the others are very good.

'Some people think Mike England can't be very strong. For the size of him he's got very slender legs. But look at the separation of those muscles, look at the definition. It's quality not quantity you want.'

Bill Nicholson was watching every movement, jogging in his track suit, keeping his own sweat on by doing some of the exercises. 'Martin. Don't hold on to your thighs. That won't help. Nice pair of toes there, Skip. Keep at it all of you. Nobody told you to stop.'

Steve Perryman, the youngest first team player, had his eyes fixed almost maniacally, pummelling himself to greater effort. Some of the older players like Mullery, though working no less hard than Perryman, from time to time exchanged looks with each other, putting on the groans. Kinnear smiled at Chivers as he was reprimanded for holding his thigh. Peters went about his work quietly, in his own world, showing no emotion.

'How many have you done, Jonesy,' said Nicholson to one of the reserves.

'Free,' said Jones.

'You mean *three*,' said Nicholson, pronouncing it for him in his flat Yorkshire accent. 'Didn't you go to school.'

Terry Naylor complained that the light blue paint – Spurs colour – was coming off the weights onto his sweaty hands. Nicholson was very scathing. Imagine worrying about a bit of paint.

Bill Nicholson missed half an hour of his lunch break that day. There was the usual count-up of balls after each session, but this time there were two missing. He and the apprentices, whose job it is to clear up, all went round the hedges at the side of the pitches but couldn't find them. The

29

professionals had raced for the showers and the dining-room the minute the last exercise had finished. They didn't care about lost balls.

The two balls never turned up – it was presumed later that some kids amongst the spectators had nicked off with them when the players were busy training. Before the afternoon session, Bill warned them to be more careful. Whoever kicked a ball into the hedge had to bring it back. He'd looked everywhere but hadn't found them. Roger Morgan asked loudly if he'd looked in Cyril Knowles' Volvo.

'You've not got to be hard on Dainesey,' said one of the older players to Eddie Baily when that day's training was over. Barry Daines is the young goal keeper, deputy to Pat Jennings.

'What do you mean,' asked Eddie, all injured innocence.

'You upset him today. You've got to be tender.'

'Tender! Christ Almighty,' said Eddie, looking round, opening his eyes wide. 'At his age I had a bloody rifle stuck in my hand.'

It was during the second week that Bill gave his little pre-season team talk, telling them details about the coming season. He told them about two friendly matches in Scotland that had been planned against Rangers and Hearts. He warned them that all travel arrangements were private and not to be told the Press. He said that if they wanted extra personal insurance, they should see him that day. He warned about any fiddles in the car park this season. He said how lucky they were to have such a car park and how he always fought on the players' behalf to get them one pass each. But some people last season had been bringing two cars in, giving their car to their wife or a friend and coming in someone else's. It wasn't fair. Because of this they'd had trouble at the last match of the season when some of the Arsenal directors couldn't park in the car park.

He also warned them about swearing during training, now that so many women were coming to watch and soon even more kids, when the schools went on holiday. 'I don't mind a few words, but you know the ones you shouldn't use. So for Christ's sake lads, cut down the swearing.'

It was during this talk that he officially introduced the

deaf and dumb boy, Bobby Scarth. He said most of them were probably aware he'd joined them. He had decided to try him out for a season and he hoped that everyone would help him as much as possible. He explained that Bobby couldn't hear at all, but he could lip read and say a few phrases. Any questions? There were none.

By the third and fourth week of the training, they got down seriously to planning the new season's tactics. They were still doing their morning physical exercises, weight training and ball skills, the sort they do all the year round in their daily training, either at Cheshunt if it's fine or in the gym or ball court at White Hart Lane, but now in the afternoons they tried to use the practice matches to develop tactical moves.

Bill Nicholson had warned them in his pre-season chat that they had a hard season ahead. With being in Europe for the first time for four years (by virtue of winning the previous season's League Cup Final at Wembley), they had a lot more matches to get through. It meant that till Christmas at least they would be playing almost every Wednesday, in one sort of Cup tournament or another, with League matches every Saturday.

Once such a season begins, and such a season is now normal for any top team in the English First Division, there is rarely any time for tactical training. If for example a set piece is going wrong, they seldom have a chance to go back to square one and correct it. It has to be dropped. The best they can do in the season between games is practise ball skills and get the injured fit.

One of their main pre-season concerns revolved round dead ball tactics. A dead ball, or a re-start, is a movement which begins when the ball is stationary, after something like a free kick, a corner, a throw-in or a goal kick. When the re-start is from a good position it's possible to create in training a move which could lead to a goal in a real match. It does work, in the case of Spurs, a surprising number of times.

You could easily miss these set pieces, even if you knew what to look out for. They don't get down in a huddle like American football. It's not like chess where set moves are

31

part of the game and everyone knows them. No two moves in football are exactly the same.

It's the free kicks, throw-ins and corners that are the most important. They're explained with diagrams, at the end of the book (see Appendix 2). They've been developed out of the unique skills of certain vital players, such as the ability of Martin Chivers to throw a ball a good fifty yards, Gilzean's unequalled gift of flicking the ball with his head and Martin Peters' talent for hitting a dead ball and sending it precisely where he wants it to go, floating it, bending it, spinning it at will.

In all the tactical talks and trials, when they went over and over the same situation, everyone had an equal chance of giving his opinion or suggestions. When Nicholson shouted at them for not doing their part correctly, there was little hesitation about arguing back, explaining why they thought it had gone wrong. At least the older players did. The younger ones tended to keep quiet. But Nicholson was keen to hear all their views.

Apart from dead ball tactics, they also practised many passing moves. Such things as wall passes, where the person receiving the ball hits it straight back at an angle for his partner to run onto, or overlapping, where a player runs up from behind and goes past on the blind side of the opponent and down the wing into space, are used by all teams.

One afternoon they practised long passes into a space on the edge of the penalty area. 'If there's nobody there to pick it up, then it looks diabolical,' shouted Nicholson. 'So everybody must be thinking all the time. I want a *placed* pass. Not a centre or a cross. It should curve round the defence and into space for the winger to run on to it. Before it's made, the player making the pass should cut in so that he leaves more space on the outside.'

When it was Jimmy Neighbour's turn to make the pass, rather than receive it, he was going too far down the wing before passing and ruining the move. Mullery ran over to him and went over what Bill had been saying, explaining that if he cut in instead of going towards the wing he would be creating more space for his pass. By going down the wing, the defence were spreading out and covering men and space.

32

It's the sort of tactic, passing into space, which is sometimes hard for the fans to appreciate. So often it can look like a wasted ball. Some players have an instinctive sense of space, like Peters, but with others it has to be developed by making them think all the time. No wonder so many footballers come off the pitch these days with a headache.

There were also many human problems being discussed during the four weeks. The arrival of Coates, apparently to play as a winger, meant that there were now five possible first team wingers. Who would be left out? There were several injured players, like Morgan and Mike England, who'd missed a lot of last season, each wondering if he'd be fit in time or if the old trouble would play up. And of course there was money.

Players don't talk about the details of their contracts – they're not allowed to – but they can go on for hours about not liking the contract they've been offered, working themselves up into a state where they feel brave or confident enough to hold out, refusing to sign unless they get better terms.

A professional with a top club like Spurs, when he signs full forms at seventeen or eighteen, can expect about £18 a week to start off with. If all goes well, he can expect, without asking, another £5 every birthday. By the time he's progressed to a regular place in the reserves, perhaps with occasional first team appearances, he can expect to be up to £40 a week. But making the jump from there to £80 or £100 a week basic, which the first team stars expect, is very difficult. That's when one or two of them start getting fed up and think about leaving in order to get a regular place in some other club's first team. But no one wants to move, while there's still a hope at Spurs.

It's not just that the first team's basic wage is so much higher than the reserves, there are all the extra bonuses to be earned. They vary, depending on what a player can negotiate for himself.

As a generalisation, a leading club usually pays about £40 extra to each first team player when the team wins and £20

33

for a draw. Some clubs have bonuses which are geared to things like long service or crowd attendance, but not at Spurs. Bonuses accumulate, depending on how well a team is playing. Winning the First Division can earn each player in the team an extra £2,000. The Arsenal players, who won the League and the Cup the previous season, were said to have made about £14,000 each for their season's work.

In a reasonably good season, the regular members of a team in the top half of the First Division can expect between £5,000 and £7,000 a year. In the lower half, it's more like £3,500. In Division Two, the wages are around the £2,500 mark. In the Third and Fourth Divisions the wages are not much more than that of a semi-skilled factory worker. When the high wages of footballers are talked about it must be remembered that it's only a minority which gets them.

The top stars in Britain get nothing like the wages which the top stars in Europe or South America can make. The average is lower abroad, but the superstars can twist clubs round their fingers and manage contracts which can give them up to £50,000 a year. It explains why so many clubs abroad are bankrupt, surviving only because of some philanthropic millionaire. (Philanthropic probably isn't the right word. Many sociologists have pointed out that it's thought to be in the interest of a local millionaire factory owner, as in the case of Juventus of Italy and Sr Agnelli of Fiat, to keep the workers happy and their minds off Communism by producing a successful football club.)

The big talk about big money in football is all very recent in Britain. Until 1961, when the maximum wage was abolished, the Football League stipulated that a player could not be paid more than £20 a week in the season or £17 in the summer. Bill Nicholson spent most of his career, even as late as the fifties, on £10 a week in the season, £8 in the summer. No wonder he's a bit ambivalent when he's paying his stars of today £200 a week.

If you don't manage to get in the first team then the next best thing is the first team pool. Last season Spurs had had a first team pool of sixteen. Everybody was waiting to see which players would be in this year's pool. Bill didn't officially announce it. On the photo call day, the only day in

34

the year on which press photographers are allowed to photograph the Spurs players at training, it looked as if the pool was going to be nineteen. This was the number of players which Bill lined up for the official team photograph, the photograph which would appear all season in football fan shops up and down the country and in football programmes whenever Spurs appeared. 'Does that mean the pool is nineteen,' someone asked Bill. He said no, it was eighteen, but he wouldn't say who was in or out. The individuals knew and that was what mattered. Mr Nicholson is very keen on individual privacy, outside and inside the club. However, by talking amongst themselves, the players soon found out which eighteen were in the pool.

Getting into the first team pool entitles each member to half the first team bonus, even when he hasn't played in the first team. For example, if the bonus for a win is around £40 per man, then the seven members of the Spurs pool who haven't played in the first team that day get £20 extra. (A substitute who comes on as 12th man, even for a second, is considered to have made a first team appearance and he gets the full bonus.)

All the same, despite such perks, the reserves in the first team pool are usually the ones in every club who feel most dissatisfied. Not being established first team players, their basic wage and their status generally is still way below that of the first team.

Those reserves who have been with the club all their lives are the ones with the biggest moans. They're naturally jealous of players like Coates who come from another club, who not only get a share of the transfer fee but manage to negotiate much better terms right from the beginning. This of course is a common moan in any business. Loyal time servers always feel the newcomers get the best treatment.

'It *is* unfair,' said Jimmy Pearce over lunch at Cheshunt one day. 'How else can we get any sort of lump sum in our hands, the way they can? I've nothing against them personally, just that they get the best of everything. Good luck to them, but the club doesn't seem to care as much about us.'

Jimmy Pearce is a winger, one of the four who felt very worried by the arrival of Coates, which partly explained why

35

he seemed so fed up. But he'd been dejected for some time. At twenty-three he was already beginning to fear he'd missed the boat.

One of the reasons he felt he'd have to go was Eddie Baily. As assistant manager, Eddie is in charge of the reserves. 'I've tried not to speak to him for two years. He did a lot for me, when I was going through the reserves and fighting to get in the first team. Bill doesn't see the reserves very often so he has to rely on reports from Eddie. He gave good reports, which helped to get me into the first team. But after a while, I was dropped back into the reserves. My first game back was away to Cardiff. Eddie was on the bench and screamed and shouted at me all through the game, you bastard this and that. Every time I got the ball he was yelling at me what to do with it. I couldn't stand it. One minute he'd been all for me, then he seemed to have turned against me. I complained to him afterwards. Later I went to see Bill, which I suppose I shouldn't have done. I never heard anything else about it, but I haven't had any relationship with Eddie ever since. We leave each other alone.'

It's Eddie's way, to shout and scream from the touchline, and he'll do it with anyone, if he thinks they're not playing well. All coaches are the same, and quite a few managers.

John Pratt, another regular reserve on the fringes of the first team, said he'd already been in to complain to Bill. 'I said I wanted another £5 a week, but he said no chance. Why did I think I deserved it? So I told him. He said he'd think about it and see what the directors thought. As I was going out, he called me back and said there was just one thing which stopped him giving me a rise: 'I lacked skill.' John paused and looked around the lunch table at his mates. They all looked suitably sympathetic. 'That was really great, wasn't it. Just what my confidence needed. I'll sign in the end of course. I'll have to.'

That afternoon, Roger Morgan's knee suddenly began to swell up during a practice match. The doctor had officially declared the knee better, but Roger had felt all the time there was still something wrong.

He told Cecil Poynton, Spurs' seventy-year-old trainer, who stretched him out on a hilly slope and began exercising his leg, bending it up and down and sideways as far as it would go. Roger yelled in pain.

'It's nothing, nothing,' muttered Cecil, as the sweat stood out on Roger's brow. 'Cliff Jones's was four times as big as this.'

'But it shouldn't have swollen at all,' yelled Roger. 'It's supposed to be better. I'm sure it's a cartilage. They should have taken it out.'

'No, no,' said Cecil. 'Jack Charlesworth had his knee swollen so bad it was hanging out like a jelly.'

Roger didn't bother to ask who Jack Charlesworth was, presumably yet another star from Cecil's past. All he was interested in was his knee, not Cecil's old memories.

'It started last night, but it was down this morning. I knew I'd be limping this morning.'

'If you believe you're going to limp, you will limp,' said Cecil flatly, still stretching away. 'Dave Mackay still limps from his breaks, but it's never stopped him playing, has it?'

'It's the knee I'm talking about. Not fucking broken legs, Cecil. I've been through that one.' Roger calmed down a bit then looked almost pleadingly at Cecil. 'I don't understand it. I really don't. What am I going to do, Cec?'

Cecil looked carefully at Roger's knee, then he began to stretch it again, as far as possible, bending it to its furthest. 'Can you feel this? And this? Hmm.'

'It's on fire Cec, what shall I do.'

'Go and cool it. Get yon hosepipe over there.'

Roger went across the pitches and turned on a hosepipe, sitting down on the grass and letting the cold spray play on his knee. Soon he was surrounded by a pool of muddy water. The groundsman, Don, came up and asked him if he'd mind doing his paddling on top of the bank, then at least the water would flow around and do some good to the sunbaked grass.

In over fifty years in football, Cecil has seen most things. Not that he's hard or unsympathetic, just that over the years he's seen footballers yelling in agony one minute and running around the next. He's known many hard men, such as

Dave Mackay, a club legend as the man who recovered from two broken legs, the second one broken on his first match back. Cecil was the first team trainer in those days. Now he's in the background, specialising in treating injuries. He went back to another pitch to attend to another player who had taken a knock, leaving Roger with his puddles.

Roger wasn't putting it on. There was no doubt about his injury. But if you're suffering from a long and serious injury it can affect you mentally, debilitating the mind as well as the body. You don't want to knock yourself out when there doesn't seem much point. Roger had been bought for £100,000 in 1969 but nothing had gone right for him from the beginning. He'd been out of first team football for ten months with an injured knee. He'd hoped all summer that he would be fit for the new season, now it looked as if his knee wasn't going to be better after all.

'I'm sure it's bad. Nobody at the club thinks it's a cartilage, but that's what it feels like to me. I'm sick. I'm back to where I began almost a year ago when it first happened. I think I'll go and see Bill and double my insurance premium. Just in case.'

4

The First Game

Joe Kinnear was first to arrive at Tottenham, looking rather pale and strained, his summer tan long since disappeared, his three-piece suit rather hot for such a bright and sunny August morning. His ear was still heavy from the battering it had taken during the so-called friendly match on Monday with Glasgow Rangers. He'd been taken off unconscious after a collision and had spent the night in a Glasgow hospital. According to Cyril Knowles, Joe had only come round when he heard them discussing whether to cut his hair off in order to put stitches in his ear. That was a Cyril Knowles joke. All the same, Joe had had two stitches in his ear and was glad that his hair was long enough to cover it and protect his looks. Being the team's eligible bachelor, he's very conscious of his appearance.

It was coming up for nine o'clock on the morning of Saturday 14 August. The stadium was deserted. For the first match of the season, Spurs were going to play away. The few players who lived south of the River were being allowed to go direct to Euston. The others had to assemble at nine to get on the team coach.

Bill Nicholson wasn't at all happy, that first sunny morning in August. I asked if he was pleased with Ralph Coates' progress so far. He made a face. I asked about the friendlies and he said they were bad. The team hadn't played at all well. He felt a few hadn't been really trying, just because it was a friendly. They'd been beaten by both Hearts (1-0) and Rangers (2-1), which he felt they shouldn't have been, not with the talent they had. Not to try was unforgivable. A player should give his all, whatever the occasion. 'It shows in the end,' he said. 'They'll regret it.'

But surely he must feel reasonably pleased that for the first match he was going to be able to field his full strength side? Wolves, today's opponents, had two players missing, their captain Bailey and their leading goal scorer, Curran.

On the contrary, said Nicholson, he wasn't at all happy. He was playing a full side, but people like Beal and Peters had had knocks in training and who was to know if they were *really* better. They didn't have injuries that could be seen. 'I have to take their word that they're fit. They might not be.'

At Euston he went to buy some newspapers. He stood in the queue, groaning and complaining, saying that it was the worst paper stall in any station. Why they didn't have a stall out in the forecourt he didn't know.

Euston was full of football supporters, either gangs arriving early from the North or London supporters setting off. On the Spurs platform, their fans were shoving autograph books through the windows or trying to get into the compartments. Some of them were travelling on the same train but most were waiting for the later and much cheaper football special.

In another first-class compartment, sitting on his own, was Fred Rhye, an elderly North London bookie, Spurs' most faithful fan who has followed them everywhere for the last forty years, even to Japan during the summer. Morris Keston, another wealthy but much younger Spurs fan, was not on the train. He also never misses a match but his presence is not exactly welcomed by the Spurs officials.

When the train had started Martin Chivers went round the compartments, asking everyone where they were going that evening. He discussed a night-club with Phil Beal. 'What colour's the key now, green is it? It isn't? Sod it, I'll have to change mine now.'

Cyril Knowles later came round, asking what books everyone had. By books he meant magazines. He picked up *Penthouse* and read out loud all the juicy bits, holding up the middle page spread and telling everyone what he could do with it. 'We've read it, Cyril,' the others kept on saying. 'Yes,

Cyril, we've seen her.' It didn't stop Cyril reading everything aloud.

'Disgusting,' he said, finally throwing it away. 'They ought to ban them. I feel right degraded. Any more?'

Someone stretched and said ah well, after today only forty-one League matches to go. The morning papers were full of the football writers giving their predictions for the season. Many were tipping Spurs to be up amongst the winners at the end of the season. They all said they didn't like that. It was a bit worrying to be over tipped. It put pressure on you. The fans expected too much.

The team was mobbed at Wolverhampton and followed out of the station into the street and across to the Victoria Hotel. They were like Pied Pipers, marching ahead with screaming and shouting kids behind them, running to keep up.

In the foyer of the Victoria Hotel there were several touts asking for tickets, but the players could safely say they had none, as the tickets had not been given out yet. For an away match, each player is given two free tickets. Most of them could have done with more, like Ralph Coates. His wife's family were coming down from Burnley to watch him. Steve Perryman said his father and brothers were coming up and would expect tickets from him.

The players pushed their way through the well-wishers in the foyer and went up to a private room where an early midday lunch had been laid out for them. Ralph Coates was teased about what it must have been like at Burnley. Did he take his own sandwiches with him when they played away? Did Burnley have a first-class compartment or did they hitch-hike?

There was a choice of poached eggs, which the majority of the team had, or filet steak. Coates had a steak, though at Burnley he'd always had eggs. Bill Nicholson had said he should, just to settle his stomach. The first things which arrived on the table were big pots of tea which they all dived into. Mr Wale, the chairman, wasn't eating with the players. He said he'd wait downstairs for the other directors who were coming by car.

Bill Nicholson ate with the players, but at a separate table.

41

Johnny Wallis, the trainer, usually ate with them but he'd disappeared. Bill was joined at his table by the Spurs scout who covers the Wolverhampton area. He'd been watching Wolves' pre-season matches and gave Bill a run-down on things to watch.

After lunch there was a rush to the TV lounge except for a couple who waited for rice pudding. They'd heard that Dave McKay, the ex-Spurs captain, was supposed to be on.

The noise was deafening in the TV lounge. They turned the sound full on and shouted out remarks as they watched. One or two residents popped their heads in and were very surprised. They soon popped their heads out again, except for one pretty young Scottish girl who sat down and stared in awe at a room full of such thoroughbred male flesh. She couldn't get over it and kept on turning round, asking them who they were. They all went strangely shy, making faces behind her back at each other, going very subdued when she turned their way. She cornered John Pratt and Steve Perryman and told them her life story while they nodded politely, like little boys in their best suits and on their best behaviour. She explained she was on a sales course, staying at the hotel for three weeks. She told them that the previous week a Dutch team had stayed at the hotel, to play a friendly against Wolves, and what a good time she'd had with them. Would they be coming back to the hotel this evening? Oh, what a shame. She was making all the running and getting nowhere. Despite all the lewd remarks on the train, when the players had been reading *Penthouse,* now that they were actually confronted by a pretty girl, none of them wanted to know.

Downstairs in the foyer Johnny Wallis was waiting, all worried. For the first time in his long career, his precious skips containing the team's equipment had gone missing. At Wolverhampton he'd gone to the guard's van to supervise them being taken off – and they weren't there. They'd been taken off at Birmingham by mistake. After a lot of desperate phone calls, he'd been promised they would be put on the next train. He hoped they would arrive in time to get them to Molineux.

It had been growing very dark outside and suddenly the

thunder and lightning started and down came the rain. Up in the TV lounge, the players were all pleased. British footballers tend to like a wet ground. They like to do sliding tackles and have the advantage of a fast skidding ball when they take a shot at goal. Goalkeepers, of course, don't like the rain. There was a sudden extra roar outside, like a victorious army arriving. Hundreds of stamping boots and raucous voices could be heard charging up the street outside, shouting in unison and clapping, TOT-EN-HAM, TOT-EN-HAM.

'It's the lovely boys,' said one of the players, and they all flew to the window and threw it up. The supporters' special train had arrived and despite the weather and the fact that none of them had coats, they were charging in formation from the station as if they owned the place, ignoring the thunder and lightning and hailstones. They were too busy shouting to look up and notice the players, cheering back at them from an upstairs window in the Victoria Hotel.

'They're not soft, that lot,' said one of the players, closing the window when at last they'd all gone past.

Alan Mullery appeared with the tickets and distributed them, two each. There was a flurry to get biros and address the envelopes to be left for friends and relations at the ticket office when they got to Molineux, the Wanderers ground.

Just before two, the missing skips arrived and they all left the hotel and made their way by coach to Molineux. The streets had turned into rivers of rain water and some stretches were flooded.

Mr Wale, the chairman, sat on the coach at the front. He was looking forward to seeing the Wolves directors again. They had good relations with Wolves, though a few years ago there had been a minor incident at Tottenham involving a previous Wolves chairman, now dead. 'He was a terrible woman hater,' said Mr Wale. 'As we at Spurs don't allow women in our Blue Room, where we entertain visiting directors, this didn't worry us. But this particular Saturday Jayne Mansfield and her husband had come to watch us play. We'd invited the husband for a drink afterwards – and she took it upon herself to follow him. No one wanted to ask her to leave. So to make it easier and less embarrassing all

43

round, I popped down and asked the other wives to come up
and have a drink. But in the meantime, the Wolves chairman arrived. He wasn't at all pleased to see women around,
especially Jayne Mansfield!'

The visitors' dressing-room at Molineux, which you enter
straight from the main road, was cold and uninviting. The
players stood around, chatting, not wanting to get undressed
till it was nearer the time. Most of them followed Bill
Nicholson on to the pitch to inspect it, a ritual at all away
matches. The drainage was working brilliantly and the pipes
were disgorging gallons of brown rainwater into a ditch
around the side of the park. There was a sudden agitation
amongst the police standing guarding the players' tunnel.
Three cops appeared from the ground, dragging a Spurs
supporter, his face streaming with blood. There was still an
hour to go but the fighting had already started between the
rival supporters.

Back in the dressing-room, Cyril Knowles and Roger
Morgan were larking about, throwing an empty bandage tin
across the room, trying to land it on a hook. Cyril then
started kicking it noisily across the room. Martin Peters was
visibly upset, wincing every time Cyril kicked the tin,
wishing he would stop and that everyone would sit down and
be quiet. But he didn't say anything. Finally Cyril threw the
tin across the room, aiming at someone, and it went out of
a window and into the street.

'You cunt, Cyril,' said someone.

'Don't call him that,' said Martin Chivers. 'A cunt's a very
useful thing.'

There was a knock at the door. It opened and Cyril's
brother came in, looking very scrubbed and neat in a short
white raincoat. He stood hesitantly in a corner, looking
round. Peter Knowles used to be one of the stars of Wolves,
and still lives in the area. He gave it all up a few years ago
to become a Jehovah's witness, something you would never
expect Cyril to do. He looked across at Bill Nicholson,
knowing that the Spurs manager doesn't normally allow
outsiders in his dressing-room, but Bill recognized him. He
didn't say anything, just caught his eye and looked at him,
then turned back and continued talking quietly to Ralph

Coates in a corner. Cyril beckoned to his brother to sit beside him and they chatted quietly for about ten minutes. Martin Peters was obviously pleased by the peaceful interruption.

'That your brother then, Cyril,' said someone when Peter had gone.

'Yeh,' said Cyril. 'Still got a lot of skill.'

'Must have,' said Alan Gilzean. 'Takes a lot of skill to read the Bible.'

Everyone laughed. Bill Nicholson even smiled. He asked Gilly if it was the Palladium he was going to tonight. Gilly said yes. Top of the bill.

Ralph Coates asked Bill Nicholson if he should play on the right or the left wing. 'As it is in the programme,' said Nicholson blankly. 'Start off like that, on the right, then change with Gilly to the left straight afterwards.'

Bill went round several other players, giving last minute instructions, and then told John Pratt to get stripped off. He would be substitute. Roger Morgan was visibly disappointed. His journey had been pointless. At the same match last season, away to Wolves, they won 3-0 and Roger had scored one of the goals, one of his few matches before he'd been injured. He knew that his injured knee, which was still swelling up in training, was the main reason for not being picked, but he'd still hoped to have been substitute. If he'd known he'd rather have stayed behind and played in the reserves, just for the sake of some sort of game, rather than drag all the way to Wolves for nothing.

Roger stood around in his sharp suit and long hair, looking very out of place beside the spotless white virgin Spurs, all booted and padded, ready to work. He said he was going for a cup of tea and went out. He was back in a few minutes. He'd been thrown out of two tearooms, for not having the proper passes, or any passes at all, and had been forced to come back, safe in Spurs only bit of territory in a foreign land.

Nobody was really taking any notice of Roger as he rab-bited on. They were too busy with their own private last minute preparations. Pat Jennings was complaining that he'd lost something, searching in his own little plastic bag, one that's always brought in the team skip and contains his

THE GLORY GAME

gloves, cap, and other bits and pieces that might be needed on certain occasions. On a sodden pitch he needed the right gloves.

Roger went out again, to get to his seat, and there was a long and artificial silence. Bill paced round, having gone through his last minute instructions several times already, thinking to himself, his brows knotted, his hands clenched. A few minutes before three, the referee came in, to tell them he wanted a good clean game and to inspect their studs in case any were dangerous. When he'd gone, everyone immediately stood up, banging their boots on the floor, chattering noisily. They processed quickly to the door, turning round to one another, wishing each other good luck and shaking hands. They always wish each other good luck before a match. It's not purely in the hope that the game goes well – but that no one gets injured.

At the doorway, Bill clapped the backs of his players, wishing them in turn and by their Christian name all the best, good luck, as each went past him, down the corridor, through the tunnel and out to the pitch.

For the first twenty minutes of the match, both teams played at full pelt, running and passing with great skill and determination, despite the terrible conditions. Spurs perhaps showed more skill, but their movements were coming to nothing in front of goal, while Wolves were playing more direct and looked more dangerous. They scored just before half-time, helped by a mistake by Jennings. He appeared to let the ball fall from his hands after he'd taken a high cross and Bobby Gould put it easily in the net. It was the first time he hadn't handled the ball cleanly and safely.

In the second half, which began in another thunderstorm, Wolves were even more confident and scored again, this time from a penalty after a solo run from Dougan. Wolves now seemed certain of victory. They were giving nothing away and were playing harder than ever while Spurs showed few creative movements. Then with just ten minutes to go, Chivers scored after Wolves' goalkeeper made a similar mistake to Jennings, letting the ball out of his hands. Four minutes later, Gilzean scored Spurs' second goal, again against the run of play. This time Wolves fell apart, shaken

46

and demoralised, and in the last five minutes, Spurs, having
been behind for ninety per cent of the game, even looked like
winning, but it ended in a draw, two goals each. It was a
great disappointment for Wolves and a great relief for Spurs,
to have got one point away from home. Wolves are always a
strong team at home. Last season they'd finished fourth in
the League with the same number of points as Spurs.

Up in the stands, Roger Morgan said that Ralph Coates
hadn't done much, perhaps with a trace of bitterness. Coates
had been playing on the wing, in Roger's position. But none
of the Spurs team had played as well as they can, particularly Mike England who failed almost every time to stop
Derek Dougan, and Pat Jennings who had made the mistake
which had led to Wolves taking the lead. If they hadn't had
a couple of bits of luck, played for and well taken though
they were, the loss of two points might have been blamed on
that mistake by Jennings. As it was, the bad luck had been
equalled out.

On the trainers' bench, where he'd ended up frantically
yelling instructions, Bill Nicholson was drained but seemed
pleased. He'd signalled towards the end that Coates should
play up and Gilly come back, which had made a big
difference and might have given them victory.

The Spurs players trooped into the dressing-room pleased
with their unexpected reprieve. None of them had really
thought they were going to do it. They all said how deflated
Bobby Gould had been when Spurs had drawn level. He'd
put his face in his hands and said that was it, it's happened
again, we won't win now.

Bill Nicholson even went so far as to make a joke. As John
Pratt came out of the showers, after his exertions of sitting on
the bench all afternoon and not being called on to play, Bill
slapped him on the back. 'You didn't play a bad ball this
afternoon, John,' he said.

The players smiled, pleased that their manager was happy
for once. 'He's made up, isn't he,' said Martin Chivers in the
corner, watching Nicholson.

'What about Mart,' said Joe Kinnear, pointing at Peters.
'Near post', he shouts, then he belts it into the crowd.

Nicholson was standing in a corner, demonstrating with

legs apart and his arms wide some position that Mullery and Coates should have taken up. They listened respectfully, naked and dripping from the bath. The rest were still in the bath, singing and shouting.

They were quickly dressed and into the coach, pushing through a crowd of fans, wanting autographs. 'Well done lads,' said Ralph, standing in the gangway of the coach, beaming round, but rather nervously, half-knowing that as a new boy he shouldn't be drawing attention to himself. There was a pause while they thought of suitable insults. 'Yes,' said Cyril Knowles at last. 'Must be strange, getting a point from a game.' Coates sat down, smiling, glad that the expected insult hadn't been too wounding. At the back of the coach Roger Morgan went 'Ralphy, Ralphy, Ralphy', in a soft high pitched voice. Coates ignored him, guessing who it was.

The Spurs fans, marching and shouting their way back to the station, banged on the windows of the coach as it threaded its way through the crowds. 'Go on, smash the town up,' said Cyril, encouraging them.

'Didn't we get at them for that first twenty minutes,' said Mullery. 'There was a few lying on the deck.'

'But they got us back,' said Joe Kinnear. He'd got cuts right across his chest after Wagstaff's boot had caught him. He didn't appear angry with Wagstaff. He always has a duel with him. Nothing personal. He only wished it had been the other way round.

Chivers had put his top front teeth back in and now looked more human. With them out he's a frightening sight, charging down the pitch, with his deep set dark eyes and towering physique.

'What would you do? With all those dolly birds watching you,' he said quietly. 'I don't like looking like this, but if I left them in I might damage someone else's chances. They once came out and went through the side of my cheek. I've still got the scars.'

Mike England was very quiet. 'I had a bad game, that's all there is to it. But I'm glad I've got it over. If you get your bad game over with early the rest is usually OK.'

Pat Jennings was saying nothing at all. He was obviously very depressed about his performance. All the same, he gave autographs to the fans with the others on Wolverhampton station.

On the train home they had dinner and plenty to drink, half of them ordering lagers and limes, two at a time. The others were on soft drinks. Steve Perryman stuck to Coke. By the end of the journey Gilzean had several empty lager tins stacked in front of him. From time to time a few fans managed to get into the dining-room and stood around, asking for autographs or just watching the players eating, till they were finally moved on.

At Euston, Gilzean was off to his car immediately, disappearing in the direction of the West End.

'Did you hear Gilly at half-time,' said Joe Kinnear. 'He said only another forty-five minutes to go then we'll be heading back to London.'

Joe said he'd once gone with Gilly on a Saturday evening on the town but had to give up half way. He couldn't stand the pace. Most footballers drink very little, except for those who like a few lagers on a Saturday after a match, such as Gilly. Nobody can understand how he still keeps so fit. But he does.

On the coach back to Spurs, they discussed where they were all going that night. Despite all the boasts about night-clubs on the way up to Wolverhampton, they were all going quietly home to their wives, after a few lagers in the British Queen, a mod pub near the ground.

In the club's car park they said cheerio to Bill Nicholson. Cyril Knowles said cheerio loudly to all the players, as if he was going straight home, but when Bill had driven away he went over to the rest of the lads, checking which pub they were going to. Joe Kinnear was sitting in his car. He took a brush out of the glove compartment of his car and brushed his hair in the mirror. Roger Morgan was in his car, dabbing on after-shave.

Outside the British Queen, a woman in tight trousers with an expensive looking tan was waiting in a white E type Jaguar. She rushed towards the players when they arrived and went in with them and stood in a corner of the bar.

The players seemed out of place, almost elderly, compared with the casual, colourful teenagers and their girls. They looked so staid in their neat three-piece suits, more like business executives or salesmen. The girl in the TV lounge of the hotel in Wolverhampton had thought at first sight that they were all salesmen, arrived in Wolverhampton for a conference.

The expensive looking E type lady was aged about thirty and she too looked out of place. The Spurs players have two or three wealthy female hangers-on who try to get them to go to parties. They seem to live in £70,000 houses in North London and have husbands, usually twice their age, who are always abroad on business.

About ten o'clock, they said cheerio to each other and headed for home, leaving the E type behind. They watched the football on TV, then messed around, trying to spin out the time, unwilling to go to bed too early. After a match, none of them find it easy to sleep. They'd been preparing all week, for four weeks in fact, for one performance and now that it was over they needed time to calm down again. It had assumed extra importance, just because it was the first.

Like the players, Bill Nicholson, already back at his home, just round the corner from the British Queen, was filling in time, putting off bed, knowing he'd never sleep. It had been an uneventful beginning to the season. Not a match to remember. But Bill still couldn't get it out of his head.

'There's never any problem about sleep during the week. I always get to bed late, exhausted, thinking I've done bloody nothing, yet I haven't stopped. But on Saturdays I can never sleep. I'm too keyed up. I go over every kick.'

5

Bill Nicholson

Bill Nicholson was born in Scarborough, one of five brothers and four sisters. His father looked after horses, working in the winter as a groom and in the summer as the driver of a horse-drawn cab along the front at Scarborough. Bill was the only one of the nine children to pass the scholarship exam for Scarborough High School. Many of the children were fee paying, the sons of local businessmen, but Bill has no memory of being out of it.

At eleven he was playing for the school's under fourteen team, but he never thought about being a professional footballer. 'I lived in a small town, an out of the way sort of place, and it didn't seem to have anything to do with us. There was nothing like the scouting system we have today.'

He wasn't much interested in academic work at school, apart from geography. He never played for any representative or district team. Scarborough High, considering itself a bit posh, didn't allow its boys to do such common things.

He left at sixteen and went into a local laundry, Alexandra Laundry, looking after a drying machine. It wasn't much of a job but he was fortunate to have it, with depression all around. He'd got it through one of his brothers who was already working there.

On Saturdays, he played football for a local team, the Young Liberals, who were looked after by a dentist, a very keen football fan. Bill doesn't know how it happened, but through the dentist he got recommended to Spurs. 'All I knew was that one day, out of the blue, I got a letter asking me to come for a month's trial. My sister's still got the letter.'

After the month's trial at Spurs, he was taken on officially as a ground staff boy at £2 a week. 'I suppose I was a good

51

lad and worked hard. And mind you, it was hard work in those days. I spent most of the summer painting the girders under the stands, from eight to five almost every day. During the winter of 1936 I hardly had my jacket on. I think the South must have softened me over the years.'

He spent two years as a ground staff boy, most of it working, very little of it playing football. The only training was on Tuesday and Thursday afternoons, but even then the boys had to fit in almost a day's work beforehand. There was no organised training. 'I remember we used to play football under the stands, using a piece of old cloth as a ball.

'Even in the close season we had to work hard. After the end of every season, us lads and the ground staff men, about eighteen altogether had to line up with rakes in our hands and go slowly across the pitch, putting new seeds down and then raking it. I had blisters on my hand with doing it.'

His first and only girl friend in Tottenham was Grace, now his wife, who lived three doors down from his digs at 17 Farningham Road. She's always been known as Darky, even as a baby.

'I had a job understanding Bill at first. He came to our house practically every night, as he didn't know anyone else in London. My father had a billiards table and he often used to come and play.'

She was very proud to be going out with a Spurs footballer. They didn't have the glamour of today, but she says he was still considered quite a catch. 'He talked a lot about it being an insecure job, he might not make it, he might break a leg one day and that would be it, but I never worried.'

In 1938 he was signed as a professional. There were even more players on Spurs staff than there are today, all desperate to succeed. 'There were eight boys and forty-six professionals when I joined, yet there were only two teams. I was one of the lucky ones.'

The next season, only three games were played before war broke out. Everything was in chaos and in October 1939 he went into the army.

He joined the Durham Light Infantry and went up to Brancepeth and then Spennymoor where he learned to take guns to pieces and put them together again. 'We trained with wooden small arms a lot of the time. Nobody knew what was going on and nobody was really organised. I conscientiously worked hard to pass the Cadre course, just as I would conscientiously work hard at anything.' He soon became a lance corporal and then eventually a sergeant.

He spent most of his six and a half years in the army at home in Britain as an instructor, first in infantry training and then eventually he moved to the Army Physical Training Corps. He didn't play much football in the army as he was too busy training or instructing. But depending on where he was stationed he guested for the local team, among them Newcastle and Darlington.

After the war, he came back to Spurs, as a centre half. Six years out of football would be a lifetime today, but he says that everyone was in the same boat so it didn't matter. No youngster had come through because there was no proper wartime football for them to play in. 'I don't know how clubs kept going at all.'

Because of his army experience on the coaching and instructing side, he decided quite early on, after he was back at Spurs, to become qualified as a coach, though it was some other players talking about it one day which encouraged him to go. 'I passed first time and got my full FA badge. It was fairly easy for me, with my army experience. It's much harder to get it today. You don't usually get your full badge till you've done two courses.'

Having got his badge, he did a lot of spare time coaching, while playing for Spurs, just as several of his younger players do today. For many seasons he travelled up to Cambridge every week and coached the university team. 'It was good working with intelligent lads. They got the hang of things quickly, but intelligence doesn't make you a good footballer. Oxford and Cambridge would have the best sides if that were true. It's a football brain that matters and that doesn't usually go with an academic brain. In fact I prefer it when it doesn't. I prefer players not to be too good or clever at other things. It means they concentrate on football.'

Bill went straight into the first team on his return from the army. In 1949 under the inspiration of Arthur Rowe, the famous push and run team, which was to dominate English football in the early fifties, soon began to emerge. In 1950 they were promoted from the Second Division and the following season they won the First Division championship, the first time they'd done it in all their forty-three seasons in League football.

Bill had become Spurs' right half, alongside Alf Ramsey. As a player he was known for consistency, his hard efficient tackles and his careful distribution of the ball. He never attracted nor courted the limelight. But he played a vital part in a long and successful Spurs team. He was substitute for the England team on several occasions but only once earned a full cap, against Portugal in 1951, scoring a goal in the first minute. He was unlucky in that during most of his career Billy Wright was England's regular wing half.

It was one of Darky's disappointments that he only played for England once. 'He was picked for the next match, but he got injured and called off. He said he wanted to get fit for Spurs rather than England. Spurs paid his wages and it was his duty to get fit for them. Not that I ever tried to persuade him. I've never been involved in any of his decisions. I see it all from the wings.'

She saw his one and only international, but that was one of the very few matches she ever saw him play in. Even today, she's not allowed to watch a match. She'd like to go, as she's a keen football fan and watches every match avidly on television and reads the sports pages, but he considers her a Jonah.

'Basically, he doesn't think women have any place in football. I never saw him play for Spurs and I'm not allowed to go and see them now. I feel an outsider really, as if I was a member of the opposition.'

Bill Nicholson never expected to be manager, which is one reason why to this day he has never signed a contract. It was all such a surprise. He'd stayed on after his playing days were over and become the Spurs coach, mastering all the new developments, working hard to bring out the best in his players. He coached the Young England team and went to Sweden with England's 1958 World Cup team.

'I came in one morning in October 1958 and the chairman

asked to see me. I had no idea what he wanted. He told me the manager was resigning and he wanted me to take over.' They never got round to a contract because Nicholson decided it was unnecessary. Success is the contract. If he has no success, he knows and expects what will happen.

'Tottenham is one of the senior clubs with tremendous facilities and enormous status. Anything less than top class would not be accepted at Spurs. I would expect to get the sack if Spurs were not successful.'

As a manager, he has never moulded his team in his own image. For such a controlled, apparently cold personality he has constantly striven for lightness and brightness, for excitement and skills and above all, for entertainment. In an era of defence, he has dreamt only of attack.

In his first five years as manager, Spurs won the FA Cup twice, the Football League and the European Cup Winners Cup, the first British team to win in Europe. Since then, he has had to rebuild a complete new team. So far it's won two major trophies, the FA Cup in 1967 and the League Cup in 1971, but without showing any real consistency. The season before last (1969-70) they had, for Spurs, one of their worst seasons, being knocked out of everything by January, ending up eleventh in the table.

Nicholson is present and takes part in every first team training session. Two seasons ago for the first time he left it to Eddie Baily in order to try and get on with the mass of administrative work he has to do. That was when they finished eleventh.

'Last season I felt I had to drag myself out of the office. It makes me feel happier. If you're going to moan at the team you've got to know what they're doing every day of the week and keep on at them all the time. I don't know if it's because of my presence we did better last season. Perhaps just a coincidence.'

It's easy to believe him when he says he was surprised to be asked to be manager. His only ambition had been to be a coach. But he realised that if he turned down the job of manager, and another manager was brought from outside, that he'd probably lose his own job as coach. There's no doubt that the coaching side of football was his first love.

That was what he loved about his army work. That's what he likes now.

'In a game you only have one chance. The ball comes at you. You either volley it or lay it off, but you can only have one go at it. So training is vital, repeating and repeating every possible action.

'Look at tennis players. You see them serving the same ball, over and over again. Footballers have got to do the same. If you don't practise, you go rusty. I can prove it. I can suddenly test a certain skill, like trapping for example. You can see the first attempts. After half an hour's practice the difference is so marked that anyone can see they're doing it better.

'There's been an all-round improvement in the game because of the better training and coaching that goes on. People say it's the high wages that makes them keener. That helps. But it's the training that brings out the best.'

He doesn't appear worried or annoyed by the size of today's transfer fees. He thinks there's less of the auctioning and behind the scenes wheeling and dealing you got in the old days. 'A club values a player when he's up for sale at such a high price that only the ones who can pay are involved. It's all very straightforward.'

What he doesn't like is the fiddling that goes on at the other end of the scale. When a schoolboy player of fifteen joins a club nobody is paid. This is the law of the game. In these days of blanket scouting systems, every club in the land has heard of every lad who can kick straight by the time he's thirteen. As for the lads who get international honours, every big club has a scout constantly panting at his back kitchen door.

'Their dads have a great old time. When we've got a big match, he'll ring and we'll give the best free tickets. Next week, I know he'll be on to Arsenal for their big match and after that Chelsea. Until his son actually signs the forms, everybody will do anything for him. I've just lost a schoolboy international, and I know what went on. It's all illegal and I can't name names. It's hypocrisy if the League and FA think the rules are working. I know we're a famous club and you'd think a boy would want to sign for us, whatever he was offered elsewhere. But if you're a working man and someone offers you several thousand pounds for your son's name on the line, a sum you know you'll never get your hands on in a lifetime of work, what would you do?

'We've never done it at Spurs. But it is done. I don't know how, mind you. Every penny here has to be accounted for.'

Nicholson's day is almost three days. The morning day is coaching and training, a job which could easily fill the whole day as he maintains that to coach properly you must think almost as much as you act. 'There must always be an object. You fall back on your past experience a lot of course, but you must know all the new developments and just *think* about the game all the time.' In the afternoon he's the administrator. 'I try to be alone in the office to get half an hour's work done, but always there's the chief scout wanting to see me or the club secretary or someone.'

It's often after midnight by the time he gets home. The evenings are when he sees other teams and other players that he or the scouts think he should see. It's not unusual for him to leave the ground in the afternoon, after a full day's work, pick up a ticket at London Airport and fly to Scotland for a second division match, coming back overnight.

It's not stamina he thinks a manager needs above all, or even money. 'In a word, it's judgement. All the time you're assessing players. Apart from skill, what I'm always looking for is character.'

He finds it difficult to relax or take his mind from football or to take part in idle chat. If he does manage an hour's TV he will suddenly jump up and say that's another hour he's wasted. He expects his wife to jump to attention when he sounds his horn outside, at whatever time he arrives back, to open the garage doors for him.

It's the same modest end of a terrace house, just off White Hart Lane, which they were living in when he was first appointed manager, some fourteen years ago. It was a club house at the time, but they eventually bought it. They've improved it and built an addition at the back and today it's probably worth about £9,000, but it's still not exactly the sort of house any of his star players would want to live in. Their houses are double that price. It's more the standard of house his reserves might have, though they would prefer something new, not pre-war.

'People are always surprised that we live in such a modest house for his position,' says Darky, 'but I insisted that we stayed in it while he's at Spurs. We could move out somewhere nice, but I'd never see him. He's in so little. We're so near that he can at least pop in for a cup of tea or come home for lunch. I'd never see him at all if we lived way out. When he retires, we might move further out.'

Inside, the house is absolutely immaculate, with every knick-knack spotless and every surface gleaming. The furnishings are very similar to those in the players' homes, though not as lush or as new as some of them. There are ornaments on the walls and on shelves brought back from South America, Japan and Israel, and other places. There's a glass alcove full of coloured wine glasses, bought on his travels.

Most of his star players don't go in for any obvious signs that they're footballers, though the younger ones do. They hide any cups or caps away in corner cabinets. But the Nicholsons have several team photographs displayed on the wall. One shows Bill opening a bottle of champagne in the dressing-room with his beloved double team. He's wearing a huge grin and a bowler hat over his ears, very untypical. There's a large painting of Wembley, given to him by the FA. There are silver trays and trophies, presented by the club on the occasion of some triumph or other. There's an inscribed silver teapot given to him by Mrs Barbara Wallace, the lady who works in the general office at the club. She's a lifelong friend of both Bill and his wife.

For many years, Darky used to teach sewing and soft furnishing at Tottenham Tech. These days she works there two afternoons a week, helping out in the office, just to give herself something to do. She never worked, on principle, while their two daughters were at home.

They're both very proud of their daughters' achievements. They both went to local schools. Bill refused to send them to anything but state schools. Linda is the elder one. She's twenty-four and was living last year at Bradford where her husband was studying a course at the university. Jean is

58

twenty-two and studied mathematical engineering at Southampton University. They're both very sporting, playing hockey and tennis. Jean got a blue for athletics and hockey at university. She was due to get married that season, in December 1971.

He obviously wishes he could have spent more time at home during their schooldays. He had tears in his eyes at Linda's wedding, much to his wife's amazement. 'I heard him beside me and I thought he's got a bad cough, then I saw his eyes. He couldn't stop. He kept on saying "I never saw her growing up".'

Bill has never been one to show emotions. Over the years, she doesn't think he's changed. Having the worries and strains of a manager hasn't made him worse. 'He's very Yorkshire. They're all like that up there. He never shows what he's thinking. When he comes in from a match I can't tell from looking at him whether they've won or lost. Now me or the girls, we're up in the air, all excited and shouting if we win something.

'He never even told me the day he was made manager. It was a Saturday and he went in as usual in the morning. It was apparently on the radio, but I was rushing around all day with the girls and didn't have it on. He didn't mention it when he came home till my mother arrived and said to him straight away, congratulations. I thought she was saying it because the team had beaten Everton 10-4. But she kept on about it and then it all came out. I said why didn't you tell me, ring me up or something? He said he hadn't had time, he'd been rushing all day. Yet he'd known from about twelve o'clock, when they'd had a special directors meeting before the match. But that's the sort of person he is.'

Mrs Nicholson is proud of his position, despite the hardship of rarely seeing him. 'Who would have thought when he arrived as a boy from Yorkshire in 1936 that he'd be lord of it all.' But she thinks he was happiest as a player. 'He's said many a time that there's only one job in football, and that's playing. When you finish playing, the enjoyment ceases. He says it's a bastard of a job, being manager. That's the word he uses. When he finishes, he says he won't go and watch football again. All he watches for is mistakes, jotting

59

them down in his little pad. I'm for it if I don't get him refills in time. It's his job to watch for mistakes and he doesn't enjoy it. Even at home, he watches it on TV in silence. I jump up at all the goals and you should see Barbara (Mrs Wallace), she really gets carried away. I like goals myself. I like to see wingers in full flight, like Cliff Jones, putting the ball over for the centre forward to pop in. I think that's lovely.'

Their phone number is ex-directory, not because of Bill's position but because of some obscene phone calls his daughters got a few years ago. It's kept very secret, especially from the Press. 'If anyone does ring I always tell the truth. Bill asks me to say he's not in but I never lie. I say he is unavailable.'

He always tells her specially not to talk about football, because she doesn't know what she's talking about. But nevertheless, unlike most of the players' wives, she is a football fan and she knows what she likes, such as goals, and she has a favourite footballer – Ralph Coates, though she feels very guilty about admitting it.

There's a little drawing of him pinned high above a door, the only sign of the present day Spurs side anywhere in the Nicholson home. I had to stretch to recognise that it was Ralph. Barbara Wallace sent it to her. It's been a family joke for years, long before he was signed by Spurs. 'He's so full of G and T, as Eddie Baily would say. Guts and Tenacity. I've always thought he was terrific. I was so disappointed when he was sent back from Mexico from the England squad.'

She had of course no influence on Bill's decision to buy Coates. That's the last thing she could ever have. 'But when he rang me up from Stoke to tell me he'd bought him he said if he turned out not to be worth the money, he'd take it out of my wages! That was a joke of course. I only hope that Ralph is going to score lots of goals. It would be so lovely.'

She couldn't remember when she was last out alone with her husband, just for a night out. They have no social life together. On the rare occasions when he does go to football dinners, he doesn't take her. In the days when there were parents' nights at the girls' school she had to go alone.

'But I'm not moaning. I accept it all. I understand why

he's got so much to do. He knows that he's missed things. He would love to have been more of a family man because he loved his own family. Even though they didn't have much, they were very happy. He's told me many a time how there was one scooter between the nine of them. They had to line up at the gate, waiting their turn while one went round the block.'

Now and again he does manage to tear himself away from football for the odd hour. He even goes to his office every Sunday morning, but sometimes tries to finish early, round about eleven o'clock. Then they both drive to Epping Forest and have a long walk and a drink in a pub. Drinking in a pub is very rare. Bill usually refuses to go into them, knowing he'll be pestered.

On an upstairs landing there's a bag of golf clubs, unused, though he's always saying he's going to have a game. In the garage there's a carpenter's tool kit which she bought him for his 21st, still hardly touched. In the fridge there's a large bottle of Sauterne, the only sliver of middle-class life style which appears to have rubbed off on him. He likes to have a glass of Sauterne with his lunch.

She worries about his health. He is incredibly fit, but he won't admit it when he is ill. He doesn't believe it and will always drag himself out of bed. He was always very proud of his daughters when they dragged themselves to school or to work when they didn't feel well. But he did collapse about three years ago, with the strain of it all, and was forcibly made to rest for a while. 'But he won't be warned. He hates being ill.

'He's been lucky as a manager, being with a club like Spurs. I feel so sorry for the managers of some clubs, and their wives. He's fortunate that it's a wealthy club, completely self-supporting so it doesn't have the money worries of some clubs. He's never had to sell players because they need the money. And he's been lucky that he's been able to make all the decisions on his own. He's had a free hand from the beginning.

'The players get so much money these days. I don't know how he can find new incentives for them. I'm not jealous of them. Even at the end of Bill's career the maximum wage was only £20, but I was quite happy with it. I thought we did well.

'I don't know what his salary is today. He never tells me and I wouldn't ask. I don't know what he's saved either. I think he's got money in the building society because I've seen the letters, but I really don't know about anything like that.'

Bill Nicholson doesn't give much away. It's not in his nature. He sees little point in talking about football, certainly not to outsiders. He feels that no one can help him to do his job so talking is just a waste of breath. All that matters is winning. Unlike some managers, he has no confidants inside his club or out, he has no pet journalists and no time for going on television.

Over the years, as one would expect, he's constantly been described as being dour. It does seem an intrinsic part of his nature which hasn't been helped by his own hard life, as a boy in a large family growing up in the Depression or as a player in the days when they got little pay and no status. He does tend to generate dourness by the way he discourages chat, or casualness or any flippancies. He finds it hard to be spontaneous.

But his dourness may be partly a mask. Perhaps in the excitements and tragedies of the season ahead he might start giving a few things away. There's no knowing what might be inside.

6

The Supporters

On the morning of the Newcastle match, Spurs' first home game of the season, John Harris left his council flat in Bethnal Green as usual to catch the eight forty electric train to White Hart Lane. And as usual, he was clutching a two-foot-wide bread pudding which his mother, aged eighty-five, had made for him the night before. She makes one every time Spurs play at home.

Playing at home is not just special for the players. It's special for every fan and every official, for the touts and the trainers, for everyone connected however remotely with the club, from the chairman to the souvenir seller. When the team's at home, they all have their own ritual which they lovingly ease themselves into.

Mr Harris is a bachelor of fifty-six and lives with his mother. He used to have the flat decorated with Spurs photographs but his mother always complained, although she is an ardent supporter. She said they attracted the dust. So when they last redecorated, the photographs went, even the ones above John's bed.

He got to Tottenham High Road at nine o'clock and got out his keys to number 744, a three storey terrace house, the official home of Spurs Supporters Club. It's the next but one building to the Spurs ground. In between is the London Co-op Funeral Parlour. Mr Harris is the full-time Secretary of the Supporters Club, a job he has had since 1966 when he gave up being a veneer panel worker.

Mr Harris was wearing his number two Supporters' Club blazer, in blue, the club's colour. His best blazer he keeps for important functions, like the Mayor's reception. His number two blazer is for work days.

He took the bread pudding to the members' bar on the

ground floor. His mother had already cut it into slices which they would sell to members for four new pence a slice. You have to be in sharp to get a piece. It goes very quickly.

From nine till about ten, when other Supporters Club officials and helpers arrived, he worked on his own, opening the mail and sorting it out, and answering the telephone. There was a call from Newcastle, saying the weather's bad up here, what's it like down there then?

'I can see the flags flying on the grandstand as I look out of my window,' said Mr Harris down the phone. 'That means the match is on.'

Mr Harris is thin and bespectacled with ears that stretch back. His manners and voice are calm and flat, like a long-suffering clerk or a minor trade-union official. It's very easy to miss his jokes, especially on the phone. When the phone rang next, he said 'Weather Information Bureau'.

A worried voice said there must be a mistake, he wanted the Spurs Supporters Club. Mr Harris said yes, speaking. 'But you just said Weather Information Bureau?'

'That's right. It's all I seem to be doing today. The match *is* on. Unless snow comes down and covers the terraces between now and the kick-off, the match is on. Thank you.'

He put the phone down and went on opening the post. It was going to be an evening match, this first match of the season, so he had a full day's office work ahead.

Every few minutes there were calls from supporters wanting travel arrangements, the price of tickets, to an elderly man who wanted the results of Spurs pre-war matches against Newcastle.

Two hours before the kick-off, the Club house had turned into a little factory, with ten committee men and twenty volunteers manning all the various departments. About half a dozen guarded the front door, getting ready to stop gatecrashers and control the crowds.

The front hall is divided with a wooden barrier running up the middle, like a turnstile, painted light blue of course. On the left, as you go in, is the shop which sells everything that any Spurs fan, however mad, could possibly want. At the last count they had 143 different items, from Spurs track suits at £4 each to buttons and balloons at 3p. Last year, the shop, which opens only on match days, took £1,300.

On the right is the bar, complete with a one-arm bandit, a colour TV and photographs of famous ex-Spurs, like McKay and Blanchflower, receiving the club's awards as Player of the Year. At the back there's a coffee bar and kitchen. Upstairs, a junior coffee bar and lounge. Before the match, the thirty workers coped with over four hundred members pushing in and out of the house, either to the bar, or to buy Spurs mementoes, or to put their names down for the special savings stamps which you can buy weekly to go towards foreign trips.

The fact that Spurs were this season in Europe again had already had a big effect on the Supporters Club. More and more people were joining, partly to take advantage of their cheap travel arrangements to foreign matches.

'It was really the thought of Europe which made me give up my job in 1966,' says Mr Harris. 'I couldn't afford yet again to miss so many days off work. The salary here is much lower than I was getting, but I don't now have the expenses of travelling to see Tottenham. My hobby always was my life, now it's my work as well.'

Most of London's first division supporters clubs are of post-war origin. The ones in the North and the Midlands are much older. Spurs Supporters Club began in 1948. They had to use the word Spurs, not Tottenham Hotspur, which they wanted to, because the club wouldn't let them. Most London clubs were a bit snooty about any supporters organisations – and many still are. They didn't want the tone lowered by any rabble elements. They also feared that supporters clubs could get too powerful and perhaps make a take over bid for the club. The Arsenal Supporters Club had the same trouble, asking for years to be allowed to exist before permission was at last graciously given.

But for the last ten years, Spurs Supporters Club has been officially recognised by Tottenham Hotspur FC and relations are now very amicable.

All the club officials that came and went that day seemed solid working men, middle aged rather than young, with their good suits on and best shirt. There's something touching about their earnestness and their eagerness to do

65

the right, respectable thing, to keep up the tone at all times. They know that Big Brother next door doesn't really need them and that they're not going to get much recognition, but all the same, they do their own things, keeping in their place, very conscious of their position, nay the honour, of being allowed to carry the Spurs name.

Tottenham Hotspur, being a wealthy club, clearly doesn't have to depend on any supporters association for financial support, which is sad for the supporters. The majority of clubs outside the first division depend on the supporters clubs and their fund-raising activities. In many cases, a supporters club can almost run a football club.

Spurs Supporters Club is aimed simply at helping supporters support Spurs. The biggest thing they do is organise cheap travel, chartering railway compartments or hiring buses for their members.

These official Supporters Club trains and coaches must be in no way confused with the specials which British Rail themselves put on. These are the ones full of skinheads. Every official supporters club in the country spends a great deal of its life disclaiming any connection with the unorganised skinhead supporters and their train wrecking activities.

'No damage has ever been done by a member of an official supporters club, yet the press still get it wrong and it rubs off on us. They send their photographers down to photograph the broken windows, and the next day the headlines talk about supporters club fans doing all the damage.

'The club's finest hour was in 1963, the year of the Great Airlift, the most fabulous supporters trip of all time! That was for the European Cup Winners' final in Amsterdam. What a day! I'll never forget it as long as I live. From dawn, we had coaches lined up all the day down Paxton Road. It was wonderful. I can see them now. We ran a shuttle service to Southend where planes were going every fifteen minutes. We had twenty-two aeroplanes in all, most of them doing double trips. I don't know where they got them all from. I think they were digging out old ones used by the Wright Brothers. Cor, what a day, We shifted 2,500 supporters by plane that day.

'Most people were going on an aeroplane for the first time. Back in those days, the ordinary working man wasn't as used to flying as he is now. Spurs were the first to win a final in Europe so naturally we were the first English club to organise foreign trips in a big way.

'It's wonderful to think it could happen again this year. It's the greatest thing in the world to go on a foreign trip with a nice crowd of supporters.'

Mr Harris is so experienced in organising football supporters' trips that during the summer he went as a courier with a rival club, Chelsea, on their trip to Athens for the European Fairs Cup Final. For that trip he wore his Chelsea Supporters Club tie. Mr Harris has twelve official supporters clubs ties which he wears on week days to Spurs, as the fancy takes him. They range from amateur clubs like Dorchester Town, through Macclesfield and Wrexham to Everton and Chelsea.

Mr Harris is a very important man in supporters club circles. He's the general secretary of the Federation of Football Supporters Clubs, an organisation which has 285 member clubs, all like the one he organises at Spurs.

It's generally accepted, so Mr Harris says, that Spurs Supporters Club is in the top six in the First Division, along with Everton, Liverpool, West Brom, Coventry and Newcastle. Each of them has about the same social and travel facilities, although most clubs envy the two Liverpool clubs the size of their club house. Each uses a converted cinema. Mr Harris put an offer in for one locally, but didn't get it. But clubs in other divisions have equally good if not better social facilities.

At the beginning of the season, Spurs Supporters Club numbered 6,400 official members. They have members all over Britain and in Malta, the United States, South Africa and Australia and every European country, particularly Scandinavia. That morning Mr Harris had a letter from a Norwegian fan called Odd Holeu who each year studies Spurs fixtures so that he can make a quick visit and cram in as many games in the shortest number of days. He sends for all the programmes of matches he misses.

Spurs Supporters Club have no branches. This time

they're a bit snooty about allowing their name to be used. 'I've got an application here from Belfast to start an official branch. We get them from all over but we find that in most cases the people are just in it for the money. They want to sell Spurs souvenirs and make a quick profit. We're not in it to make a profit. We're simply here to help supporters.'

Firms pester them all the time to get them to sponsor or sell souvenirs. Most of them are turned down as being shoddy or just plain daft. Mr Harris had just got a doll from Hong Kong, at least it said on the outside it was a doll but when he blew it up, he couldn't make out what it was. The idea was it would wear the Spurs strip. 'Very nasty,' said all the club officials when they saw it.

Mr Harris has a season ticket for Spurs, the same one for over twenty years, but he's very often late getting into the ground, having to lock up the supporters' club. 'I'm allowed to go through the directors' entrance to my seat, which means I don't have to queue or go through any turnstiles. It's very nice of them.'

All people on the fringes are terribly grateful for any crumbs or signs of recognition from Tottenham. Fred Rhye, who was on the train to Wolves, has the unique privilege for an ordinary supporter of having a pass to the club's car park, a privilege which is impossible to buy.

Fred Rhye is seventy-four and no other Spurs supporter comes near him, when it comes to supporting Spurs. He's given a lifetime's devotion to the club. In the last forty years he has missed only three games. He's been a widower for three years, but even when his wife was alive, it never stopped him travelling all over the world with Spurs. 'She got used to it in the end. She had to. I said I was off and I went.'

During the close season, he was the only Spurs supporter who followed them to Japan, paying all his own expenses, just to see their three games. He never travels with the official party, but always manages to get a seat in the next compartment or a hotel room on the next floor. He's always alone, just sitting there, very quiet, never pushing. He doesn't seem to mind not being invited into the inner party. Being near to their presence seems to be enough for him. They all

68

know him, of course, from the chairman to the newest first team player, and when they notice him, they always say hello Fred, how's it going. He's a large, lumbering giant of a man with a pock-marked face, a very dark suit and grey hair pushed back in a middle parting. You'd think he couldn't be missed, but because he never talks and hardly seems to move, he fades into the walls till you suddenly realise his watery eyes are watching, like a genial toad in the corner, taking it all in.

He was born Fred Broderick but is known by eveyone as Fred Rhye, which was his boxing name and now the name he uses in his betting shop business.

He doesn't know how much he spends a year on following Spurs, but with trips like the two and a half weeks tour of Japan thrown in, it must come to about £3,000 a year.

He always talks about the club as 'we' as if he was a player, or at least an official. After forty years of organising his life round the club's movements, he lives his life through them. He can't remember when he didn't do it. He's used to people saying he's daft but when pressed about why he does it, or to describe the pleasure he gets, he finds it hard to explain. 'It's my hobby, isn't it, that's why I do it. It's a hobby I've made into my life.'

He never watches any other team, not even on TV. Only Spurs. This is what particularly endears him to Spurs officials. They mutter darkly about some of the so-called supporters, the flash ones, who throw their money about at all top players, holding parties for them, offering them money or presents, trying to get them to go to dinners. If they can't get a Spurs player, they'll turn to another club. In Fred's life, there's only Spurs.

He thinks he was closer to the players in the old days than he is now. 'Ted Ditchburn was a good friend, and Eddie Baily. And Alf Ramsey. He was a right gentleman.' In one of the many dusty drawers in his office, he keeps a letter written from Bill Nicholson in 1958, thanking Fred for his kind letter of congratulations on being appointed manager. He also thanks Fred for a couple of boxing tickets, which Fred had thoughtfully sent as well. Since Bill Nicholson's arrival, he's never been in the dressing-room, but then very

very few people have.

He lives alone in a large terraced house in the Caledonian Road. It's old fashioned and Dickensian, full of photographs of bygone Spurs stars. His office is just as Dickensian, strangely silent and untouched somehow, with men sitting silently in corners on high stools in front of roll-top desks, waiting for something to happen.

'It's going to be a great season. Coates will make all the difference. I have nothing to look forward to when they're not playing. I'm always glad when the season starts again. I've felt out of sorts all summer.'

While John Harris was supporting his supporters and while Fred Rhye was easing himself into his Rover and into life's routine, the spivs and touts and salesmen were flocking towards Tottenham High Road, getting ready their wares for the first haul of the season.

This season, at long last, Spurs were going to open their own club shop, something they should have had years ago. They'd advertised for a manager and were busily interviewing. Thousands of pounds are made each week from selling Spurs souvenirs, yet the club itself, the source of all the goodies, has never profited.

Tom Mann, who has a souvenir shop in the High Road, not far from the ground, wasn't at all worried by the prospect of some official competition. He's made a living out of Spurs for five years and sees no reason why it shouldn't continue.

He started by selling Spurs programmes in the street, as a part-time job on a Saturday. The rest of the week he was a window cleaner. He'd been a Spurs fan for years and wanted extra money to follow them around. When he found he was being asked for last week's programmes and away match programmes, apart from the current programme, he started specialising in football programmes for all teams and for all matches, going back sometimes for years.

During the week, he runs the shop on his own with one part-timer. But when Spurs are at home, he needs a staff of seven to cope with the crowds. As the kick-off approached for the Newcastle game, the first home game of the season, the crowds were jamming the entrance. A policeman came over

70

and made them stand in an orderly fashion.

'I don't know how many people I serve on an average Saturday. All I know is that Spurs average home gate is thirty-six thousand and they all seem to be in here at once.' On a good Saturday, he can take £300.

He sells about a thousand Spurs programmes every Saturday, but even more surprising, he also sells four hundred Manchester United programmes. He has a bulk order sent down from Manchester every week and sells them to London based Manchester United fans who haven't managed to get to Manchester. That day a young boy came in with a battered Addidas bag full of old and tattered programmes. He said there was four hundred in the bag. Tom Mann glanced at the bag quickly and offered the boy £5, take it or leave it. The boy thought for a bit, then accepted the money.

'The dearest programme I've ever heard tell of was for the 1946 Cup Final between Charlton and Derby. That fetched £26.

'The most expensive thing I had was a 1905 Spurs handbook, the first they ever did. It was published by the White Hart pub. I had an offer for £80 for it, but I wanted to keep it myself. Then when I was away on holiday, my Dad was looking after the shop and he sold it to a Norwegian Spurs fan for four bob. He's dead now, my Dad, God rest his soul.'

His most consistent line is books about Spurs, either ghosted autobiographies by the star players or assorted annuals. He estimates that in nine years, counting selling stuff on the street on a Saturday and then in the shop, he's sold sixty thousand Spurs books. 'Greaves, Mackay, Blanchflower, they were the best. Mullery's book was the worst. I think it's because today they don't have the personal following of the sixties. Greaves was the last individual player. My shop was almost empty for two weeks after he was transferred. The fans didn't want to know.'

He's never had any trouble over copyright, though the scores of mugs, plates, pennants, scarves, pens, wallets, dolls and other such stuff littering his shop all either have photographs of footballers or club crests. 'There's not a lot a club can do to stop it. I wish they could. Look at this Spurs mug. If you study it closely, you'll see that heraldically it's not quite right. The spurs on the legs of the cock are missing. The manufacturers usually change things slightly so that a club can't sue. Not that the manufacturers really worry. It mostly comes from Hong Kong.'

Just before the kick-off, as Tottenham High Road had grown suddenly quiet and empty, Tom Mann shut up shop and raced to the ground to take up his seat. Like John Harris and Fred Rhye, he has his season ticket which entitles him to the same seat, season after season.

The players aren't interested in these lives which revolve round the club. They're protected from it by the club and by their own exclusiveness. They've got their own routines to concentrate on. In many ways they're suspicious of supporters. They put on a public face should they meet them, keeping their private jokes and their real personalities to themselves. They know only too well that when things start to go wrong, there are always those supporters who can suddenly turn against you.

The Newcastle match itself turned out not to be worth the build-up, both from outside and inside the club. There was little football, no goals and no signs of future successes or future failings. It was frustrating for the players and eminently forgettable. But there were two bits of drama, both of which had repercussions for the rest of the season.

The drama happened right from the beginning. Unknown to most people, 18 August 1971 turned out to be the first big day of the new interpretation of the laws of the game by the referees. From now on, every little transgression was going to be heavily penalised. It was a complete shock, according to the football managers and directors, who all said later that they hadn't been warned. And as for the players, they were choked. (Players are always choked, that's when they're not sick. When things go right, they're well pleased. Bad decisions are always diabolical. Places they don't like are hateful. Players they don't like are wankers.)

The referee booked five players in all that evening, three from Newcastle and two from Spurs. Mike England was booked for a tackle from behind, an offence which up to then had been punished, if at all, by a free kick. Joe Kinnear, even more surprisingly, was booked for stopping the ball with his hands. The ball had been going out of play when he touched it, so he hadn't been interfering with play. But the new interpretation of the rules said that a deliberate hand ball had to result in a booking. (In the dressing-room afterwards, Joe said he'd protested to the referee. 'He said he was sorry he did it, but he had to under the new rules.')

Being booked is a very serious offence for a player. Three bookings in a season and he will be disciplined, either by a fine or by being suspended, or both. That same day, forty-one players were booked in English League matches. The total for the week rose to 123 players, about five times the normal amount.

The League was trying to clean up English football which was said to have become nasty and brutish. It was probably true, compared with many foreign countries. But it was the manner in which the rules had suddenly been announced and the inconsistency of their application which kept the football writers in a state of apoplexy for weeks and the managers frothing at the mouth.

Once the book started coming out on the field, it was obvious that the players on both sides didn't know what to do. They were penalised for actions that had been part of their training since they were thirteen. They were perplexed by the amount of infringements and the game lost any rhythm it might have had.

The second bit of drama concerned the crowd. Just after half-time, the Newcastle goal keeper, Ian McFaul, went down, struck by a missile thrown by someone in the Park Lane crowd. Apparently other missiles had been thrown at the Newcastle players earlier in the match. At half-time they'd protested to the referee, saying they wanted protection. When their goalkeeper was struck and injured, the referee this time stopped the match. Police went into the crowd, to find the culprits, and two youths were brought out. The referee broadcast an announcement, asking the crowd to report any idiots seen to be throwing things. If it happened again, he would stop the game for good.

The missiles were later found to be half inch long steel staples, fired from a catapult. It was about the worst thing that could have happened to the club, right at the beginning of the season. Both Leeds United and Manchester United had been heavily penalised the season before for crowd incidents. Spurs were likely to have their ground closed. That was what had happened to Leeds.

The chairman and the board ordered a quick investigation and worked out plans to take every precaution to stop it happening again. The majority of supporters were just as upset, furious that a couple of hooligans could ruin things for everyone else.

And as for the match itself, a goal-less draw rarely provides enjoyment for anyone. 'I'm not the sort of supporter who gets depressed when Spurs don't win,' said John Harris afterwards. 'I'm happy when they win, but I don't get upset if they lose or draw. It's football I like and the friendship of being with other supporters.'

7

Alan Mullery

Alan Mullery left his home in Cheam, down in suburban Surrey, just before midday for the Liverpool home match. Most of the team live north of Tottenham, in places like Enfield and Waltham Cross. For a home match, many of them are still getting up or lolling about over their poached eggs when Mullery is already on the road.

They'd trained very hard all week, the hardest so far. Bill had told them that if they had any pretensions to being a top team, they had to do well against Liverpool. During Friday's team talk, he'd said he rated them the best team in the League.

After some rather dreary draws which had opened the season, they'd suffered a terrible humiliation at Manchester City, just the week before, being beaten 4-0. The game had been lost in the midfield and both Mullery and Peters had had poor games. Bill Nicholson hadn't named the guilty men, even in the dressing-room afterwards, but simply criticised the whole team for lack of effort. 'Some players were hiding out there,' he said before slamming out of the dressing room.

But in a way, the defeat acted as a vital spark. The following Wednesday, Spurs had flown to Italy to play Torino in the first leg of the Anglo-Italian League Cup Winners Cup. Spurs won 1-0, their best performance of the season so far. Coates had looked good. Mullery was back on form.

It was a very hot day, hotter even than it had been during the week in Turin, and Mullery had some difficulty getting through the crowds. The sun, and Liverpool, always a glamorous team, had brought them out, over fifty thousand of them, the biggest gate of the season so far.

75

When he got to the ground, Mullery learned to his surprise that Cyril Knowles was back in the team. He'd been injured in the first match of the season at Wolves. Tony Want, Cyril's deputy, had played very well in his place and had been named again to play, but earlier that morning Tony had suddenly dropped out, reportedly suffering from a stomach upset.

Most of the team, like Mullery, had arrived early to avoid the crowds, well before the two o'clock deadline stipulated by the manager. Martin Peters was standing in Mrs Wallace's office, drinking a cup of tea and signing the inevitable football books that had been sent in by fans.

Tommy Smith, Liverpool's captain, came to the window of the office, a hatch window through which Mrs Wallace answers callers, and asked if he could have an envelope. The Liverpool coach had just arrived in the car park and their first concern, like all players, was to leave their complimentary tickets for friends and relations at the ticket office.

'Envelope, did you say Tom?' said Martin, putting down his cup of tea. Mr Smith gave no sign of recognition. On the field he looks about the toughest and most menacing player in the League. In his good suit, he didn't look any less welcoming, staring dourly through Martin, his face set tight. There was a piece of sticking plaster on his neck. It looked as if he'd cut himself shaving, though Mr Smith appears to be the sort of person who uses a blow lamp for shaving, like Desperate Dan, not an ordinary razor.

'Here you are, Tom,' said Martin, all smiles as he handed over some envelopes he'd taken from one of Mrs Wallace's cupboards. Mr Smith took them without a word and walked off into the car park.

'Got to keep in with Tom,' said Martin when he'd gone.

Amongst the fifty-thousand crowd were many famous football faces. Sir Alf Ramsey had turned up, to watch his England players, or prospective England players. He was sitting in the directors' box beside Mr Wale. Denis Follows of the FA was there, Ken Aston, the World Cup referee, and Joao Saldanha, the ex-manager of the Brazilian team. Lord Willis (Ted Willis that was) was also in the box. He's been a regular Spurs supporter for many years. Yes, Tony Want would have had the quality watching him, if only he'd been playing. Even more important, the winger he would have been marking, Peter Thomson, turned out to have a very poor game and was taken off fifteen minutes before the end.

In the first half, both teams played at top speed, but from the beginning Spurs always had the edge. They scored after ten minutes from one of their well worked out free kick movements. Chivers back-headed a Joe Kinnear free kick for Gilzean to score. In the second half, Martin Peters scored from another rehearsed move, a far post cross from Cyril Knowles which he headed into the net. Spurs won decisively, 2-0.

In the dressing-room afterwards Bill Nicholson said they'd done well. A rare compliment. He'd especially liked their performance in the first half but he was disappointed they'd fallen away slightly in the second half.

The players themselves were delighted. It was all laughs and jokes, even though two of them had been booked, Perryman and Chivers for hard tackles. 'I didn't realise it was Smithy,' said Chivers, talking about his booking. 'I wouldn't have fouled him if I'd known who it was.'

Cyril Knowles was going round collecting autographs for a young friend. He got all the Spurs names then went down the corridor to the visitors' dressing-room to get the Liverpool team. 'You should have seen them with their teeth out,' he said when he came back. 'What a sight.' He handed the autograph book to Steve Perryman. Steve said he'd already signed. 'I want you to sign John Toshack's name across here. I didn't get him.'

Mike England asked if anyone wanted to play cricket tomorrow and they all booed. The football results came through on the loudspeaker. There were soft boos when Arsenal's victory came through and slight whistles when they heard that Sheffield United had won again, away from home. Sheffield United, newly promoted from the Second Division, were the sensations of the season, having raced straight to the top of the Division.

Up in the Oak Room, the directors were having their hands shaken by friends. Each was being warmly congratulated, as if they personally had beaten Liverpool. Outside

in the car park, at the door to the players' entrance, Bill
Shankly, the manager of Liverpool, was spitting out a few
well chosen words for the Press as they crowded round him.
He was telling them to ignore Tottenham in their reports.
The man they should all be writing about was Keegan, his
new discovery. 'He *is* a player now.' He had a few remarks
to make about the referee, saying a computer could have
done a better job.

Bill Nicholson, when he eventually appeared, was also
approached by the Press, but they respectfully kept their
distance, awkward and artificial, hesitating when they called
him Bill, laughing nervously at anything that might be
meant as a joke. His hands were still shaking from the
tension of the match. But he gave them some quotes good
humouredly, without naming names. Mr Nicholson doesn't
go in for talking to the Press but when he can't avoid it, he's
always very careful with what he says. He doesn't believe in
publicly saying what he really thinks.

'That wasn't bad,' said a reporter when the impromptu
press conference had finished. 'I think he's mellowing with
the years.'

'He's impossible before a match,' said another reporter.
'Always has been, but I find him OK afterwards. In a good
mood, he can be a good bloke. At least he's honest, not like
some of them.'

Mullery was the last player to come out into the car park.
He'd been into the studio to be interviewed by BBC TV for
Match of the Day. He'd been talking them through the
Spurs goals. There was still a crowd hanging around outside
when he appeared, players signing autograph books belonging to the handful of privileged kids who'd managed to get
into the car park, players talking to their girl friends or
wives, plus hangers-on generally, all looking affluent in their
leather coats, just waiting around to catch a glimpse of the
stars.

'How did my goal look, Skip,' said Chivers, looking up
from an autograph book.

'It looked great,' said Mullery.

'Did you see my chip which gave Martin his goal,' said
Ralph Coates. He was smiling widely, getting very cheeky for

him, considering he hadn't yet settled down or found his top form, or most of all, scored a goal.

'It looked lovely,' said Mullery, walking to his car. 'Lovely.'

Alan Mullery lives in a large detached house in a leafy road in Cheam. There's a huge garden at the back, all lawn which looks about the size of a football pitch. 'A third of an acre, actually.' He moved in in 1969, from a smaller suburban house in nearby Worcester Park. It cost £14,500 and is now worth about £20,000.

The furnishings are very much like those in all the established first team players' houses: plush sofas and rich soft furnishings with everything smelling new as if it had just been unwrapped and the kids warned not to touch it. In Alan's case, three-year-old Samantha gets very few warnings, not from him anyway. His wife June is a bit stricter.

They would like a large family. They've been married nine years in all. 'We've tried everything,' said June. 'Even artificial insemination. We just keep on hoping.' They miss other kids for Samantha to play with, which is one of the problems of being young rich in a middle-aged rich area.

He was glad to be home. 'Every time I get in the car to drive across London, especially to Cheshunt for training, I think bloody hell. But it's never as bad when I get there.' Despite what many of the younger players think, he's very home loving and domestic. They mutter behind his back about it's OK for him being captain, on a big wage with all the perks and getting all the invitations to the big occasions, but in fact he hardly goes out. It's just that living so far away, with no contact with any other Spurs player, they presume he must be out living it up.

June isn't the sort to let him live it up. Some players get away with murder and their wives have a lot to put up with, but she is very strong and sensible and far from being a yes girl. She'll criticise him strongly if he's playing badly or if he's lost his temper on the pitch. He in turn relies on her a lot. He may be captain but at home he's far from being an Andy Capp.

He takes an equal share in the domestic chores, which is very rare for a footballer, drying the dishes, and when it's

Coronation Street on TV, he washes and dries. 'Juny loves Coronation Street, but I hate it.' He tries to take his fair share with Samantha. He changed her nappies as a baby and still baths her when he's at home. 'I love it. I wouldn't miss it for anything. I love seeing her going in all dirty and coming out a shiny new little girl. Sometimes I get in the bath with her.

'I think I should do my share. Juny has a hard day in the house so it's only fair I should help.' It's mainly for his wife's sake that their house is so far away from Tottenham.

'We've lived round here ever since we were married. We don't know North London where most of the lads live. As I'm away from home so much, travelling with the club or England, it's much easier for June to be in an area she knows. She feels happier here. When I've finished with football, I intend to stay here, so why change just for a few years.'

He's very proud of his success and conscious of how much he's advanced, in social and economic terms, since his early days in a slum area. 'All this from football,' he said, throwing his arms in the direction of the garden and settling down in an easy chair.

He was born in Notting Hill in 1941, the son of an electrician. At school he played football and cricket and boxed but by thirteen, when he was an eleven stone centre forward, playing for London Schoolboys, he decided to be a footballer. Several clubs made approaches. After talking it over with his Dad, he chose Fulham as it would be easy for him to travel there, compared with the other clubs, and it seemed a better place to get quickly into the first team. Fulham were then in Division Two, though strong challengers to be promoted. He joined them on the ground staff in April 1956 when he was fifteen.

Four days after he started, he was sitting in the boiler room, about to stoke the boiler for the afternoon match, when he was told to get his boots, he was playing for the reserves at Tottenham. 'I was shaking like a leaf. I couldn't believe it. Maurice Pratt, a young left winger, hadn't turned up. I'd never played on the left wing before. I got on the team coach and sat petrified as we set off through London.

80

We hadn't gone far when the coach stopped at some traffic lights. Maurice Pratt suddenly came running up and jumped on. I never got a game.'

On his seventeenth birthday, he signed full professional forms with Fulham. He asked for a £1,000 signing-on fee. Some of the other lads had put him up to it, telling him that most people got a few quid when they signed as a full pro. Being very cocky and cheeky, he went in and demanded it, as if it were a right. The manager swore at him. Even Johnny Haynes, the big star at Fulham, had received only a £10 signing-on fee. He held out for days, having got himself in such a daft position, but was eventually pacified when the manager said that if he wasn't in the first team within six months he'd pay him the £1,000 out of his own pocket. Within two months he was a regular in the first team.

'I developed my own style at Fulham and have always stuck to it. A lot of bustle and energy if not a wealth of natural skill.

'I enjoyed all my years at Fulham; but I think it was *too* much of a happy family. Some of the stars would wander into the board room after training and pour a drink. Everyone was so easy going that no one wanted to leave. I think at one stage they went seven years without one request for a transfer. Yet we were nearly always struggling. Looking back, I'd have preferred a set-up where a manager or trainer was giving us some stick. I think the discipline could have been much tighter.'

Mullery signed for Spurs in March 1964 for a fee of £72,500, a record fee at the time for a half back. By that time he was twenty-three and had played 193 League games for Fulham, had had six seasons as a full professional and won three Under 23 international caps. He hadn't asked for a transfer and was dumbfounded when the manager told him he was going. 'Frank apparently didn't want me to go, but the board had overruled him. They wanted the money for ground improvements. When I went to Frank's house and was told the news, Mrs Osborne had been in tears. They were both very upset.'

When Alan told his family he was leaving Fulham for Tottenham, they thought he was an idiot. Even his own team players wouldn't believe it when they heard.

'June thought I was stupid to leave Fulham and go to such a big club. She was very scared. My Dad didn't think I was good enough to make the grade at Spurs. After a couple of matches he said I'd be dumped. I was very worried. I'd gone as a back street kid to Fulham and I'd grown up there and been very happy. Now the club didn't want me.'

Throughout his first year at Spurs, Mullery was very unhappy. He was one of Nicholson's major buys in rebuilding after the retirement of the old double side, along with Pat Jennings, Alan Gilzean and Cyril Knowles, who all joined the club the same year, 1964. It was an interim period and the rejuvenation wasn't yet working.

'I was very depressed. I came home in bloody awful moods. The crowd were barracking me. They didn't like me and preferred Blanchflower who I was replacing. He had so much more skill than me and I could see why the crowds didn't want me. He could thrill them with his precise passes. My big points were hard tackles and lots of energy. We were poles apart.

'I was abused in the street as well as on the terraces. I got letters saying how bloody useless I was. I'd go home almost in tears and June, having watched the game, would say "Hopeless". When I went to Tottenham I was really in love with the game. After six months, I was ready for a transfer.

'Watching Dave Mackay desperately training to get fit after his broken legs was a big inspiration. He'd chase painfully up and down the terraces, determined to get back, though many people thought he'd had it. He was so cheerful as well. I used to think to myself, I'm playing every week in the first team and this fellow is sweating it out, never believing for one moment that he might never play again. What have I got to complain about?'

The turning point for Mullery came about a year after he joined Spurs. He suddenly became aware that he was at last succeeding when one day he heard a man shouting at him in the crowd.

'I was taking a throw-in. You can hear every word when you do that because they're breathing down your neck. I heard this voice say "Come on the tank". There was a sudden silence at the time and everyone heard him. I sort of nodded my head and got really stuck in. It was not being compared to Danny Blanchflower that bucked me up. I'm not sure whether he meant it as a compliment or not, but it gave me an identity at last.'

Mullery's tank-like qualities, plus his quick temper and aggressiveness have led to rows, on and off the pitch. It has lessened slightly over the years, but he can still be explosive. It's not really temper, more over-eagerness. He throws himself into things so strongly that he can't bear disappointment or things going wrong. He can't simply walk away after an incident, the way Martin Peters can. He always has to be in there, shouting, whether he's been involved or not, a habit both Nicholson and Sir Alf Ramsey have tried to break.

He's had several arguments with Nicholson himself over the years, particularly when they've won a match and he's thought Bill has been more concerned with criticising things the team did badly, rather than praising them for winning.

'I remember in 1967 when we won the FA Cup against Chelsea. Bill gave a little speech afterwards at the hotel reception. He said he didn't want us to become big headed. We hadn't won anything yet.

'He was right in many ways, I admit. Bill is a perfectionist and his double side was the nearest thing to perfection in football so far. We know we haven't won anything till we've won again in Europe. That's what Bill would call success. Let's hope we have it this season.'

Everyone talks about Bill being sparing with his praise, but he has given it, as he had after the win against Liverpool. Mullery remembers one game in which he played particularly well and Bill actually rang up on the Sunday morning to tell him so. 'When I told the lads, none of them would believe me.'

Their biggest row was in 1968 when they beat Ipswich 1-0 and Bill, so he says, swept into the dressing-room afterwards saying, terrible, disgusting.

'He said the way we played in the second half we didn't deserve to win. I said, but we did. We stood bawling at each other for about ten minutes. The younger lads went to hide in the bath to keep out of the way.'

Mullery received his first full cap for England in 1964 against Holland, but it was nearly three years before he received his second. Illness prevented him once, but it was mainly Nobby Stiles who kept him out of the team.

'It went on for so long that I thought, that's you, Mullers old son. You're going to be one of those fellers who only has one cap. You better be proud of that one.

'I think now that Alf did have faith in me all the time, it was just that he preferred Nobby. Nobby's name was always mentioned first by everyone. If he was fit, the position was his. When I did eventually get a game, my name wasn't even in the bleeding programme. They'd expected it would be Nobby as usual. I came home and the wife said have you got those couple of programmes for the boys in the street. I hadn't brought any I was so fed-up. Even the buggers printing the programme at Wembley thought I wasn't up to it.'

When he did get his place back, he made history, of the worst sort. In June 1968 against Yugoslavia he was sent off – the first Englishman to be sent off in a full international. Englishmen shouldn't do such things. 'The next day I came back to the hotel and found there was a telephone call for me. It was June. "You're a disgrace to the family." I know I shouldn't have kicked the bloke back. The thing is, I will rise to any bait. If somebody shouts at me in the crowd, I shout back. I know it's daft but I can't ignore them.

'A bloke in the crowd not long ago shouted at me, "Mullery, you're fucking overweight." I shouted back at him "Why don't you fucking come and do better then." I'm a bit like that. I've got a terrible temper. I can go so far, and then no further.

'Last season I got myself in the worse scrap so far. I was in the Spurs car park getting into the car after a match, with June beside me and me Dad behind, when this yob opened the door and pushed my wife and said I was fucking useless. I got out, took me jacket off, and knocked him out. The police were rushing round, trying to calm me, and I began fighting the police. I must have been mad. It took three cops to control me and get me back in my car and out of the ground.

'That night, I sat at home, dead worried. The phone was going all the time. June said I was out. About twelve there was a knock at the door and two reporters were there, from one of the Sunday papers. They said they'd interviewed the boy and got a full statement. He was going to prosecute me for assault. They read out his statement and it was right, word for word.

'I let him finish then I said if one word of that was printed, I'd sue their newspaper for everything they'd got. Then I slammed the door on them. I couldn't sleep for worry. But the next day, there wasn't a word in the papers.'

At the club on Monday, there was a huge inquest. Bill Nicholson called him in. The boy was already there. There were apologies from Mullery and the boy agreed not to sue.

'He was a long-time Spurs fan as well. However, it was all settled in the end. Luckily nothing ever came out in the papers about it.'

Despite such minor local difficulties off the pitch, Mullery went on from strength to strength for England and Spurs. He's never been sent off since that 1967 incident or been involved in any ugly scenes on the pitch, although he would still be relatively easy to provoke.

'With Spurs, I think we could do with a bit more of the killer instinct. I don't mean thumping them physically. I mean when you're leading three-nil you should really go at them and play them into the ground. Players will go out on the field when we're playing sides at the bottom of the league in a sort of complacent frame of mind. I think this is diabolical, when they're receiving such good wages. It's a lack of professionalism. Footballers must play to win at all times. If we can correct this fault this season, we could win anything. We've got the talent.'

As an England player, Mullery thinks he is still developing, season by season. Perhaps his best matches so far were in 1970, during the World Cup in Mexico when he played so effectively against Pele.

'During the World Cup, I used to hear little groups of our players discussing on the coaches who'd been doing what. I was always hearing the name of Mullery coming up. On my bed afterwards, I'd go over it, thinking, they're talking about

85

me. I came back from Mexico with a new dimension.

'It's strange, isn't it, that at twenty-nine I should seem to be getting better.

'With Spurs, the team has developed to suit me. I'm even scoring goals – eight last season. I've never scored so many. I've no reason to think I won't play even better.

'Perhaps it's with confidence and experience. I don't think my basic skills are any greater than they were. All I'm hoping is that this season will be the best I've had.'

8

The Directors

Sidney Wale, as chairman of Spurs, was involved throughout in the signing of Coates but the other Spurs directors knew nothing about it till they read the news in the papers.

'It was helped by our good relations with Burnley. My father was very friendly with Bob Lord. They got on very well and understood each other. I often heard my father say "Don't be a bloody fool, Bob." Burnley had always promised us that if they were demoted they would let us know first about Coates. They kept their promise.

'You can't have too many friends in this game. By and large Spurs do well and have good relations with everyone.'

Mr Wale has been a director since 1957 and chairman since 1969. Although he inherited some of his shares from his father, Frederick Wale, who was also chairman, Spurs is not a family concern the way many clubs are, such as Chelsea where the Mears family, who were in at the foundation of Chelsea, have practically run it ever since. Mr Wale, like his father before him, is a self-made business man. He went to Tottenham Grammar School (where the boys were banned from going to Spurs ground), trained as a chartered accountant and then worked his way up to be managing director of a North London bolts and nuts firm, C. Lindley and Company. He's fifty-eight and like Bill Nicholson has two daughters. He is the largest single shareholder at Spurs (he had 586 shares in 1970 whereas the other directors between them had only 155) but he won't necessarily be passing his shares on to his daughters. He was surprised at the idea. 'There's never been a female director of a football team, not that I've heard of anyway, although I was told once about a lady club secretary.'

He lives in stockbroker Hadley Wood, quite modestly, and drives a Rover, like Bill Nicholson. Spurs takes up most of his time. At the beginning of the season, he retired from full-time business, though he is still a director of his old firm.

He never interferes with Bill Nicholson's work as a manager. Anything to do with the team is Bill's concern, but like everyone else concerned with the club, outside and inside, he was wondering privately how the season would go and how Coates would affect the others.

'I can't see Gilly lasting the season. He was very slow at the end of last season, especially in the Arsenal match. I can see the wingers eventually being Morgan and Coates with Gilly becoming substitute. But you never know, Gilly might get a new lease of life. As a spectator, I love watching Gilly. But as chairman, my thinking has got to be harder and I've got to face the fact that the time is drawing nearer for him to finish.'

Like Bill Nicholson, he's not very worried about the big transfer fees. 'You have to pay the money to get the star player, though it was embarrassing for me when we paid £200,000 for Martin Peters. My father had gone on record the previous year as saying that anyone who paid £200,000 for a player was barmy. I did have qualms when he took some time to settle in, but not now.

'You just can't replace a team of the quality of Spurs purely from home grown players, so you have to buy. On balance, I think it's a good thing to buy. A bit of competition does no harm. It makes the existing players that bit keener to keep their place.'

The Spurs board is a very tight little circle, like the boards of all successful clubs. Getting into something like the Athenaeum is easy compared with getting on the board at Spurs. To be a director the qualification is ten shares, but, even if you found someone willing to sell you ten shares, the board has to approve every transfer. If they don't want you, even as a shareholder, that's it. Under their articles, they don't even have to give any reason for turning you down.

The public image of a football director is of a bluff and hearty, self-made, middle-aged businessman, someone who's fought his way up ruthlessly from the bottom of the local pile, starting as a messenger boy in a pie shop and ending with a string of butcher's stops throughout the town. He's followed the local team since he was a boy, so he's a genuine fan, but he sees the football club as an extension of his empire and of his personality.

This sort of dominant, bulldozing football director is in fact very rare. They tend to be gentle committee men who become directors more through family connections than by empire building and they see their position almost as a public service, carrying the flag.

None of the present Spurs directors has ever had to put a penny of his own money into the club. They presumably would, if it ever became necessary, but it doesn't look likely. When they go abroad, they get pocket money, just like the players, but they get no salaries as directors. The FA doesn't allow directors to be paid. As shareholders, they might get a few pence every year, but that's about all. The FA limits the dividend which a club can give to shareholders to seven-and-a-half per cent before tax or five per cent tax free.

All clubs try not to be left at the end of the tax year with large profits which can be taxed. If a club spends money on buying a player, the tax people, in their wisdom, consider it a running cost and therefore not taxed, but if you spend the same money on a new stand, then that is counted as adding to your capital and it is taxable. If Spurs had simply left the £190,000, they spent on Ralph Coates just lying in the bank, they would have lost a big chunk of it in tax. So in one way, they *had* to spend it. All very strange, but then a football club can't be considered as a normal commercial company nor the directors as normal company directors.

Charles Cox is the vice-chairman of Spurs. He's the oldest director, aged seventy-four, a widower who lives with his daughter. His father, George Cox, became a director of Spurs back in 1907.

He's very approachable and friendly and prides himself on getting on well with people, as a good salesman should. He retired about ten years ago after a lifetime with Car Mart, part of the Kenning car sales group. He ended up as sales promotion manager. He dealt a lot with the Royal Family, supplying them with their motor cars.

He agrees that normally it would be difficult for a salaried executive, as he was, to be a football director, but as a salesman he always found it fitted in quite well. 'The firm was quite proud that I was a Spurs director. I met a lot of people travelling round the country. It was good for business. Kennings have branches everywhere. It created interest.'

Arthur Richardson is the next most senior director. He's sixty-seven and, like all the other directors, he was born, brought up and has always worked in North London. He runs a waste paper firm in Kentish Town which was begun by his grandfather in 1863. He has expanded it into other enterprises, such as property, and today it employs about fifty people.

As a boy he played football and once had a trial for London Schoolboys. (None of the other directors showed any football skill.) He's a keen Rotarian and mason and for many years was a local Conservative Councillor. He's slender and rather dapper and looks a lot younger than his years.

Godfrey Groves is also in his sixties, though he's a fairly recent addition to the board. He's a quantity surveyor by profession, with a London practice in Bedford Row. He also owns half the shares of a very successful building firm in Tottenham, G. Groves and Son, which was founded by his grandfather in 1850.

He's a mild mannered bachelor, shy and self-effacing, who wears old-fashioned tweed suits and speaks slowly and quietly. He's quite a surprise to find on a football board. One of his passions in life is history and the preservation of old buildings. He lives in an exquisite Elizabethan manor house in Enfield. He often lets local societies use it for meetings. His life seems to be an endless succession of meetings – he's an Enfield Borough Councillor, a JP, and chairman of the Southgate Conservative Association.

He would appear to be the wealthiest of the Spurs directors – his house alone must be worth £100,000 – but his possessions are things of beauty rather than anything flash or ostentatious. He does have a Rolls, as well as a Rover and an MGB, but sticks to the Rover when his chauffeur takes him to Spurs on match days.

He went to Tottenham Grammar School, though several

The 1971-72 season began with the ceremonial unveiling of Spurs record signing, Ralph Coates. He kneels modestly, despite his £190,000 fee.

Frank Herrmann

The photographers then capture for posterity the other stars, each hoping to shine in the new season ahead.

Frank Herrmann

Straining, training: once a week every team's performance is public and glamorous, but every weekday in private they have their bodies and souls beaten into shape. Frank Herrmann

Basic skills in the ball court: Barry Daines bowls, Mullery strolls, Perryman lifts a dainty foot, Chivers collects, and Joe Kinnear kicks. Frank Herrmann

Sunshine exercises in rural Cheshunt, at Spurs own training ground: Roger Morgan, one of that season's jokers, finds time to grin while Bill Nick bends. Frank Herrmann

Travelling: in the 1971-72 season Spurs did 7,750 miles round England and 10,238 miles round Europe. Steve Perryman, the season's Boy Wonder, manages a smile. Gilzean, behind, has seen it all. Frank Herrmann

Our heroes put in the travelling hours, whether it's to Manchester or Milan, by playing cards. Left to right: Mullery, Gilzean, Kinnear.

Frank Herrmann

Away the lads. Johnny Wallis and Bill Nicholson, both still at Spurs today, exhort the troops.

The classic goal, the classic photo: Chivers and Neighbour cuddle, Peters and Gilzean rejoice.

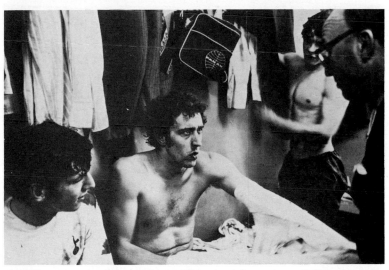

Dressing room analysis: Martin Chivers, superstar – or Bill Nicholson's cross in life?

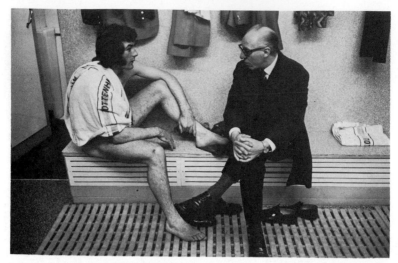

Meanwhile Pat Jennings listens to the thoughts of Eddie Baily, assistant manager.

Young boys who have seen a lot: Steve Perryman and John Pratt, two of the 1972 players, still at Spurs today.

More post-match words of wisdom from Bill Nicholson – but is Alan Gilzean by now too knackered to hear?

Teachers and pupils: Bill Nicholson keeps up the advice, but even Eddie Baily, right, is tiring, while Terry Naylor starts to dress.

Still life in the dressing room: Cyril Knowles, left (now Darlington manager), Martin Chivers, Mike England (now Wales manager) and Joe Kinnear.

Frank Herrmann

Victory in our time: a fitting climax to the pains and pleasures of the 1971-72 season. Spurs won the UEFA Cup for the first time.

Carleton

years ahead of Mr Wale, and has always been a keen Spurs fan. He still has a cuttings book, lovingly preserved amongst his Elizabethan paintings and *objets d'art,* in which as a boy of twelve he pasted the newspaper reports of Spurs' 1921 Cup Final success. 'One of my brothers was an Arsenal supporter. I quarrelled with him all the time.'

He says he was surprised to be invited to be a director and didn't realise at the time what a sought after prize it was. Now he knows how many people are trying all the time, by various means, to become a Spurs director. 'I suppose the harder you try for something, the less chance you have of getting it.

'I'm not quite sure why they asked me. It was wheels within wheels. I knew friends of the chairman. They thought as a surveyor and with my local connections I might be useful to the club.'

The fifth and final director of Spurs is Geoffrey Richardson, the son of Arthur Richardson. He became a director in 1970, at the age of only twenty-nine, which made him one of the youngest football directors in the country. The other directors were no doubt becoming a bit self-conscious about their ages – the average of the other four is sixty-five – so it was Geoffrey's youth as much as his family connections which was a major factor in getting him invited on the board.

'At board meetings I do get asked for the young viewpoint, as a member of the younger generation.' At thirty-one, he's the same age as some of the senior players, and in Alan Gilzean's case, a few years younger. Like his father, he's very smart and well turned out, but without being trendy. He gets on well with the players. People like Mullery call him by his Christian name – and so does Bill Nicholson for that matter – whereas the rest of the directors are studiously referred to by everyone as Mr.

He went to Highgate School, which makes him the only director from a public school, but left at sixteen after his O levels to study paper making and then enter the family firm where he still works.

As the only son amongst all the directors, it seems obvious that he would have become a director eventually, but he says

91

it happened out of the blue. 'Mr Wale asked me if I'd be prepared to give up the time. It would mean an awful lot of travelling. I discussed it with my wife. She was as highly delighted as I was. It was always my ambition, but I didn't hope it would come quickly.'

As a member of the younger generation, he's far from being radical. Mr Cox, the oldest director, can be more radical on some issues, such as the perennial question of allowing advertising in the ground. Spurs is one of the very few clubs which doesn't allow advertisements anywhere in the ground. Even Wembley, the sacred heart of English football, sells advertising space round the pitch. It can make them about £20,000 a match from the internationals.

Mr Cox, perhaps through his training as a salesman, thinks it's bound to come, but young Mr Richardson is definitely against it. 'I voted against advertising the last time it was brought up. We've got an image at Spurs which we must maintain. You don't have to lower it to get money. I don't want disc jockeys on the pitch or other things which some clubs have.'

But it's the voice of the chairman, most of all, which appears to prevail on such topics. 'It's a personal thing with me,' says Mr Wale. 'We've never had it and I wouldn't like to be the chairman which started it. I like the look of the ground much better the way it is, without all the clutter of adverts. If we were really hard up then perhaps we'd have to get money any way we can, even from adverts. But it's not true to say we're not interested in making money. We're constantly looking at new ways. The club shop which we hope to open this season is just one of the ways.'

They're lucky, of course, to be able to stick to their principles. A successful team is the source of their income and as long as it's successful, they don't have to scurry around for other means.

Each director has his own sphere of influence. Mr Groves, for example, being a surveyor and also a Councillor who's worked on planning committees, is looking after the new gym and ball court which is being built this season. One of Geoffrey Richardson's little spheres of influence is officially timing the goals. You can see him sitting in the directors' box at Spurs, stop-watch at the ready. It's an important job and one which must be above suspicion. At each match, they sell goal time tickets and if you get the lucky one, you get a prize. Spurs might be above selling advertising space but they do approve of raffles.

The Spurs board meet once a fortnight. The first thing is always Bill Nicholson's report in which he reads out his view of the progress of the team, how matches have gone from his point of view, the state of the injured and any other developments

The directors also meet together before every home match. Any urgent business can be done then, instead of waiting for the next official meeting. (Bill Nicholson was appointed manager on a Saturday before the match.) They all arrive at the club about midday. The chairman's usually there from eleven thirty, discussing various matters with the club secretary, Geoffrey Jones.

The five directors and their guests have lunch together in the board room – four courses followed by brandy. About two o'clock, one director is detailed to welcome the visiting directors and offer them cigars and drinks in the Blue Room. The other directors, when they've finished lunch, join the visitors later, going to their own box to watch the match, just before three. Each director has a seat for himself and three guests. Visiting directors are allocated a total of twelve seats, which is what the Spurs directors and officials are given when they play away.

It all sounds a pleasant and not too arduous job, being a director of Spurs, as long as you don't mind travelling. But would they be so keen if it was Hartlepool?

Mr Wale once overheard another Spurs director (whose name he won't mention) refer to someone as being 'only a Third Division director'. He was soundly reprimanded and told not to say such a thing again. 'A Third Division director probably has to take all the kicks and carry the club himself and guarantee the club's overdraft.'

They do have quite a lot to do, though the normal fan on the terraces might not appreciate it. Behind the scenes at Tottenham, there is a little factory of workers who have to be administered, an income of half a million pounds to be collected and spent, property worth half a million to be cared for and forty players worth a million pounds to be paid and kept happy.

It's such a big business now for the top clubs that many people think that directors have too much to do, not too little. The day of the part-time amateur, running a business in which they themselves have never worked, might one day be over. Mr Wale disagrees with the inference that there should be more footballers running football. 'They wouldn't be up to handling the financial side.' But he thinks the day will come when at least one director will have to be paid. 'He would be a sort of managing director figure, paid a large enough salary to make it worth his while to run a football club as his full-time profession.'

Traditionally the Spurs directors have always been rather aloof. 'You never see us making statements to the Press the way some clubs do,' says Arthur Richardson. 'Some directors are always replying when their club is attacked. We say nothing. Anything we want to say is printed in the programme.'

But as the policy of the programme is also very traditional, with no advertising or personalised opinions or anything remotely controversial or sensational, it would be very hard, from reading the programme, to find out what the board really thinks.

The directors know their place, which basically is looking after the finances, and they stick to it. But as they're always saying, they're football fans first and foremost, which leads at times to an interesting dichotomy. As fans, they have their heroes in the team, especially when the team is successful, but as directors, they have very little in common with them. They're with them often for days on end, yet they're miles apart.

Some of them would like to go down to the dressing-room after a match, but at Spurs it's not done. 'I have done it on occasions,' says Mr Wale, 'but I don't make a practice of it. When I do, I never hang around. You want to do it when they've won, but if you only did it when they won it would look bad. When I was first appointed a director in 1957, I went down to the dressing-room and the man on guard wouldn't let me in. He was very apologetic when he found out who I was. I told him he was only doing his duty.'

During the year, I never once saw the directors in the dressing-room at Tottenham, not even the chairman, but now and again they appeared briefly when the team was abroad, but more in the way of checking in, rejoining the party for the journey home. I could sense them glancing round, rather embarrassed, taking in quickly all the little rituals. The players aren't the slightest bit interested in what happens in the privacy of the board room, but the directors would like to know more about the dressing-room dramas.

Mr Groves, being a newcomer to the board and one who had had no previous family connection with the club, seems to have been quite surprised by the gap between the directors and the players when he joined. He was grateful for the Japanese trip for giving him a chance to get closer.

'I got to know the team quite well. They're a nice bunch of lads. There were a few escapades and some were a bit boisterous at times, but there were no troubles or incidents. That's quite good, when you consider what some touring teams are supposed to get up to.'

He would like to know them all a great deal better, but doesn't want to push himself. He wants to keep his place and not force himself upon them. 'Sometimes I think we should go down more to the dressing-room, but it's not the custom at Spurs. I think the tone is set by the chairman. In our case Sidney is fairly reserved and so we all tend to hold back. In my case, I couldn't push forward anyway. I'm not a very communicative sort of person. I don't slap people on the back.

'It's not an easy relationship, on either side. It's very hard to establish a wavelength. You can't really be buddies with them. I'm only too pleased when they speak to me.

'I don't wish to be apart from them. It's just the way it happens. I suppose it's a bit like the colour question. *They* want to be apart. It's not that you make them keep apart. Personally, I welcome any opportunities to be with them, such as the close season tour. I got to know Pat Jennings quite well in Japan and found him delightful. "That dreamy Irishman", as Bill Nicholson calls him. Joe Kinnear's a nice

95

young boy. They all are. And Philip Beal, he's a greatly underrated player.

'I don't think the difference between the directors and the players is a class thing. I wouldn't say it was like officers and men, or school masters and pupils, or even directors and workers. At my firm there are no distinctions between directors and staff. Everyone is very friendly and close. It's just a matter of age. That's what makes all the difference.'

But they are united on many things. Arsenal is the traditional rival, for the directors just as much as the players. The players in the dressing-room afterwards always want to know how Arsenal has got on, hoping they've been beaten. The directors are polite with Arsenal, but there's not a lot of warmth. They were obviously pleased to sign Coates, especially keeping it all so secret, so that Arsenal couldn't have him. When they play at Arsenal, the Spurs directors aren't invited for lunch with the Arsenal board, but when Spurs go to Chelsea, they always have lunch with their board.

As for the fans, the directors are very much against any they think are a bad influence, such as the rag trade hangers-on. The players are always defending their friends, rather insulted at the suggestion that they are easily conned. With the rank and file supporters, the vast majority of the crowds, directors and players alike don't have a lot of contact. The players think the crowd is too fickle, on your side one minute and turning on you the next, while the directors shy away from any contact with supporters.

The so-called hooligans at the Park Lane end, the ones who cheer the team regardless, are quite fondly regarded by the players. That time at Wolverhampton, they were genuinely pleased to see them as they stampeded through the thunderstorm. They exchange obscenities with them on platforms or on trains. As lads themselves, the players weren't much different.

But the directors and the management generally think that the hooligans give football a bad name, with some justification. It was the Park Lane end which threw the missiles at the Newcastle team. The directors were quick and severe in dealing with them. After that match, for the rest of the season, the terraces immediately behind were barricaded off and guarded by police. It looked rather strange, a great expanse of nothingness surrounded by acres of cheering fans, as if the Royal Family had made a block booking and then decided not to come. Like the Spurs directors, the Royal Family wouldn't care for this sort of fan. They do rather lower the tone.

9

The Skinhead Special

As far as British Rail is concerned, there are two sorts of football supporters – football supporters and hooligans. You can tell the hooligan train by the police patrolling up and down every carriage.

For the Coventry match, the special train was the twelve forty. It wasn't billed on the train departures board, just in case any innocent passenger going to Coventry should get on it by mistake.

They were arriving in their hundreds from about eleven o'clock, looking for excitement from the minute they got onto the forecourt at Euston, chanting Spurs songs, drawing attention to themselves as much as possible, hoping someone would be silly enough to stand in their way. One of their constant rationalisations is that they don't look for trouble, but if anyone else does, they go right in. Not looking for trouble means running in gangs and scattering everyone before them, upturning people or objects in the way and jeering and swearing at anyone who looks remotely like a supporter from another club.

This morning they were looking out for any Everton supporters arriving at Euston for their match in London against Crystal Palace. The massed Spurs fans stood at the doorways, their knotted scarves at their side, daring the Everton fans to walk between them, ready to trip them up. It was all good hearted, really. It was too early for a fight. They were just flexing muscles. However, it didn't fool the police. They suddenly pounced and half a dozen Spurs fans were dragged off by the ears across the forecourt, shouting they'd done nothing. The rest immediately calmed down and made their way in little huddles to the ticket office.

As a species they used to be called skinheads, and still are

98

by the Press, but that term was already about a year out of date. Almost all of them had long hair and many could have passed for hippies, except for their big heavy boots. The average age was fifteen. They called themselves Smooths, if they called themselves anything. There was none of the uniformity of the previous season, when they all had Dr Martin boots and dark blue Crombie overcoats and very short hair, though there were remnants of the old style here and there. The term Smooth had come about because of their smoother hair and more colourful clothes compared with the drabness of the skinheads. They don't like being mistaken for hippies, a breed they consider filthy.

The train was full and there must have been a thousand supporters altogether. They hung out of windows, cheering their friends, jeering at other trains. There was a big roar when a couple of the kids who'd been strong-armed by the police reappeared and came racing down the platform to leap onto the train as it started. But a few had been kept behind. The police policy is to grab any ringleaders creating a disturbance and put them in a room, letting them out *after* the train has gone.

For the first half hour of the journey they kept up the noise at the windows, shouting and singing, then they settled down, some playing cards, some fighting each other on the seats. No damage was being done, except to each other. The police patrols were very good humoured, breaking up the fighting by trying to make everyone sit one to a seat instead of jamming twenty to a table.

I sat down with three of the noisiest. Two of them had their arms covered with tattoos. 'Ben Gunn in Chingford done it for me, didn't he.' One of them turned down his bottom lip to reveal a tattoo on the inside and asked me to read it out. It looked like fuck. He laughed and said look again. It said Nick, which was his name.

Nick said he was eighteen and worked on a building site. He'd been up since six-thirty that morning. His mother, who didn't approve of his habits, wouldn't give him breakfast so he'd gone round as usual to his mate's house and had his breakfast there. His mate said he'd been an apprentice bricklayer at one time, but after they both got put away for

99

three months, he lost his apprenticeship and now he was a labourer.

'It was at Manchester City last season,' explained Nick. 'We got beat 1-0 and we were right cheesed off. We saw a gang of them. They threw a brick at us so we went and done them. We got three months detention in Nottingham. First month was the worst. We were on remand in Liverpool. A month in a little room about the size of this table. Not nice. Not nice at all. Poor little Nicky.'

Nick put on a funny Charlie Drake voice and everyone laughed. Encouraged by his success, he took off his polo neck to show his muscles, challenging the rest of his gang to compete with him in arm locks. One of the policemen going past on his rounds and seeing Nick naked to the waist stopped and asked if he wasn't going to go the whole hog.

'Cheeky,' said Nick blowing him a kiss. 'And I'll have two tickets for your ball.'

Everyone cheered and the policeman continued down the gangway, smiling.

That morning, so they said, they'd walked around the streets after breakfast till the pubs opened. They'd been drinking till it had been time to go to Euston. Nick's mate said he'd started the day with £7.50. He now had £3 left for the day's football and drinking.

I asked what they thought about the steel staples thrown by two fourteen-year-old kids at the Newcastle match. 'Out of order', said Nick. 'Stupid. They just spoil it for us and everyone. Stupid.'

They all agreed, nodding their heads, saying they would never throw things at players. Hitting rival supporters, that was different. 'Or an Arsenal player', said one lad. 'That would be different. I'd like to kill all the Arsenal players and then burn the stand down.'

They argued amongst themselves over this, most people disagreeing. They hated Arsenal but they wouldn't actually kill an Arsenal player. That was also out of order.

They seemed knowledgeable but completely uncritical in their loyalty to Spurs. They hadn't a bad word for any player. They loved each and every one. There was no one they wouldn't have in their team. But Gilzean was clearly

100

the most popular single player. At the mention of his name, they burst into his song, to the tune of the Christmas carol Noël, Noël. 'Gilzean, Gilzean, Gilzean, Gilzean, born is the King of White Hart Lane.'

After Gilly came Chivers, but none of them had many good words for him off the field. 'He's a monkey git. He won't sign autographs. But on the field he's fantastic. I'd go anywhere to watch him.'

The policeman came past again and made the same remark to Nick who was still sitting stripped to the waist.

'I knew you fancied me,' said Nick, standing up on the table and unbuttoning his flies. He pulled his pants down and turned round, showing his bare arse to the policeman. 'There you are, ducky. Now he'll nick me for indecent exposure.'

The policeman laughed and went on. When he'd gone, Nick put all his clothes back on. 'Bloody cold. Always the same when you go Norf wif all them natives.'

Ipswich was his favourite place and his mates agreed. 'More cunt,' said one of them. 'They ain't got no supporters. All the geezers up there don't know what it's for. We always stay the night there and chase their birds.'

The worst places were Manchester and Liverpool, though they wouldn't miss either for anything. 'It's a long way from the station to the grounds and the police just let you get kicked. They don't look after you or nuffink. Just let you run into trouble. You go around a corner and there's a hundred of their supporters. They down you and nick everything from you, even your clothes. The police don't give a bugger. Diabolical. The cops should protect you. Leeds is easy. Pushover up there. Same as Coventry. We'll eat them today.

'The club call us hooligans, but who'd cheer them on if we didn't come? You have to stand there and take it when Spurs are losing and the others are jeering at you. It's not easy. We support them everywhere, but we get no thanks.'

'I don't think Nicholson's appreciated by the Press,' said another. 'He's a great manager. Yet the only fucking face you see on the telly is Shankly. He's on it all the time. It's all this Northern thing. Makes you sick. They hardly mentioned Nick. Look what he's done. That '61 team. Fantastic.'

They all went into raptures about the '61 team. John White was their favourite. They had pictures of him on their bedroom walls, ringed in black, as a sign of perpetual mourning for his death. (Killed by lightening on a golf course.) They'd all gone to Spurs even then, taken by their dads.

'Nick gives entertainment. You never see Spurs play defensive. Even today. They'll attack against Coventry. You see.'

One or two had the audacity to say that they hoped Mike England was back on form. If not, they wanted Collins back. They all agreed they liked Collins. And they hoped Mullery was also back to form, though it wasn't his fault he hadn't started off the season so well. 'Too much football.'

Most of them had blue and white scarves, in either wool or silk, which they had knotted round their middles. Some wore rosettes, but not on their chests. That season's fashion was to pin rosettes on their thighs. Nick didn't have a scarf or any Spurs sign.

'It draws attention to you. The police nick you before you do nuffink. I tried last week to emigrate but they said I can't till I'm twenty-four because of my prison record. I don't want no more of that.'

In the corner a bespectacled hippie-looking supporter was asleep. He was said to be the leader of their gang, a boy named Tony. If you woke him, you'd be for it. His mates were sitting peaceably by his side reading comics, *Scorcher, Shoot* and others. He had a coloured shirt and beads round his neck. He looked tubby and innocuous, more like the Owl of the Remove than a hooligan. I said excuse me, Tony, could I have a word. He said no, fuck off. He wouldn't talk. I'd talked to Nick and that lot before him. I should have spoken to him first, as the leader. Then he closed his eyes again.

There were a few girls on the train, travelling in couples, not with any of the gangs of boys. They were dressed alike, in trousers and men's jackets, swearing at any boy who tried to sit beside them, suspicious and very aggressive. They didn't want to talk at all.

I went back to the famous Tony and this time he kindly

consented to be talked to. I admired his beads. 'Got them this morning. I became a hippie when I decided it was better to make love not war. I'm not mad.'

I asked how many grounds he'd been chucked out of. 'You mean this week?' He looked round, leering while his mates laughed. 'Tony raped his teacher at five,' shouted one of them. 'Go on, ask him. Didn't you Tony.'

'Let's see,' said Tony, taking off his specs and pretending to think. He was medium height, fat rather than well built but he had a presence, at least his admirers seemed to think so, waiting breathless for his answer.

'Arsenal five times, Tottenham six times, Carlisle, Palace, Coventry, I forget . . .'

He'd been in court six times, the last for attacking a policeman. 'He was trying to chuck me out so I grabbed his walkie-talkie and tried to break it. He was calling for help. But I haven't been sent away. I'm too lovable to send away.'

One of his mates with a skinhead haircut said the first day he went to Spurs with Tony he got three months' detention for being in the same fight, yet Tony had got nothing. It must be Tony's looks, so studious, blinking through his glasses, not the sort you'd immediately suspect. He said he was living in Kentish Town at the moment, but that was temporary. His family were squatting.

Of all the fifty or so in his gang, he was the only one who said he actually looked for fights. Nick and everyone else maintained they only fought when attacked, making a big pretence of it all being self-defence.

'It's more exciting if you hit someone,' said Tony, 'especially some Northern bastard. I hate all Northerners. You've got to show them the cockneys are best. It's satisfying to hit someone. It feels good. Now get lost. I'm going back to sleep.'

As we got into Coventry, they raced for the doors, swinging them open before the train had halted. They lined up on the platform then charged over the bridge, cheering and shouting, taking over the station by the suddenness and volume of their arrival.

At the bottom of the steps, the police were waiting. There were about twenty of them, with sergeants issuing orders and talking into their walkie-talkies, all ready for the attack.

We were all stopped and herded into orderly lines as the police made gauntlets for us. As each person went through, he was quickly searched. Pockets and legs seemed to be the main object. It was done speedily, without the queue being held up. I hardly felt the policeman who searched me, but he obviously knew what he was doing and what he was looking for. Nobody in the gang I was with seemed to have anything illegal hidden in his pockets. But on the pavement outside, I saw a couple of lads being strong-armed into a black maria.

We set off in formation, singing songs and clapping, to let Coventry know that the Spurs boys had arrived. The ones at the front set off at a trot, but eventually slowed down to let the others catch up. The police set off at the same time, spreading out at intervals along the long line of supporters, directing them along a pre-arranged route, keeping them away from trouble or temptation.

Our numbers had swollen to well over a thousand by now. Supporters who'd come on earlier trains or by car or coach had been waiting for the special. Tony's gang was joined by two old-fashioned skinheads with Crombie coats and blue handkerchiefs in their top pockets. They had strong Wolverhampton accents, but were covered in Spurs badges. They said they never missed a Spurs match, home or away, even though it costs them a fortune. There was a girl who'd come from Birmingham. She was the girlfriend of one of Tony's pals, but Tony immediately had his arm round her, kissing her like the demon lover he said he was.

Nick was marching abreast of one of the policemen, facetiously chatting him up, thanking him for his consideration and help, awfully good of him, guiding them to the ground, he was a toff. The policeman seemed amused rather than annoyed.

I fell in line with the policeman and asked about the searching at the railway station. He was very proud of that. Coventry police had a Task Force of fifty policemen, he said, created especially for football crowds. Policemen came from all over the country, and abroad, to watch them at work. He explained that they were split into what they called serials of eight policemen, each with a sergeant in charge and one constantly on the walkie-talkie. 'If a fight started now,' he said, looking at Tony's gang, 'I could have the whole Task Force here in seconds. But these seem good lads to me. More like students than skinheads.'

I said that London hooligans didn't look like hooligans any more. He admitted it was only his second week in the Task Force so he wasn't really experienced. We passed a gang of old-fashioned Coventry skinheads, standing across the road, keeping their distance. The Spurs lads jeered at them. The policeman looked across at them with interest. As he did so, some of Tony's gang filled their pockets with fruit from an open air stall.

I asked the policeman if he'd had any trouble on his two matches so far. He said no, nothing serious. Coventry had had no serious disturbance since the Task Force started eighteen months ago.

'But the magistrates don't help. They let them off very lightly. Now at Leicester, they put them away. One football hooligan's just got eighteen months. We want more like that. That's the way to stop them.'

I asked if he was worried. 'I'm scared stiff. I stand at the back surrounded by them and I think if one pulls a knife, I've had it.'

He knew that only one or two might have a knife. Most of the lads were probably OK. But all the same, he couldn't understand why any of them came. They couldn't possibly enjoy the match.

I said it was the crowd excitement. I'd already felt it when they were stampeding off the train. In the middle of all the noise and shouting, you really did feel you'd taken over the city. I said they were all in rotten jobs, from rotten homes, all the usual things. There was no other excitement or meaning in their lives.

'I suppose I can understand that. I'm in the police for the excitement. I'm longing for that call in the middle of the night and we'll have to go belting down the street. I suppose I'm lucky. My excitement's legal. Theirs isn't.'

At Coventry City's ground, all the Spurs boys made for the West stand knowing that was where the home bred hooligans would be. The police also knew and were already there, guarding every entrance and every queue. Once again, everyone was searched for weapons, but more thoroughly this time, even down to their feet. A policewoman asked me to lift my shoes up one at a time. They were perfectly ordinary Saxone slip-on shoes, but she still wanted to check I had no studs or toe caps fastened underneath. Beside her was a large pile of boots and heavy shoes which fans had been forced to take off. They'd had to go in to watch the match in their stockinged feet, collecting their boots afterwards.

Most of the Spurs boys weren't wearing boots. It was the Coventry fans who were still on that fashion, being skinheads. Two-tone heavy welted brown shoes seemed to be the new fashion, bright and colourful, like their skinny striped sleeveless pullovers.

Another policeman was guarding a pile of lethal looking metal combs, the sort you use on dogs, but presumably ideal for combing long straggling hair. They seemed such effeminate weapons, but no doubt very handy for scarring faces.

One of Tony's gang was being forced to hand over his comb. He'd had it sticking out of his top pocket for all to see. Tony jeered at him. 'If you had more brains you'd be dangerous.'

Inside, they charged for the middle of the West stand. The police had made out the demarcation lines, the Coventry fans one side, Spurs the other. Down the middle was a line of policemen, shoulder to shoulder, splitting the West stand in half. The Coventry fans were outnumbered so far. The sudden arrival of a thousand or so Spurs troops a good hour before the kick-off was no match for the handful of local skinheads.

On the pitch, a gymnastic display was being given by some healthy-looking girls, part of Coventry's policy of trying to entertain the fans and make their ground as much a social centre as possible.

'WHAT A LOAD OF SCRUBBERS,' the Spurs fans all shouted, delighted at their own wit. The noise was deafening, echoing up to the roof as they chanted it over and over in unison. At the same time as they were shouting, little gangs of them were carefully manoeuvring around the police.

Once through the police, they infiltrated down into the Coventry groups and started pushing them. Nothing savage, just slowly moving them over by their sheer pressure of numbers. The police were forced to move the demarcation line further over, now that the Spurs had expanded. It had been done without any apparent cohesion, no general had masterminded the invasion. But now, instead of having half the area of the West stand, as the police had planned, the Spurs territory had grown to two-thirds. 'WE'VE GOT THE WEST STAND IN OUR HANDS' they suddenly started singing. 'WE'VE GOT THE WHOLE WEST STAND, IN OUR HANDS.'

The police let them stay where they were, but as the Coventry supporters slowly grew in number, the Coventry songs and shouts got louder, beginning to equal the volume of the Spurs songs. It became a dialogue, with each side of the thin blue line taking it in turns to sing insults at the other.

'IF YOU ALL HATE CITY, CLAP YOUR HANDS,' sang Spurs, and the claps that followed shook the ground.

'MAN-CHESTER CITY, MAN-CHESTER CITY,' shouted Coventry in reply, very nastily, getting in one below the belt. It had been Manchester City who'd hammered Spurs earlier in the season, 4-0.

When they'd finished this chant, they continued with shouts of CITY, CITY, this time meaning their own club. The Spurs boys punctuated it by shouting SHIT after each shout.

There seemed to be no leader of each group, yet the shouts were instantaneous. There is a well-known repertoire and it was only a matter of which one was used at which time. Sometimes it was obvious – if they shout CITY, or whatever their team is, you shout SHIT. But other times, the quickest wit or the loudest voice would start a chant and the rest would immediately follow.

'FERTILISER,' shouted one Coventry fan as a polite counterpoint to Shit. All Coventry seemed to take up the shout.

'SEE YOU ALL OUTSIDE,' sang Spurs in reply.

Now and again, Spurs went into some of the songs used by

107

all football supporters, like 'You'll Never Walk Alone' or 'We Hate Nottingham Forest'. A few of the Coventry fans joined in, knowing the words so well, not realising the rival fans had started it.

Then they went back to taunts. 'RUN, RUN, RUN, COVENTRY.' Most chants have only a couple of lines which are put to well-known pop songs and repeated over and over again. 'POWER TO THE PARK LANE,' to the tune of 'Power to the People', kept the Spurs fans going for a long time, clapping and chanting it.

For an hour, they kept up the songs, solidly and without ceasing, one leading to another. I couldn't understand a lot of them. Many of the chants had actions with them, like 'We hate Arsenal', where you punch one fist in the air in front of you, like a Nazi salute. My ears were numb, being right in amongst them. There was a definite feeling of power and excitement, but we were deafening ourselves more than anyone else.

By about half-an-hour before kick-off, the Coventry fans outnumbered the Spurs contingent. This was when the fights began in earnest, though the singing still went on.

'Right, let's go,' said one lad beside me. 'Round the back and get them.' He and a little party moved off through the singing sea of fans and approached Coventry from the other side, getting in amongst them and kicking, hoping other Spurs gangs would attack from the other side. But this time Coventry were strong enough to fight back. The supporters not involved swayed violently to one side. Immediately there was a human tidal wave as a great mass of bodies retreated from the action, or at least tried to, causing more damage and knocking down more people than the actual fighting. If you didn't see the wave coming and swayed with it, you got trodden on.

The police saw it as it happened and charged bravely into the thick of it, coming out with arm locks round the ring leaders. I saw Nick being led away by his ear, screaming and shouting that he hadn't hit anybody.

Tony was leaning against a barrier, all on his own, with a circle of space around him for about ten yards. The whole terrace was by now jam packed, yet Tony had space to spare.

He was leaning forward, glowering round from time to time.

There was a group of the young kids, not his own gang, watching expectantly at a distance, waiting for him to make a move. He'd taken up his stance right in the middle of no man's land. On one side was Spurs, the other Coventry. The Spurs fans were egging Tony on, wanting him to lunge and beat up any poor Coventry fan who dared to get near to him. He knew they were watching him. He was flexing his muscles, going through his primaeval posturing, like something out of *The Naked Ape*.

Further down the slope of the stand towards the pitch, other little circles had arisen, as other gang leaders took up their stances. The police had seen Tony's performance and were slowly moving in, circling the watching kids, just waiting for him to do something before pouncing. By the look of Tony's shirt, which was torn and blood-stained, he'd already been in a fight. Suddenly he saw the police and turned and muttered something to a few of his henchmen. I hadn't noticed them amongst the mass of gaping kids. Then he turned his back on his troops and threaded his way through the crowd and disappeared.

'We're pulling out,' said one of his mates to the other. They pushed their way across the stand, individually, without following each other but obviously knowing where the next rendezvous was to be.

I saw a scuffling across a mass of heads. Some innocent had got in their way. A boy was on the ground and being kicked. The police threw themselves into the crowd, but at that moment the teams came out and there was a roar which shook the stand. Everyone turned to the pitch and the fighting was forgotten. The Spurs fans went in turn through each member of their team, chanting his name, with a different chant for each, depending on the number of syllables in his name. You can't sing Ralph Coates to the same tune as Alan Mullery, for example. With Coates it's just a long low monotonous chant, splitting up his surname into two syllables 'RALPH CO-OATES, RALPH CO-OATES'. Mullery is very different. It's a much quicker and livelier 'RA, RA, RA-RA, MUL-ER-EE'. Each fan knew the right tune, but no one knew where the Ra Ra had

109

come from. Somebody somewhere is doing a PhD on the folk culture of football fans, then we'll know all the answers.

Gilzean has his own special song, being the King of White Hart Lane. They began and finished with Pat Jen-nings. He raised his right hand in a quick, Papal-like thanks as he ran to his goal. He only started acknowledging the crowd two years ago when they all wrote to him and protested. No other Spurs player acknowledged the cheers, apart from Mullery who gave a quick grin. The rest looked very serious. At home, safe at Tottenham, they each give a magnanimous wave to the Park Lane end when their name is sung, but not on foreign soil.

For the first fifteen minutes, I found it impossible to watch the play. They continued going through their Spurs songs, for at least the hundredth time, but this time they were also raising their Spurs scarves horizontally in the air in front of them, making layer upon layer of blue and white. Because of this, I couldn't see anything and neither could they. They swayed back and forward in time to their songs, forcing everyone around to do the same.

Eventually they lowered their scarves, but without giving up their chants. It was still very difficult to watch the play, with all their pushing and shouting and interruptions. What they were straining to see was a Spurs player have a shot at goal. This brought out incredible cheers, however big the miss or however weak the shot. And what they wanted most of all was a goal. They were paying little attention to Spurs' build-ups or to any of Coventry's movements. All they wanted was simple action and excitement.

It would be too easy to say they weren't interested in the game, only in the result. But by the very nature of standing physically and precipitously so close together and by making so much noise and raising their scarves and pushing each other, it is hard to believe that they can ever follow the details of the game. Coventry did win, by one goal to nil. Unlike Bill Nicholson, the fans didn't criticise the Spurs players. They didn't even admit that Cyril Knowles had had a bad game, which he had. Cyril was bloody unlucky, they all said. He was fouled. It wasn't his fault. The referee was useless.

110

Just before the end, I went round into the main stand to see if the West stand could be heard throughout the ground. The Spurs fans were definitely making more noise, right to the end, than Coventry, but looking at them from a distance they seemed so puny. When you're with them, you feel you've taken over. But they hadn't taken over anything, just been corralled into one part of one stand and tolerated.

'No guts,' said Bill Nicholson afterwards in the dressing-room. 'No guts.' The players said later they thought he was near to tears, but it looked more like fury to me, the way he shook his head, bowing it, not looking anyone in the eye. He went over the Coventry goal, saying what Knowles should have done.

Knowles and Beal had both been going for the Coventry winger, Young, but only succeeded in getting in each other's way without either getting in a tackle. Young cleverly went between them, seeing their mistake, and Carr scored from his cross. For a Coventry fan, it was an excellent and well-taken goal. But in the Spurs dressing-room, interested only in their own mistakes not the opposition's skills, most people put it down to Knowles' mistake. He should have made a tackle right away. Before the end, Knowles had been taken off and substituted by Pearce. A rare event, for a full back to be taken off through bad play.

'You've got to go in to get beaten,' said Nicholson. 'It's no use hanging back. Tackles have got to be made. You were all back pedalling for most of the match. No guts. Terrible, terrible.' He moved off, shaking his head. 'They're not a good team, Coventry. That's what really gets me.'

The day before he had obviously been aware of what might happen. Spurs have a habit, especially away from home, of crumbling before a hard but inferior team. He'd said in the team talk that he knew Coventry were a funny team, one they'd always found hard to do well against, so nobody must feel confident and hope to rely on skill. But this was what had happened. The guts had been missing.

They were all invited into Coventry's players' lounge. They trooped in, rather sadly, and stood around, talking to each other. Only Martin Chivers was mixing, which of course he couldn't help. He's the one that everyone wants to

111

talk to or gape at. Footballers are just as interested in seeing what the big stars look like in the flesh as anyone else.

Cyril wasn't admitting he had a poor game. He was his usual self, on the surface anyway, slating the Coventry team, attacking the ref.

Nobody answered. They realised that Cyril knew the truth, but couldn't admit it. It was just his way. They nodded in silent agreement, helping him with his excuses.

Martin Peters, who'd missed Spurs' only real chance, early in the first half, openly admitted his mistake. 'I was slow, I should have controlled the ball quicker.' He said it quietly, matter of factly, condemning himself, biting his lip as he said it, hoping the purging of his guilt would stop it happening again.

On the coach home, they were still going over the match, far more than on a day in which they've won. Mike England especially couldn't stop talking about it. He was trying to cheer Cyril up, knowing how Cyril must feel inside. 'You've got the skill. He's got none.' Cyril laughed bitterly.

The coach was taking them all the way home for once, as it was easier to go straight down the M1 than get a train. We'd been going about half an hour when Cyril started again. This time he said their centre half Blockley had played well. He wasn't being funny or skitty. He obviously meant it. It was true. Blockley hadn't given Chivers much room, though watching the game, it looked towards the end as if Chivers wasn't trying any of his bursts, even when he had half a chance.

Cyril, by going so far as to praise the opposition, was obviously softening. He'd moved on from his initial twisted, bitter reaction. Mike England joined in, going over Blockley's game.

In a corner, Coates, remarked on Mike's obsessions with the game. He'd never heard him talk so much. Phil Beal said Mike had been the same during the game. 'He kept shouting at me not to worry, or telling Cyril he was playing well after he'd given a bad pass. I told him to shut up in the end.'

A huge hamper appeared and out came a picnic dinner. There were chicken legs, sandwiches, lagers, soft drinks, apples, oranges, pears, plums and a basket of fresh straw-

112

berries for everyone in the party. Even the card playing stopped until they'd all finished eating.

'You're tucking in, Ralph,' said Martin Chivers, standing up and stretching his enormous body, radiating muscles and confidence if not exactly charm, but his remark wasn't meant to be nasty, just gentle teasing. Ralph was eating as if his life depended on it. 'Shouldn't be hungry after the match, you know, Ralph.'

After the meal, while most people were playing cards or dozing, I chatted at the back with Phil Beal about the 'no guts' remark which Bill Nicholson had made in the dressing-room.

'On the field, you're not aware of people not trying or not showing guts. You see things differently from the stand. I've noticed it myself when I've watched matches. It's easier to see then who's not going for the hard balls. Good passes and bad passes can look very different, when you're watching the whole field from the stand.

'Cyril took the hard way out today. His placed passes were going astray, but he would keep on with them. When it happens to me, I belt a few up the middle, getting rid of them quickly till I get my confidence back. A belted ball doesn't look as bad if it goes to one of their men, but a short pass which goes to an opponent looks diabolical. Cyril kept on trying to give really clever balls. He's a skilful player. But today they didn't work.'

He said that when bad balls start being given by a defender, the forward receiving them can make them look worse by not trying hard enough to pick them up. Chivers, by really throwing himself at a ball, can make a poor pass look a good one, just by getting it.

He was full of praise for Steve Perryman. He was one who definitely ran his heart out for everything and everyone, regardless of the chances against him succeeding. No one could say he didn't have guts. 'I couldn't do his midfield job. I wouldn't have the breath. I can do my job by thinking. That saves me breath.'

Steve, as usual, wasn't saying much, sitting alone looking out of the window. But he said he wasn't too depressed. Not as bad as he used to feel when the team was defeated. That

113

ruined the whole weekend. Now he could cope with it more, though it was still terrible.

But something that had happened two weeks previously, up at Sheffield, was still on his mind. He'd been substituted by John Pratt, when he thought he'd been playing well. He still couldn't understand it. 'I worried about it all weekend.'

It had been a sad day for everyone. The skinheads got home safely, without any serious incidents and without any of them being taken into custody. The Coventry supporters, delighted by their team, had been very kind and not presented too many challenges which the Spurs boys, of course, would not have been able to ignore.

Until today, the team had had a very good run. Their fine win against Liverpool had been the real start to their season and they'd gone seven games without defeat.

But being beaten by a team they didn't rate as highly as themselves was worrying. They'd got into a spell the previous season of doing badly away. They didn't want it to happen again. Most of all, they didn't want to see Chivers starting to fade in away games, the way he'd done today. Cyril Knowles' lapse was bad, but it had happened before and would no doubt happen again. Chivers is the man who wins matches. Chivers has got to be on form, every match, home or away.

10

Martin Chivers

In the next match, Mr Chivers scored a hat trick. Admittedly it was against Keflavik of Iceland which wasn't really fair. Spurs won 9-0, going through easily into the second round of the UEFA Cup. Even Ralph Coates scored. He still hadn't scored a League goal yet, but with the Icelanders being so generous, Ralph managed to slip on to the score list.

In the match after that, Mr Chivers pulled Spurs out of the fire when they looked as if they might lose to Ipswich. He scored the equalising goal. Against Torquay he scored twice to take Spurs into the fourth round of the League Cup.

Then Mr Chivers heard that he'd been chosen for the England party against Switzerland – along with Mullery and Peters. In just two months of the season, he'd become the most feared striker in the English League – with twelve goals so far to his credit. And in just a handful of games for England, starting only that summer, he'd become the best known centre forward in Europe.

'I feel very strong and confident. I'd like to think I could improve even more, but certainly I've never played as well as I am now.'

If Spurs could be said to be standing or falling by one player, then at that time it was Martin Chivers. He is the most exciting player in the team. You can *feel* the excitement, home and away, whenever he gets the ball.

As a player, he appears to have all the football skills. For a big man, he's so delicate and graceful, apparently unhurried, apparently about to go too far and lose the ball. Being a big man, he can hold the ball with his body and shrug them off like flies. When he gets his head down, when he's in a head-getting-down mood, there are few defences who can stop him.

115

But on a day in which Chivers isn't in the game, Spurs aren't in the game either. Which comes first? Does he affect the team or is it perhaps the team affecting Chivers?

By the very formation of the team, he has responsibility thrust upon him. In a 4-3-3 formation, which means four defenders, three midfield men and three forwards, Chivers is the striker in the middle. Coates was playing as a roving wing forward, along with Gilzean, but they are both essentially ancillary players, flicking or fetching the ball for Chivers. Chivers is the one expected to go forward for goal whenever he has the opportunity. Chivers takes all the knocks, but at the same time, as football is all about scoring goals, Chivers takes all the glamour.

He was having breakfast when the phone rang. A weekly newspaper wanted to interview him. They were doing three players who had made tremendous recoveries from serious injuries and wanted him to be one of them. He said how much. After a lot of huffing, they said ten pounds. 'Ten pounds' said Chivers. 'Do you think I'm going to give away the biggest story in my whole playing career for ten pounds? You must be joking!' and he hung up.

The phone rang again later. It was the same reporter. He'd had a word with his editor. The final offer was £15. Chivers told him what to do with it.

'Footballers are the most exploited people in England,' he said. 'We should earn a lot more. Look at all the entertainment we provide. Newspapers use your name to sell copies. They should pay through the nose, instead of getting it all for free.'

The previous week he'd been paid very handsomely by the *Daily Mirror* for his choice of the six best strikers in the country. It had entailed no work, just a straightforward little telephone conversation. The *Mirror* had then gone on to film Mr Chivers on Hampstead Heath, kicking a ball in the air, and were going to use this film in a TV commercial for the paper, urging the millions to buy the *Mirror* and read Martin Chivers. They'd played fair, and paid him well, acknowledging that a famous player's name can be used as a selling line to bring in readers.

Compared with all that, £10 for his life story was a bit

derisory. It was only in the last year he'd become hard on people, so he said. Life was short and he now had to cash in quick.

He's twenty-six and was born in Southampton where his dad was a stevedore on the docks. He passed his eleven plus and went to Grammar School, which is unusual for a footballer, a highly regarded local grammar school called Taunton's. It was a surprise to him, and the family, that he passed. Martin had been considered simply as a sportsman, spending his childhood kicking a ball and doing no school work.

The same happened at grammar school, even more so. Being such a naturally gifted all-round athlete, strong, fast and agile, he won everything in sight, all of it effortlessly. The only fault, for a perfect physical specimen, is his teeth. He has a couple of false ones on a plate at the front. It wasn't an accident. They decayed. 'It runs in the family. We've all got bad teeth.'

To everyone's surprise, as he seemed completely pre-occupied with sport, he passed his O levels in five subjects, including German. His mother is German which helped him to learn the language.

He'd been spotted by Southampton when he played for Southampton Boys and later Hampshire Schoolboys, but his headmaster wanted him to stay on for A levels. But at sixteen he decided to leave.

In 1967, he was in the Southampton team which got back into the First Division. He'd already earned a dozen England Under 23 caps (he still holds the record number at the moment, seventeen) and was chosen that year for the Football League team. He began to realise he should look for a bigger club. 'I talked to Jimmy Greaves in that Football League international and he said I could do well elsewhere.' In that match, Martin scored three goals.

He was transferred to Spurs in 1968 for £125,000 and on his first match scored the winning goal against Sheffield Wednesday. In his second match, a 2-2 draw with Manchester United, he scored both goals. 'I struck gold from the beginning and I kept it up for quite a while. When I did begin to fade a bit, the fans were very disappointed. I think they expected too much because I'd started so well. They'd been spoiled. I don't know why I faded. It was towards the end of the season and we'd been knocked out of everything. That was probably it.'

He started the next season well, scoring six goals in ten games, but on his eleventh he received his injury. This was on 21 September 1968, at home against Nottingham Forest. He twisted his knee and fell. It wasn't a collision. No one was to blame. Jimmy Greaves went to help him, but he couldn't get up. He just lay there. It was the front of his left knee which was damaged. He was rushed straight to hospital but they couldn't operate immediately as he'd had a cup of tea at half-time. They operated at eight in the evening. The lower patella ligament had been severed and they had to knit it up.

'When I woke up in the morning, Bill was there, looking at me, very worried. I was told I'd be out for at least six months. I can remember all their faces vividly. I was shattered. So were they.

'I think they held an emergency board meeting afterwards. I'm sure they thought my career was finished.'

It had been a big investment for Spurs – £125,000 was the record at the time – but it was the man that mattered. They saw Chivers in the Bobby Smith tradition, their big, bustling double team centre forward. Jimmy Greaves was now on his own, to take the knocks and score all the goals.

The six m nths' estimate proved to be optimistic. He never played again that season and in all he was out for a whole year, from the September to the following August.

'I can remember all the stages. Like the first time I could fully bend my knee. That took four months. When the first six months were up, which I'd believed would see me back on the field, I kept on at the surgeon, when can I get back, can I play in the reserves. But he said give it the summer. It mustn't be rushed. I was very depressed.

'The club was very good to me. I had a seat in the directors' box for every match. For the first time I learned a lot by watching. I could see how Jimmy Greaves was so good. I could see how vital it is to keep moving all the time. When you're playing, there often doesn't seem any point.

118

But from above, you can see the movements being built up.

'I trained very hard to get fit again, once the injury had cleared up. Bill paid me the biggest compliment of all time by saying I'd tried hard – I'd even done as well as Dave McKay had done! That made me feel really good. I was at the ground morning and afternoon, building myself up. I never thought I had it in me. It brought out good things in my character.'

But at home, he was very miserable, feeling out of it and useless. He did some gardening, laying paving stones, generally hanging around. 'I was very irritable with the wife. I wasn't fit company. But I don't think I ever seriously thought it was the end of my career. If I'd known from the beginning it was going to take a whole year, I might have done. As they'd only said six months, I'd believed them and worked with that in mind. It kept on being put back and put back, but all the time I felt it wouldn't be long.'

His wife Carol was more worried. She genuinely thought it was the end, but never said this to Martin. 'My job was to keep him cheerful.'

He came back at the start of the 1969 season but in many ways the worst was to come. 'I was cured and I was fit, but I suppose I didn't believe it. I worried and I was very tentative with everything I did. The crowd was very impatient and had a go at me. Bill was impatient as well and gave me some stick. My confidence had gone.'

I remember watching him at this period and like most fans on the terraces, I was convinced he'd had it. Inwardly, it might have been his confidence which was lacking, but outwardly, he just seemed to show few signs of any talent at all. It wasn't that he was getting rid of the ball quickly or showing his skills in very small doses, he just seemed generally to be a big clumsy player, with no finesse, who could do nothing right.

For most of that season, very few matches went well for him. But very slowly in the next season he began to pick up. He's not sure when it began to happen, which match or even which month he found himself again. He thinks several factors helped to make him confident again.

The most important happened inside the club where

everyone, manager and players, tried to make him realise what a strong and gifted player he was. They told him continuously that he was ruining his own career by not asserting himself and using his own gifts.

'Despite all my success, I'd always been a timid player. At Southampton I'd never had to fight because everything had come easy. It was the way I'd been brought up. I'd had a very easy-going childhood and school days. I did everything easily without really trying. I'd never had to fight. From the beginning people had called me a gentle giant which was true. It's always the little fellers who do all the fighting, in football as in other things. They never forget they're little, so all the time they're trying to prove how good they are. Big players like me, and I suppose John Charles, don't continually have to prove anything.'

Bill Nicholson deliberately set out to bring out the aggressive side to his nature, by keeping on at him, taunting him for being soft, trying to rouse him, goading him into action. 'He never stopped moaning at me all that season – he still hasn't stopped. I still get it. But that season was terrible. I remember Mullers saying to him, "You'll ruin that lad."'

In all practice matches, the clubs' two big centre halfs, Mike England and Peter Collins, were encouraged by Nicholson to give Chivers as many knocks as possible, which they willingly did. They too didn't like to see him ruining the team's chances by being soft and slow and not throwing himself around.

'They're both tough lads and very good defenders. Having to play hard against them did me a lot of good. They worked on me all the time.'

On one occasion it went too far. After Mike England had been particularly hard against him in a practice match at Cheshunt it led to a fight between them. They stood shouting and kicking each other till they were pulled apart.

'They had to put a tough streak into me. As a striker, you've got to use your strength. I wasn't using my strength because my confidence had gone.'

There was perhaps more to it than that. There's also a stubborn streak in him which makes him sometimes not do things he's told to do. Some players like young Steve

Perryman flog themselves to death at the slightest sight of the ball. Perhaps Chivers is too clever and rationalises his actions and his chances and holds himself back, even if it's done subconsciously.

All the work on making him aggressive at last began to pay dividends. Chivers thinks that the final element in making it all click was the transfer of Jimmy Greaves to West Ham.

'It was probably the best thing that happened to me, though I didn't realise it at the time. I was left with a real job. Up to then I'd been playing with Jimmy, as the number two striker to him. Now I was on my own. It was a hell of a responsibility but it made me more responsible. I then had two defenders opposing me, which meant I had to be aggressive all the time, to withstand them. It was from then on I began to think if I didn't play well, Tottenham didn't play well.'

It was last season, 1970-1, that the difference dramatically began to show. Chivers had the best season he'd ever had. The team finished third in the League, compared with eleventh the year before. Chivers was in every way the star of the team, playing in most games (54) and scoring most goals, (29). The crowd, having booed him mercilessly the season before, started to cheer. Their cries of 'Chivers for England' were at last rewarded and at the end of the season, Chivers got his first full cap. It was his first representative honour for almost four years. If nothing else, that showed how long and seriously he'd been suffering.

There's another minor element in his revival which he doesn't really admit. It's one of those elements anyway which are hard to prove – the arrival of Peters. Chivers himself puts his improvement down to Greaves going, but Peters coming must also have helped. (Mrs Peters definitely thinks her Martin played a big part in Chivers' transformation, but says, very bitterly, that it has never been acknowledged.)

'Sometimes I think he's now a bit too tough,' said Carol. 'A bit too blunt and outspoken. I tend not to be, but I know, really, it's the best thing to be. People know where you stand if you say what you really feel. But it doesn't do his image any good.

121

'He was more of a worrier in the old days. He used to take tranquillizers before a match at Southampton and even when he first came to Spurs. Now he doesn't do that, but he still worries. All good players worry, I'm sure. He still gets upset when Mr Nicholson goes on about the goals he missed, especially when he's scored a hat trick and the team has won.'

The Chivers live in Epping with their two daughters, Andrea and Melanie near the middle of the village, in an exclusive enclave of what are called Georgian Town Houses. They'd had an offer of £20,250 and were thinking of moving to something more detached and secluded, surrounded by a large garden, though still in the same area.

Martin spends a lot of his spare time playing golf, which his wife puts up with, quietly, though she'd obviously like him more at home. 'I sometimes think I wouldn't like my daughters to marry footballers.'

She doesn't worry as much as some of the wives about being alone – it's Martin who hates to be alone. There must be some deep psychological reason for it – perhaps despite all his new aggressiveness and confidence he is still insecure. On the occasions when he's been alone in the house – when Carol has been down in Southampton visiting her parents – Martin has found it so unbearable that he's had Joe Kinnear to stay the night with him.

'I really am scared. I don't know why. I don't like the dark and going to bed on my own. I worry if I've locked everything up. I never read books and I don't like TV and I can't cook anything for myself, so I go to pieces on my own. I *must* have company. I must be doing something all the time and have other people around me.'

It seemed strange, for such a huge bloke. He'd even used the word scared, surely he didn't mean he was worried about a burglar attacking him? Yes, he was physically scared. He didn't know what of.

He has several business interests outside football, but nothing very big. He would like to have something, if just for the future security of his family. His main commitment is with a local garage in Epping, Leford Motors, who have him as a sort of sales representative. He doesn't do any work, except roll up now and again, but they use his name in any way they can. They advertise a car as "Martin Chivers' Choice of the Week" and get prospective buyers to come and meet Martin Chivers.

In return for his name, he gets a free car which he can change every year. At present he has a huge Ford Zodiac automatic.

He has an agent for any advertising or press articles but finds he gets most such work on his own. 'It's money for old rope so I might as well do it myself. I make myself a bit more amiable to reporters, if they're paying.

'They only want to know me now I'm a success. I understand that and it doesn't worry me. When I was struggling to get back they didn't care. That's the only thing that hurt me. I hated them for not believing in me, nor believing that I could come back. I suppose the Press have a right to their opinions. They don't have to give me the benefit of the doubt by saying I was just lacking in confidence. I would have liked them to have said that. But they never did.'

'They were terribly unfair to him,' said Carol. 'There's one fellow whose name I vowed never to forget. He was writing in the supporters' magazine and he was saying what a bad buy Martin was. I've forgotten his name now. . .'

There's no doubt he now has the will to win and confidence in his own powers and ability. So what happens on those days when the team, including Chivers, seem to fade, to hide, to be lacking in guts?

'I don't know. We're all aware of it. Bill makes it perfectly clear. I know Eddie usually blames me. Perhaps the other players are waiting for me, hoping I can pull something out. I tell myself I'll have to do something to liven the match up. I keep trying for that first goal, knowing that the whole team will play well if only I can get it.

'The pressure is never there at home. I always play marvellously at home and so does the whole team. But away from home, I'm more over-worked. We're defending more and I don't get the service. I've got to make my own openings.

'I know Eddie would have me on my knees. But I couldn't do what he wants, chase every little ball. I'm not a fitness fanatic. I'm just not made like Steve, wanting to run myself into the ground in every match. I reserve my strength for when I'm going forward with a reasonable chance. It's very tiring, fighting every ball with their centre half. It's a thankless job.'

11

Nantes

We had to be at London Airport at two o'clock on the
Tuesday to board a BEA charter plane for Nantes in France.
As we were checking in, a TV crew were standing waiting,
their lights at the ready. 'Must be waiting for Martin,' said
someone and the others agreed. But when Martin appeared,
the one and only Martin of the moment, the cameramen
weren't at all interested.

The Spurs party consisted of thirty-five people. There were
sixteen players, eight directors and officials, ten journalists
and Mr Broderick of Cooks who'd arranged the trip.

It was a normal sized party for a British football team
going into Europe. The cost of the plane was about £1,500.
Spurs usually hire their own plane when they play abroad as
it's more convenient, letting the Press for once join the inner
sanctum. But no fans are allowed on the team plane.

Mr Broderick spends his whole life organising football
trips, for clubs like Spurs, Chelsea and others, plus the
England team. He'd recently taken the England party to
Switzerland. He prefers going with the England team,
though not for snob reasons. 'With the England team, there's
a nice atmosphere because it's mainly old friends meeting
each other again. With a club, they see each other every day
of the week.'

At Nantes airport, there were photographers and a TV
crew waiting to meet the Spurs team as they climbed out of
the plane. Greetings were exchanged with the Nantes officials who said there would be a reception next day, Wednesday, for the Spurs directors and the Press. Bill Nicholson
thanked them but said he was more interested in visiting the
stadium. It was agreed he could see it at eleven the next day.

The local Press went straight for Chivers, running after
him and shouting Mee-ster Chee-vers. They got him to pose

with a toy pistol, pretending to shoot. His legend had preceded him, even to Nantes, wherever Nantes was. None of the players had the slightest idea, or were even interested.

We went by coach to the Central Hotel in Nantes, a modest, medium sized hotel, nothing like as posh as most of the English hotels Spurs use. Bill Nicholson had chosen it personally, vetting the rooms and meals. He'd come over on a quick trip the week before, mainly to scout on the Nantes team. As usual, he'd left nothing to chance, but he'd been even more meticulous this time, as it was Europe.

Playing in Europe is both an end and a beginning for the top British clubs. It's in their minds all season, knowing that if they finish high enough in the English League, they will end up qualifying for one of the three European competitions the following season.

Spurs were now in the second round of what's called the UEFA Cup – the Union of European Football Associations Cup. Each round is played on a home and away basis, with the winner on aggregate of the two matches going into the next round.

Sixty-four teams had started off from every footballing country in Europe back in September and several famous ones had already been knocked out, such as Leeds United and Atletico Madrid, though traditionally the first round is looked upon as a walk-over for the big clubs. It had been for Spurs, playing the Icelandic amateurs. But now it was serious. Having a good run in Europe can keep a club going for nine months, a whole season in fact. It keeps the players on their toes, the fans happy and brings in money to the club.

They knew they would have a hard struggle with Nantes. They had twice won the French League in recent years so they'd had good experience of European football (Celtic had knocked them out of the European Cup in 1966). Although French football journalism is of a high, nay, intense level, French football is not as well supported as English. Nantes' average gate is considered very good for France, eighteen thousand, only half that of Spurs.

The Spurs directors were making no bones about what a pleasure it was to be in Europe again, but many of the players were coming on strong about it being a drag. The ones who'd played in France before were telling the others there was no chance of any talent after the match. The French didn't like the English. Their girls wouldn't even dance with you, unless you paid them a fortune. Now Germany, you always had a good time in Germany.

We checked in quickly at the hotel and the players went into their own dining-room for a light tea while the Press and directors went into the main dining-room.

As they waited for their meal, the players were all comparing their rooms. 'How's your TV? Only one of mine's got colour. Got a bar? We've got a bar. Cyril's got a swimming pool in his room.' They were complaining, in their usual inverted fashion, about the hotel. They all thought it was pretty crummy with no facilities. It wasn't luxury by any means, but very French with a kind staff and a friendly atmosphere. The players ordered toast and tea and had hysterics when the toast arrived wrapped in plastic, like babies' rusks. They tried to butter it and immediately it disintegrated into crumbs. But there was strawberry jam which they loved.

After tea most players put their heads out of the front door. It was raining and dark. Several had wanted a walk but when they saw the rain, they went back to the foyer, sat chatting or played cards. The regular card players, Joe, Gilly, Mike and Cyril had got down to it the minute tea was over without looking at the weather.

Phil, Roger, Jimmy Neighbour and myself decided to chance it and we made a dash between showers. We got fifty yards from the hotel and took shelter in a souvenir shop. Phil picked up a pair of moccasins and indicated that he wanted a larger size. The assistant nodded and went to get bigger ones. Phil spread his arms about two feet wide and she nodded, though beginning to think she'd got the order wrong, or was serving a madman. Phil put one finger up and said One, he only wanted one, then left the shop.

Roger picked up a paper knife and was pretending he was going to throw it at the wall. The lady took it from him and held it in front of her chest, defending herself, convinced they were madmen, trying to push Roger out of the shop.

127

Roger came out at last, laughing. 'She said Sootie, Sootie. What does that mean?'

Dinner for the players was at seven thirty, served in the same dining-room. Bill spent at least an hour going through the menu, standing in the middle of the room and reading it out, getting them to choose by a show of hands what they wanted. Not just for the meal they were about to have, but for the next day's meals as well. It was a job Johnny Wallis could have done, or Mullery, or the head waiter, or anyone.

The choice of main course was veal or steak. At the table I was at, Phil and Roger and Jimmy had steak but left almost all of it. It arrived with a little daub of garlic butter on the top and they tore at it furiously, swearing, and wiped all marks of it from their steak. They all said they hated garlic. Phil even washed his hands on his napkin, pouring water on them from a jug, in case he'd been contaminated. I ordered beer but the players couldn't. The hotel staff had been given instructions that no player could have beer or alcohol of any kind, at the table or in his room, not till the match was over.

Bill, his orders finally completed, went to eat with the directors in the main dining-room. When he'd gone, the bread pellets started flying and then the grapes, but nothing out of hand and no clothes or tables were ruined. The waiters were amused, when they weren't pointing out to each other which one was Cheevers.

Throughout the entire meal, all four courses of it, the card school played cards non-stop, dealing on the table over the vegetable soup, trout meunière, the steak and the fruit salad, all of which was delicious, much better than any English hotel food, that's if you don't mind garlic.

As we left the dining-room, Roger saw a notice above the door which said 'Sortie' and asked what it meant. I said exit. 'That's it. Sootie. That's what she said.'

After dinner, they all sat around in the hall, the card players still hard at it. The Press decided they'd go out and see the town, plus me, and Mr Broderick, the Cooks man. We all discussed our plans loudly, about the night-clubs we were going to, knowing the players were confined to barracks.

As we went out the front door, Eddie Baily and Johnny Wallis were standing there, four square and resolute. They were on guard to make sure that no players sneaked out with us.

Next day the morning paper, *Nantes Océan,* had a picture of me on their front page, coming down the ladder from the plane. Beside me was David Miller from the *Telegraph,* Colin Malam of the *Sun,* Steve Curry of the *Express* and Nigel Clarke of the *Mirror.* The caption underneath said 'The stars of the celebrated Tottenham team arriving at Nantes airport yesterday.' That kept the team in jokes all day.

At eleven o'clock, I went with the players for a brief visit to the stadium, then they went back to the hotel to put in the time till lunch, going through their usual monastic rituals, no fun and no alcohol, simply playing cards or taking an occasional walk round the block, hour after boring hour.

Meanwhile, I went with the Press and the Spurs directors to a slap-up reception at a hotel ten kilometres out of Nantes, given by the Nantes Football Club. We had lots of wine, a three-hour lunch and several speeches. The big lads from the Paris Press had now arrived, wheeled out for the match, to show the local lads how to write correct captions. They knew the names of every Spurs player. All of them seemed to be from *L'Equipe.*

Back in Nantes, I went shopping in the afternoon with a couple of directors. We went to a superb cheese shop, taken by a Nantes director. Mr Groves, the bachelor, bought six. Then he bought six bottles of Muscatel. Back at the hotel, you could tell the players from the directors. One lot had bought souvenir dolls and the other carried wine bottles and smelled very strongly of cheese.

While the Press and the directors had been enjoying themselves hugely all day, lapping up the entertainment which the players' success had brought them, the players themselves had still been hanging about the hotel. They were obviously feeling the strain of waiting. They'd just finished a one and a half hour team talk from Bill. He'd gone through every Nantes player in detail. They couldn't wait for the match. They were all fed-up and bored rigid with waiting.

We left the hotel by coach at seven fifteen. By now the

hotel was full of Spurs supporters – seventy of whom had just arrived. Suddenly the foyer had become crowded with middle-aged Englishmen in their best Sunday suits and supporters club ties, wandering round wearing blue and white rosettes and ogling the players.

The streets to the stadium were crowded but the bus got through fairly easily. Along the final stretch were rows and rows of stalls selling nougat, hot dogs, sweets and drinks, ham rolls and other delicacies. Unlike a British ground before a match, nobody seemed to be selling rosettes, scarves, badges or other football souvenirs. Food and drink seemed to be the only line for all the street traders. The crowds too appeared different, older and better behaved, a lot of them wearing tartan berries. There were no gangs of young hooligans trying to assert themselves or looking for fights. But inside the stadium, they made just as much noise if not more than a British crowd. When the songs started, the whole crowd joined in. At Tottenham, it's just the Park Lane end who sing the songs. The French crowd communally sing, the way they do at Welsh Rugby Union matches.

The dressing-room, like the stadium, was spartan and seemed to be made entirely of concrete. On the benches round the dressing-room was a new bar of soap and a new blue towel for each player to use, still in their wrapping papers. Most of the players pocketed the soap in its wrapper. 'Another free present for the wife.'

Peter Collins, who was suffering from diarrhoea, was given some pills by the Spurs doctor and told not to eat anything for twenty-four hours. Then, along with the directors, the doctor discreetly withdrew, leaving the manager and the players to get on with their rituals.

A French official opened the dressing-room door and looked in and Philip Beal shouted at him. Philip beckoned with his hand, wiping his bottom and saying in English that there was no lavatory paper. Everyone laughed, thinking it was another Philip Beal joke. A few minutes later the official reappeared with a packet of paper and everyone cheered as he threw it across the room to Philip.

'Well played,' said Roger Morgan. That was his catch phrase of the moment. He'd said it to every waiter in the hotel since we'd arrived in Nantes.

'It's good to have one joker in the team,' said Eddie Baily heavily and sarcastically. 'A joker always helps.' He was busily massaging Steve Perryman's thighs with warm oil.

'Is that why you bought Roger,' someone shouted. Everyone was looking at Roger, to see how he reacted. They were no doubt thinking of an article in the previous week's *People* in which Roger Morgan had been described as one of Bill Nicholson's expensive mistakes. Roger must have been very hurt. It hadn't been his fault that he'd been injured and not played in the first team for a year.

Roger made a face, his head bowed, pretending to be hurt and embarrassed, but laughing, putting it on, not at all worried by the joke at his expense. Roger is one player who'd be very difficult to humiliate by sarcasm. Not because he's thick skinned, or even conceited, but because he takes it all as a joke anyway. He'll try hard, but not playing for the first team is not the end of the world to Roger.

Underneath the table was a brown cardboard box. Bill Nicholson picked it up, put it on the table and opened it, saying there was a present inside for everyone.

'They asked me for a list of things you'd like, but I don't know which one they chose,' explained Bill. 'If it had been me, I'd have given you a comb and a pair of scissors each.'

The players ignored the joke, having heard it a hundred times before, and rushed forward to get their presents. They'd been individually wrapped in green paper and tied with a bow, just like a Christmas present. Roger was first to tear his open so they all watched, deciding to keep theirs nicely wrapped up. Another free present for the wife. Inside was a black present box containing a Waterman's propelling pencil. 'Great', said Roger. 'The box on its own will do as a present.'

'Made in Hong Kong, mine says,' said someone, pretending to read the label.

'Nantes,' said Mullery.

'Nantes-sense,' said Chivers, walking across the room to the shower, repeating his joke on the way, but still nobody got it.

An official appeared and told Bill that the teams were to

come out five minutes before the kick-off. The match was to begin at eight thirty. It was now ten past eight. The room was getting quieter. The time for jokes was over, if you could call them jokes. It had been self-conscious noise and chatter, an outlet for their nerves.

Joe Kinnear was doing exercises on his own in a corner. Outside, inspecting the pitch, he'd been shivering. An evening chill had descended, but he was obviously nervous.

Martin Peters asked Bill if he knew the referee. Bill said he was an East German but he'd forgotten the name, which was unlike Bill Nicholson. Martin thought he might be the same East German ref they'd had in the World Cup. Bill said he didn't think so.

None of the players had programmes. In an English dressing-room, the players are always amply supplied with free programmes. I had got one at the hotel from a French journalist. It was a simple four-page, folded-over programme, full of adverts. Leslie Yates, a freelance journalist who writes the Spurs programmes, had come specially to Nantes so that his sixteen-page Spurs programme would be full of information about the Nantes players and club. I handed the Nantes programme to Bill. No, it wasn't a ref he knew.

Martin Peters went into the shower room with a ball and started banging it back and forward against the walls. Eddie Baily moved on from Perryman's thighs to rubbing Gilzean's chest. Johnny Wallis was strapping up ankles. Mike England was putting a new strip of elastoplast on a cut on his forehead. Phil Beal and Mullery were rubbing vaseline on their faces – to stop the sweat going into their eyes during the match. Bill Nicholson went out of the room again. He told Eddie to lock it and let no one in. He'd knock three times to get back. The room was hot and fetid with embrocation. It was more of a crowded concrete cavern than a dressing-room, with no direct light and no ventillation, just a couple of small holes in one corner of the ceiling.

Bill came back, almost bursting the door down in his rage, swearing and cursing. 'They've changed their bloody strip. They told me last week they'd play in yellow. They always play in yellow. That's why they're called the bloody canaries.'

132

The players tried to look equally concerned and serious. A
few joined in the curses, pleased to have something to vent
their anger on, an outside body they could all have a go at.
Mullery asked why they'd changed their minds.

'For the bloody French TV,' said Nicholson. 'The TV
want them to play in green.'

Everyone groaned even louder this time, all cursing TV,
saying you should never do anything for those TV cunts. I
couldn't see what all the fuss was about. As Spurs were going
to play in white, their normal colour, it could make no
difference if Nantes played in green as opposed to their
normal yellow.

'Have you brought any others,' said Nicholson to Johnny
Wallis. 'Pat will have to get changed.'

Pat was out at the lavatory. I'd forgotten he always plays
in a green jumper. Someone shouted down the corridor for
him. When he came back, he was already wearing green. He
looked annoyed, when he heard what had happened. Roger
handed him a red shirt, to try it on, but Pat said it was OK.
He went to his corner and searched around till he found a
yellow shirt. He said that would do. Bill went to wash his
hands.

Everyone calmed down again, the curses dying out as the
talking stopped once again and only the stamping of boots
could be heard and the stretching of arms and legs in last
minute exercises. Eddie Baily called out the time – fifteen
minutes to go. There was a knock at the door and the referee
came in, very quickly, catching everyone by surprise. He
tapped Pat on the shoulder and pointed to his boots. Pat
turned them over to be inspected. He moved on as Pat was
holding up his boots, going round the room so quickly that
he hardly seemed to look at more than one pair of boots. Bill
tried to grab him as he came round the room and was going
out of the door.

'They've changed their shirts,' began Bill. 'It means our
goalie is now in yellow, will that be. . .'

But the ref had gone, pushing straight past Nicholson,
ignoring him. Bill made a face when he'd gone. The players
whistled. 'Not much of an inspection that,' said someone.

'East German, eh,' said Eddie. 'I wonder if he was a POW

133

in the. . .' But he tailed off in mid-sentence, unable to think of a suitable insult.

Bill went to the middle of the room and began addressing his players. They sat silently, each of them taut and gleaming, ready for action. Bill had his head bowed and was moving his hands and arms nervously, walking back and forwards, talking loudly and urgently. There was a feeling of embarrassment, as if the players felt worried on his behalf. They were already completely keyed up. Their minds were on the match. There was only three minutes to go. Nothing he could say now could make much difference, not at this late stage.

'The last time we played in France,' began Bill, 'I know you all remember it. You know what happened. I don't have to go over it. We thought we'd have it easy. But we didn't, did we. I don't want a repeat of that. I want you to go hard, but keep your feet down. Even one foot off the ground and you'll be for it. Don't give that referee any excuses.'

The last time in France had been four years ago at Lyons. Olympique Lyonnais had beaten Spurs 1-0 and went on to knock them out of Europe. That was the night that Mullery was sent off, a night not to remember.

Bill went over a few more points, then finished suddenly. It was as if all he'd been doing was nervously clearing his throat, thinking aloud. His mind was seething with details but he knew that it was too late. He stood in silence, the players watching.

'Now no arguing with the ref either,' said Mullery, taking over the silence, becoming keen and captain-like, clapping his hands, moving forward so everyone could see him. 'We've got to go very hard for the first ten minutes. Don't let them get settled. *Hard* all the time. OK lads.'

They were sitting with their heads bowed. A couple of the reserves exchanged looks as Mullery spoke, quickly, and then looked away. All five reserves were in bulky blue canvas track suits – Roger Morgan, Collins, Daines, Ray Evans and John Pratt. They looked like convicts in a work party.

'One minute to go,' said Eddie Baily. Nobody spoke. It was now like a death cell. As if they were all going out to an execution.

134

'If you beat this lot,' said Eddie, 'you'll be in the last sixteen. Then after that you'll be in the last sixty-four.'

He was trying to reduce the tension, but as always they were ignoring Eddie's jokes.

'Right, bayonets on,' shouted Eddie as a whistle went in the corridor. 'Over the top. Let's have you!'

They all stood up, stamping their feet. Bill had been busily tidying up the already tidy room as Eddie had been joking. He suddenly beamed and looked expansive and benevolent. As usual, he patted them on the back and wished each one by name the best of luck. Then he went to the shower room where he washed his hands yet again and put on his jacket. He helped Eddie to lock the dressing-room door and then followed the players into the tunnel where they were waiting, lined up, just below the entrance. There was a roar as both teams went out together and a blaze of fireworks lit up the night sky.

The trainers' bench reserved for the Spurs team was just to the left of the centre stand, three wooden forms which we all crowded on to. Just a couple of yards behind us, well within spitting distance, was the crowd, separated by a six foot high wire fence. The crowd were in good temper and gave Bill, Eddie and the Spurs substitutes a cheer as they sat down.

'Get out there,' said Bill, turning to his reserves. 'Get the feel of the turf.' They were a bit embarrassed, not wanting to draw attention to themselves in their baggy blue track suits, only being reserves, but they went out reluctantly to join the first team in white for the pre-match kick around, then they returned hurriedly and sat down. The crowd gave them a derisive cheer. They were screaming in our ears, trying to get us to turn round, shoving beer and bread through the wires, but nobody did. 'Bloody frogs,' said Eddie Baily.

The ball was wet and greasy and from the beginning the Spurs forwards seemed unable to control it. When they tried to collect the ball it bounced off their legs to a Nantes player. When they did get a passing move going, it ended with someone hitting it too far in front. Chivers at last collected a ball well but was robbed before he was ready and gave up without chasing the man who'd robbed him. Eddie screamed abuse. Bill hung his head.

135

The Nantes team came tearing through the middle right from the beginning, very confident on the ball and in their running. They were doing immaculate wall passes, scattering the Spurs midfield before them, and the crowd was roaring and cheering. For the first half hour, they had it almost all their own way, apart from a couple of isolated raids by Spurs. Even high balls up the middle to the tall Spurs strikers were getting nowhere. Chivers and Gilzean were having no luck. Only Jimmy Neighbour looked dangerous, beating their full back easily and tearing up the wing, but his centres were not finding their men and he was soon starting to take on one man too many and losing the ball. But he alone looked sharp and on form.

My ears were numb well before half-time. Eddie kept up a continuous stream of abuse, cursing every Spurs mistake when they lost the ball and then screaming orders when the Nantes forwards started thundering towards the Spurs penalty area.

He screamed at Steve to mark number 8, or Gilly to come back, or Jimmy to run wide. He was working himself into a frenzy, yet none of them could hear him. Only when a Spurs player was running down our side of the pitch, right beside us, could his voice be heard. He yelled at Phil Beal, but Phil deliberately ignored him. He yelled at Mullery to urge the team on. Mullery shouted back that he was fucking doing it.

Bill was shouting as well, yelling at Chivers to get moving, but mostly his shouts were sudden blurted-out oaths of panic and fury, burying his face in his hands as once more the Spurs forwards failed to get anywhere. Eddie literally never stopped. His instructions were really a running commentary, shouting out what people should be doing even when he knew they were miles away, hoping by osmosis he might get through to them. Sometimes he just shouted out names, over and over again, screaming at the top of his voice. Sometimes it was sheer gibberish. He jumped on the bench once, putting his knees up in the air, his signal for Chivers to get running, hoping he might be seen by Chivers if not heard. The crowd behind furiously booed and jeered, thinking he wanted Chivers to get the boot in. This wasn't true. Not once did either of them exhort any player to rough stuff. They were concerned with their players getting rid of the ball quickly and intelligently, avoiding bodily contact if anything. When a foul was given against Spurs they were furious with their own players for having got into such a position, though it didn't stop them from cursing the ref whenever he seemed to be favouring the opposition.

When it was one of Spurs' three big stars at fault, Eddie was all the more abusive. 'Bloody internationals,' Eddie was screaming. 'Look at them. Play for England but they won't play for us. GET MOVING! DON'T BLOODY STAND THERE! Useless. Too much publicity. It's gone to his head. He won't try any more.'

Half-time came suddenly, in the middle of a stream of Eddie's curses. We followed the players slowly to the dressing-room, letting them get settled. They sat quietly, not looking at each other. Johnny Wallis got some bottles out of a crate which had been left for the Spurs players. It was all Vichy water. There was no tea, which was what the players wanted. They were too limp to be furious. They stared into space, avoiding each other's eyes, hanging their heads, exhausted on their benches.

Bill stood silently for a bit, his face red and contorted, controlling himself as much as possible.

'You're not getting in. You've got to get in first. You're just letting them do those wall passes.'

He went round the defenders individually. He told Mike England and Phil Beal to keep up their covering and to watch numbers 7 and 10 breaking through from behind. He said nothing to the forwards. He was furious with them and they knew it. They were furious with themselves, dejected and utterly miserable. Slowly they all started to stand up, looking round, bemused, asking for a drink, looking for some stimulus, some diversion, anything to avoid Bill.

'It's just Fishy water,' said Eddie. 'And there's no bloody glasses either.' I went down the corridor and got some glass coffee cups which was all I could find.

'We don't want any mistakes at the back,' Bill was saying when I returned. 'No silly goals.'

The second half was much the same. Nantes had most of the ball and were still as quick and inventive as ever,

137

especially in midfield. Spurs were sluggish and had no inspiration up front, but the defence was still managing each
time to break down the Nantes attack on the edge of the
penalty area.

Everyone on the Spurs bench knew that the Spurs forwards were playing badly. It was one of those away games
where they seem to hide, to go numb, to stop thinking at the
vital moments. Jimmy Neighbour was still trying hard, but
Chivers was showing little of his skills. Admittedly he was
getting few good balls from his harassed midfield men and
not once did the ball bounce his way, but all the same, he
made not one chance for himself. You could sense the team
praying for him to turn a half chance into a goal by sheer
brilliance and bring himself and the whole team to life.

Gilly was showing a lot of heart, but was getting nowhere.
Fifteen minutes before the end, he was brought off and
Roger Morgan was sent on, his first appearance in the first
team since he'd been injured exactly a year ago. It seemed a
rather desperate measure considering he was a long way from
being back to first team form, but Bill was obviously hoping
for some miracle.

'Do it for us, Roger,' exhorted Eddie, pushing him on.

The reserves stood up to make room for Gilly on the
bench. Someone gave him Roger's track suit and helped him
to put it on. He sat at the end of the bench, his face shattered with effort, sweat streaming from every pore. Around
his head was a halo of steam. He was like a defeated
racehorse, frothing and steaming from being pushed almost
beyond endurance.

Roger had no chance to show what he could do, though he
made one good cross, which was what Bill had told him to
do.

Eddie kept up his screams. The crowd behind were now
getting angry with him. They'd started by laughing, then
had taunted him and now they were furious. They were
convinced that he was egging on his players on to foul. When
Chivers got his name taken, just before the end, Eddie had
tomatoes thrown at him from behind.

It was a goal-less draw.   Spurs could have scored, when
Jimmy had a chance towards the end, but it would have

been unfair if Nantes had been beaten. They had played well and had the majority of the play. They'd been well drilled, had run well and intelligently, and their defence had successfully blotted Chivers out of the game. They'd showed none of the inferiority complex about Chivers the local press had led us to believe.

In the dressing-room the players were a mixture of anger, sadness and disappointment. On the way into the tunnel, as we followed the team, a couple of reserves whispered that now we'd see something. Bill would have to say something. No, he wouldn't go for Martin, said one of them. The Big Fellow's now too famous for anyone to criticise him, even on a bad game.

The players collapsed exhausted. Bill stood in the middle, his head bowed, saying nothing.

Martin Chivers was the last to sit down. As he did so he muttered loudly, 'Poor team, poor team'. It was a sort of reflex remark, getting in first, as if he expected to be assaulted.

'I never said they were a poor team,' said Bill sharply, looking at Chivers, suddenly angry. 'Never at any time did I tell you they were a poor team.'

Chivers hadn't meant it like that. By criticising them he was really blaming Spurs for not doing better, and himself. He hadn't meant to accuse Bill of misleading them. Bill couldn't have warned them more about Nantes, piling on the details of the strength of their team. In turning on Chivers' remark, Bill was really attacking Chivers, as they both knew.

'They were a poor team,' repeated Chivers sullenly, knowing that Bill had said the opposite. Perhaps he meant that Spurs might have beaten them if they'd been told beforehand they were a poor team. If so, it was a silly line of attack. On the night Spurs had been the poorer team.

Chivers was looking for something to say, a way of getting words out, any words, to convey an emotion, a feeling of depression. 'A poor team,' he said again, shaking his head. The lack of logic was a red rag to Bill but he was struggling to control himself.

'You mean *we* had some poor players,' said Bill. He was standing feet apart, shaking slightly, his head up, looking

139

straight at Chivers. He hadn't named any names, but there was no doubt which poor player he was referring to.

'What do you mean,' said Chivers, becoming suddenly violent and animated. Up to now he'd been deliberately sullen, waiting for the real attack to come so that he could plead self-defence.

'What do you know about it ? You never praise us when we do well. Never. You never do. What do you know about it? You weren't out there. You didn't have to do it. It's easy to say we didn't do well, bloody easy . . . '

'I've bloody well been out there,' said Bill, determined to finish the argument. 'I know what it's like. I've been through it. What are you talking about? We had some poor players tonight. That's what I'm saying. Some of our players weren't trying. That's what I'm saying.'

'You weren't out there,' continued Chivers, repeating himself once again, but beginning to weaken. It was too early to admit any failings. In his mood of tension, fraught and straight from the field, he was still caught up in his confused mood of bitterness.

Bill waited for him to continue, more than willing to see the argument through, to say to his face what he really wanted to say, but there was a sudden commotion behind him on the table. The anger and the heat and the half-finished fury suddenly began to disintegrate.

Someone had asked for a towel. In throwing a clean one across the table, Eddie Baily accidently knocked one of the glass cups onto the floor where it shattered, spreading broken glass under the players' bare feet.

Bill left Chivers and got down on the floor and used some soiled tie-ups to sweep the glass under the table out of the way. The players all started talking loudly, jeering at Eddie for his mistake, trooping into the showers to get washed. Soon there were the normal post-match noises and discussions, players showing injuries to Johnny and asking for bandages, going over mistakes made, chances lost.

Chivers didn't move. Everyone else was soon back from the showers and busy putting on their clean clothes, but Chivers sat in his filthy, sweat-sodden, matted strip, just as he'd come from the field. He had one leg across the other,

140

leaning on one elbow, staring straight ahead, menacing, and threatening, yet beaten and fed-up. What's the point. What do I get out of it. Why do I bother. I tried my hardest out there. I wanted to win. I didn't go out there not to try. But that's all I get.

Mullery started singing 'Oh what a beautiful morning' very loudly and badly, knowing he was singing it badly, going right through with all the words, carrying on when people groaned and told him to shut up. After all, it had been a goal-less draw, a good away result. There was the home match still to come.

Someone shouted to Eddie to open the door. They couldn't breathe. The place was like an oven. Eddie unlocked it and opened both doors, swinging them back and forward to make a breeze.

'Close the bloody door,' said Mike England, who was getting dressed just beside the doors. French officials were hanging around outside, trying to stare in. 'They're like monkeys out there.'

'One says open it, one says close,' said Eddie. 'Bloody hell.' He closed both doors and locked them, banging them hard. There was a knock, then another knock, then another. He opened them furiously, ready to give a mouthful to some monkey. Mr Wale, the chairman, came in followed by the directors. They crept in rather than walked in, nodding to Bill, not saying anything, sensing the atmosphere, standing demurely against the wall, looking round, talking quietly to each other.

There was another knock and in came Mr Broderick, the Cooks organiser. He went to help Johnny pick up all the dirty clothes and pack the bags – they'd brought a huge canvas holdall this time, not their normal basketwork skips. Bill helped as well, passing over filthy boots and dirty socks. When Bill finished, Mr Wale went into a corner with him where they talked very solemnly.

'The chairman wants you all to go to this reception,' announced Bill apologetically when the directors had trooped out again. 'Don't worry. We'll only stay fifteen minutes. There'll be a buffet there but don't forget there's a meal back at the hotel, if you want it.'

Chivers had started to move at last. He was now in the shower, having peeled off his dirty clothes in a pile at his bench. He'd brightened up a bit, now he'd pushed himself back to life. Bill, Johnny and Broderick were packing away Chivers' dirty strip with the rest of the gear.

Chivers came back to his seat and stood drying himself beside Mike England. 'Did you hear that supporter,' said Chivers. 'Shouting at me I should have scored six.'

'They know nothing,' said Mike, quickly, eagerly. 'They know bloody nothing. I heard one as well. They know nothing.'

'You're right. Nothing at all.'

Mike started gently whistling, quietly and in tune, not a pop song but a piece of Tchaikowsky, from the Nutcracker Suite. He was in his smart three piece suit. He'd washed the vaseline out of his hair and the battle out of his body and looked like a young managing director about to summon his board of directors.

Some British reporters arrived when the players were ready and were allowed in. They went to Chivers and to Mullery, taking it in turns to talk confidentially in their ears. One had heard the rest of the evening's football results and everyone stopped talking to listen to his news.

On the coach Bill Stevens, Spurs' assistant secretary, was given the job of chucking off the French kids. While it had been waiting, quite a few had crept on and were hiding behind the seats. Chivers was their main target. He signed autographs good humouredly. The bus was surrounded by French fans, waving and smiling. If the crowd felt they'd been robbed by the draw, which is what an English crowd would have thought after a similar performance, they weren't showing it. They were still as fascinated and as pleased to see the Tottenham team, especially Chivers, as they'd been before the match.

The reception was being given by the Mayor of Nantes at the Château des Ducs, a towering castle in the middle of the city, with a drawbridge and a wide moat.

It was all lit up when we got there with powdered flunkeys everywhere and a magnificent buffet laid out. The reception was in two large rooms, with a closed circuit TV in the

142

smaller room, so that the guests there wouldn't miss the speeches being made in the other. The Press were also invited, French and British, plus both teams and officials and assorted local dignitaries. Mr Wale and Mr Cox replied in English on behalf of Spurs, thanking the Mayor and people of Nantes for their excellent hospitality, the best they'd experienced in many years of going abroad.

The players stayed about half an hour in all, then Bill said they could go back to their hotel.

Most of them drank lagers in the hotel bar till about one or two o'clock and then went to bed, glad it was all over.

On the plane next morning, only Gilzean was moaning, at least moaning on about France, saying it was his third French trip and he still didn't like it. He preferred any country except France. But the rest were all very cheerful, greatly relieved to be going home, carrying dolls, bottles, souvenirs and other presents.

Champagne was served on the plane, though it was only eleven o'clock in the morning, but I didn't see any of the players drinking it. The directors and the Press managed to have their share.

Chivers was now agreeing he'd had a bad game. He admitted it. He said nothing had gone right for him. He'd been heavily marked and had lashed out in the end out of anger, which had been silly.

Bill Nicholson chatted to a few of the reporters, saying who had had a good game, such as Phil Beal. Jimmy Neighbour had tried hard, he said, though he might have got the ball over more often. He had no praise for Chivers, Peters or Mullery. He nodded towards them as he spoke, not wanting them or the other players to hear.

Later, he told me that he was worried that Chivers was becoming a player who could only play brilliantly at home.

'All they have to do is play it simple. That's the answer, but they won't do it. When you get into difficulties, when the opposing team are doing well and not letting you do anything, all you do is play it very simple till things go your way.'

He opened a newspaper and divided the page in three with his fingers, describing how play could be kept safely in

143

the middle third if things were going badly, even if it meant changing from one flank to another without beating anyone or going forward. He went over passes which had been thrown away. He analysed one move where Peters had tried to pass between two Nantes players and failed when he should have made two simple angle passes.

'I don't know what comes over them. Mackay and Blanchflower, they could get a grip when things were going badly, but this team doesn't seem to be able to do it. They've been told often enough what to do. And they *can* do it. I know they can. I don't know why they don't. It sickens me.'

In the cool clear light of a new day, did he agree with some of Eddie's screams in the heat of the match that some of the players suffered from too much publicity? Surely that couldn't have any effect on their play?

'Players can easily become too confident and arrogant. I don't mind confidence, but it leads to lack of self-criticism. That was what was wrong with some of them last night. They weren't self-critical. Good players like that shouldn't make mistakes, ever. That should be the aim. But if they do make one mistake, that should be it. They should be so furious with themselves that they vow never to do it again. But they won't admit mistakes, so they don't try harder and do better. *Everyone* can do better.'

It was a perfect flight, completely different from the dark and rain and turbulence which we'd had when flying out to the unknown. There was sunshine all the way home and we had a perfect landing at London Airport.

So what can be done, if his players won't do things simply and they won't be self-critical?

'Work at it,' said Bill grimly. 'Work at it. That's all we can do.'

12

Reserves and Nerves

Reserves suffer from many pressures. They analyse and over-interpret every decision, every remark the manager makes, tying themselves in knots, sometimes forcing themselves into opinions and actions they later regret.

They have a sense of being failures. If they were good enough, they'd be in the first team. They're not in the first team, so they're failures. John Pratt had been telling himself this for months. He felt his chance would never come. What made things worse was the conviction that he could do better than Mullery, the player he was understudying, at least on Mullery's present form. After Nantes, Mullery had several other poor games. Eventually, he was taken off in a match and it was announced he was suffering from a serious groin strain, an injury which would take weeks to clear up. This explained his run of poor games. John Pratt was no longer a failure. Through no effort on his part, through no sudden display of brilliant form, he was in the first team.

Tony Want, much earlier in the season, hadn't been so lucky. He's the reserve who acts as deputy for Cyril Knowles. He was given a run of several games, when Cyril was injured, but before the home match against Liverpool, the sort of big glamorous match all reserves dream about playing in, he withdrew at the last minute from the team, injured. It was reported at the time that he'd gone down with a stomach upset. Unbeknown to Bill, Tony had apparently suffered what can only be called a pyschological brain storm.

Perhaps the strangest part of it was that it should be Tony Want. He's everything a good reserve should be, solid, reliable, hard working, enthusiastic, punctual, polite. He's had over seventy first games in four seasons, without ever becoming an established first team player, yet he doesn't complain or argue or demand more money.

'I've always understood Bill's problems and felt that he knows best what he's doing. I've never questioned anything. I think Eddie is a brilliant coach. I've always been happy, despite having to go back to the reserves every time. I was very pleased to be picked again for the Liverpool match. Sometimes in the past I've not played well when I've had my chance in the first team and I've deserved to be put back. But this time when Cyril was injured, I had two good games in his place and I felt on top of the world.'

The day before the Liverpool match Bill called Tony into his office. Although he had been picked again, Bill said it didn't mean that the position was now his. Cyril would be back in the team next week, whatever happened. Cyril was his first team choice as left full back and he still considered him the better player.

According to Tony, he was too stunned to argue. He sat silently as Bill made the position clear. According to Bill, he was simply stopping Tony from having any illusions.

Tony went home to his parents' council flat in Shoreditch. He's unmarried so he hadn't got the comfort of a wife to discuss his problems with. He couldn't sleep for thinking about what Bill had said. 'I couldn't get over Bill telling me *before* I played that I'd had it. That's what upset me. Bill obviously *wanted* me to play badly against Liverpool. That would then give him a straightforward reason for dropping me next week. Even if I played well, it still wouldn't help, so what was the point of trying? I'd got to face facts. I'm a failure. I'm obviously never going to be good enough to make the top.'

Next morning, he decided, in his own twisted way, that he would get his own back. He rang up and said he had a stomach upset. Bill, after all, had to play Cyril, though he hadn't played first team football for several weeks. By his own decision, Tony had deliberately thrown away the game he'd most wanted to play in.

On Monday, Tony went in to see Bill again. 'This time I got it all off my chest, which did me a lot of good, instead of bottling it up. Bill said I was vital to the club. He had the

146

best first team pool he'd had for a long time and he didn't want me to leave the club. He said he knew that really I didn't want to go either. That's true. I don't. I realised I'd been stupid. Now I'm back in the groove again.'

But Cyril was the player who was back in the first team. There's an unwritten rule in football that a first team player who's out injured, always gets his place back afterwards. It's the sort of rule which all reserves moan about, especially when they think they've been playing well.

But in the case of Joe Kinnear, the team's eligible bachelor, it didn't happen. About the same time as Mullery was injured, Joe hurt his ankle and Ray Evans, his deputy, came into the first team as right back. Ray played very well, so well that several observers thought he might turn out to be as good as Joe.

Joe was apprehensive when he was first injured, as all players are, but he wasn't worried. There seemed no reason to be. As the established right back, he felt sure of his place in the nature of things. At the age of twenty-four and an Eire international, he'd already experienced most things that can happen in football and had come through triumphantly.

In 1967, still just a youngster, fresh to the first team, Joe was in the Spurs team which won the Cup Final at Wembley against Chelsea. He was only nineteen, the youngest player on the pitch. He was voted the man of the match by many newspapers. The sudden rush of money went to his head.

His bonuses just for winning the Cup, came to £2,500. He gave £500 at once to his mother, gave each of his four sisters £30 and a complete new outfit, bought his grandmother in Dublin a TV and an armchair, bought himself a Corsair at £600 and then took the whole family of eight, including his grandmother, for a six-week holiday in Ireland till the rest of the money ran out. 'I couldn't get rid of it quick enough.'

Then he broke his leg and was out of football for twelve months. His mother couldn't sleep at night for worry. She lost three and a half stones in weight in the year. Joe thought it was the end. 'I can hardly believe it now that in that year nobody came out of the cheque book to fill my place.'

All the Spurs players who work their way up internally, starting with the club as youngsters, say they have this

147

constant worry that Spurs, because of their resources and reputation, will buy somebody better, or perhaps just more famous, and they'll be out of the team.

'It's very unsettling. You might be only nineteen with a great future but you know if they buy a famous player of twenty-four in your position you might as well leave. The crowds like new players. It brings them in if a big star is signed.'

'Big stars bought from outside always have the advantage,' says Joe's mother. 'They're always making allowances for them. If a big star doesn't play well they say he's got a headache or backache, but when a youngster who only cost the club £10 plays badly it's out, out, out.'

'But I got over the broken leg,' says Joe. 'In the last two years I've felt much better. It was when I started reading bits of gossip that Manchester United were after me and would pay £70,000. That's when I started believing in myself again. Not that I read football gossip – it's always a load of rubbish.

'It doesn't matter what the papers say or the fans. All that matters to me is Bill saying well done. He goes through worse things than we do. A season ago it was "Nick must go" banners. Last season it was "Arise Sir Nick".'

This season, Joe had every right to feel confident, until he twisted his ankle against Nottingham Forest and had to come off. Week after week, Bill encouraged him to get really fit, saying he wanted him to hurry back, but there was a sting in the tail. 'You'll have to hurry,' added Bill, 'because Ray's a good player, you know.'

Ray was playing well and Joe knew it. It was becoming a strange experience for him to have to *watch* the first team playing, especially when he felt his injury was better.

'I've been around long enough to know when they're using an excuse so I asked Bill straight if he preferred Ray to me. He should say so if he did because it would mean there was no point in me staying. He said I was jumping the gun. That sort of talk was far too early. When I'd proved I was a hundred per cent fit, then I'd be in the running for the first team. That's all there was to it. I had to prove myself first. I said fair enough.'

So Joe had his run-out with the reserves, away at Swansea,

which he didn't like at all. 'The atmosphere is so different. It was just a brawl, kicking each other up in the air. My ankle did hurt a bit, so Bill was right, but it came through OK.'

He'd been very depressed by Roger Morgan, listening to him after the match mentioning the reserve matches to come, working out the easy ones. 'Roger now *expects* to be in the reserves, at least that's how it looked to me. He seems quite happy. I think it's vital not to lose heart. You mustn't let your ambition go. You've got to be determined to get back in your own place.

'Since my ankle got better I've at least been training with the first team so I feel more in touch, but you still feel out of it, not playing with them. When you're out, you're forgotten. Bill comes into the treatment room and never speaks to you. You might as well not exist.

'I've nothing against Ray personally. We're both in the same position, both wanting in. If he hurt his leg I'd have a chuckle and if I hurt mine again, he'd have a chuckle because it would be his chance. That's the way it is. We both know it.

'What's really hateful is that I thought I'd been playing well all season. I've not had a bad game till I was injured. Some of the team haven't been playing well at all and they've kept their place. I said this to Bill and he said that was no concern of mine, which of course it isn't. But he agreed I had been playing well. Well, he didn't say I hadn't been.

'The Press have been driving me mad, ringing up and asking why he's taking it out of me. I've said nothing. I've seen so many people at Spurs down the years who start shouting and complaining when this happens to them, they moan all the time at the club or take it out of their family at home. I try to keep it to myself. I try to keep it separate. It's just between me and Bill. The big thing is not to lose heart. I'll try to do my best, but if it's not getting me back in the first team, well, I don't know. What else can I do?

'With Ray being younger than me, Bill might decide he's a better prospect. Tony Want seems to have accepted being Cyril's deputy, signing year after year, but Ray hasn't. He won't accept so easily. So Bill's got to make up his mind.'

149

Joe at least had his property business to take his mind off his worries. He'd bought two large houses in his home town of Watford, converted them into flats and was making quite a bit of money. Although he was losing a large amount by being out of the first team (in bonuses he was probably losing about £70 a game), the money was the least of his worries.

He still had enough to run his flash car and buy records. His aim of saving £2,000 a season to put down on another house, plus always having a few hundred in the bank for personal whims, didn't look like being affected. But there wasn't much consolation in being affluent, not when he wasn't in the first team.

Ray Evans, who was replacing him in the first team, was far from affluent. He was living with his wife Sandra, a comptometer operator, in a rented flat in Edmonton. He had a car, an old Vauxhall Victor, but he wasn't on the telephone, the only first team pool player who wasn't. They were saving for a house, but didn't know where they would get the deposit from. First team stars get ample help when they want to buy a new £15,000 house, even if they've only arrived at the club, like Ralph Coates, but reserves find it much tougher, even if all they want is a little semi, half that price.

Joe Kinnear is very sociable and outgoing, with a smile for everyone. Outsiders always find Joe and Alan Mullery the two easiest to get to know. Each of them remembers people's names and always has time to stop and chat. Ray Evans is much quieter and keeps in the background, as if suspicious of strangers. But then reserves are forced into the background. It's often hard to tell their true character. Only an obvious extrovert like Roger Morgan stands out, regardless of whether he's been reduced to the reserves or not. But Ray in many ways *looks* like a reserve.

He's bigger than Joe, strong and strapping, almost on the Chivers mould, though a couple of inches shorter. But somehow he never looked as imposing as Joe, nor as smooth or as confident. But success can soon make people look successful.

Last season Ray had only seven first team appearances

150

compared with Joe's forty-seven. But Ray at last had got into the first team pool, which was some progress, though according to him, it still wasn't bringing him in the money he thought he deserved. This was why he'd been determined when this season began to hold out for a better contract.

He thinks his three seasons of being Joe's understudy have at least helped to make him stronger, in his game and in character. 'You can't talk in certainties in football. You just have to try your best and then wait. I don't believe in luck. Luck is more of an excuse than a fact. I'm not saying there isn't luck. Everyone refers to it in football. It's just that I don't think it's real. I've been waiting a long time for this break, not for luck.'

Ray certainly made the most of his break, coming in and playing solidly and carefully, giving nothing away. He was tending to belt the ball up field, playing safe rather than trying any dangerous short passes near his own goal, but his big belts were good ones, well up for Chivers, in the outside space where he likes to receive them.

'I suppose I feel confident because after holding out for months, I've got what I wanted from Bill. He's agreed to the contract terms I wanted. I had a down to earth chat with him a couple of weeks ago and he said I had a future at the club. It was nice to hear it. I believed him.'

As the weeks went on, with Ray getting the place each time, Joe was forced into the humiliating position of being an also-ran. For most of the matches, especially at home, Bill named a party of fourteen players, each of whom had to turn up at the ground, ready to play.

For the home match against Blackpool, in the fifth round of the League Cup, Joe didn't know if he was in or not till he walked into the dressing-room, like Ray Evans, to see if his boots were laid out. Ray's were, but there was no sign of Joe's size eight boots.

Bill hadn't told him he wouldn't be playing. Joe had had to find out for himself. He walked straight back out of the dressing-room again and into the car park to find Bonnie his girl friend.

She was with a group of his friends and once again there were commiserations all round. 'Footballers are more intelligent and more sensitive than in the old days,' said one of Joe's friends. 'Yet they still get treated as thick heads.'

Yet again, the Press were buzzing round Joe, asking him questions. Was he going to ask for a transfer, had there been a row, what were his plans. Joe said he was going into the stand to watch the match, that was his only immediate plan.

Spurs won that match easily, 2-0, with goals from Peters and Chivers. Coates, who'd also been injured but had got his place back at once, didn't play well and obviously wasn't match fit. It wasn't a great match. Nobody really distinguished themselves. But Ray Evans played very well, once again, which wasn't much fun for Joe, watching up in the stand.

'There's nothing personal between me and Joe,' said Ray later that week. 'I'm sure he would say the same. I hope he would. I was lucky to get another chance because of his injury. I've played well and kept the place. It's just a matter of who's in and who's out. I've had a long spell waiting. Now it's Joe's turn. I don't know if he'll be prepared to play for any length of time in the reserves. But you never know, after tomorrow, that might be it. I'll have lost my chance yet again.'

In the next match, against West Bromwich Albion, Ray played even better. Spurs won 3-2. It was a big day for Barry Daines, Spurs' reserve goalkeeper, making his first team debut. Pat Jennings had taken a knock in the previous match, nothing serious, but he wasn't a hundred per cent fit. Barry did well, but no one for one moment expected him to get Pat's place. Like Ray, Barry played for England Youth, but he's much younger and with nothing like Ray's experience. And in the case of Pat Jennings, he wasn't just understudying one of Spurs' biggest stars, but one of the best goalkeepers in the country. Barry is one reserve with apparently years of waiting ahead of him.

Ray Evans, however, really consolidated his position that day. He wasn't simply being solid in defence. Thanks to his new confidence, he was coming up well and overlapping. He made several good runs up the right wing, ending with strong crosses into the middle. He also centred two short corner kicks from Jimmy Neighbour, cleverly coming up on

152

the blind side and hitting them first time, very dangerously into the goal mouth. It was a ploy he'd started a few weeks previously but it was now becoming almost a set piece.

In the dressing-room afterwards, Bill even publicly praised him, though slightly obliquely and worst of all for Ray's pride, *after* Ray had left the room.

Jimmy Neighbour was standing in front of the mirror. As he put his tie on, he let out a sigh. Bill started to smile. There were definite traces of it at the corner of his mouth, which showed a joke was coming.

'You can't be tired,' said Bill sarcastically, shouting across the room to Jimmy. 'If you'd been putting across centres like Ray Evans, then you might be tired.'

Being in the first team was making Ray better while being in the reserves wasn't helping Joe at all. Joe still had experience on his side, though as the weeks went on, Ray was getting more and more. Joe in many ways is the classier, more skilful player, very polished and precise. But Ray is much stronger and faster. He's more menacing and aggressive when he comes forward. He's bigger than Joe, but size isn't so vital in full backs these days. It's skill and thought which matter. Ray's heading is weak, though he was working on it in training. Most people, watching both of them, found it very hard to choose between them. But most people don't have any say, only Bill Nicholson.

13

Scouting for Boys

Charlie Faulkner is fifty-eight and very dapper with a cigarette holder, suede shoes and a sparkle of gold teeth. He's very friendly and open with none of the tough no-nonsense attitude to outsiders which officials in football so often have. Charlie has been Spurs' chief scout since 1966. For most of his working life before that he was a barber.

For eleven years he was a part-time scout with Brighton, doing it every weekend and every evening after barbering. For three years he was with West Ham. Looking back, he thinks he got round just as many matches in those days, by working round the clock.

Spurs have two full-time scouts – himself and Dick Walker – who do nothing else but scout for Spurs. Then there are eight scouts who are exclusively under contract for Spurs. They have weekday jobs as well, as Charlie used to have, and range from teachers to office workers, but every Saturday and Sunday and several evenings a week they work for Spurs. These eight are scattered round the British Isles – two in the London area, two in Wales and one each in Scotland, Northern Ireland, Birmingham and Rotherham.

Spurs also use occasional free-lance scouts, who are paid or given expenses to cover a match which a regular Spurs scout can't get to. Each scout, of every level, has also got his own network of unofficial scouts and contacts, in schools, local leagues, youth organisations, factories up and down the country, who every year pass on information about hundreds of boys that Spurs might be interested in.

Players already playing for professional teams are of course scouted just as much as schoolboys and amateur players. This is the area which Charlie Faulkner specialises in – Dick Walker is more the specialist on schoolboys. Charlie is ex-

154

pected to know the name of every professional on the books of every Second, Third and Fourth Division team. Whenever a new name appears on a team sheet, he's got to be scouted and a report made, just in case Spurs should ever be interested in him for any reason – either because they might want to buy him or simply because Spurs are going to play against a team which he's in.

Charlie doesn't scout in the First Division. That's Bill Nicholson's area. Bill knows every First Division player. He has to, to brief Spurs each week before they play them, and also to keep an eye on likely players Spurs might want.

Every top football club has a similar scouting system, blanketing the country with their scouts and contacts, so the number of reports on players that flow into the clubs every week must run into thousands. It's surprising that anyone ever gets missed.

When it does happen, there's usually an investigation. Ade Coker, for example, the young Nigerian star of West Ham had recently appeared. All the old records and reports had to be looked up because Bill demanded to know why the Spurs scouting system hadn't spotted him. It turned out he had been reported on, right from the beginning when the first tip-off came in. A part-time scout had been detailed to vet him, but for some reason he hadn't gone personally to see the boy's parents, the normal follow-up whenever anyone plays well. He'd sent a friend along instead. Because of this in-direct approach and the ensuing delays, West Ham had got him before Spurs could talk to him personally.

Even more important was the case of Liverpool's new star, Kevin Keegan, a player signed apparently out of the blue from a Fourth Division club, Scunthorpe. Bill was very impressed when he saw him play at the beginning of the season and wanted to know why Spurs hadn't spotted him first.

'In our records,' says Charlie, 'I found we had sent a scout to see him and he'd given a good report. A second scout was sent but his report was a bad one. I'd then decided I would go and see him myself, but I'd already arranged to go to Scotland on a vital scouting mission. When I got back, I'd missed the last match of the season. During the summer,

Liverpool signed him, and that was that. But we had known about him.'

Every Friday, Charlie produces a list of around thirty matches for the coming week which he proposes to get covered by the Spurs scouts. He brings them in to Bill and they discuss them together, with Bill adding any others he might want covered. Then it's worked out which scout will scout which match and what he will look for.

About three quarters of the time, a scout is being sent specifically to see one or two players. The scout is given the player's name and position and he has to make a personal report. These names are a result of previous scouting reports. About a quarter of the matches are being covered to look at a team generally, a new team which perhaps hasn't been scouted for a while, just to see what their new players are like, making first reports on any individuals who look likely.

It was by covering such a match like this, on spec for no specific reason, that Charlie discovered Steve Perryman in 1966. Steve still considers it fantastic luck that he was seen by a real live scout on his first match for Ealing Schoolboys. But the luck was really on Charlie's side, seeing Steve before anyone else had got wind of him. It's these sort of discoveries which keep scouts going, which keep their spirits up week after week, standing in the rain, along with perhaps only half a dozen other spectators, knowing that it's ninety-five per cent sure that the player they've come to see is going to turn out to be a load of rubbish.

'It was the first game of the season. I don't know why I chose Ealing, perhaps just because it was a game near my home. I didn't know any of the players and had nobody to look at, but Steve stood out a mile. While he was still playing, I rushed around, trying to find his teacher. I found him, but he wouldn't give me Steve's address or any details.

'I'd arranged that afternoon to go up to Leicester for a League match but I cancelled it. Steve was too promising to miss. I eventually got his address and went round to his house at one o'clock. His brother Ted opened the door and said "Hello Mr Faulkner. I saw you at the match this morning. We had a nice letter from you last year."'

Charlie didn't understand what he meant. Ted then

brought a letter, written by Charlie on Queens Park Rangers notepaper. The previous year, when Charlie had been chief scout at Rangers, he'd got a note, one of scores, from Steve's father, asking if Rangers could give him a trial. It was the end of the season and Charlie had written back to say the trials were over but they would contact him later on. He'd never done so. 'Steve might already have been on Rangers' books if I'd seen him then.

'From then on, I kept in contact with Steve and Mr Perryman every week, either going round or ringing him. I became a friend of the family. They asked my advice about what to do about the other clubs and I said fine, go and look at them. I knew they would anyway – parents with a star on their hands always do.'

The chase went on for well over a year. Because Steve couldn't make up his mind, both Bill Nicholson and Eddie feared they'd lost him. It had gone on too long. They were sure some other club must be nobbling him. 'Mr Perryman himself was getting fed-up. In the end he said Steve would make up his mind, once and for all, in the next two weeks. I cancelled my holidays. I couldn't be away in case anything happened. On the last day I got a phone call, asking me to come round. When I arrived, I knew the situation was very dicey. Steve had obviously decided in favour of Queens Park Rangers, though his father still preferred Tottenham and a brother preferred West Ham. The other clubs, such as Arsenal, were out of it.

'I told him that all three were good clubs. I'd worked for them all. I said forget Spurs. If it's a choice between West Ham and Queens Park Rangers, I'd recommend West Ham. They're a big club, with good facilities and excellent coaching. At Queens Park Rangers, the apprentices have a lot of cleaning work to do, being a small club.

'I let it all sink in. After a lot of pauses and thinking, they decided on Spurs. I was so relieved. It was the close season and everyone at Tottenham was away on the summer tour. I took Steve back to the club, typed out the forms and signed him on myself.'

This whole field of signing-on schoolboy stars is a night-mare for chief scouts because of the illegal payments which many clubs offer to parents, as an inducement for their son's name on the dotted line. 'The biggest illegal payment I've personally heard of is £10,000. But Dads being told to pick any car they fancy as a present is not unusual. I don't know how clubs get away with it. Spurs have never gone in for any illegal payments, which of course makes my job very hard. The chairman is very well aware of the problem, and so is Bill. It means that a boy has to come to Spurs because he wants to come. I know that Spurs is the best club in the country. It's up to me to persuade *him* that it's true.'

The team's success helps a lot, the glamour of their name and reputation. On the day that Spurs beat Liverpool at White Hart Lane, Charlie had quite a few parents with their sons, sitting in the stands, as guests of the club. All clubs lash out the free tickets when they've got a big match on. 'I knew that many of those boys had had approaches from Liverpool as well as us. The fact that we won and played so well must have had an effect on their decisions.'

Charlie wasn't there at the match. He was only told that the first team had played well. He's always out scouting when they're playing. The only chance he gets is when they play at Wemble *y*. When that happens the whole of the Spurs staff closes up shop and goes en fête to the match. Since Charlie came to Spurs, that's happened twice – 1967 and 1971.

Once the boys have been signed on as apprentices, his job is finished. As chief scout, he gets nothing extra, though ordinary scouts get a bonus when their discovery finally signs. He rarely sees the result of his work, though perhaps once or twice in a season he might see the reserves or youth team play when he's casting an eye over the opposition. Charlie has had a major hand in many of the present youngsters, including Barry Daines, the reserve goalie who'd just made his first team debut. 'He was an easy one, compared with Steve. From first hearing about him, we'd given him a trial, brought him and his parents to the club and signed him as a schoolboy, all in a week.'

What Charlie is looking for most of all is ability. 'This means positional play, quick thinking, shooting, heading, ball control, balance, all the skills that a footballer needs.

'Physical powers come into it, but I don't put that first, not like Eddie. If I came back and said a boy was six foot, then he'd really be excited. Eddie likes the big 'uns.'

Charlie has a corner in Eddie's room at Spurs, with a typewriter and a phone and a filing cabinet. Eddie was sitting quietly writing out a report of a match he'd seen on Saturday.

'Trust you to talk about yourself, mate,' said Eddie. 'Don't bring me into it. Who have you found anyway, apart from Steve?'

Charlie reeled off a few names but Eddie wasn't impressed.

'What about you then,' said Charlie. 'Who have *you* found?'

'I just happen to do some coaching and training and looking after the reserves, that's all,' said Eddie. 'Apart from doing reports.'

'Yes, and I've got your report on a certain player,' said Charlie. 'I've got it locked in my file. You're not getting your hands on it.'

Eddie smiled. When this particular young professional had been scouted, Eddie had been one of the people to write a good report on him. Now he bitterly regretted it. At that moment in time, Eddie had decided that the player, now in the reserves, wasn't trying hard enough.

'It's difficult to write a report which will stand for always,' said Charlie as Eddie put his head down and continued writing his own report. 'Players fluctuate so much. He can show in one game and not be seen in another. I like to see a player three or four times.'

I asked why there weren't more coloured kids at Tottenham – West Ham had three in or on the verges of the first team. There were none at Spurs amongst the apprentices or professionals and only a couple amongst the schoolboys training after school.

'There are bound to be lots of them in the years to come, especially the Africans. But so far, the ones I've looked at don't have the determination.'

Eddie went on writing in the corner, refusing to be drawn.

'How do you spell "elementary",' he said.

Charlie then made a telephone call to the parents of a

schoolboy called Atkins, whom he'd been chasing for a long time. He'd had a tip-off that the boy was going to get picked for England. He chatted up the parent, arranging to take the family to some matches in the near future, as Spurs' guests. In the course of his chat he discovered that fourteen clubs were now after the boy, including Manchester United. When he'd finished, Charlie then got out the standard Report on Player's form and wrote out what he'd just learned.

'How do you spell "defensively",' said Eddie, jokingly.

It was a rainy, cold Monday afternoon. The first team had the day off and would be in their £20,000 luxury homes slumped in front of the children's programme on TV. But that evening's scouting work of knocking at council house back doors when dads come home from work had still to be done.

Viewed from outside, it could be said that Spurs' whole scouting system, however well organised, hadn't produced all that much. Leeds United, on the other hand, had seven players out of the first eleven whom Leeds themselves had discovered and taken on as schoolboys – Cooper, Madeley, Bremner, Charlton, Hunter, Grey and Lorimer – all of whom had become internationals. Only four had come from other clubs – Giles, Sprake, Clarke and Jones.

Spurs' team was balanced almost exactly the other way round. Only three were home grown players – Evans, Beal and Perryman. The other eight were all bought. Surely that wasn't a very good reflection of the power of Spurs' scouting?

'Other clubs are always saying this about Spurs when they're trying to persuade boys not to sign for us. But today it's just not true. This season so far ten home grown players have played for the first team, people like Pratt, Neighbour, Pearce, Want and Naylor. All the top reserves waiting in the wings are home grown – Souness, Clarke, Holder, Daines and the rest. And don't forget that the reserves are top of their league, and so are the youth team. That shows how good they are.

'I think ten players getting a chance in the first team is a very high proportion. I tell every parent that every boy, if he has the ability, has as good a chance as anywhere of getting in the first team.

160

'We're looking at players all the time, every day of the year, but they're very rarely anywhere near as good as the players we have already. Some clubs have got to depend on getting bargains from the Third and Fourth Divisions.'

If the reserve pool is so good, who then is the replacement for Alan Gilzean when he eventually retires? Charlie admitted there wasn't a comparable striker in the reserves, for all their success in the Reserves League. Nor was there one for Chivers. So would Spurs be on the transfer market for a striker soon, perhaps before the season was out?

'I'm looking at strikers all the time, with the problem of Gilly in mind. But it's hard to find any who are better than what we've got. Every club in the country wants good strikers. Scoring goals is what it's all about. It's the same at all levels, professional and schoolboy. We're all looking for good strikers.'

When the schoolboys eventually sign as apprentices at fifteen they come under the care of Pat Welton, the youth team manager, a job he has had since 1969. He also has a desk in Eddie Baily's office. He was ringing up getting tickets for a youth game, Charlton Youth versus Fulham Youth. Like Bill Nicholson with the first team, he tries to see the rivals play as much as possible. 'You've got to see teams all the time so that you're not taken by surprise when you play them. Every team has a pattern of play. Whether they're doing it successfully or not, they have a plan they're trying to achieve, even if it's just knocking it up the middle for everyone to run after it. If you know how they play, then you can prepare your own team to meet them.'

New ideas are rare, but they do happen. He thinks the last innovation in English football was probably back around 1962 when overlapping full backs were first widely used. (A full back who suddenly comes up on the flank and becomes a wing forward.) 'Chelsea was the first team I saw doing this. You can't just copy new ideas. You've got to have the right players. Our first team does it, but in the youth team one of our backs isn't up to it yet. The main job of the backs is to defend so that must be mastered and perfected first.

'An overlapping left back would be very difficult in the

present youth team anyway because Bobby Scarth, the left winger, is the boy who's deaf and dumb. An overlapping full back has got to be *heard* coming up behind the wingers.'

Pat is tall, handsome and young looking. He might be a dashing young sportsmaster at a smart school, which is what he was for a time, though unqualified. Bill and Eddie by comparison look more like factory foremen. But as far as footballing careers went, Pat's was mediocre. He spent his time as a goalkeeper in the Third Division, mainly with Leyton Orient.

During the first ten years after the end of his playing career, he had many and varied coaching jobs, all of them outside League football. From 1962 he was an FA staff coach, a job which led to the FA making him manager of the England Youth team. He was asked to come to Spurs in 1969. He was by then forty, but at last he was back in League football. Spurs were re-organising their youth programme and had seen what a good job he'd made of the England Youth team – twice winning the Little World Cup (an annual international tournament for youth teams) and twice getting into the final. In Pat's first season with the Spurs Youth team, they won the Youth League and Cup.

Every season, up to about five hundred schoolboys are seriously considered by the Spurs scouting staff. Trials are held, at Cheshunt or the ground, throughout the year, holidays included. Every year about twenty of these youngsters are asked to sign schoolboy forms. Until this year, this could be done on a boy's thirteenth birthday. But after this season, the age is being put up to fourteen. But from as early as twelve, youngsters are invited along to the ground for trials or for coaching, although nothing can be official until they are fourteen.

The twenty or so boys who've signed schoolboy forms train at the ground every Tuesday and Thursday after school. Pat coaches them, perhaps with the help of senior reserves like John Pratt and Tony Want. The boys are continually assessed, notes are kept, they're tried out in trial matches and then eventually a meeting is held on each one to decide whether they are good enough to become apprentice professionals.

162

Present at these meetings are the two scouts, Charlie Faulkner and Dick Walker, Eddie Baily, Pat Welton, and Bill Nicholson who is in the chair. Bill knows each schoolboy who has been training and he has the last word on whether he should be taken or not, but everyone has a say in deciding which of the twenty schoolboys each year should become apprentice professionals.

Pat admits there is a large wastage, that the majority of the schoolboys never make it, but he doesn't think it's as tragic for the boys as it looks. He doesn't think their lives are ruined, having been brought to Spurs at twelve or thirteen and then two or even four years later being told they're no longer wanted.

'Even if we decided not to take them in the end as professionals, they've had a very good grounding, the best there is. They've mixed with world class players. They might not measure up to our standards, because we demand the highest, but they can always go elsewhere.'

What Pat says he is looking for most of all is character. By this he means a determination to win, a willingness all the time to want to play and to do well. Then comes ability. He says this is easier to spot than character. 'Simple things show ability, like receiving a ball, passing it back. But it's no use having ability if he doesn't care.' Thirdly he puts running ability and strength. 'It's not his height or his weight we're primarily interested in, but what he does with what he's got. Obviously, if they're very small or light this is worrying. In that case we look at the family history, the size of their father or brothers and work out how big he might become, or could be developed to with the right exercises.

'Height can be a handicap. Leggy boys can look very awkward, but this might disappear with age and maturity. We've got to decide whether in trying to get the ball he's doing the right thing, but his legs are not developed enough to let him do it properly. Only experience in watching boys and how they develop can tell you this.'

Fourthly, there's the ability to read the game, a natural football brain, which is the hardest of all to pinpoint. 'This is what's most lacking in schoolboy football. You watch most schoolboy matches and you see them either all running after the ball at once or just standing still, waiting for the ball, thinking becau~e the ball is fifty yards away there's no need to be doing anything.

'You've got to see how he solves problems. Is he doing what the situation demands. When he's winning three-nil he might be different from when he's losing three-nil. You want to see if he rolls his sleeves up when he's losing. If it's a goalie, you want to see him make a mistake. This is the test. Does a mistake destroy him or is he saying to himself, that was the first and *last* mistake today.

'We can make him faster, we can improve his skills, but it's difficult to improve his character. He's got to be aggressive. Martin Peters is not aggressive in a physical sense, but it's so obvious he *wants* to win. It matters to him so much. These are vital players when so many these days, even at the top, have a flaw in their character which can make them inconsistent. Positive players, that's what every team wants.'

He made it all sound like battery farming, looking for types rather than individuals. Flair and individuality didn't seem to come into his reckoning.

He said that real flair *is* the most vital thing of all, but it is very rare, which was why he hadn't mentioned it. When you did get it, it could be let down by going with the wrong character. This was so often the problem of flair. It was a bonus when it appeared, but it was good footballers they were looking for. Genius couldn't be waited for.

Having passed all the right tests, of character and of footballing abilities, and survived under the microscope from twelve to fifteen, the first really big hurdle for the boys is the first six months of their lives as apprentice professionals.

Living football as a job, day after day, instead of as a pure and innocent hobby is very difficult. Their individuality is taken away from them and they have to play to a pattern not for fun. It comes as quite a shock. Having been the star of their schoolboy team and allowed to play as they liked, they now find themselves shouted at and made to do things they don't particularly enjoy. Physically it's hard work, doing weight training and cross countries and endless practising. It's like going straight from the Wolf Cubs into a paratroop assault course. Few concessions are made to their tender ages or tender muscles.

Then there's the problem of living away from home for the first time in their lives – none of them have been to boarding schools or are used to fending for themselves. They're all very homesick. They've jumped into a rarified athletic atmosphere and they're not equipped emotionally or culturally for all the changes. From the age of ten, when they first realised they could be professional footballers, they've been interested in very little else. Straight away they have men's problems to deal with. No wonder it takes a strong character to be able to cope and overcome this first six months. 'It is very hard for them. We worry all the time, will they cope? We've done our best to pick the ones who will, but it's still a chancy time.'

Then of course, having survived the homesick period, girls begin to rear their lovely heads.

'When they first arrive at fifteen there is never any problem. There's only one thing in their minds and always has been – football. Girls start after about six months. I can tell by then how they're going to react. I know who'll settle down and get a regular girl and stick to her and who'll flit around. You can't stop them. All you do is give advice and try to help them.'

Talking about one boy (Gary Mabee) whom he expected to start having a lot of girl friends any week now, he said he wasn't worried really as long as it didn't affect his play. He was an extrovert, on and off the field. What was good in his character was the fact that he always bounced back.

Pat, naturally, becomes their father figure. Bill Nicholson hasn't the time or the personality to attract personal confessions or confidences, nor has Eddie Baily with his various dislikes about the modern world. Pat *looks* kind.

He's with them every hour of the day. It's rather touching the way they come to him with a new suit for his approval, or ask him about their hair styles. He doesn't actually approve of long hair, but he never tries to force them. 'It would be wrong to press my will on them. I just encourage them to look like pro footballers. That means looking smart and clean. I instruct them in hygiene and the care of their body and keep a close eye on what they eat.'

Far more time and energy and personal attention is lavished on the youth team than the first team. No one, for example, bothers about what the first team eat at home. Nobody really knows about their private lives, unless it comes to the attention of the club or somehow affects their play.

With the apprentices, Pat is in loco parentis until they are eighteen. It's part of his duty to keep them on the straight and narrow. He's continually in touch with parents and they come to see him and find out how their boys are getting on.

He's rather saddened that he can never get his boys to sing. Even back in the mid-sixties, when he was managing the England Youth team, he always had them singing on the way to matches. 'As we entered the stadium we always sang "Keep Right On to the End of the Road". We even sang it in the dressing-room.'

But now it's all gone, for the young players and the old ones. He doesn't think it's simply because of the present day pop music, which he says can't be sung anyway. He doesn't really think it's the worries and pressures. After all, his youth team shouldn't have the worries that the first team have.

'Singing gave a tremendous feeling. One for all and all for one. It helped you to play better. The communal feeling of the coach transferred itself to the field.

'When I was a player, it was kept up all the time, even on long trips. And everyone had to do a turn. Football is an attitude of mind. You've got to *feel* good. The average professional today never gets in the mood until he's in the dressing-room. That's when mentally he starts. I'm sure a few songs on the way there would help a lot. But it's got to be within you, this spirit. It seems to have gone.'

He disapproves of all the card playing. He sees cards as a fragmenting game, dividing people rather than bringing them together, especially when there's money involved. He won't allow his boys to gamble and discourages card games generally, although he doesn't stop them.

'I admit there were some heavy gamblers when I was a player. I saw a lot of unhappiness through that. That's why I'm biased against cards.

'It was a different world in those days. Our big night out

was fish and chips and a pint, now it's the Top of the Town or whatever it's called. They take taxis here, chauffeurs even, drink wine, and as for the clothes, well, it's a completely changed life today.'

14

Mullery's Injury

Alan Mullery celebrated his thirtieth birthday on 23 November 1971. Not that he had anything to celebrate. By then he'd been out of action for a whole month. But long before that he'd obviously been struggling, as everybody saw in the Nantes match. Many critics had begun to think that Mullery was too old for an arduous midfield job.

He'd been playing all season with stomach pains. He'd hoped he could play it out, that the pains would just fade away, but they hadn't. He'd been using a corset for some time, a broad elasticated stomach corset to hold his stomach muscles in place. This had helped slightly at first, but then the pains had grown worse.

'The end came at Stoke. One of their blokes got past Phil Beal and I started running back to tackle him. It was about thirty yards but I just physically couldn't run. Bill just had to take me off.'

For several weeks he had deep heat treatment twice a day at the ground. The diagnosis was strained pelvic muscles. An X-ray had shown no break. There was no damage whatsoever to be seen. It was the sort of injury footballers hate most – where the cause isn't known, the injury can't be seen and there is no known time scale of treatment.

'I've no idea how it first happened or when. I just suppose it's general wear and tear on the groin muscles. These muscles control so much – they control your running, your passing, your body movements, stopping, starting, everything. I've probably been doing too much for too long.

'I felt a bit of staleness at the end of last season, which was probably the first sign, though I didn't know it. That was why I asked not to be considered for the England home matches in the summer. I got to the stage where I found

168

going off for training a burden. League games seemed a strain somehow, even though we desperately wanted to end up third and win our bonuses. There were great incentives right up to the last game of the season, yet I was finding it all boring. I didn't want to kick a ball. It was a bad feeling. I'd never had it before.'

But by the beginning of this season, he felt very good, completely recovered, fit and with his appetite back, looking forward to his best season so far. 'In the first few matches I felt a couple of stomach twinges, but I thought it was just indigestion.

'In eight seasons with the club I've hardly ever been injured. In almost four hundred games, I've only missed about six. It's a funny old club, this one. You're expected to keep going if you can. You're expected to be tough. Well, that's what I think anyway. I just wanted to play.

'But in my mind I began to worry, which made it even worse. I look upon myself as one of the fittest in the team normally, yet I found myself being unable to do things I know I can do.

'I didn't want to complain about it or moan, that's why I didn't tell the lads for a long time. I didn't really want to tell Bill. His first reaction was what I knew he'd say. He said Dave McKay had it and he played on till it went.

'When the crowd and the Press started getting on at me, I just had to take it. It worried me, but I was more worried about myself and getting better. The crowd always thinks you're a hundred per cent fit, just because you're out there, but many times you're not. They don't make allowances. I know Bill doesn't either. If he considers you're fit, he expects your very best.

'I was beginning to feel the pain at home. Many a time I was in agony. The wife said I was stupid. I should tell them all and not play till I was completely better. It was silly to carry on. She's very pleased now it's out.

'Now all I've got to do is rest and get better. I don't know how long it'll take, but it's the only way. I should have done it earlier. I've probably made it worse all these weeks, playing when I haven't been fit.'

I suggested that if it was going to be six weeks of treatment and rest, then a week completely away from the club, somewhere nice in the sun, might be the best thing. He made a face.

'This club doesn't do that sort of thing. I've never heard of any player here ever being sent away on a holiday. They do it at other clubs, not here: Anyway, I've still got to have the heat and electric treatment twice a day. They don't know if that'll do the trick, but they've got to try.'

For the home match against Everton, he turned up to watch with Samantha, his two-year-old daughter. Gilzean, in true Scottish fashion, did the doting uncle bit and pressed a ten pence bit into her hand. Mrs Wallace got her a bottle of lemonade. As she was opening the lemonade, Alan answered the telephone which, as usual, was ringing non-stop. One of the calls was a group of Arsenal fans, singing obscene songs down the telephone. Very witty. Presumably in idle moments the Park Lane bright boys do the same with Highbury. But most of the calls were enquiries about tickets for the next round of the UEFA Cup, their long awaited home tie against Rapid of Bucharest.

Samantha asked if she could answer the next call. Mrs Wallace, with a wink at Pat Welton, said yes. Pat was sitting eating his sandwiches at a desk in the corner. He'd just come in from Cheshunt where his Youth team, back on form again, had beaten Chelsea 4-3. He picked up the phone on his desk and rang the Spurs main number. When Mrs. Wallace's phone rang, she picked it up and handed it straight to Samantha. Pat said down the telephone, 'Is your Daddy playing today, Samantha?'

'No, he's not,' said Samantha, very seriously. 'He's injured.'.

Pat then went on to ask if it was true she was wearing a shiny brown raincoat and purple trousers. Samantha got very excited, unable to work out how somebody could see her down the telephone. Football might be a big tough nasty world but there are always incidents to touch your heart.

The door opened and in came Alan Ball, the Everton captain, his red hair gleaming.

'Pain here, isn't it,' said Ball, feeling his own stomach. 'Don't tell me, right here. And when you try a long ball

across the field like this . . .' He demonstrated the sort of kick
he meant. 'You get a pain here.'

'That's it! Exactly,' said Mullery, very excited.

'I knew it,' said Ball. 'As soon as I saw it in the paper, I
said to the wife, Mullers has got the same as me. Bloody
terrible. I was out six weeks.'

Mullery asked what did they do. Ball said he got three
injections, he didn't know what, but it was mainly rest. They
were both very excited at having a common complaint,
slapping each other on the back. Ball then went off to get
changed. Mullery took Samantha to a seat in the stands. As
she went out, Mrs Wallace gave her a bag of crisps.

Alan Ball had a terrible game. Sir Alf Ramsey, who was
in the directors' box, must have been very disappointed. Ball
had obviously not got over his injury. But as far as Spurs
were concerned, it was one of their best matches of the
season. Martin Peters, as captain once again, had one of his
best games, perhaps *because* Alf Ramsey was there. (It's a
team joke that he always turns it on for Alf.) Ray Evans did
very well again and so did Chivers, scoring two excellent
goals. But the man of the match, according to the evening
papers that night, was John Pratt, playing in Mullery's
midfield position. He scored one brilliant goal – his first for
Spurs at any level for two years – and gave the through ball
for one of Chiver's goals. Spurs won decisively, 3-0. For once
there were no aggravations for Bill Nicholson. He couldn't
have been more pleased. But what with Ball obviously suffering, and Peters and Pratt playing brilliantly, as captain
and number 4 respectively, it wasn't much fun for Alan
Mullery.

Mullery went to watch the team play at Chelsea and this
time let his aggravation get the better of him, though for the
best of motives. This was a sad match for Spurs, beaten 1-0.
At half-time, Bill lashed into them for not trying. Mullery,
who'd been sitting on the trainers' bench watching the
match, joined in Bill's criticism of them, saying he thought
they hadn't been trying either. It was the wrong thing to
have said. They can take it from the manager but not from
an injured player, someone who's merely been watching
them, even if he is the captain.

After the match, several newspapers tried to get a row going, phoning up the players at home and asking if it was true they were furious with Mullers for interfering. Somebody managed to get a quote out of Phil Beal and Coates, both of whom denied it later, saying words had been put in their mouth. Luckily, it never came to anything, but Mullers got the message. When you're out of the team, for whatever reason, you've got to stay out, in every way.

Mullery also missed the home match against Rapid of Bucharest, although he seemed to be responding to the rest and treatment at last and it was thought he might soon start full training.

Against Rapid, Spurs were back on form, showing a lot more aggression than against Chelsea. For this match there were five substitutes, all sitting ready and waiting on the bench. Joe Kinnear wasn't one of them.

This was the evening Joe decided he'd had enough. He'd been playing hard for weeks and weeks in the reserves, but getting nowhere. For the Rapid match, his name had at last gone up on the team sheets as one of the five substitutes. At one time, being named as a substitute would have been a great humiliation for Joe, but at this stage in the nadir of his career, he considered it was an improvement at last. But at seven o'clock, just half an hour before the kick-off, Bill Nicholson changed his mind. He told Tony Want to get ready to be one of the substitutes, not Joe.

'I don't understand what he's doing,' said Joe, coming out into the car park, looking very bemused. 'I don't know what's going on. I'm going to go and see him tomorrow. It's the only way.'

Joe did go in next day, saying he wanted to leave. He saw no future at the club. Bill was calm, but adamant. He was letting none of his first team squad leave. There were too many important cup matches for him to lose anybody. They were doing well in Europe. They were in the semi-finals of the League Cup. The FA Cup was still to come. He couldn't possibly spare anyone.

So Joe had to be content, though Bill was sympathetic. 'The fact that Joe is out of the first team doesn't mean he's a worse player than Ray,' said Bill afterwards. 'Ray is playing so well that he can't be displaced. It's unfortunate, but Joe is suffering from one of the hazards of the game.

'He was unlucky to lose his place, but he might be back in at any time, with so many matches ahead. I can understand his disappointment. I know how he feels. He understands my position as well.'

People began to wonder if the same sort of thing would happen to Mullery. John Pratt was playing well in his place. Perhaps he would keep the position when Mullers was finally fit?

One of the most important matches before Christmas which Mullery missed was the away match at Leicester on 11 December. It wasn't a very exciting match to watch, being bitterly cold with very little for the supporters of either side to get excited about. Martin Peters got the only goal of the match, a header after a long, high cross from Ray Evans. But it was Spurs' first away win in the League that season. It was also the first time they'd set out with a deliberate 4-4-2 formation – meaning they had only two attacking forwards up field, four people behind in midfield, with four at the back. Jimmy Neighbour, who'd played on the wing in most of the recent matches, home and away, was dropped. Instead, John Pratt was in midfield – along with Coates. After half a season playing mainly as winger, though coming back to help when necessary, Coates' lack of success was openly recognised. He was now being brought back, taking up Mullery's position in midfield. He'd said all along, privately, that he preferred playing in midfield, as he'd done at Burnley, but had been prepared to play as a forward for Spurs, which was what Bill had originally wanted him to do. Now with Mullery out for so long, with the midfield losing its impetus and with the appalling away record, Bill had been forced to revise his plans. even his philosophy.

'It wasn't a great win,' he said after the Leicester game, 'but we got the two points. We play the way we have to. It's as simple as that.'

An arrangement of having only two forwards (in Spurs' case Chivers and Gilzean) but four midfield men (Peters, Perryman, Pratt and Coates) is looked upon by some football experts as an admission of defeat. It's considered a defensive

173

formation. In Tottenham's great days, in the fifties and sixties, they would never have considered such an arrangement. They'd always played at least one conventional winger, such as Cliff Jones, and the emphasis had always been on attacking, flowing, creative football. While other teams, such as the England team, had given up wingers and made no bones about concentrating on midfield and defence, Spurs had gone blithely on with a policy of attack, a policy which had been very successful.

It was only one little away win, against a not particularly feared team, but it had been done with 4-4-2 and it looked as if, through force of circumstances, it might have to be continued. Not that every expert considers it a defensive line-up. Martin Peters doesn't think it is. 'You can still get a lot of people up in attack, more sometimes with 4-4-2. When you're moving forward, two midfield men can go up into the attack, such as me and Ralph, which means you then have four forwards.'

Bill Nicholson doesn't care for any airy fairy technicalities. He maintains that when a team is attacking, the whole team attacks, from the full backs onwards. He's not in favour of demarcations. But he admitted the change of policy, perhaps even sadly.

'The teams of the fifties and sixties played football that was right for the times. The game has got more defensive, more negative. We have to do what's necessary. Supporters aren't interested in good teams that lose. This is professional football. The first rule in a manager's bible is "don't lose". That's the way it is.'

If the new system worked, and in many ways it looked as if it *had* to work because playing conventional wingers, whether Coates or Neighbour, had patently not worked, at least away from home, then it could have a further effect on Mullery's return to the team. If Coates proved to be a success in midfield, it would be even harder for Alan to get back.

Mullery himself had been slogging away, week after week, to get fit. Then he had a relapse. In training one day the pains came back. He went to see specialists who said he'd been rushing it. He must now start again, have a complete rest, much longer than last time, then gradually ease himself

174

into light training, without forcing it this time.

He came home from the ground one day, convinced this time his career was now in jeopardy. Whatever happened, he must start planning his future. If he was never going to be fit again to play football, he had to make sure his family was secure.

'It's them I worry about. What'll happen to June and Samantha. They're now used to a certain standard of living. Samantha knows nothing else. How can I possibly get £5,000 a year when I'm finished as a player? I'm looking all the time for things I might do. I'll have the house which will be worth a bit, though I haven't paid for it. But apart from that, I'll have no real money. My sports shop brings in a little money, but I couldn't live on it. I have life insurance policies, but only on my death. I have none of those policies which mature when you're thirty-five, the way some players have.'

What he really fancied, he said, was driving around in a big car, with an open neck shirt and an expensive tan, just looking at his businesses. 'There's someone who lives near us who does this,' said June. 'Alan thinks he'd like it. He's such a boring bloke.'

Over the years, many people have approached him with ideas, wanting his name. But everyone at Spurs is very wary, after Bill Brown and Cliff Jones, the double team stars, came to grief with their businesses. 'The people that Bill calls the "fringe mob" are always putting up schemes, but I've kept well out of them.'

He'd ruled out any possibility of going into football management. He couldn't stand that. I was surprised. Of all the present team, he seemed the one with leader qualities, not just because he's the captain but because he's by far and away the best and most fluent at talking football. Martin Peters might know more, but he doesn't talk much or impose himself. Martin Chivers might be more intelligent and have more O levels, but Mullery always appeared the most direct, most coherent when it comes to imposing his ideas.

'I've met managers who I used to play with as players – and they're different people. I couldn't have Bill's dedication. I first met him years ago, long before I joined Spurs, when he came to Fulham with his England Youth team to have a practice match with our youth team. Even then, in a little knock-around, he was completely engrossed, so worried and worked up. If I was a manager, I might not be like him. My temperament's different. But even so, being a manager takes over your life and wrecks you.

'You just have to watch Bill before a match. His hands are shaking so much he can't hold a cup and saucer. Really, you can see it rattling. It's terrible. I feel so sorry for him. Nobody would want to be like that. I don't know how he stands it. I'd be in the loony bin.

'You've got to sit there, unable to do anything, yet seeing everything going wrong. You know we're the better side, but it's not happening. It drives you round the bend. Really, I get more exhausted watching than I do playing.

'It's worst at a club like Spurs. You have three games in a row without a win and it's like the end of the world. Bill's in a terrible state. Yet someone like Matt Gillies of Notts Forest would give his right arm to be in our position at the moment.

'Bill has the problem of always having been at Spurs. He knows no other club except a big successful one. He's *got* to have success. He's had such experience and seen everything, so you can't argue with him. Like telling me the wonders Dave McKay performed after his injury. You want to say it's *me,* it's my injury, this is how I feel and I'm not putting it on. Those other people don't matter to me.

'But you can't deny he's a great manager. No one can question that. His record speaks for itself. You can't argue. He's one of the best ever. I have great admiration for him. But I don't know him. I would count as a friend of his, I suppose. I've been with him eight years so I must know him as well as anyone. But I don't. I couldn't describe him if I had to. He's a great football manager who thinks about nothing else except football. That's all I could say.'

Looking at the immediate future, to the time when his injury would at last be better, was he worried about getting his place back? John Pratt, despite doing so well, was still convinced that the old rule would apply – that established first team players would always get their place back after

176

injury. Joe Kinnear admittedly hadn't got his place back, but then Joe hadn't been a bought player, a famous England international or captain of the team. Mullery, surprisingly, agreed with John Pratt.

'I think it's an unfair rule though it does seem to have grown up. I don't see why established players should be treated differently. If I'm out for twenty games and John Pratt plays twenty good games in my place and the team wins twenty times, then obviously he shouldn't have to step down for me. You've got to let the lad have his chance. If he's doing better than me, he should be kept in. Better men than me have been dropped from the team.

'Mind you, I wouldn't stay in the reserves. Reserve football is not for me. I'd leave. Just as I couldn't be at Spurs and not be captain. If they took that away from me, I wouldn't want to stay. If I went to a new club and I wasn't made captain there, that wouldn't worry me. But at Spurs, if I wasn't captain I wouldn't want to stay.'

I said that if he felt like that, and presumably Bill Nicholson must guess he did, then it made it all the more difficult for Bill to drop him, or any of the big stars, just because of a bad spell. It would be such a loss of face and such a loss of confidence. Dropping a young reserve must be so much easier.

'I know it's difficult, but if I was manager, I'd always have the best team at the time. For example I'd have kept Cyril Knowles out of the team that time, when Wanty had all that trouble. That was a different problem I know, but Cyril just wasn't fit. He was puffing and panting before the end.

'It is always a difficult decision, picking a team. It's easy for me to talk. I don't have to do it. And I don't want to. I couldn't put up with the worries.'

His wife smiled. She can't believe that when the time does come, whether it's sooner or later, he'll be able to pack up the game completely. She reminded him that at one time he used to say he would like to be a manager. 'That was about ten years ago, when I was young. OK, I do feel there is so much I could give to the game, I know that, but I'm not going to.'

'What about coaching youngsters,' she said. 'You know

you love children. He always has crowds of them round him and he loves playing with them.'

'I would enjoy that, but you can't just do that for a bit of fun. You've got to do it properly. Television, I would quite fancy that. I like talking about football on the telly. But no one's asked me. Telly would be good for the money. It might be the sort of job which would allow us to carry on with the sort of life we have now. I don't want to go back to Notting Hill now.'

'We haven't much in common with our old background now,' agreed his wife. 'But round here we haven't got many real friends either. They're a bit snooty in this area.'

'Perhaps we are a bit out of it,' said Alan, thoughtfully. 'A fellow like me of my age is a bit different from all the middle-aged professional people. They've accumulated wealth over a long time whereas me, I'm sort of precocious. It's suddenly happened.'

All the same, they were digging themselves in. They had been round a few weeks previously to look at a local private school for Samantha and had been very impressed. They were planning to send her in January, to the kindergarten department, when she'd be three years old.

'She could go right through there to the end,' said June enthusiastically. 'If we still have the money . . . I hope she doesn't look down on us when she grows up, going to her little private school.' June smiled nervously, turning to her husband.

'I'll punch her nose if she does,' said Alan. 'I think she's very clever, so she's got to have a good education. I wouldn't like her to say her father and mother stopped her having any advantages. She'll just have ten kids in her class, not forty the way we had as kids. That way she'll learn very quickly.

'No, whatever happens now we're staying here. Once you've arrived you don't want to go back. That's why it's so important for me to find some sort of job for the future. It's all very worrying.'

15

The Battle of Bucharest

There had been rumours that the Rumanian food might be
unsuitable for the Spurs' sophisticated palates, so Bill
Stevens (the club's assistant secretary) was sent running
round Tottenham all morning in his car, buying up chicken
and steaks and lamb for the players' meals during their stay
in Bucharest. It was stowed away on board the plane, in a
special deep freeze box, under the care of a BEA catering
man.

Spurs left for Bucharest at lunchtime on Monday, 13
December, giving themselves two days to arrive and settle
down before the match on Wednesday afternoon. They were
leaving a long time ahead, but they were taking no chances.
Being midwinter, there might well be delays because of bad
weather at London or Bucharest. They couldn't have had a
longer trip – Bucharest was the furthest town still left in the
competition.

Although Spurs were 3-0 up from the home game,
everyone knew it was going to be a hard match. Rapid had
already won both their home ties by large margins. They'd
obviously been unsettled by Spurs' early goal in London.
The same sort of thing could easily happen in Bucharest,
only the other way round.

At Bucharest Airport we were met by a man from the
British Embassy. He issued an invitation to the directors and
officials to come to a party the next evening. The Press didn't
appear to be invited, the way they had been in Nantes, not
that they were interested. They said they'd been to enough
draggy Embassy parties during their years of reporting
foreign matches.

There was a small crowd of sightseers and one solitary
photographer with a wide trilby and a very worried look.
The players larked around as he lined them up, much to his

non-amusement. Geoffrey Green of *The Times* was at the front of the Spurs group and as the photograph was taken, he made the sign of the cross and shouted 'Il Pape'.

In the foyer of the Intercontinental Hotel it was the usual jokes from the players, followed by groans, as lots of complicated forms had to be filled in. Usually they don't have to do anything. Bill signs them in. But now they were behind the Iron Curtain. Joe Kinnear was putting on his idiot abroad look. As an official was telling him where to fill in his passport number Joe kept on repeating 'But I don't smoke. I've told you. I don't smoke.' The official gave up in the end and went away.

Gilzean collapsed exhausted on a sofa. 'You do it all Steve,' he shouted to Perryman, his room-mate. 'Fill in anything you like.'

It was obvious on the journey from the airport that Bucharest was going to be yet another town unseen by the players. But with good reason this time. For a city of one and a half million, it looked unbelievably drab. Not dirty or poor. Just monotonous and utterly boring. The Intercontinental, as an isolated piece of Western decadence, seemed positively flash.

In my well appointed hotel bedroom, there was a bedside radio with four different channels, like a TWA aeroplane, each with its own brand of non-stop taped music. I turned on channel one and it was the Beatles 'Sergeant Pepper'.

After dinner, I joined a few players and Press in a walk round the block with a Rumanian interpreter called Nick. Someone remarked on the absence of police. 'You don't have to wear uniform to be in the police,' said Nick. The Rapid team, when they'd gone to London to play Spurs, had taken a security man with them, to make sure no one had absconded. With a ballet company, he said, the ratio of security men to dancers was much greater, almost one security man per dancer. Footballers were not considered a great risk. In Rumania they had enormous status. Why, he knew at least two of the Rapid team who had their own cars! Footballers, he said, were better paid than doctors. But he thought the best paid people were waiters in any bars foreigners went to, because of all the tips. The top prostitutes, the ones who

180

hung around the Intercontinental, they also made a lot of money.

I had breakfast next morning with Arthur Richardson, the Spurs director. His day was ruined right from the beginning when he was given stale cornflakes and hot milk, two things he really hates. But he cheered up at the thought of the Embassy party. They'd heard nothing so far from the Rapid directors, or at least committee men. The last time he'd gone to a football reception in an Iron Curtain country, in Prague, he was sitting at the top table and had seen the committee men pinching bottles from the table and putting them in their pockets.

At eleven o'clock a coach arrived to take the players to a training session at the Rapid ground. As we got on, the taped music being played was 'Georgy Girl', sung in Rumanian. There was a long delay as everyone waited for Johnny Wallis. Someone was sent to find him. He was standing waiting at reception. He'd ordered twenty-four towels. When he'd enquired what the delay was he'd discovered they were preparing twenty-four pieces of toast.

There was ice on the ground round the pitch, but the pitch itself was clear and quite firm. 'I don't mind ice,' said Martin Chivers. 'Especially in Bacardi.'

The doctor advised Mike England not to train, as his foot was slightly swollen. But Mike said he wanted to, just to test it out. He'd take it easy.

Eddie Baily, in a blue track suit, explained to the players what he wanted them to do. He wanted them to go out two by two and do a few laps, sprinting and walking, the usual Friday morning light training sessions. Then they'd do a few ball exercises, just passing, and finish off with an eight-a-side.

'We're not doing much, but I want you to take it seriously. No messing around. There's people watching. Look as if you mean it.'

'Who's going out with me then,' said Joe Kinnear as the players jogged out of the dressing-room in twos. As Martin Peters came out he joined Joe. 'Thanks, Mart. I'm set now. Running with the acting captain. I'm bound to be in the team.'

It was Joe's first trip with the first team for many weeks,

since he'd been demoted to the reserves. Ray Evans was still playing consistently well and seemed in little danger of losing his place for the match tomorrow.

As the players trained, Bill Nicholson walked round, watching. He said there was actually no reason to train. The object was to give them something to do to stop them getting bored during the two days of waiting. A couple of hundred workmen were sitting in the deserted stadium, giving good humoured cheers every time a Spurs player made a mistake.

Afterwards, there was lemon tea provided in the dressing-room, served in a big metal pot, with a ladle to dish it out. Several Rumanian faces appeared through an open window, watching fascinated as the Spurs stripped and went for their shower.

After lunch at the hotel, the players had their team talk. For an hour and a half, Bill went through the Rapid team, their strengths and weaknesses, saying that he was going to play 4-4-2 again, as at Leicester. Peters, Perryman, Pratt and Coates would be in midfield with just two forwards, Chivers and Gilzean. They wouldn't be playing any wingers so the outside of the midfield men would be expected to go for the wings or to cover the full backs if they overlapped. The Rumanians would play 4-2-4, so he suspected, having four forwards up, including two wingers, to try to score. Spurs would be four against two in midfield, so they must win the midfield.

· At six thirty I went with the directors and Bill Nicholson to the long awaited British Embassy do. The Ambassador himself turned up, which was only what the Spurs directors had expected. They usually get the Ambassador when they go to a capital.

Bill Nicholson was the centre of attention. It was strange to watch him, with his broad Yorkshire accent and no nonsense manner, surrounded by a gaggle of Oxbridge faces, yet perfectly at ease and in command. They were hanging on his words, especially some of the women, hoping they'd be given a Spurs button-hole badge. One of the ladies had a row of them pinned to her bosom – mementoes from Liverpool, Dynamo and other visiting teams of firemen.

The players, once again, went to bed early that night.

Despite the long wait for the match, and the lack of entertainment or sights to be seen in Bucharest, there was a noticeable lack of card playing. They'd each been given £10 in Rumanian currency, but had been unable to spend it. The only shops with anything to buy were all dollar shops – shops for people with foreign currency.

At ten o'clock, every player was in bed, except Mike England who stayed up a bit later in the bar on the twenty-first floor. It had now been decided that because of his injury he wouldn't be playing tomorrow. He fancied a walk round the block. He went downstairs, only to see Eddie Baily sitting in the foyer guarding the front door, and came back up again. Even an injured player is not allowed to flout the rules.

I felt exhausted with all the hanging about. Hanging around in any city for two days is boring, but Bucharest must be about the worst. I don't know how the players ever survive, anywhere. They seem to go into a trance, become soporific, until they get into the dressing-room. No wonder a home team always has the advantage. The away team is numb and disorientated before anything begins.

Next day, the players had an early light lunch, at eleven in the morning, and at last it was time to leave for the ground, the August 23 Stadium (named after the day in 1947 when Rumania became a People's Republic). It's the national stadium used for all the international matches and can hold eighty thousand.

I looked for crowds all the way to the ground, but there were none. We saw one supporter, carrying a red banner, who waved and held up four fingers to the coach – meaning Rapid were going to beat Spurs 4-0 and therefore win the tie. It was the same sign the players had had since Monday whenever people saw them in the street, especially during the training session. As at Nantes, every fan was good at spotting Chivers, with Peters a close second. Football is the national sport in Rumania and every match is televised live. They have a daily sports paper, like *L'Equipe*, which is more than Britain has. I'd met their reporter at the training sessions and he knew the name of every Spurs first team player.

We arrived at the ground at twelve thirty, just an hour

183

before kick-off, and even there the streets leading to it were deserted. I thought perhaps there had been a mistake. The kick-off had originally been going to be two. Now it was one thirty. Perhaps it had been changed again. Someone said perhaps the match was over. It felt eerie, arriving at a huge deserted stadium. The players seemed on edge and keyed up. With every match they play, home and abroad, they're accustomed to crawling through dense traffic, often with police escorts to keep back the crowds.

At the players' entrance, a crowd of uniformed police stood waiting, silently. We went inside the stadium, which was like a grand but rather old fashioned hotel. There were long corridors full of large vases and potted plants. The players couldn't believe the dressing-room. It was exactly like someone's front parlour, only larger. There was a green carpet in the centre (the first dressing-room I'd ever seen with a carpet), and in the middle of that a small circular table with a potted plant on top. At the edge of the carpet was a row of elderly chairs arranged round the walls. It looked as if the room had been cleared ready for folk dancing. There was no sign of showers or lavatories. Someone finally found them, across the corridor and further down, two showers, neither with soap. In a corner of the dressing-room was a pile of faded towelling dressing gowns, presumably for players to put on when they padded down the corridor for a shower.

Having inspected the dressing-room, everyone went back along the endless corridors and down a huge tunnel leading to the pitch. The tunnel was even bigger than Wembley's, big enough to drive a couple of lorries down. In the middle of it ran a narrow wired-in cage which led out onto the pitch itself. This was to protect the players, before and after their march into the lion's den.

The stadium still looked deserted, till we got out onto the pitch and were greeted by a blast of kettle drums and shouts. There could only have been a couple of thousand Rapid fans, all crowded into a strip of the terraces beside the tunnel, but they went mad, shouting, screaming, roaring. The Press had to go across the pitch to get to their box on the opposite side and they too were screamed at as they

184

crossed. Geoffrey Green, as ever, rose to the bait and waved his fist back at them, which led to even louder roars.

Back in the dressing-room, the players stood around, putting off the time before getting undressed. It was very quiet. It wasn't just the strangeness of the room and the stadium, but nervousness. It was the sort of silence which nobody remarked on, being too aware of it. Ralph Coates was the first ready. He stood in the middle of the carpet, doing press-ups. The bump could be seen on his thigh where his ham string injury still hadn't completely cleared up. Mike England, with his ordinary clothes on as he wasn't playing, took down his trousers and bent over while the doctor gave him an injection, a pain killer, to help his infected toe. Cyril Knowles, the biggest fearty in the team when it comes to injections, looked the other way.

Bill was going in and out, busying himself, but not talking. Johnny Wallis went round giving out kit and bandages. Eddie silently rubbed oils into Gilly's body and massaged Steve's legs. The five reserves got changed into their playing gear, going through all their usual rituals of rubbing and massaging, elaborately stretching their socks, testing their leg muscles, even though the chances were against them playing. When they were ready, they sat huddled in a corner in their blue canvas tracksuits. They whispered and nudged each other. Joe Kinnear *looked* like a reserve, hunched and rather self-conscious, not the big strapping, self-assured star who'd begun the season.

'No complaints?' said Johnny, half to himself as he went round asking everyone if they wanted anything else, more bandages, tie-ups, more oils. Nobody wanted anything. 'I can't get over it.'

Three of the reserves in the corner suddenly started giggling – Terry Naylor, Joe Kinnear and Jimmy Pearce. Mike, standing silently in his good clothes beside them, asked what the joke was. 'What does a midget do in a football team,' said Terry Naylor. 'He takes short corners.' All three of them collapsed, unable to stop giggling. All the players, the real players, the ones who definitely knew they would have to go out there and perform, stared at them blankly, unable to take in even the stupidity of the joke.

'Right lads,' said Eddie Baily, clapping his hands. 'Fifteen minutes to go.' It was time for Bill's pep talk but he seemed to have disappeared from the dressing-room.

'I want you to go over the top, get the bayonet right in and twist it.' It was Eddie's usual wartime metaphors. They exchanged looks behind his back.

'Where's all the chewing gum,' said Martin Peters, coming back from a short walk to the lavatory.

'I put twenty packets on that table,' said Johnny Wallis, pointing to the centre of the room. The little table was now covered with his medicine and equipment. The potted plant had been placed carefully on the carpet underneath.

'Yeh,' said a voice. 'And seventeen of them are in Cyril's pocket.'

Everyone was ready. Chivers, Gilzean and Ray Evans, the last to get changed, had had their ankles strapped and were now stretching their feet, easing themselves into their boots. Bill reappeared, holding a piece of paper. He'd got the team sheet. Earlier he'd been saying that three of their regular players wouldn't be playing. Now he'd got the news that Dumitru, Rapid's best player, had made a recovery and was in the team after all. He hurried on to tell everyone that the tactics would still be the same, 4-4-2 once again. In the midfield, the two on the outside would have to take their winger leaving the two in the middle to mark their two front runners. When a midfield man went for the winger, the full back had to give him cover, and vice versa. Pete Collins, playing centre half in place of England, was told to have no worries. He would be able to beat Dumitru in the air. Bill went over each person's role quickly, player by player, except for Pat Jennings. Chivers and Gilzean were told they would have to work very hard, to keep at it, even on their own.

'Above all,' said Bill finally, when there was only five minutes to go, looking up and round at everyone, 'I want no retaliation. You've got to keep your tempers. It'll be hard, but you'll be penalised if you step out of line. So no re-taliation.'

There was a knock at the door. It was opened to reveal the Italian referee standing there, spruce and shining. He didn't come in and made no attempt to inspect anyone's boots. He asked for the captain. Martin Peters came forward. The referee shook his hand, still standing in the doorway, and then turned and walked away. There was a pause of about ten seconds, while everybody looked at each other, then a whistle blew in the corridor and everybody started talking, banging, slapping, wishing each other as usual the best of luck and shaking hands. At the doorway Bill's face came to light and life as he threw off his twitches and his expression of panic.

Rapid were already on the pitch. They'd been warming up for almost twenty minutes, to the delight of the crowd, which now numbered about ten thousand. Their noise was deafening, yet nine tenths of the vast stadium was empty. The terraces were uncovered and were simply layers and layers of concrete, going up miles into the sky. When the weather gets bad in Rumania the football season breaks for the mid-winter till the spring thaw begins.

I sat on the bench beside Bill and Eddie and Broderick, the Thos Cook's man who'd taken it upon himself to help Johnny Wallis the trainer with the kit. The five substitutes in blue sat at the other end, away from Bill and Eddie. Some of them had put cotton wool in their ears, knowing that sitting beside Eddie in a match can lead to deafness.

Eddie was up and shouting from the first kick, screaming at the ref for fouls he'd spotted. Bill just hung his head in silent fury. Five minutes later Bill himself was on his feet, tearing towards the touchline, shouting and screaming. Gilly had been brutally and openly punched in the kidneys by the Rumanian number 4, unseen by the referee who was at least fifty yards away.

As they stood shouting, ignored by the referee, it happened again. This time the number 4 took a running jump at Gilly, going through the air and bringing both his upturned boots down against Gilly's legs. It had again been completely unprovoked, yet once again, Gilzean did nothing in reply.

Slowly, Gilly shook his head and moved out of reach of the number 4, shrugging his arms to Bill on the touchline, signalling there was nothing he could do. A younger, less experienced player would certainly have retaliated. Yet Gilzean, miraculously, had just stood there, taking it.

187

Bill and Eddie were hysterical. I thought they'd both have heart attacks. The powerlessness of their position was making them froth at the mouth. It had been Gilly's brilliant back header in the first minute of the match at Tottenham which had led to their downfall. There had obviously been instructions this time to get Gilly.

Play moved on, the number 4 had to run for the ball, and Gilly escaped, limping. Bill and Eddie collapsed back on the bench, their heads in their hands, moaning.

Spurs soaked up all the Rumanian pressure, slowly but surely, and all their fouls and kicks. Chivers was being brutally kicked, on and off the ball, but being bigger and stronger than Gilly, he was managing to shrug them off, so far.

The Rumanians created several good chances, only to be saved by Jennings, Collins and Ray Evans, which made their policy of fouling seem all the pettier. If they'd concentrated on playing they might even have scored. Their policy of physical aggression betrayed cowardice, not confidence.

Spurs at last managed a good move, but Coates shot wide. Rapid had the best opportunity of all. Ene picked up a terrible back pass by Perryman and was through, with only Jennings to beat. Pat dived at his feet and Ray Evans cleared the rebound. There was no score at half-time.

Rapid had had more chances, but had wasted them. Spurs had taken everything thrown at them and were becoming more confident all the time. By keeping their heads, they'd given nothing away. Gilly was limping but worst of all Perryman had badly injured his shoulder. He'd come off for a few minutes midway through the half, after a bad tackle on him had resulted in an awkward fall. The doctor had treated him on the touchline. A bone had become dislocated in his shoulder, but had gone back into place. Steve had insisted on going back on, though he must have been in considerable pain.

In the dressing-room at half-time, Bill and the doctor examined Steve. Terry Naylor was told he was going on instead. Terry left almost immediately, going out on the field to warm up. Johnny and Eddie attended to all the other bruises. Gilly and Collins had both been kicked in the chest and needed their ribs strapped.

Bill said they were doing well, keeping cool, but they must keep the game even quieter and give nothing away. He told them to watch out for the quick one-twos near the penalty area. Several times Rapid had got through that way. He told Ralph to head for the wings, to give himself space along the touchline, beating his man when he could, but without losing the ball.

Bill's criticisms were mild, nothing compared with what both he and Eddie had been shouting from the bench in the heat of the game, unheard by the players on the pitch. Peters, Coates and Chivers had all come in for unprintable abuse as each in turn made some mistake or failed to take a chance which Bill thought they should have done. Eddie particularly had kept up non-stop screams at Chivers, shouting as usual that he wasn't trying hard enough. Bill finished by complimenting them on not retaliating.

In the second half, Spurs gradually got on top. It became obvious that Rapid knew they could never score four goals, and their tackles and fouls became even worse. Eventually Gilly had to go off and was replaced by Jimmy Pearce. It was Pearce who got the first and vital goal of the match. Chivers was put through by Pratt but the goalkeeper blocked his shot. Jimmy hooked in the rebound.

Once again Jimmy had come on as a substitute late in a game and scored the vital goal. But this time he went off just as suddenly, sent off, after only twelve minutes on the field. He got into a tussle with their number 2, out on the wing. They both aimed blows at each other, though neither connected. Jimmy's swing was a joke punch, ending it by scratching his head, hoping the referee thought he really had only been scratching his head. Immediately they were surrounded by other players, all tugging and pushing at each other. Bill and Eddie joined in from the touchline, screaming and shouting at the referee, an action which could have had them severely penalised in an English League game. Jimmy was given the red card, and so was their number two, and both left the field.

As a piece of brutality it had been nothing compared with what had gone before. Neither Jimmy nor the Rapid player had been vicious, simply squaring up to one another. But Jimmy had made the mistake of appearing to retaliate, using threatening behaviour which until then the Spurs players had avoided, despite continual provocation. After that the Rapid players kept up non-stop fouling to the end, knowing they hadn't a chance. Cyril Knowles eventually got in his bit of retaliatory fouling and had his name taken. In all, three Rapid players had their names taken, plus the one sent off. The worst, and most farcical, incident concerned their eccentric goalkeeper, Raducanu, after Jimmy's goal. He was so furious, maintaining Chivers had been off side, that he ran a good thirty yards and threw the ball viciously at the referee, scoring a direct hit on his back. Amazingly, he wasn't sent off but merely cautioned. As usually happens in a match full of fouls the referee appears to turn a blind eye to the home team, as if he fears the crowd will storm the barriers and lynch him. Where we were sitting, two bottles did come over the wire fence behind us and smash into pieces at our feet.

But the referee did award a penalty to Spurs, when Coates was brought down from behind. Martin Peters, the penalty expert, missed it. The goalie had moved before the ball was kicked, which is illegal, and had come a good couple of yards out from his line, but all the same, Martin's shot went weakly past the left hand post.

Just before the end, Chivers scored, a brilliant and typical individual Chivers' shot. Up until that moment, Eddie's screams had been constant and terrifying, shouting that Chivers was letting the team down, the club down, he wouldn't have him in his side, he was useless, etc. Eventually, Chivers himself had heard some of the oaths when he came near. He could be seen quite clearly swearing back at Eddie.

Chivers beat two men by swerving out to the edge of the penalty area and shrugging off their brutal tackles, then he began to hone in on goal. Almost on the goal line, he shot, scoring from the narrowest of angles. Everyone on the bench was in the air, cheering and clapping the best and only piece of individual play in the whole sordid match.

The subs immediately all turned to Eddie, watching him, wondering what he had to say now. After all his terrible abuse, Martin had done it once again, proving Eddie wrong.

'The bugger,' said Eddie, sitting down, mopping his brow in a state of bemused hysteria. It was almost as if he couldn't stop his abuse, as if he still wasn't aware that the object of his hatred had produced a piece of genius. Slowly he came to his feet again and ran to the line, clapping and cheering, shouting to Martin that he'd done it, he was brilliant, he was great. Martin obviously heard every word this time but he studiously ignored him, deliberately turning his back on him. Eddie sat down, drained but satisfied.

When the final whistle blew, Bill and Eddie ran forward onto the pitch to help the team off, putting their arms round them, congratulating, commiserating, asking if they were in pain. In the dressing-room, there was a controlled but excited noise, not the excitement which a brilliantly played match would have brought, just a general loud noise as everyone in turn said it was the worst team they'd ever played against.

'Now be careful with the Press,' said Bill Nicholson, going to the middle of the room. 'They're bound to ask you what it was like. Just be careful what you say.' There was a pause as everyone stopped talking and listened.

'But as far as I'm concerned,' Bill continued, 'it was the dirtiest team I've seen in thirty years. If this is European football, I'd rather have a Combination match. Diabolical. I've never seen such dirty fouls.'

Even the players were a bit taken aback. There was nothing anyone of them could possibly have said which was stronger than that. (Later, when the first pressman, Bernard Joy, was allowed in Bill repeated the same remarks – that Rapid was the dirtiest team he'd ever seen. Nobody bothered to try to get quotes from the players, not when they had a manager saying such things to them, all on the record.)

Bill went round inspecting the injuries as the players began to undress. As they each padded back, wet and exhausted, with their dressing gowns wrapped round them, the old fashioned parlour turned into a hospital casualty ward.

'What about that miss then Ralph,' Bill said to Coates, going back to his normal self, unable to forget the chances missed despite all the achievements.

'What?' said Ralph, obviously hurt. 'What about that penalty I got you? You forget that, don't you.'

'Never mind,' said Bill, smiling, playfully punching him. He went to the middle of the room and told everyone he was proud of them. That was the phrase he used: proud of them. The players looked amazed. It was the first time he'd used such words all season.

'Yes, I'm proud of you. You showed them how to do it. You didn't retaliate. We've had the last laugh. Well done.'

Steve Perryman, in his street clothes, had his arm in a sling. He and the doctor had missed a lot of the second half, staying in the dressing-room to attend to his injury. He'd been given a pain killing injection, but the pain was still there.

Peter Collins carefully unwrapped the plaster and strapping from his ribs. In the second half, he'd been punched in the stomach. Phil Beal was being treated for a calf injury. Knowles had an ankle injury, plus a knee injury and he'd also been kicked in the arse behind the referee's back, which he said had annoyed him most of all. Everyone smiled. Steve said that in the first half, when he'd been clearing a ball on the touchline, one of the players had grabbed him by the balls. In Steve's case, not wearing underpants, it must have been very painful.

Gilzean was getting both legs and his back attended to. Jennings was nursing his arms where he'd been trodden on. Chivers was rubbing his head. He had bruises all over his body but the most painful was his head where he'd been punched.

There was no tea or any refreshments but the groans didn't last long. They could do without tea, fuck them. They certainly had no intention of having a drink with the Rapid players, as they'd been invited to before the game. They just wanted to get away. Everyone was pleased that we were flying home at once, not spending another night in Bucharest.

The trip home was very noisy, with the drink and food flowing freely. The players talked excitedly and hardly played cards. Perhaps card playing is an escape, when players don't want to talk to each other or think about the game. Everyone was very excited and pleased.

Every newspaper except one carried horrifying accounts next day of the match. Peter Batt in the *Sun* said it was 'the most shameful exhibition of thuggery I have ever seen by the brutes of Bucharest'. Norman Giller in the *Express* said Spurs were 'hacked and kicked about like rag dolls'. Jeff Powell in the *Mail* said it was one of the most 'savage matches in the riot-torn history of European football' and was 'another bloody chapter in the Rumanian catalogue of brutality'.

Even the *Daily Telegraph* reporter, Robert Oxby, let himself go, describing it as 'the most cynical exhibition of deliberate fouling I have ever witnessed'. The *Guardian* headlined it as a 'Kind of War' and their reporter Albert Barham talked of 'sly cynical fouls ending in pure viciousness'.

Only Geoffrey Green in *The Times* avoided any emotion, though he talked about the 'fur flying' and quoted Nicholson, as everyone else did, on Rapid being the dirtiest side he'd seen. He managed to stay relatively calm in his report, pointing out, which nobody else did, that in the first half Rapid had three good chances and if they'd scored, the game might have been very different.

It's difficult to avoid prejudice, following one team and concentrating on what they do. Naturally, this leads to seeing life through their eyes, which is permissable perhaps in a book about the year in the life of one team, but a newspaper reporter is supposed to be unbiased. With a foreign trip, when it's a British team against the rest, then chauvinism always comes into it. It's much easier to let yourself fly, calling a foreign team the dirtiest in the world. It's relatively safe. No reporter, or manager, would ever use such words about another British team. There are no come-backs when you slander a foreign team.

All the same, notwithstanding and nevertheless, it was a brutal display. Spurs didn't play much good football, apart from Chivers' goal, but their calmness and maturity in the face of constant provocation was a lesson for every team. I would never have believed they had such strength of character. It had been their manager's last instruction, on leaving the dressing-room, and they'd resolutely stuck to it.

16

Background Staff

Eddie has the office next door to Bill Nicholson's. On his wooden door it has 'Asst Manager, E. Baily', in old fashioned script. Eddie was making notes in a surprisingly beautiful italic handwriting about the art of trapping the ball. In front of him he had a 1934 FA manual on coaching and a 1965 book written by a Hungarian on how the great Hungarian team did their training. He was using both of them, plus his own knowledge, to assemble some notes on the gentle art of trapping the ball. All for his own benefit, not for publication. He likes to have notes he can refer to when he prepares training sessions.

'The basic things haven't changed all that much,' he said, pointing to a diagram in the 1934 book. 'The skills you have to work on are much the same. Trapping a ball under the foot is as sensible now as it was then. The big difference is speed. The quicker you can do things, the better, because time is space.

'Even top professionals can make a mistake in trapping a ball. A great player is the one who makes least mistakes. A truthful player comes off the field concerned about the mistakes he's made, not boasting about all the good things he's done. Some players can make the same mistake week after week. There is obviously something wrong. It's got to be corrected in training.'

Eddie Baily is a strange mixture. When talking about the theory of football he is calm and in control. When he moves onto personalities a demoniac look can come into his eyes. His Alf Garnett prejudices about immigrants and his hatred of the players with the 'wrong character', which he never disguises, can verge on the violent. He can rant and rave, yet

194

he can suddenly calm down and tail off, without finishing his sentences, as if he realises what's the point, deportation is the only cure for some people.

As a player himself, he was never a toughy, never a hard man. He was a star forward of Spurs' great side of the fifties and won eleven England caps. He was a ball player, quick and intelligent, with great individual skill and flair. Now as coach, it's the hard men he seems to love, ones who run themselves into the ground, like Steve Perryman in the first team or Terry Naylor in the reserves. These are the players his heart warms to. They have the character he admires. 'I know many players resent being told to do something. They often think it's a waste of time. But standing still is the biggest waste of time. Moving is doing something, even if the ball is forty yards away. It's human nature to have spasms when you don't move enough. I know that. So you've got to keep at them. You use anything to motivate them. Shouting, insulting them, touching their ego. I understand my missus. I know what affects her. A coach has got to understand each player and what has an effect on him.

'When you know it's not skill that's lacking, you've got to get at them. If they don't do it voluntary, the way Steve does it, you've got to make them do it involuntary, even if they hate you for it.'

Chivers wouldn't exactly agree with this theory, nor would motivation experts in other management fields, but over the previous weeks I had noticed a big difference in Roger Morgan. During most of the season so far, he was so fed-up being in the reserves that it was obvious his heart wasn't really in it. Eddie was now full of praise for his effort and was giving Bill good reports.

'I would sack the ones who don't try. There's no good applying skill standing still. You want to be on the London Palladium if you want paying for standing still. I wouldn't have them in the club. And I know which ones I wouldn't have.

'It all comes down to character. I can tell by a face whether a person has a weak character. I know by looking at people who will be the fighters and who won't.

'If you've got a fighter, you can improve him all the time.

I want them *all* to do better all the time. I know that Roger
Morgan is never going to be able to lift weights like Spud
Collins, but all I've wanted him to do is try harder every
time. I know what he's been saying under his breath at me.
All I want is for him to be a fighter so people will see what
a good player he is.'

He was by this time very worked up, banging the table
and spluttering on the books in front of him. Then he
subsided and went back to his notes.

While Eddie was writing, the club secretary was in the
counting house, counting out the money, the laundry ladies
were laundering, the trainers were training and the doctor
was doctoring. Altogether there's a total of thirty full-time
people behind the scenes at Tottenham, apart from the forty
full-time footballers.

On a match day the full-time staff suddenly increases to
three hundred, ranging from a hundred Mecca catering staff,
who man the thirty bars and restaurants, to the fifty
policemen on duty *inside* the ground. The annual bill for
these policemen comes to over £10,000. (Police *outside* the
ground come for free.)

The biggest single item on the expenditure sheet is salaries
for the players and staff – this comes to almost £200,000 a
year. Buying strips for the players and footballs for them to
kick comes to £6,000 a year. Travelling to matches, at home
and abroad, costs almost £40,000. Playing football isn't
cheap.

Cecil Poynton, who was in the treatment room clamping
an ultra sonic lamp on to an injured leg, is the longest
serving member of the staff. He's seventy and joined the club
as a player back in 1921. Now he's the trainer who attends
to injuries. The electronic equipment which he has in his
treatment room, next door to the dressing-room, cost over
£3,000 to install. It's like a little hospital with a battery of
micro wave, ultra sonic, radiant heat and other frightening-
looking machines, plus beds and medicines.

Tony Want was the player with the electric pad on his leg.
'Is this the one Cecil where you could bore a hole in my bone
if you turned it up too high?'

'I don't know about that,' said Cecil. 'But this little one here could kill a tank of goldfish.'

In the boot room, Johnny Wallis, another ex-Spurs player, was polishing the boots with black Kiwi polish. (Dubbin went out with middle partings.) Next door in the first team dressing-room the apprentices were swilling down and mopping up, paddling round in old gym shoes with their trousers rolled up. I said I thought the boys cleaned the first team's boots. That was one of football's traditions.

'Not here they don't,' said Johnny. 'Cec or I do them. I couldn't trust these buggers. They wouldn't clean them properly or tighten the studs the right way.'

When he'd finished the boots and when the boys had cleaned the dressing-room to his satisfaction, he started to lay out the first team's shirts, boots and shorts, putting them in neat little piles around the dressing-room. It was like the preparations for a very clean party.

'The minute the team sheet goes up at Friday lunchtime I start getting ready. When I know who's playing I know which boots to lay out.'

He laid out pads for those who wanted pads, moaning as usual about the ones who refuse to wear them. It drives both him and Cecil mad. They both say there are far more leg and ankle injuries than in their day, yet some players like Gilzean and Knowles, won't wear pads. 'If it was my decision, I'd make them all wear them.' Chivers, Perryman, England and Mullery always wear pads, without fail. As for the rest, they sometimes do and sometimes don't.

He got ready the bandages and tubular sleeving – a special bandage material which many players wrap round their ankles to give extra protection, such as Chivers, Ray Evans, Phil Beal and Mike England. Then he went to blow up the two brand new footballs (Minerva Supreme at £12 each) which he has ready for every first team match. The one that is used is kept for the reserves for their next home match. After that it goes into the pool for training, in the gym or at Cheshunt.

On the table in the middle of the dressing-room he arranged his bottles of warming oils (eucalyptus or camphorated oils which many players like to have rubbed

197

into their chest and legs) and jars of Vaseline. Vaseline on the brow is supposed to stop the sweat running into your eyes. On dry days it's often put on the knees as well. If you slide on the hard ground you're not supposed to hurt yourself as much. Johnny is very sceptical about things like Vaseline. He calls them gimmicks. But if a player gets it into his head he needs Vaseline, then he's got to have it.

'In a bad game when nobody has played well they all moan afterwards about the little things – the studs being too low, the Vaseline too thick. When they play well, there are none of those moans. If they want the top brick off the chimney, you have to let them have it. If they miss a goal I don't want to be blamed, do I.'

Most of his centre table stuff comprises bandages, sticking plasters, strip dressings and tapes for tie-ups (tying up their socks). There's a first-aid set, scissors and smelling salts (ammonia) in a bottle to bring people round after concussion. Several players have a quick whiff before they go out to clear their head. Then there's a leg splint, though you wouldn't tell by the look of it. It's a plastic, inflatable one. You pull it on like a sock, zip it up and blow and it goes rigid in a matter of seconds.

When Johnny, as first team trainer, has to run out on the field he carries an assortment of gimmicks in his little bag. Smelling salts, of course, and a wet sponge. An antibiotic spray, in case anyone has an open wound, and a cold spray which freezes any part of the anatomy which has been injured and deadens the pain. Johnny didn't know what chemical was in the cold spray. It was just a temporary measure, lasting ten minutes.

'The sprays are a bit psychological. Some just need a quick rub and they're up and playing, but others like the full treatment to make them feel better.'

In his bag he also carries bandages, tie-ups, laces, spare shorts and shirts, studs, pliers (to tighten or loosen studs) and chewing gum. Before every match he lays out a dozen packets of PK chewing gum for those who want them. Most spit it out the minute they get on the pitch.

What about shampoos and deodorants? Many clubs today now provide them for their players.

'Get out. They're supposed to be footballers, not bloody poofs.'

Well then, a hair dryer? Surely that would be a good thing after all the hair washing they do in the showers.

'You want to turn the place into a beauty parlour, you do. Hair dryers would be bad. They'd get their death of cold going outside with their heads warm. The only beauty extras we lay on are those green square things in the bath. Carbolic. You can't beat it.'

Although he's scathing about the gimmicky stuff the players insist on, and all their pre-match neuroses, he's very proud that at Spurs they spare no expense.

'I had one trainer in here a few weeks ago, from a First Division club as well, and he couldn't believe all the stuff I'd got laid out. I told him that three-quarters of the stuff would be used that day. He didn't believe me. He's allowed only two rolls of Elastoplast per match. We get through seven or eight!

'It's nerves with a lot of them, things like pouring on all that oil, or just habit. Mind you, being nervous is good. You should be keyed up before a match. It keeps you on your toes. But personally, I think they're too pampered.'

Cecil came in from his chores and sat down beside Johnny in the dressing room. He agreed. Footballers were all too pampered these days.

'There's a different atmosphere with the reserves,' said Cecil. 'They're all equal and they shout at each other, on and off the pitch. In the first team you couldn't imagine someone like Jimmy Neighbour giving someone like Chivers a bollocking.'

'I think our lads are a bit frightened to make a mistake,' said Johnny. 'In Dave Mackay's day there was a lot of shouting. He was fantastic. The minute the ball was kicked off, he was screaming, urging everybody on, swearing at every mistake. We want more of that. There aren't the characters like Dave today.'

They were back once again to the good old days when luckily in came the doctor, checking on any of the injured.

Dr Brian Curtin, Spurs' medical officer, is forty-three, well-built and stocky in the way a Rugby player is stocky and well-built. He spends one day a week in Harley Street, but basically he's a GP in partnership with his brother Maurice in Edmonton.

He was born in Enfield but he's very Irish, in his conversation, in his liking for a gargle or two and in his general friendliness. He was sent back to Ireland to be educated, to a public school and university, and when he gets going, even his accent becomes Irish.

Over the years he's become a father confessor to many of the players. Not just because he's the family GP to many of them (players like England, Jennings, Knowles, who live in his area, and also Bill Nicholson and his family) but through his personality. The players often find it easier to tell him their personal problems rather than Bill Nicholson.

There is an ascetic, puritanical streak which runs through the club, from boardroom to managerial level, so it's surprising and refreshing to come across Brian Curtin. He says, half as a joke, that one of the reasons he's not usually allowed to travel away with the team is because he would start enjoying himself too much. 'When I'm with the directors in a hotel, I always order the best food and wine. I can understand why Bill doesn't want me on tour. Curses.'

Good times apart, Dr Curtin's contribution on the medical side is vital to the success of the club. He stresses that he's their medical *adviser*. He has no executive power. 'Bill makes the final decisions. I give him the medical report but he takes the decision whether to play a player or not.

'In sending a player on there are other aspects to be considered apart from the purely medical. Bill knows for example the pain threshold of each player. He can watch a player on the field and tell far better than I can if his play is being affected. The fans can't tell and sometimes even the player can't tell, but Bill can. He knows which player will allow pain to affect him mentally and which won't. Cyril Knowles, for example, is a player you could send on eighty per cent fit because he has such heart. He can rise above pain on the field. Yet surprisingly in the treatment room he's the one who yells when he's being treated and doesn't like injections.

'There is also the matter of charisma. It is often vital for the team to have a certain player playing. Cliff Jones, for example, was often sent out when he wasn't a hundred per cent fit because he mattered so much to the team – and he worried the opposition even more. Two men would always be made to mark Cliff Jones.'

Sometimes the doctor declares a player fit but Bill says he's not and puts a reserve in his place. 'I picked up the paper one morning and read that a certain Spurs player had been declared unfit by the club doctor and wouldn't be playing. Yet the day before I'd told Bill he was fit.' In this case Bill had decided the player needed a run-out in the reserves but didn't want to hurt his feelings.

At the beginning of every season the doctor gives a talk to all the players, telling them to inform him at the first sign of any injury or illness, at home or abroad, He gives them general health and diet warnings and warns the younger players about the dangers of VD, what signs to look for and how it can be treated if reported immediately. He also talks about contraception, explaining their responsibility not to get girls pregnant. There's usually one incident every season when a father comes to the club to complain about what one of their players is supposed to have done, as if it was the club's fault. It's not officially the club's responsibility of course – the players only work there – but everyone is encouraged to confess all at once so that the best legal or medical advice can be hired immediately and the club's good name protected.

'We've got forty very active, very healthy young men to look after, some of them with a lot of money and a lot of temptations. You can't expect all forty of them not to go astray at some time.

'At one time players were encouraged not to get married young. It was felt that they hadn't the money to take on the problems of a house and a family. But today it's the opposite. We like them to get married young. They have the money and the club will even lend them more to buy a good house.

'Marriage is considered a good thing to settle them down and keep them from going to night-clubs and such places. But the first months of marriage are difficult. I've noticed

201

that it takes them two months to settle down. They put on weight and get sluggish and it affects their play.'

When he first took over as doctor, he relied heavily on Cecil Poynton's long experience with football injuries. 'I never played football myself. I went to a rugby school. I'm not even quite sure of the rules. Cecil knows so much about football that he can tell from a player's walk at forty yards' distance what is wrong with him and what sort of knock he must have had. Cecil might not know much about physiology, but his practical experience and common sense is unbeatable. He can go over similar injuries which happened forty years ago and describe what caused them and how they were cured. Basically, football injuries are still the same.'

The most common single injury is the sprained ankle. Recovery depends on the age of the player. For a player aged between 16 and 22, the recovery period is two weeks. For those aged 22-27, the period is three weeks. For the 27-33 age group, it will take four weeks.

He's a bit suspect of players who pride themselves on being quick recoverers, although of course he's all for players thinking this. 'But it can worry them if things seem to be taking a long time. Ralph Coates got very worried about his pulled ham string. I'm sure he usually does recover quickly, but a ham string is one thing that has just got to be given time. You can't hurry it. But of course this hunger to get better and the hunger to play well is a vital part of every good player.

'Ralph is an exception in being such a hungry *bought* player. In my experience I've noticed as a general rule that the hungriest players are the home grown players. They've got everything to prove.

'Oh, but the biggest exception to this, now I think back, was Dave Mackay. He was the most all round footballer I've met. He was so hungry it was incredible. How he recovered from those two broken legs was a miracle of guts and perseverance.'

He was very worried by Mullery's injury. He felt this sort of pelvic injury was becoming all too common in football, brought about simply by overstrain – by playing too many hard matches and by having to train so hard to be a hundred per cent fit for every match. 'They also have physical strains outside football, living the good life, coping with adulation. When players were on £10 a week, they all went home every night. Now they get invited everywhere. A few can get away with it. The younger players hear stories about people like Georgie Best and Bobby Moore going to clubs, or they see Gilly knocking back the lagers. But these are all exceptional players. They train twice as hard next day after a night out. But this is very rare and not to be encouraged.'

He's noticed, and so has Pat England, the orthopaedic surgeon who advises the club, that early signs of osteoarthritis are becoming more common. Even players in their mid-twenties are having traces of arthritis in their knee joints, ankles and thighs. 'It's because their joints are being subjected to major pressures from a very young age. They're going to be in great pain in the years to come. The way things are going in football I think players will retire in future at twenty-seven. The stress will be too great after that age.'

He has a very high opinion of Bill, as a manager and a man, though in many ways they are very different. 'People keep on saying he's dour and callous and brutal but he's not. Underneath he's a soft bastard. It's just the initial reaction which some people find hard to take. It's because he's so truthful and straightforward and highly intelligent.

'You should see him when he goes through my medical reports, the ones I have to fill in if a player is going to hospital. I always like to write them as well as I can. Bill takes them to pieces. He sees things so logically. I get told to cut the flam, cut out all the rubbish and just put it down straight, one two and three. I'm supposed to be the educated one and he isn't, yet he can précis far better than I can.'

Dr Curtin checked on Tony Want's injured leg and then got into his car and went home, back to his beautiful mansion in Enfield, his beautiful young wife Jilly and his four beautiful children.

The light burned late in Bill's office. He'd begun his evening's paper work. During the morning he's always involved in training. In the afternoon, people are queueing up to see him. It's only in the evening that he can read all the scouting and other reports that flood into his office every day. The next day the team were playing Chelsea in the first leg of the League Cup Semi-Finals, the cup that Spurs won last year at Wembley. The thought of choosing the substitute was still hanging over him.

17

Cyril Gets Dropped

Alan Mullery was chatting to friends in the corridor outside the dressing-room, at Chelsea, looking very depressed. He'd had three games in the reserves but now his stomach was beginning to hurt again. He'd been in pain during a reserve match the night before, against Queens Park Rangers, and his abdominal muscles had been so sore he could hardly run.

Steve Perryman was also around the dressing-room. He wasn't better, but he was much happier. His dislocated shoulder, injured in Bucharest, had responded well and wasn't as serious as had been thought. 'I should be ready for West Ham on Boxing Day.'

There was a large Spurs contingent amongst the 43,000 crowd and right from the beginning they made themselves heard, particularly with 'Osgood is a Fairy'. As usual at Chelsea, the east stand was crawling with actors, show business people and rag trade moguls, far more than at Spurs. I could hardly get to my seat for the blinding flash of leather coats and the heavy smell of aramis.

The first half was fairly even, with both teams playing cautiously, sizing each other up, trying nothing rash or daring, except for a few sly kicks at each other behind the referee's back. Just before half-time, Chelsea scored, rather luckily. Jennings came out to clear from the edge of his box. There wasn't much danger but his kick somehow rebounded off Naylor right into the path of Osgood, who kicked the ball into an empty goal.

Just a few minutes after half-time, Spurs scored twice. Cyril Knowles set up the first goal with a long run up the left and then a far post cross to Coates. Ralph headed back and down to Naylor who scored, his first goal ever for Spurs.

205

Then a couple of minutes later, Naylor won the ball near Chelsea's penalty area, passed to Pratt who put it through to Chivers.

The game then turned into a real battle compared with the formalities of the first half. Pratt retaliated after being badly tackled and had his name taken. Osgood kicked England on the chest while both were on the ground and he got his name taken. Others were warned, others got kicked. Cyril Knowles, who'd been marking very heavily, was lucky not to be cautioned.

Spurs momentarily began to slacken off, appearing a bit too confident now they were winning. Cyril started messing around, teasing the opposition and almost gave away a goal. Chivers shot over from far range when with a bit more thought he might have scored from closer in. Then Garland, who came on as substitute, scored with a brilliant header. Chelsea were now level.

With only a few minutes to go, Chelsea then had their second big bit of luck of the evening. Jennings had caused the first goal. This time Naylor, Spurs' scoring hero, accidentally handled in the penalty area and Hollins scored from the spot.

From being 2-1, Spurs were beaten 3-2. In the dressing-room everyone was shouting about the penalty, cursing Chelsea's luck. Nobody was moving, a real sign of defeat, just sitting, unable to take their clothes off.

'Never mind,' said Mullery, coming into the dressing-room. in his good clothes. 'We'll send Ossie a bottle of champagne from Wembley.'

Everyone started cursing Osgood, remembering the things he'd done, saying what they'd like to do with him.

'We're not at Wembley yet,' said Nicholson, ever the pessimist. He had his head down, talking half to himself. The team had played well. There wasn't really a great deal he could criticise, except generally to say that a team 2-1 up should never lose. The doctor arrived and got out his syringes. There were a lot of injuries, almost as many as Bucharest. Philip Beal, when he was ready, had both arms and legs swathed in bandages. I had to button his shirt for him as he was unable to move his arms. Mike England was

206

a mass of bruises, on his thighs and chest where Osgood had kicked him. Others had also been injured.

Terry Naylor was the first dressed. Everyone had sympathised with him. The ball had just bounced up and hit Terry on the hands. It had been a complete accident. But all the same, Terry was very upset. He would have been the hero, if Spurs had won.

It now meant Spurs had to win the return leg at Tottenham. It wasn't just the chance of winning a Cup Final which was so important. It was a way into Europe next season. Not even the fanatics could see the team getting into Europe any other way – Manchester United seemed too far ahead in the League to be caught.

Bill slowly put his jacket on, went to wash his hands, then left the dressing-room to meet his directors upstairs. When he'd gone, Martin Chivers turned to Cyril, laughing.

'You were lucky, pissing around that time. Bill forgot didn't he. What were you doing anyway?'

Cyril just swore. There was no excuse he could give.

'Never mind, my lads,' said Peters. He too was smiling, as if he'd already got over the defeat. But Terry and Pat Jennings were still looking completely miserable.

'I'll never sleep tonight,' said Pat as he dragged himself slowly to the coach. 'I don't want to. It doesn't seem to matter how old you get, or how many matches you've played. Being beaten never gets any better. It gets worse if anything.'

But if anything it was worse for Terry Naylor. As a young reserve with only a handful of first team games so far that season, he'd been very near to his big break-through, having scored one goal and had a hand in the other. By the time he got home, on the bus and tube as he hasn't got a car, his wife Linda had already seen the highlights of the game on TV. She's not much of a football fan. In fact when the commentator said penalty she thought it was a penalty *for* Tottenham. When he made it clear that Terry had handled the ball and had given away the penalty, she burst into tears in front of the TV set.

Terry was out of the team for the return match against Chelsea two weeks later. Steve Perryman had by then recovered. If they'd beaten Chelsea the first time, as looked so likely, Terry might have kept a place somewhere. There is always a temptation to keep a winning side. But for the return match everyone was fit (except Mullery) and Bill was able to field his strongest and most experienced team.

The atmosphere from the fifty-two thousand crowd was the noisiest of the season, more intense even than the Arsenal match. People were literally shaking with excitement. When the teams came out I expected a few heart failures. At least nobody would be cold for the next two hours.

Spurs got off the mark like animals unleashed, tearing into everything and by their sheer pressure forced Chelsea right back from the beginning. As Chelsea were a goal ahead it was vital to score quickly. They threw themselves forward like Japanese suicide troops. Chelsea tried to keep cool, but they were overrun. Yet a goal wouldn't come. The more Spurs battered, the more Chelsea stayed cool.

With seconds to go before half-time, Spurs at last scored. Mike England, of all people, dribbled upfield, beating three players before sending Coates free down the wing. From a difficult position, Coates crossed into the middle. Gilzean nodded it down to Chivers who seemed to stop in slow motion before taking aim and firing into the far left hand corner of the net.

The screams and roars were deafening. The whistle blew for half-time but the shouts continued, getting louder if anything. Throughout half-time the stadium was ablaze. It had almost been a scripted goal, scored at the crucial psychological moment. Spurs must win now.

Perhaps if there had been no half-time, Spurs might have continued blindly at the same pressure. But the break seemed to take something away from them. When they came out, they'd cooled down and seemed a bit puzzled. Their clearances became wild, furious and mostly pointless. Chelsea pressed forward, with more flair and intelligence than Spurs had done in the first half. They took over the midfield by sheer skill and aggression. Peters seemed slow. Pratt seemed exhausted. Perryman seemed to lack skill. The whole team seemed lost.

Jennings saved several point-blank attacks before Chelsea

finally scored, a fine shot just outside the penalty box by Garland. It seemed inconceivable that so one-sided a first half should be followed by a half with Chelsea so clearly on top. It was as if the first half had never existed. It wasn't lack of confidence or character. Spurs were obviously trying. But they were just unable to do it.

Then Spurs got a penalty, quite undeserved and quite out of the blue. Their first bit of luck in the match, in either of the matches. This time Hudson had accidentally handled in the area under little pressure, under no danger. The Spurs players couldn't watch. Ray Evans was on his knees, his head on the ground, as Peters took the kick. It was low, not very hard, going for the middle of the left of the goal. Bonetti had moved, going the wrong way. Spurs were ahead again. With such a stroke of luck, surely Chelsea would now collapse.

The penalty had come with only eight minutes to go. It looked as if nothing would happen now before the whistle and extra time. Spurs might then get their second wind. They had stolen the psychological advantage again. A breather might transform their bodies.

The game seemed clearly to have found a pattern, as if the rise and falls in fortune had been carefully timed. Now, with Spurs leading 2-1, making it 4-4 and all square on aggregate, it seemed only fair that extra time should decide who went to Wembley.

Hudson, the Chelsea player who'd given away the penalty, was quietly taking a free kick right beside the corner flag. None of Chelsea's free kicks or corner kicks had been remotely dangerous. Everyone had been well cleared. Hudson appeared to mis-kick this one. It was heading straight for goal, harmlessly, low and very easy to stop. He should have aimed high into the middle of the box for his waiting forwards. It was a wasted shot.

Cyril Knowles had it covered easily, with no Chelsea player around him and Jennings right behind him, just in case. Knowles changed feet to hit it with his left, his best foot, rather than his right, though either foot could have done as there was so little danger. He stumbled, fell over and missed the ball completely. Behind him Jennings was unsighted. He watched unbelieving as the ball rolled gently past him. It bounced against the far post then trickled slowly into the net. It was a freak goal, a cruel unfair freak goal, the worst possible piece of bad luck at the worst possible time. The whistle blew almost immediately. The Chelsea players went wild. The Spurs crowd were stunned.

It was the first time I'd heard the fan going in the dressing-room. I hadn't realised before that there was one. It's low, insistent hum seemed to reverberate round the walls, getting louder and louder, as if trying to drive everyone mad, an Orwell 1984 room, a torture chamber where everyone is face to face with his worst fears.

They sat like shipwrecked hulks, naked, with their heads bowed, their faces in their hands, unable to move. Knowles seemed to be crying. His eyes were red and swollen. His arms were shaking. No one could look at anyone else.

Of course it wasn't the end of the world. It was only a game. There would be many more. What's so extraordinary about football anyway. But at that moment their little disaster seemed to be a microcosm of all human disasters.

Eddie and Bill were both sitting silently and alone on the bench, their coats on, their heads bowed. Suddenly they stood up and came together, speaking to each other in whispers, urgently, each going over movements, each talking for his own sake without listening to the other. They were relieving their own agonies, not wanting to criticise the players.

Bill took his coat off. He walked round, put it on again, then took it off. One or two players had at last started to move, getting quickly dressed to escape the tensions. John Pratt, who'd been taken off, was first away. But most were frozen in various stages of undress, trapped by their thoughts. Gilly was in a daze, his head going from side to side, struck dumb with disbelief.

The doctor came in from the treatment room, all jaunty and chirpy. People avoided his gaze and his remarks. He checked on Cyril, Ray and Gilly, all of whom had had colds in the chest before the match.

'Now take one after every meal,' he said to Cyril, handing him some pills. 'I've never known a time when we've had so much chest trouble. Do you know that Bill? Very bad.'

'He shouldn't have played if it was that bad,' said Bill bitterly.

'Nobody could have stopped him,' said the doc, all smiles, looking round.

'Well, I'm going to the reception. Get a few noggins in.' The doctor went out, still smiling. Nobody moved. There was silence again. Bill walked round and round the dressing-room, ending up in the middle beside the treatment table.

'Well,' he said slowly, addressing everyone, though no one was watching him. 'That's it. It's over. There's no need to worry about it now. Not any more.'

He looked blank and stiff. He was saying the right things, realising they'd reached the depths and had to be pulled out of it. But he lacked any conviction. He put his coat on and left.

They took a long time combing their hair. Standing behind one another, staring into the mirror, combing and re-combing, not wanting to go outside. Every time the door opened the shouts of delight from the Chelsea team could be heard down the corridor.

'We said beforehand if we got a goal before half-time that would be it,' said Mike England. 'Somebody said it anyway.'

'Fucking tragic,'' said Gilly, still shaking his head.

Cyril still hadn't spoken. He was putting on his tie very slowly. It was black, to go with his dark blue shirt.

'You've got the right tie there, Cyril,' said Martin Chivers grinning, the first grin of the evening. No one had dared to talk or even look at Cyril up till then. All season he'd almost been caught in the act, trying to do something fancy with the ball instead of clearing first time. Now it had happened.

Cyril's face was contorted. At other times in other games he would have laughed it off, denied it was his fault, blamed the referee or simply sworn back at Chivers. But this time he was incapable of any reply.

'You'll have to keep it on all week,' said Chivers, unable to resist driving it home a little more. Cyril's eyes were almost closed. He stood with his black tie in his hand, looking into space.

'Well then,' said Chivers, 'I'm going to the reception. If

nobody else is going. I'll represent you. I'll see you on Friday, if I'm sober.' See you, then.

'I thought when we got the penalty,' said Mike England, still gnawing away at the game, 'that was it.'

On the table was a telegram, a large greetings telegram from an unnamed Spurs supporter in Leek, Staffordshire. It was addressed to Bill Nicholson and the team, wishing them the best of luck. As the players left the room, they picked it up in a trance, looking at it but not taking it in.

'I'm going upstairs, Mike,' said Ralph Coates at the door. 'You bring the girls up.'

'No,' said Mike. 'Don't be so bloody lazy. You know Gwen will have been waiting outside. You go and get them now.'

'No,' said Coates, rushing out and banging the door.

'Bloody hell, what's wrong with him.'

Johnny Wallis had cleared up and was sitting in the corner, waiting for the last ones to go.

'Never mind,' he said. 'Worse things happen at sea.'

'What a fucking goal,' said Gilly. 'I've never seen such a fucking goal. I'm definitely not going upstairs. They can stick their reception.'

'Worse things happen . . .' said Johnny, not even bothering to finish his cliché this time.

'There'll be some spewing up in Tottenham tonight,' said Gilly standing up. 'I couldn't stand seeing anyone. I'm going straight home.'

Outside in the streets, there were mass arrests as Tottenham fans ran riot in the streets. In all, forty-two people were arrested, each to be charged next morning with causing an obstruction.

Later that night the Chelsea team were running riot as well. Peter Osgood, along with two other Chelsea players, was picked up by the police at three twenty-five in the morning. He was accused of being drunk and disorderly in the King's Road. (He was later acquitted).)

Bill Nicholson put on a brave face when the Press grabbed him in the car park. 'A lot of our players were very tired with so many games. This now gives us a breathing space. We can go to Cheshunt and work on tactics and iron out the faults.'

It was all true. Spurs had played more games than any

other English club so far, with doing so well in Europe, in the League Cup and in the Anglo-Italian cup matches.

But Bill, like every Spurs player and every Spurs fan, had wanted to get to Wembley. The game might be full of burdens, compared with Eddie's day, but the glories are great. Wembley would have meant national fame and a couple of thousand quid extra for each player.

The Press tried hard to get him to criticise his players, but he was very careful when they brought up the question of Chelsea's last goal. 'It was diabolical, that's all there is to it. *We* don't get goals like that.'

Cyril's aberration was the talking point of football all the next day. It had been seen only too clearly on TV by millions of people. Luckily for Cyril, when the news that he was dropped came out the following Friday, when the team sheets went up, George Best had taken over the sports headlines and Cyril was left in peace with his miseries.

It had been a strange season for Cyril. After four years in the wilderness as far as the England team was concerned, he'd been suddenly called up for the England party to go to Greece just a few weeks previously. He hadn't played, simply sat on the substitutes' bench, but it made being dropped by Spurs all the more dramatic.

His early career had been equally dramatic. He comes from a mining village in Yorkshire and for three years he worked down the mines, having been turned down in turn by Manchester United and Wolves. He'd given up all thoughts of football when Middlesborough, in the Second Division, signed him on. He'd hardly had a season at Middlesborough when in 1964 Bill came along and paid £45,000 for him.

On Saturday, when Spurs played their next match at home against Manchester City (a 1-1 draw) Cyril stayed at home all day with his wife Betty (who's from the same mining village as Cyril) and his two young children. All afternoon and evening he sat slumped in front of the TV.

'I couldn't bear to go to the reception after the Chelsea match, or talk to anyone, so I just got in my car and slipped off. I couldn't sleep that night. Next day wasn't much better. I just hung around the house. I didn't want to go out and meet people. I couldn't bear it. The Press were ringing me all day, but I said nothing.

'Bill didn't speak to me on Friday morning at first. There was about three times when he passed me and could have said something. I was alone with him in the dressing-room, but he still said nothing. I began to think nothing was going to happen. Then just before the sheets were due to go up, he called me into his office.

'I told him the ball had just popped up and went over my leg. I was trying to clear it, not do anything clever. It just sort of went up and I missed it. But I said it was my fault. It was there for the hitting and I missed it – so did Pat, standing just behind me. I said I was more sickened than anyone else.

'He said he was dropping me. I started to say that it wasn't fair. I was being made the scapegoat, but I didn't get much chance. I know Bill. This is my eighth season with him so I know there's no use arguing. He'll go on till he's made his point and you've got to accept it. He told me to be a man and accept it and not go round talking to anyone.' He said it wasn't just because of that one mistake, but because I'd been off form for a while.

'I think it *was* just because of that one mistake. I'm sure if I'd cleared off the line we'd have gone into extra time and the whole thing would have been forgotten and I'd have been playing this afternoon. That's what really sickens me. One mistake and I'm out. I can understand Bill's feeling. I know how much it meant to him.

'Over fifty thousand people saw me make the mistake then millions later on television. If it had been a normal League match I might have been forgiven and kept my place. Because it was a semi-final and so much was at stake, I've got to carry the can. That's football.'

According to Cyril's assessment of himself, he didn't think he'd been playing badly. He admitted a similar slip at Chelsea in the first leg, when he'd fallen over the ball and nearly given a goal away, but he thinks he had a good match that day. 'People forget the cross I gave which led to our first goal. They just remember the mistakes.' But it's not really in Cyril's character to admit mistakes. Instead he gets himself

214

into a series of complicated rationalisations, seeing himself as the martyr for the team's errors, not just his own.

'Forwards make loads of mistakes, but nothing happens to them. When a back makes a mistake, it's a goal. I feel really sick.

'If only I could have played today I would have got rid of it right away. I'd have made up for it and got over it now. Now I don't know when I'll get it out of my system. Worrying about it is going to make it worse. I know the crowd won't help when I do get back. They don't really like me. They're not a good crowd that way. But they don't get me down. Whatever they say, I just laugh. But I'd like to have got straight back and forgotten about it quickly.'

The Hangers-On

There are three sorts of fanatical fans, fans fanatical enough to follow their team anywhere. There's the Kids who move in gangs and strut and prance and look for action. There's the Supporters, the honest working men who form the backbone of the supporters' club. Then there's the Hangers-on.

The Hangers-on hate being called hangers-on. They're the ones in the expensive leather coats who look as if they've just had their hair done. They have money to burn and their ambition in life is to burn it on the players.

The nearest a Kid gets to his hero is an autograph on the platform. The nearest a Supporter gets is when his hero condescends to present the prizes at the supporters' ball. But the Hanger-on, if he plays his cards properly, he can have his hero home for dinner.

Morris Keston has hung on so successfully over the years, despite endless discouragement from the club, that he is now about the closest to the players of all the outside fans. He spends about £3,000 every year in following Spurs. Wherever the team stays, no matter where it is in the world, Morris Keston stays, usually in a bigger and better suite.

He's forty, married with two children and lives in a very posh block of flats at Marble Arch. He has a firm in the East End of London, in Bethnal Green Road, which sells ladies' dresses and coats. He employs a staff of fourteen people and has a turnover of about £800,000 a year. They must be very keen, loyal workers. Morris never seems to be there.

In his office he has large photographs of himself. There are many with Bobby Moore, at balls and dinners, beaming in a splendid dinner suit. There's a photograph of Morris shaking hands with Prince Philip. Morris helped to organise a do which raised money for the British Olympic team to go to Mexico. And there's Morris shaking hands with Lord Mountbatten – thanks to Morris helping to raise money for the Commonwealth Games team.

Morris is a great fund raiser, a form of expression beloved by many self-made, affluent East Enders. He's helped many charities, but mostly those connected with sport, either for sporting charities or benefits for individual sportsmen.

'My life really revolves round Spurs. I probably only know about twenty people in the rag trade, but thousands know me through football. Everywhere I go, people say there's Morris Keston of Spurs.'

That's the sort of boast which could give a Spurs director apoplexy, but all fans are possessive about their club and talk about our team and our lads and our club. Every big club has a fan like Morris Keston, but few have them as big as Morris.

Fred Rhye, the elderly bookie, is an equally ardent Spurs fan, but he seems almost in a trance as he moves round the world, following Spurs. In many ways Spurs is all he's got. But Morris has a young family, an expanding business, his non-stop social life, his charity stuff. Why waste so much time and energy with Spurs.?

'I don't understand it myself. I've had ups and downs in business, lots of them, but I just seem to accept them. But Spurs worry me all the time. I don't actually enjoy watching them. I'm too worried. I must be a masochist. There's a magnetism that draws me to them, yet honestly I'd rather pick up the paper and read the result than go and see them. But I've got to go. I can't keep away.

'I chain smoke all the way through a match and get all worked up. These days I often leave about fifteen minutes before the end because I can't stand it any more.

'Even if they're winning 1-0, there's no point in suffering any longer. I can't stand the agony of watching them perhaps lose their lead.'

If Spurs have a good win, then it's champagne all round at his works on Monday morning. If they lose, then he's miserable and irritable, bad tempered with his family all weekend and refuses to take his wife out.

'My wife's given me up for lost as far as football's concerned. There's nothing she can do about it. Now and again she comes with me, for the ride. She picks her trips, like New York or Greece. She wouldn't come to Iceland or Carlisle.'

When Spurs have a really big win, like the FA Cup in 1967 or the League Cup in 1971, then Morris throws a big party at the Hilton for several hundred people which costs him at least £1,000. It was this 1967 party which led to the open rift between him and the club.

The club had their official celebration party at the Savoy. All clubs who get to Wembley celebrate at a big London hotel, treating the wives and officials as well as players, whether they win or not.

The Spurs Savoy party was a very nice affair, from most accounts, but long before it was over the players, so they say, got bored with the speeches and decided to leave and get taxis across London to Morris's party at the Hilton. The directors have never forgiven him for it. They were left with a celebration party which didn't contain the reasons for the celebration. 'Morris had better groups at his party,' says one player. 'Our party was deadly.'

'I didn't make them come,' says Morris. 'They came of their own accord. I was having a celebration party for the Spurs win, whether the Spurs players came or not. I had over two hundred guests. It would still have gone on and been a success, though of course it was great to have the players there.'

Since then, no official at the club has spoken to him. They're always seeing him of course, but they avoid him and he goes out of his way to avoid them. Things weren't helped a couple of years ago in a train coming back from a match when one of his mates, a ticket tout, physically assaulted one director, incensed by the way he thought Morris was being treated.

From Spurs' point of view, you wouldn't expect them to actively encourage the Morris Kestons of this world. The players are supposed to be superfit athletes. How could they possibly ever approve of someone who wanted to take them out to clubs and hotels?

'I can hold my head high,' says Morris. 'They're surrounded by lots of people and get offers all the time from

Garth Crooks: elegant striker, but suffered somewhat during the season.   Professional Sport

Steve Perryman: Captain Steve, the only player still performing for Spurs from the 1971-72 team. Professional Sport

Chris Hughton: overlapping full-back but carrying worries in an unsettled season.

Two present day England stars, Gary Stevens and Glenn Hoddle.

Tony Galvin: Spurs star with the BA in Russian Studies, a sign of the social and educational changes in football in the last decade.

Kicksports Foto

Some emotions never change: Mark Falco, Clive Allen, Graham Roberts rejoice.   Professional Sport

Clive Allen: cost £700,000, the present day most expensive Spurs player.

Professional Sport

John Chiedozie: one of four black players, now first team regulars. In 1972 there were none.

Professional Sport

Ray Clemence: from Liverpool to Spurs, but still at the top.

Professional Sport

Glenn Hoddle: the most naturally talented player ever to grace the Spurs team . . . ?

Mike Hazard: midfield master, but so often in the shadow of the Blessed Hoddle.

Professional Sport

Ossie Ardiles: Spurs import from Argentina – who DID go to Wembley.

Professional Sport

Mr O. Ardiles: law student, Times *reader, chess player. Also plays a bit of football.*

Cheers: salutes to each other from Hoddle, Falco and Perryman.

Professional Sport

Paul Miller: behind that dour, uncompromising exterior, today's dressing room joker.

Professional Sport

Graham Roberts: iron man with greying hair, one of nine present Spurs players with England experience. Professional Sport

all over. They come to my parties because I'm genuine. I live for Spurs. I don't want them to do badly.

'Fans never get any credit, not of any sort. I feel sorry for those kids who travel up and down screaming their heads off for Spurs. Their hardships are never recognised. But if gates were to fall, you'd soon hear the club complaining.

'A few years ago I found someone willing to sell me five Spurs shares. I paid him £10 each, which he agreed. I wanted them for sentimental value. The club refused to register the sale. I wrote to them and asked for a reason but they never gave me any. They're quite entitled to of course, under their regulations, but I was very upset.

'I'd give anything to be a director of Tottenham, any money. I'd enjoy the fame. It's a human reaction.'

Morris doesn't know why so many of the Hangers-on seem to be from the rag trade. 'There's always been a big following amongst Jewish people in the East End for clubs like Tottenham and Arsenal. Chelsea's a bit different. They get the show business crowd.' I asked if it was because as emigrés, once they get any success they want to identify with something very English like a local football team, but he didn't think so. 'It's probably just that Jewish fans draw attention to themselves so much. There always *looks* a lot of them around.'

One of the many social functions which Morris helped to organise during the season took place on the Sunday after one of Spurs' best wins of the season, their 1-0 defeat of Leeds United. Morris couldn't have chosen a better time. There's nothing that footballers like better than being seen after a good victory. The do was actually in honour of Colin Milburn, a cricketer who had lost an eye, but it was the famous footballers everyone wanted to see and be seen with.

The invitations were very posh. First of all it said 'Ball', nothing so common or garden as a dinner-dance. Dress was black tie and 'Carriages', so the invitation said, were for two am. Cabaret was to be by 'the sensational Lovelace Watkins'.

The women were in beautiful ornate dresses, dripping with jewels, their hair high and immaculate and their faces tanned and expensive. And as for the men's evening suits, I couldn't get over the variety of designs – brocade lapels, satin

219

collars, embroidered jackets and shirts in every colour and material. And, like the women, the men were dripping with rings and jewellery and expensive tans.

Morris Keston, in a green creation, seemed to be known by everyone as he glided round saying hello Denis (who turned out to be Denis Howell, the MP and former Minister of Sport) and kissing Liz (who turned out to be the actress, Liz Fraser).

The tickets were £10 each. Drinks were extra. Most of the footballers I talked to had been given their ticket free, by Morris. Not only had he organised it all, he'd paid for many of the tickets. It would have been simpler to have handed over a large cheque, but of course there would have been no fun, no glamour, no rubbing shoulders with the famous.

A lot of the guests seemed to be connected with sport in some way:TV sports people like Jimmy Hill and Peter Lorenzo, sports agents like Bagnell Harvey. There was also a sprinkling of film and TV people, like Richard Baker, who reads the news on BBC TV, Mike Aspel, and Moira Lister the actress.

I sat down very quickly at my table, table 40, trying to keep my old fashioned evening suit hidden. I sat alone for some time till luckily Martin Chivers and his wife Carol arrived. He was with Stephen Rutland, a business partner and friend. Also at the table was Billy Walker, the boxer, and his wife, plus two partners of Bobby Moore's. The place seemed to be full of Bobby Moore's business partners. The girl next to me said she worked in his Mayfair shirt shop.

The menu was good but safe, just the job for footballers, smart without being in any way worrying. It was melon, followed by soup, followed by steak and two veg followed by a meringue.

Martin Chivers and his friend Stephen had just come up from Brighton where Stephen has a night-club. He has another one opening soon in London which he talked a lot about. The main reason for going to Brighton was a toy fair. Martin had been making personal appearances, endorsing goods with his name.

Stephen talked over dinner about an idea he'd just had for Martin – a gramophone record of Martin Chivers telling

220

people how to score goals. It would be part of a package
deal, with a big photograph of Martin scoring one of his
famous goals, plus a booklet about his technique. 'It's what
every parent and uncle wants. It solves their problems at
Christmas. Every kid wants to be able to score goals like
Martin. At fifty pence, it could make a packet. Don't you
think so? I'm going to organise a demo.'

I said I thought there would be people to buy it, but what
could Martin actually *say* on the record? Scoring goals is a
physical not a verbal activity. How can it be explained in
words?

Stephen said the record would perhaps be a come-on to a
certain extent. No one could really expect to be *taught* to
score goals like Martin. 'It's just part of packaging Martin.
The whole of commercialisation of footballers is still in
infancy. Nobody yet realises the millions of people out there,
all fanatics, all untapped, all interested in *anything* to do with
a famous footballer.' Everybody nodded their heads and
agreed, especially Martin.

The first speaker after the meal was Morris Keston, who
briefly thanked everyone for coming, and then a much longer
speech was made by Denis Compton. This led into an
amazing ritual which apparently happens at every sportsmen's evening. Each famous star in turn had to stand up
when his name was called. He took a bow while everyone
clapped him, then he sat down again. He didn't have to
make a speech or say a word, just stand up and be seen by
all. There was such a crowd that evening – over five
hundred guests in all – that it seemed to go on for hours. The
footballers who were clapped, just for existing, included
Bobby Moore, Geoff Hurst, Alan Ball, Rodney Marsh, Martin
Peters and Phil Beal. Martin Chivers got an extra loud clap
for having scored yesterday's goal against Leeds.

Looking round the tables, I watched the expectation on
every passing famous face as they wondered if they too
would be announced and have to stand up. There were two
faces not announced who seemed very familiar but I couldn't
place them. I was sure I'd seen both at Tottenham, but in
open necked shirts and looking very shifty. Now they were
resplendent in brocade evening suits and purple dress shirts.

I pointed them out to Martin. He knew them at once. Ticket touts. They came to every big do at the Hilton. The flashest tout of all won a big prize later in a raffle and got a standing ovation.

Martin Chivers said he'd seen Lovelace Watkins three times in the last few weeks, at one place or another. He discussed with other people at the table whether the accoustics for cabaret was better in their experience, at the Savoy, the Hilton or the Talk of the Town. All of them seemed to have spent half their lives at such places. I thought of Bill Nicholson and Eddie Baily back in their days, celebrating with a pint and pie and a game of darts.

The band struck up, the sensational Joe Loss no less, with songs like 'I Love to Go A-wandering'. Quicksteps seemed to be in order. At last I felt that my 1962 evening suit might not be too old fashioned after all. But I hadn't got the energy. I left around midnight, too tired to continue. Being a footballer is a hard life. Being a successful footballer, lapping up the social life which the hangers-on love to provide, must be absolutely exhausting.

19

Bill Goes to Bristol

One evening in February I went with Bill Nicholson to Bristol. He was going to watch his reserves play Bristol City reserves. He'd hardly seen them all season, with the first team having so many more matches than usual. In the back of his Rover he had a pair of heavy Wellington boots. When you're watching amateur matches or schoolboy games, even First Division managers have to stand out in the rain.

His wife Darky would have liked to have come with him, just for the ride, but he prefers going on his own. He'd taken her with him only once that season, on a scouting mission to Southend to look at a player. Once again, she brought him bad luck. 'We had fish and chips on the front after the match. When he got back to the car it wouldn't start. It was all my fault of course.'

But at least she had seen one first team match that season, one more than usual. It hadn't been a League match. She doesn't know when she was last allowed to watch a League match. It was the second leg of the first UEFA match, against Keflavik of Iceland. Even she couldn't have ruined the team's chances that night, not when they were already 6-1 ahead. 'Mr Wale rang me and said I just had to go. They couldn't possibly lose. So I went and enjoyed it very much, especially when Ralph scored.

'Mr Wale rang me again for the Nantes match. They'd drawn nil-nil away but I knew from Bill how hard it had been out there. I didn't dare go to that one.'

So as usual she stayed at home, keeping the back window open as she does for every home match, trying to catch the roar of the crowd. When the wind is in the right direction she can hear every goal that Spurs scores. Just to make sure, she's also got an arrangement whereby one of the office staff rings her after every Spurs goal.

223

I felt suitably honoured, being allowed to drive in state with Bill. The reserves, under Eddie Baily and accompanied by Mr Cox the vice-chairman, had left by train at lunchtime. They were having a pre-match meal at a hotel in Bristol.

Bill was looking forward to the match. 'I always like to watch our reserves. They're such good lads. They train so hard and they play so well.' He knew a few of the players in the Bristol team, particularly one called Spiring whom he'd seen a few times last season. But there were none he was going to scout. He was going simply to see his own reserve team.

They didn't know he was coming so they would be very pleased. Reserves tend to feel a bit overlooked and hard done by. They know that the manager can't see them very often and has to rely on reports.

On his car radio he tried to get the result of the Leeds-Liverpool Cup replay which had taken place in the afternoon. He talked about the Liverpool team, how he'd rated them highly at the beginning of the season but now it looked as if the replacements weren't as good as the previous team. He'd been worried by Heighway and now that he wasn't showing such promise he felt his worries had been proved right. 'You see a player doing good things but sometimes there's a nagging feeling he's having a bit of luck. When he keeps on doing it, you begin to wonder if you're wrong. With Heighway I always felt he was lucky. I think Keegan is Bill Shankly's best new discovery.

'Luck is a strange thing. We had a lot of it last season. We won several away games that I knew we shouldn't have done. We had a terrific away record, only letting in fourteen goals in twenty-one matches. That was the same as Liverpool. We were the best two in the League. But we had a lot of luck. This season we're not getting much luck, at home or away.

'I believe in luck happening, but the most important thing is to make chances. Chances can be made all the time. Look at Martin Chivers against Leeds. By running for a half chance he pressured Sprake into making a mistake. You can say it was luck, but I'd say it was a chance which was made to happen. If you're always trying, always running off the ball, then you make chances happen, but you've got to be looking for them. In the old days you were rated as good depending on how good you were on the ball. These days it's more important what you do off the ball. The whole idea of one-touch matches in training is to teach running off the ball. You've always got to be ready.'

I asked if Joe Kinnear was going to be in the reserves tonight. Bill said no, Joe was injured. I'd hoped he might go on and talk about his reasons for dropping Joe from the first team, but he drove on in silence for several miles.

I said how well Ray Evans had done and he agreed. What he liked best about Ray was his speed. 'You've got to be quick as a full back these days, otherwise you've had it. His heading isn't good, but neither is Joe's. Joe's much more experienced of course, but Ray deserved his chance. Even if Joe hadn't got injured I would have given Ray a proper chance.'

Ray had been the only deliberate team change that season so far – the midfield changes had been brought about by Mullery's long and serious injury. Making a deliberate change, promoting a reserve and dropping an established player, must be a very difficult decision.

'One of the first things I learned as a manager was that there's no point in simply making changes for the sake of changes. You should always know at any time what is your best team and you should stick to it. It's only through playing together that a team can get better. That's the way they whip up enthusiasm and understanding. It's very easy to be disappointed by a team's performance and start making quick changes. If you consider one player to be better than another player, you can't just drop him and bring the other one in.

'You have players in the reserves because you consider them not as good as the first team. By sticking them in when you know they've still got weaknesses, all you're doing is exposing them. Players can come into the first team and be lucky. I know Roger Morgan's weaknesses but against Leeds he did well. I expected his weaknesses to be exposed, but they weren't. But that might be his best game of the season.'

He mentioned one manager who went in for a lot of changes, always bringing in new people. The Press and public liked him because he was a great enthusiast, always going on about his latest player, but later he tended to drop them, which led to trouble all round. And if the player had been bought from outside, it landed the club with a huge salary which had to be paid long after the player had been dropped.

Then there is the policy of equality which is favoured by several managers. With this system you try to have a large and completely equal first team pool, with the idea that everyone is considered each week for a first team place. 'I'm against that as well. It's just unsettling. I know Eddie for example would drop certain players because they don't play well away, but if he was a manager he'd probably change his views. The manager has to make his decision on his best team, and barring injuries it's best to stick to it. If someone starts to prove to you that he's better than someone in the first team, then that's different. But that doesn't happen overnight.

'It's ridiculous to drop a player because he's played one bad game. What do you do then? You have to bring in a reserve whom you've always considered the poorer player, when he might not have played a match since the last time you saw him. He could turn round to you and say, why am I playing? I haven't touched the ball since I was last in, so why do you choose me now? No, you can't defend change for the sake of change. All that happens is that you upset people. The following week you send the reserve back to reserves and you've succeeded in upsetting two players, the first team player and the reserve.

'It's different when a player comes into the team through injury. That's a special circumstance and he's got to be well aware of it and not kid himself. It's his chance to show what he can do, but it's not his chance to get into the team for good. It's hard for him to take but it's the only way.'

I mentioned the case of Tony Want. How upset he was that time when Bill had told him that Cyril would be back for the next game, whatever happened, just because Cyril was the first team player. Bill had been sticking to his principles, but wasn't there a better way of explaining them?

Bill thought for a long time. 'I don't think Tony can

grumble. He knows he's not the first choice. He was being included through injury. If he was the first choice, he would know it, wouldn't he? No, there's no use giving people false hopes. They have to be told the truth.

'But when I *do* include a player in the team through choice, because I've come to the conclusion that he is now better than the first team player, I always tell him he's in on his merits, not through injury, and he's going to be given a run of three or four games. I give him a fair crack of the whip. I don't want to make him feel it all depends on one game. If then he fails, he's only himself to blame.

'You have to drop players if you think someone can do the job better. As a player I was dropped into the reserves to give Danny Blanchflower a chance. And then as manager I dropped Danny to give a young kid his chance.

'I know the reserves grumble about not being put in when they think someone in the first team isn't playing well. I know only too quickly when someone's not playing well. It's happening to Steve at the moment. He hasn't progressed this season as much as he should have done. And Mike England hasn't yet regained his confidence. But I'm too aware of the weakness of the reserves who could take their places to start chopping and changing. We have to live with it. All the players know the principle. They can have few real grumbles.

'Each week the first team is easy to pick. Unless there's injuries it picks itself. Each week my biggest problem is the substitute. Sometimes I can take two hours deciding who will be the twelfth man.'

Basically, all the players understand his problem and agree with his principles. But couldn't he perhaps be a bit more cheerful and encouraging in handling his players . . .?

Again, he thought for a long time, then he started talking about the old days. He knew that some players thought he went on about the old days too much, but really, the fifties team he'd played in and the sixties team he'd managed, both of them had been better teams than today's. He ran through the people he'd played with. 'Look at Ron Burgess, Ted Ditchburn. They would have been first choice players at any time. They were the best in their position in the country. Then look at the sixties team. Who was better than

227

Blanchflower, or McKay, or Bobby Smith, or tell me a winger better than Cliff Jones?

'I suppose it is unfortunate for the present team that I should have been involved in two excellent teams, but I think that should be a help not a hindrance. By having seen so much, it should help me to get the best out of them. The team can only benefit by my experience. I should know what I'm talking about. If I was a player in the present team, that's what I'd think. But I know some of them don't accept it. They think I'm living in the past.'

It was strange that he should have said this. I'd not heard one player say such a thing. To a man, they're all in awe of his record, as a player and as a manager. They know he's had more success than they'll ever have. They might think he's old fashioned in some senses, being against long hair, but that didn't worry them. That was a joke. But as a football manager, they had the utmost respect for him. The only moan I'd ever heard was that he didn't praise enough.

'I was no different with the sixties team. I only ever wanted the best. There is satisfaction for everyone in doing things right. There's no use being satisfied when things are done wrongly. I want to get perfection. It's no use telling players they're good when they're not. That doesn't help them.

'I read about managers who "get the best out of players". I don't know what that means. What does it mean? You tell me.

'I've spent all my life learning to read character. In the army I spent six and a half years handling people. I've discovered that it's best to tell people there's always a bit to go, that they must try harder, that they can do better.

'I get no pleasure out of being a manager. It's a job. I prefer coaching. I was happy as chief coach and didn't want to do anything else. Coaching is still what I like best, though now I can't give as much time and thought to it. When I was the coach and nothing else I used to try to spend two hours every afternoon, just sitting thinking things out, scribbling ideas on a bit of paper. I'd throw most of them away because nothing was coming. But sometimes they'd make a pattern which I could carry out in training. It might be a pattern which would keep me going for two or three weeks, with other ideas and patterns coming from it. I enjoy that very much. I still do it today, when I have time. Very often when I'm sitting at home I'm thinking of coaching routines. The thing about coaching is that you never stop thinking about it.

'When I took over as manager I introduced the best training schedules which any club had at the time. I can't tell you how we were trained when I was a player. I just can't. It was too bad to talk about, even now. I was one of the first to introduce the sort of organised training which all clubs have today. Danny Blanchflower once asked if I didn't think we were doing too much. Now it's accepted by everyone.

'I enjoyed discussing things with Danny. He's a great talker and he was a bloody good player and a good captain. He was as proud as I was of the success of the sixties team. I ran everything, but as today, any player in the team-talk can suggest ideas or changes. I *want* them to talk about the game, to think about it, but few of them do today. But Danny, he always did. He was a good captain in that sense and I backed to the hilt any decision he took on the field.

'Since Danny went, I've never been able to talk as well to anyone about the team. I miss that sometimes.'

He talked for a long time about Danny, as if he was worried about something. He kept on stressing how well they'd got on and how good Danny had been. When his playing days were over, Bill had made him assistant to the manager – not assistant manager as is sometimes thought – to help him with coaching and training. But it hadn't lasted long. Danny Blanchflower is now out of football, working as a sports journalist.

We were making such good time to Bristol, thanks to the new M4, that Bill suggested a cup of tea and a sandwich. We stopped at the next service station and sat down at an empty table. We were joined after a few minutes by a man who asked if there was a seat free. 'I might as well sit down with Billy Nicholson,' added the man, smiling in Bill's face.

Bill looked stern and his face showed no change of expression. The man wasn't at all aggressive or pushy. He was well dressed and rather hesitant. We all sat in silence for a few minutes. The man sensed the atmosphere but wasn't quite sure why.

'You are Billy Nicholson?' he said, stirring his tea, thinking perhaps he'd made a mistake.

Bill looked at him, then grunted an admittance.

'I thought you were. When are Spurs going to come good, then? Been a while now, hasn't it? Do you think they'll win the FA Cup?'

Bill said nothing. He was tearing open the cellophane wrapping of his ham sandwich. He started to eat the sandwich slowly and deliberately, staring straight through the man.

I felt sorry for the man, saying all the wrong things, yet doing it politely and pleasantly.

'My lad will be thrilled when I tell him I've met you,' said the man cheerfully drinking his tea. 'Who is it you play in the Cup? I've forgotten.'

I said it was Everton, away, and he nodded. I wasn't sure if Bill wanted him encouraged in any way, or whether he was hoping he'd just simply give up and disappear into a hole in the ground.

'This is not a new signing is it,' said the man looking at me, smiling. 'I'm not a reporter, don't get me wrong,' he added quickly. Bill gave a quick smile at this but still didn't reply.

'You know Billy, I used to watch you play at Tottenham. You and Ron Burgess playing together. I remember it well. What a team.'

He'd now revealed something about himself and I could feel Bill softening. He didn't mind talking, as long as it wasn't to reply to questions about today's team. He asked the man if he lived round Tottenham. He said no, but he'd been born there. He'd played in the district team as a schoolboy and even played once at White Hart Lane. Bill was very interested. The chat from then on became quite animated as Bill asked the man details about the district team and who else had been in it.

Back in the car, heading for Bristol, he said he hated being recognised by people. 'They always ask the same inane

230

questions about football. There's nothing I can say, so I prefer to say nothing.'

At Bristol City's ground, the doorman at the directors' entrance smiled at once when he saw Bill and welcomed him in. There was a murmuring round the box as Bill sat down. One or two leaned across and said hello but most people gave a quick stare and then nudged each other. We sat down just as the whistle blew for the kick-off.

I'd been looking forward to the match. I'd only seen Spurs reserves once that season, with always following the first team around, and it had been a scrappy, disappointing game, a 1-0 win at home against Plymouth reserves.

The Bristol crowd looked much bigger, more like a real match and less like a shadow game, the way it had done at Tottenham. But the first half was just as poor as the previous reserve match I'd seen, full of bad passes and bad positional play. Peter (Spud) Collins was continually misjudging the ball, going forward to head it, missing it and having to run back. I said perhaps there was a deceptive wind. 'There can't be a wind just out there,' said Bill.

Tony Want looked aggressive, but in coming forward he was losing the ball. The two wingers, Jimmy Pearce and John Cutbush were getting nowhere. 'Why don't they swap,' Bill kept on saying to himself. Only two Spurs players looked convincing – Terry Lee in goal who was brave, self-assured and made no mistakes, though twice he punched the ball away rather dangerously. Bill was very pleased, as he should have been, considering Terry was only Spurs' third choice goalkeeper. The other Spurs player who was showing any real signs of skill or class was little Phil Holder, all five foot three of him. Various people were leaning over to Bill and asking who he was. Bill sang Phil's praises, saying what a worker, what a tackler.

I followed Bill down to the dressing-room at half-time, but I didn't stay long.

I'd never heard Eddie in such a rage. I'd seen him many a time frothing at the mouth on the bench, screaming abuse at the first team, almost without realising it. But this time he was uncontrollable, shouting at Spud Collins, lashing into him about his diabolical game. Spud started to make a reply but Eddie turned and shrieked at him to shut up. He was only good with his mouth. The other players were hiding, keeping well out of the way. Bill stood silently in a corner.

I left and went upstairs and joined Mr Cox in the directors' room, where I had a cup of tea with the Bristol City directors. I knew why Eddie was so furious. Spud is one of his best reserves, one he admires tremendously, one he has great hopes for, one he would personally find a first team place for, if it was his decision. He'd been telling Bill for several weeks about how well Pete was doing in the reserves. Yet here he was, his big chance to really impress the manager, and he was throwing it away. He was letting himself down and he was letting Eddie down.

In the second half, Spurs played a bit better, but not much. Spiring for Bristol still looked the most dangerous player. 'They're never going to score,' groaned Bill. Seconds later, almost as if they'd heard him, Spurs did score. From a throw-in the ball went into the penalty area where Jenkins headed it across the goal for Jimmy Pearce to score. Not long afterwards, Spurs got another goal from a free kick headed in by Clarke. They won 2-0 which rather flattered them.

'Amazing isn't it,' said Eddie afterwards in the dressing-room, walking round and shaking his head. 'They do nothing yet score twice from a throw-in and a free kick. I don't understand it.'

John Pratt was coughing alarmingly in the corner. Graeme Sounness looked white. He'd come on for the last five minutes for Jenkins who'd been injured. 'I can feel blood in my mouth,' said Graeme, feeling his chest. 'I think it's with sitting in the cold for so long then suddenly coming on.'

Johnny Wallis was silently packing up the gear as usual. The coach driver from Tottenham had arrived and was standing waiting.

'Terry Lee did well,' said Bill walking round. Terry was in the bath and didn't hear the praise, alas for him. 'He got down very well,' continued Bill. Eddie nodded but said nothing. He'd exhausted his invective at half-time. Despite all his screaming and shouting they'd managed to win, yet without playing very much better.

Bill went up to the directors' room. The City manager

congratulated him, said Spurs had done well, and Bill said thanks, they were a good set of lads. Bill had a glass of sweet sherry and asked the best way out of Bristol to get on to the motorway.

Mr Cox came back with us in Bill's car rather than in the team coach. Bill religiously referred to him as Mr Cox and was very attentive and polite. He'd come a long way on a cold night for a football match, considering he was seventy-four, but he said he enjoyed it. Being a widower and being retired he could get away for midweek matches easier than some of the other directors who had family and business commitments.

Bill talked for a while about the match, especially about how well Phil Holder had played. He said it wasn't really a worry about his height. 'Every team can stand one small player.'

While Mr Cox dozed on the back seat Bill got onto his next day's problems, planning what he was going to do in training. He'd already done a thirteen-hour day that day, training all morning at Cheshunt, working in his office at the ground in the afternoon and then Bristol for the evening. But his mind as ever was still on football, thinking out new training patterns. I asked if he didn't think there was too much training today. A lot of the old timers maintain that teams have become regimented and soulless with in-dividuality gone.

'I regret the day that the theories of 4-3-3 or 4-4-2 came in. People think that one is an attacking formation and the other defensive. There's no such thing. It misleads people, including players. Players think they are there to defend rather than attack. It makes a so-called defensive midfield man think he should always drop back rather than push forward, even when he's got the chance. I never talk about 4-3-3 or 4-4-2. It restricts thinking.'

He then moved on to his other perennial problem, scout-ing for new players. There's hardly a week goes by without him showing an interest in some player. Even when he knows there's not a hope of the player moving, he might still ring up the manager and register interest. 'Some you never bother to ask about. Would a manager ever ring me up and ask to

233

buy Chivers?' He half smiled. Chivers might think from time to time that his manager doesn't love him enough, but Chivers just has to think about the rivals for his position, then he's bound to smile all the way to the bank.

Bill said he'd gone the previous Saturday morning to watch some primary schoolboys play. That means eleven-year-olds, kids hardly out of the cradle. Scouts don't usually start till boys are thirteen and fourteen.

'There was a boy there who scored a text-book goal. He got the ball on the half line almost, came forward, beat his man and shot from twenty yards. It made me smile to see it. You couldn't have wished for a better goal.'

He'd got the boy's name, contacted his teacher and generally made himself known. It's illegal to sign boys at eleven but you can make contact. The chances are that a precocious boy of eleven might never develop any further, but it's still worth showing an interest. At eleven, Bill himself was playing for an Under 14 team.

It was misty and rainy at Spurs. Bill got out of his car and went across to Mr Cox's car and wiped his windows for him and saw him safely out of the car park. Then he turned his car round and drove up White Hart Lane and home.

It was just after midnight. Darky was pleased to see him home so early. When he goes to the North or to Scotland for evening matches, then he's home a lot later.

Their thirtieth wedding anniversary was coming up soon – on 1 March 1972. She'd mentioned it a few weeks previously but didn't want to mention it again. 'Thirty years?' said Bill when she pointed it out to him. 'Have I put up with you that long?'

Bill went to bed almost straight away, leaving her to lock up. When she came to bed, he checked that she had done everything she was supposed to have done.

'It's the same routine every night he's at home. Have I locked the front, have I locked the back, have I taken out the TV plug. I say yes, yes, yes, then if he can, he'll find an excuse to go downstairs, just to prove I've forgotten something. With Bill, it's very hard to do anything right.'

It's very noticeable in his football work, this passion for looking after every little detail himself. I'd noticed many

234

times that he will do little jobs which could quite easily be left to other people.

Like all his players, and his staff, his wife values any morsel of praise which Bill happens to give. 'If you get a compliment from Bill you feel ten feet tall. His idea is that by not giving out the compliments very often you'll try to keep up your standards all the time. He was the same with the children and they did very well, in their school work and in sport. If he ever does say something nice I say "Can I have that in writing." I rarely get complimented on my meals. I'm not one for cooking. I don't like it and I'm not very good. Sewing and soft furnishing is my thing. But when I do serve up something good the whole family will say "How did you make this mistake."'

In his manner, his humour and his views, Bill is very Yorkshire, which he himself is proud of. He reprimanded me that evening on the journey to Bristol for asking what he considered an impudent question. I'd asked him what his date of birth was. He almost stopped the car.

'Where I come from that's looked upon as very cheeky, asking someone their age. You just don't do that sort of thing.' I smiled, but he obviously didn't think it was at all funny. 'I hope you haven't been asking the players their ages? I make a rule at the ground that no one is to give out a player's address, phone number or date of birth.'

Bill Nicholson is stuck with his personality. It's obviously and patently a good one for his job, even though it might make him difficult at times to live with or work for. In a shifting world he is a man of steadfast principle.

His wife thinks the clue to him is the army. He probably would still have been a soldier today, if it hadn't been for football.

'Bill's never come out of the army. He imposes army discipline at work and he's like a sergeant major at home. He's very fussy about everything in the house. He wants everything spotless. His suits have to be absolutely right. All his shirts are hung up on a hanger. When I've ironed them he inspects each collar and if it's not right I have to do it again.

'I don't think he'll change now. He's been like that since

he was a boy when I first met him. His mother was just as fussy. You should have seen her laundering. Spotless. And she had a family of nine to look after! It didn't do her any harm. She died at eighty-four, about eight years ago. Bill loved his mother. She was a wonderful woman. Bill's like his mother, a perfectionist.'

20

Mullery Misses a Party

Mike England couldn't have picked a worse night to have a party. All footballers hate social occasions when they've been beaten. But when it's been *your* particular fault, then showing your face is almost unbearable. After a run of so many good performances, Mike had suddenly got nothing to celebrate. That afternoon Spurs had been beaten 1-0 by Derby at home – the goal coming from Mike's bad back pass. But there was no way out of it, even if he'd wanted to cancel everything. Invitations had gone out over a month ago. The caterers were booked. The champagne was ordered. The mobile discotheque was coming, complete with flashing lights, amplifiers and all the other gear which no smart 1972 party could be without.

All that was missing to have made it a really smart 1972 middle-class party would have been a few reefers, but footballers wouldn't touch such things. Some footballers might have moved into the middle classes but there are two things they won't have at their parties – drugs and homosexuals.

Most players, despite their money and their big houses, stand out from their neighbours and find it hard to mix, especially the wives. When they move in beside the architects and the solicitors and the doctors, fresh and rather flash from their council estates, they become the talk of the neighbourhood, but the novelty soon wears off, apart from amongst the neighbours' children, and they eventually tend to be left alone. It doesn't matter so much for the husband, who's so often away touring the world, but the wife has very little in common with her new neighbours. They are very alone when their husbands are away. But Mike and his wife Gwen have assimilated well. Mike is an active member of the local Round Table. Acceptance doesn't come higher.

They live with their two boys, Darren and Wayne, and

baby Gabrielle, in a large architect-designed house in the village of Broxbourne, a few miles further along the road to Cambridge from the club's training ground at Cheshunt. It looks the sort of house a smart young businessman would have, all careful good taste, nothing flash or nasty. There's a Victorian chaise longue in the entrance hall and louvred doors behind, contrasting nicely with the brand new bright thick pile carpets and gleaming sofas and chairs. There's a huge lawn at the back where the two boys feed squirrels. Once, they even had a pheasant in the garden. The house is worth £25,000. Mike has come a long way from his council house in North Wales.

There were about sixty people at the party from different walks of life, reflecting Mike and Gwen's local social position and his professional life. As befitted an active member of the Round Table, there were doctors, solicitors and similar professional people, plus young businessmen with county set wives. I got talking to one very smooth man in a velvet suit who said he had an art gallery in Mayfair. He was talking about having just been to see Mr Heath, the Prime Minister. One of his artists was doing a painting of *Morning Cloud.* There was even a well-known girl pop singer at the party, Olivia Newton-John.

About three-quarters of the Spurs team were there. The younger ones like Ray Evans, John Pratt and Jimmy Neighbour stood around with their wives or girlfriends, glowing freshness and eagerness, obviously very pleased to be there. But one or two of their ladies looked a bit nervous, watching their husbands for a lead, wanting to say and do the right thing, but not getting much help as the boys tended to talk to each other. The main joke of the evening was Ralph Coates, once again. He'd played in a practice match that morning, not being fit enough for the first team, and had actually scored a goal. 'Did you hear what Bill said to me afterwards,' said Ralph, telling everyone in turn. 'He said who was I trying to pass to? Bloody cheek.'

All the younger players, including Ralph, seemed to be wearing identical flared trousers, immaculately creased and pressed, and printed cotton shirts with long collars. Ray had arrived in a suit and tie but once he saw the others were

238

casual, his jacket, waistcoat and tie came right off. He folded them very carefully on a chair in a corner.

The wives were just as immaculate, with lacquered hair and long elaborate party dresses. Martin Peters' wife was in trousers, the only player's wife confident enough to be really casual, but of course her husband was now the team captain. She was trying to pull Martin onto the dance floor from the moment she arrived. Joe Kinnear was there, with his girl friend Bonnie, but he hardly left the kitchen. Brian Curtin, the club doctor and his wife Jilly, were in the thick of it all. 'I'm driving home,' said Jilly as Brian was knocking it back. 'When he's awake he always back seat drives. I prefer it when he just falls asleep in his seat.'

Pat Jennings and his wife Eleanor, heavily pregnant, kept mainly to themselves and didn't go in for any jumping around on the dance floor. Alan Gilzean arrived late, looking as usual unlike any of the other footballers. He was in an old fashioned twopiece dark suit and white shirt. He slipped quietly in, as if it was a business call, come to read the meter. There were none of the quick smiles or hurried glances in the mirror to check his hair and shirt, the way the younger ones had done. He was hardly noticed as he picked out a vacant seat and went straight to it, drink in hand. You could feel he'd been to many parties and had got his priorities right. He wasn't going to waste time on any social chit-chat.

The local middle classes hardly spoke to the footballers in their floral shirts, sticking mainly to their own groups. Footballers anyway are hard to talk to. Outside football, they're underdeveloped personalities with no outside interests or chit-chat, apart from in-jokes at each other's expense, unintelligible to outsiders. Yet they were all confident and at ease. Since the age of eleven they've had the respect of their peers, through being good at football, so they don't lack in self-confidence, even in a non-footballing milieu. They wouldn't want any middle class cocktail chit-chat, even if they were capable of it.

Mike England, the exception to all this, a player who actively likes the middle class life, was doing his bit as a good host, going round introducing people along with his wife Gwen. On his walls, discreetly displayed, were the two original paintings he'd brought back from Rumania, pretty water colours in gilt frames. The rest of them had brought back fluffy dolls.

For the sake of the party atmosphere, they'd added round the walls a few colour photographs of half-naked black girls in provocative but artistic positions. 'I know I'm prejudiced,' said Ray Evans eyeing one up, 'But I wouldn't say no to her.' He and his wife had found another house to buy, having lost three in the last six months. They were looking confident and prosperous, as befitted a regular first team member. Joe Kinnear, on the other hand, was still hovering in the kitchen, away from the other players.

Ray's wife said he now felt confident of his position in the first team. 'But he's only seventy-five per cent happy, that's all.' It had been discovered that a stomach upset he'd had a few weeks ago, causing him to miss a game, was now going to be with him for life. 'It started with gastroenteritis last year,' said Ray. 'I had it very bad. It's left colitis. The doctor says I'll never get rid of it. It can come again at any time. It upsets your bowels and makes you weak. I don't know what brings it on. It might be psychological I don't know. All that worrying about my contract in the early part of the season didn't help. What the doctor's been doing now is giving me an injection twenty-four hours before a match. It's just a tonic, to counter any trouble I might get. I had it today and I felt great. It's just something I've got to live with.'

Cyril Knowles was there, making wisecracks and giggling with the younger players. He'd been back for some time in his regular first team position. Tony Want had only lasted a few games and hadn't played very well. Cyril was once again as confident as he'd ever been.

About the only famous Spurs face who wasn't there to hear all the chat, to partake at the lavish buffet, to lap up all the champagne, was Alan Mullery. No one mentioned him.

As they all danced and enjoyed themselves, basking in their own success and affluence, Alan Mullery was trudging back in a second-class carriage from Hull with a group of lowly Second Division footballers. Alan Mullery had started the season with the best years ahead of him, for Spurs and for England. Now it looked as if his future was behind him.

Earlier that week, after four months out of first team football, Mullery had gone in to see Bill Nicholson. He was desperate to get back in the first team. He'd had four games in the reserves, in gruelling conditions, and had felt no ill effects.

'I was beginning to think they weren't in a hurry to have me better, that they didn't want me any more, now that the team was doing so well.

'Bill said the side was doing well, so he couldn't change it. The way they were playing, I'd have to continue in the reserves for the rest of the season, unless someone was injured. Bill is a very shrewd and a very clever man. I understood his embarrassment, having me, the club captain, better, but not able to give him a place. It didn't matter to him that I was captain or played for England. He simply didn't want to change his team.

'I said how disappointed I was at missing the game earlier in the week. If only I'd gone as sub, he could have shoved me on for ten minutes at the end, as they were doing so well. It would have given me a little first team run-out. He didn't like that at all! He said he didn't do such things. He said he wasn't sentimental.

'I could see his dilemma but I said reserve football wasn't any good to me. I wanted to play in a first team, anybody's first team, so I might as well get away. I said I'd heard that Fulham had been after me. He said I wasn't being transferred. So I said what about a loan. He said he'd have to see the directors. The answer came back quicker than I expected. I was off to Fulham the next day. But as I went, Bill reminded me I was still captain and still a Tottenham Hotspur player.

'I need to *play*. I must have competition. I couldn't stick two months till the end of the season in Spurs reserves. I've had too many good years at Tottenham to play in the reserves. Fulham is the only club who've approached for me, so I'm going there. I didn't have any choice of clubs. I needn't have gone anywhere, but it's better than reserve football. But Tottenham is still the only club I want to play for.'

So on Saturday 11 March, while Spurs were at home to

241

Derby, Mullers made the trail up to Hull with Fulham. They went second class, which Spurs never do, and didn't stay at the sort of luxury hotel which Spurs usually use. 'It was a very strange feeling.'

People on the train, in the crowded second class compartments, actually asked Mullery who he was. That never happens at Spurs. There's always somebody on a train or a platform who recognises the team, then the buzz goes round.

'As we sat down in the train, a woman said are you a football team. I said yes and she said which one. I nearly said Tottenham but managed to say Fulham just in time. She said "Oh".'

It was a long journey for nothing – they got beaten 4-0. Mullery injured an ankle before the end and had to come off. 'I seem to have a sign on me. It can happen in football. You get a plague of injuries, a run of bad luck, and nothing seems to go right.

'When we gave away the first goal the heads dropped and they looked beaten already. That would never happen at Spurs. I think at Fulham they take the manager a bit more for granted than we do at Spurs. If Spurs get beaten, there's silence in the dressing-room. Nobody speaks. Nobody looks at each other. You daren't look at Bill, not when you get beaten. But the Fulham lads were soon laughing and joking, almost as if they'd won. They seem to accept losing.'

Mullery had been rather brave, hiding his pride and going voluntarily to play for a lowly Second Division club. It would have been easy to have continued at Spurs, resting in the wings, his status as club captain and an England star still intact, till at least the end of the season. By deliberately severing himself from the club he might well be precipitating the end. Bill had stressed it was just a month's loan, but few people in football thought he would ever come back. Mullery himself had few hopes. He was now over thirty. Playing as a midfield man is a gruelling job at any age, but someone ten years younger, like Phil Holder, the young reserve who'd just made his debut, was obviously a much better prospect.

Looking ahead, he presumed that he would see the season out with Fulham, then during the summer Spurs would quietly and officially transfer him. He'd already decided in his mind he wouldn't go to Fulham. He wasn't going to a Third Division, or even a Second Division club.

'If Spurs finally decide they don't want me, I'm going to try for another First Division club. I'm only thirty, for God's sake. I've got some good years yet. I *know* I have.'

21

Super Leeds

Leeds had not been talked about in training all week, which is normal, but there wasn't a great feeling of confidence. On paper, Leeds were on form and stood the better chance of getting into the FA Cup semi-finals. Though Spurs had already taken three out of four points from Leeds in their two League games, few of the experts gave them a chance. Martin Peters, writing his first column as captain of Spurs in the *Evening Standard* (the first since Mullery went to Fulham) said Spurs weren't going for the ride, but he didn't sound very convincing.

'This is the big one,' said Geoffrey Richardson as we got on the five o'clock train to Leeds on Friday evening. He was there with his wife, as was the chairman, Mr Wale. A party of fourteen players had been chosen, but no one yet knew which eleven would play. Phil Holder, despite his good work at home the previous week against Derby, wasn't included. For such a big match his lack of experience might tell.

It was presumed by most people that the vacant number 4 position would be taken by either Ralph Coates or John Pratt. Ralph Coates had at last been declared match fit, having missed the previous five games. Not being included against Leeds would be a big blow to his pride. Two first team players had already that season failed to get their place back after an injury – Joe Kinnear and Mullery. Would Ralph be the third international star to be dropped? His track record so far at Spurs had been very disappointing.

Over dinner on the train, sitting in state on the Pullman, Phil Beal was boasting about The Clan, a group of seven star players from different clubs whose photographs had been in the papers that week. They included Geoff Hurst, Rodney Marsh, Francis Lee and Phil Beal, the only Spurs player in the group. They were photographed, posed round a table, in frilly shirts, smoking cigars and trying hard to look like swingers. Phil explained that it was a publicity gimmick dreamt up to make money.

'But where do you get the money from?' said Ray Evans.

'When we've established the image of The Clan, we'll get a lot of sponsorship, see. We've already had a free suit each. We might sell ourselves to a big company, the way Georgie Best has done. We're just starting. Whatever happens, we can't lose.'

'Got a club tie,' asked someone. 'How about a club jock strap,' said another. But despite the jokes, they obviously wished they were in on something which could make such easy money. Most of them get approached by agents with a view to sponsorship, but very few of the big ideas ever happen.

The Queens Hotel in Leeds was already full of Spurs supporters, the well-heeled ones, from rag trade moguls to car salesmen, who'd driven up during the day in their limousines. Morris Keston was already there, installed in his suite. So was Phil Issacs, boss of the Sportsman, the Tottenham Court Road club well frequented by footballers. (Their names go up in the foyer to let more humble members know which big stars are in tonight.) Some of the players' relations had arrived – Ray Evans' sister was sitting in the lounge. Bill Nicholson was wandering round the reception looking worried, waiting for his daughter Linda and husband John who were coming over from Bradford. The next day, approximately eleven thousand Spurs fans were due to make the journey up from London, the biggest contingent of the season. There's nothing like a big Cup match against a big team for bringing out the big crowds.

Linda, Bill's daughter, eventually arrived. She was very excited about the match. 'I probably won't sleep tonight.' She joined her father for sandwiches. Bill's son-in-law John had remarkably long hair for a member of the Nicholson family. It was as long as any of his players', apart from Roger Morgan's. Roger was having his sandwiches in a far corner, talking to some friends from the motor trade.

Just before ten o'clock, two of the Leeds stars, Eddie Gray and Peter Lorimer, popped their heads into the lounge on

245

their way to bed. 'We stay here every Friday night before a home match,' said Eddie Gray. 'Room 303, always the same one. We've both got young babies who keep us awake. Don rings us at ten to make sure we're in bed.'

In one corner Steve Perryman and Pat Jennings were being chatted up by two blokes trying to interest them in using their names for sponsorship. One was the managing director of a Leeds sportswear firm and the other turned out to be someone I knew, Paul Trevillion. Fresh from his success as an artist drawing footballers (he did the diagrams at the end of this book, which proves how successful he is). Trevillion now apparently was moving into new fields. I knew nothing about it till I went across and listened to his spiel.

'I'll be the biggest name in sport in a year,' he was telling Steve and Pat in his usual modest way. They didn't blink, being too polite to laugh in anyone's face. 'I've taken over the Leeds team in just six weeks, haven't I, Harvey,' he said, turning to his friend for confirmation. 'Tomorrow Leeds will come out and do things which have never been seen on a football field before. I promise you.'

'It's true,' said Harvey, on cue this time. 'When the Beaver says something, he does it.' Trevillion is known by himself, and hopefully by others, as the Beaver. It can be rather confusing for strangers when he starts talking about himself in the third person as the Beaver.

'It might not be tomorrow,' added Trevillion, for once being careful. 'Don might keep it back for next week's home game against Arsenal. But you'll see in the end. The Beaver's done it again!'

Steve and Pat looked polite but unimpressed. I got the feeling they didn't understand what was going on.

'I only want five *special* players and I've got two already, Francis Lee and Terry Cooper.' He pulled out a portfolio of drawings and plans and started ranting about something called the TC6, which was a new training shoe, so revolutionary he couldn't reveal the details.

'It's no use doing something irrelevant like The Clan. They've gone for the wrong image, concentrating on being swingers and chasing birds. That's going to put the mums

246

off. It's the mums who buy most football shirts and track suits. The Clan should stick to its image as *footballers*. Nothing else.'

Steve and Pat nodded. They'd been thinking this on the train. 'I want you two on my list because you're both special.' Steve and Pat sat up waiting to hear what was so special about them, wondering why Chivers or Peters hadn't been picked to benefit from the Beaver's brilliance.

'You're playing very well, Steve,' said Trevillion, pausing for breath, giving his hard sell a chance to sink in.

'No I'm not,' said Steve quickly. 'I'm not playing well at all.'

Trevillion had slipped up on his homework for once. Any close study of Spurs that season should have told Trevillion that. And any close study of Perryman would have shown him that flattery would get him nowhere. Steve is nothing if not a realist.

'I know you've got an agent, Pat,' said Trevillion, changing the subject.

'He's done very little for me . . .' said Pat.

'But I don't want to be your agent,' said Trevillion, giving Pat no chance to continue. 'I'm not after your twenty per cent. If you decide to sponsor any of the goods we have in mind, *you* keep it all.'

'So what's in it for you?' I asked Trevillion.

'I get a copyright fee as the designer of the products,' he said.

'It's got to be gloves for you, Pat, for a start. From this minute on I want you to deny you've got big hands, OK? In interviews you say it's not true'. Pat held up his huge hands, great slabs of them, as if amazed himself by their size. 'It's not your big hands which help you Pat. It's your specially designed gloves. Isn't it? Yes! Well don't forget it.

'What would you say are your best points Steve,' said Trevillion. 'Tackling? I'd say you were a brilliant tackler. Harvey, we'll do a special tackling boot for Steve.'

'It's getting in the right position for a tackle that matters most,' said Steve quietly.

'Yes, I'd say it was your tackling, plus your non-stop energy,' continued Trevillion. 'Energy, that's it. Perryman

247

Dextrose tablets! I can see them now. It's what the chemical industry's been waiting for. When you give interviews or go on telly you'll suck them all the time. OK? As the whistle blows, you put one in your mouth, facing the cameras. OK? And when reporters ask you afterwards if you're tired, you say you're *never* tired. You could do with another ninety minutes, you've got so much energy left.'

'What if the tablets are no good,' said Steve. 'You can sell things once, but not a second time. It wouldn't do Pat or me any good, or Spurs.'

'They will be good. If you believe in them, others will. Listen, you've got just ninety minutes a week to project yourself. Life is short. You've got to look after yourself. In that ninety minutes you've got millions watching. Spurs are on TV every week aren't they?'

'Almost,' said Pat.

'So it's the biggest free commercial slot in the world! You could do anything, yet no one's tried. Tomorrow you'll see something which will kill you. Leeds have seen sense. The players went in to see Don saying we want the Beaver. He refused at first, now he's agreed.'

'Bill would never agree . . .' said Steve.

'I've cracked harder nuts than him,' said Trevillion. They both smiled.

'Look at your team,' said Trevillion. 'You're all faceless. Apart from Chivers who is there? Who does the public know? Look at Coates. A British record at £190,000 and the only thing people know about him is his dodgy knee. I could guarantee to increase Spurs gates by ten thousand a time, just by promoting the players. The club does everything wrong. The manager only moans. The directors are faceless. Look at Shankley, screaming about his new star Keegan. People come specially to see him. When has Bill ever said any of his players are great?' There was no answer to that one.

Saturday morning was very misty. The directors and their lady wives were up early and went window shopping along the Leeds boulevards. Most of the players had a late breakfast, spinning out the morning.

Over in the Leeds camp they were all quietly confident of victory. Don Revie had said publicly that with the home advantage they could have no excuses. As at Spurs, the scouts and spies had produced masses of notes on the rival team. I talked to one of the Leeds spies who'd been sent specially to see Spurs on three occasions in recent weeks. His report was very damning. Each Spurs player sounded like a condemned man about to be sentenced for life. These reports are meant to be destructive. The scout was looking purely for weaknesses which could be exploited, not for points to praise.

'Spurs are not co-ordinating as a team,' he said. 'They have too many individuals who are not giving enough. Personally, I wouldn't have Peters on my side. When a side is winning he plays very well, getting round the blind side into space, but he lacks the strength to contain the opposition in midfield when things are going badly.

'I wouldn't have Coates either in my side. All he can do is run, usually into people or through people. He has no distribution. To have an ace team you need people who can play well in all circumstances. Peters and Coates can't.

'Spurs' big weakness is in midfield, mainly because of Peters and Coates. I only hope they don't put Holder in. When I've seen Spurs play recently he's been their best midfield man. I can understand the decision if he's not picked because of his lack of experience, but personally I'd take a chance and play him.

'I rate Perryman, but he hasn't yet developed into the great player that seemed likely last season. It might just be lack of help. A midfield player has to be a winner *and* a creator. It's pointless winning the ball if you can't then do something with it, which is what often happens to Perryman. But Perryman might be able to create more chances with more help around him.

'As for Morgan, I've never rated him. But I must admit he's fighting hard at the moment, now he's been moved back to midfield. But I wouldn't have bought him.

'Amongst the forwards, Chivers can be magnificent. He's so powerful and strong and deceptive, accelerating just when you think he's going to stop. But away from home he's being left too much on his own. He needs someone like our Alan

249

Clarke beside him, capitalising on his work. I'm not saying that Clarke and Jones together don't do well, but Clarke and Chivers would be unstoppable.

'Gilzean is an enigma. He's a good asset in set pieces, with his flicks, but he's too easy to blot out. He hasn't got the strength or the aggression to burst the skin off a rice pudding. He doesn't want to know if anyone comes in hard. You can't afford this sort of player in any team.

'The defence is fairly sound. Beal and England are doing grand jobs. I didn't think much of Evans earlier on. I thought he was very ordinary but he's getting better all the time. But Knowles, he's not to my taste. I think he's awkwardly aggressive.

'Pratt has never played when I've been scouting Spurs. I didn't give a report on him.

'That leaves Jennings. I take my bloody hat off to him. I've thought once or twice I've spotted his weakness. I saw him once go for the near post a bit early, leaving his far post empty. I thought that's it, that's his weakness. But he never did it again. Every time I've seen him he's been magnificent.

'These are just my personal views. All I've done is put them in my report and give them to Don Revie. He has his own views, from his own observations. He alone decides the tactics. I'm sure the Spurs scouts will have picked on Sprake and Charlton as our two weaknesses, but they always underrate Jack. They think because he's thirty-seven he's past it. But we've only had one game a week recently and it's been just what he's needed.

'People still underestimate the Leeds team. Most of the players were not rated at all by other clubs at one time, now the whole team is blossoming, just the way we all knew it would. Spurs are a good team. No one ever underrates what they can do. But at this moment the whole is not co-ordinating. Their weakness in midfield is stopping the rest from developing.'

Back at the Spurs' hotel, John Pratt came out of the team meeting looking quietly pleased. Ralph Coates looked straight ahead, catching no one's eye. John was in the team. Ralph wasn't. Then they all went into the dining-room for an early lunch.

Even by Bill's standards, he'd been unusually pessimistic in the meeting, telling them not to worry if they got beaten 2-0. 'Someone's got to lose,' he'd said. 'And if we're losing, just keep playing as well as you can.' In going through the Leeds team he'd made them all sound like superstars. As his players all knew that anyway, it didn't help their confidence very much.

On the coach to Elland Road Bill spread himself out on a double seat and beamed round. 'OK Martin,' he said, smiling at Martin Chivers who was grimly looking out of the window. 'You could put the fear of death into them today. Sprake's scared of you and so is Charlton. That's two for a start Martin. That's not bad, is it?' Martin smiled bravely but didn't reply. He was sitting alone, knowing only too well how everyone, manager, player and supporter alike, was expecting miracles from him.

The Leeds United ground was already full of chanting fans with still an hour to go. The players as usual went straight onto the pitch to inspect it and were greated with a welcoming cheer from the eleven thousand Spurs fans who'd collected at one end. The Leeds fans at the other end replied with the usual obscenities – Tottenham Shit – just to get the right party spirit.

Bill was talking to Martin Peters in the middle of the pitch, working out which way the sun would be in the second half. The others prodded the surface, trying to ignore the screaming fans. Pat Jennings had his hands behind his back in the best Prince Philip style. I could see them visibly shaking. I pointed it out to Dr. Curtin.

'I've noticed it for some time,' he said. 'It means nothing. But footballers who are going to get diseases in later life can perhaps get the signs earlier than other people. Their physical training is so hard that it can bring out weakness that wouldn't normally be apparent in such young men.'

They all trailed slowly back into their dressing-room. Spurs were to play in yellow, being the away team, while Leeds would be in their normal all white. In the corridor, Bill asked Ralph if he was fit. Ralph said he felt great. In that case he was to be sub.

Inside the dressing-room, unaware yet that Ralph had

251

been chosen as sub, Jimmy Pearce and Peter Collins were sitting in a corner in their good suits watching the first eleven getting undressed. 'Have you seen the boots yet?' whispered Pete to Jimmy. They both stared round looking for signs. Ralph came in and started taking his clothes off. 'You owe me a quid, Spud,' said Jimmy.

'Any of you players want oiled,' said Ralph, smiling and looking round. 'I might as well help out.'

John Pratt came back from the lavatory and announced that he'd seen a sign on the Leeds dressing-room as he'd come past. It had said 'Keep Fighting'.

Nobody said anything. They knew that it was true. It was the first time I'd been consciously aware of the Spurs team worrying about their opponents. Against Nantes, earlier in the season, Spurs had been tense but more because of the strangeness of the setting than worry.

About two thirty, Bill started going round the players in turn, going over what they each had to do. 'Watch Eddie Gray when he drags the ball back,' he told Ray Evans. 'He does it with either foot, then he suddenly moves forward. Don't be fooled by it.' Ray nodded solemnly.

He went over to Steve and John Pratt about their roles in midfield, working out who would take whom. 'I'll take Giles,' said Steve. 'I'd prefer to.' Bill looked at him and said what about Bremner, wouldn't he be better with Bremner? Steve said no, he thought he'd be best marking Giles. Bill then moved on to Roger Morgan. He was told to make a tackle only when he had a good chance. 'I don't want you throwing yourself around when you haven't a chance. I don't want you on the ground. Keep on your feet. Only commit yourself if you've got a chance.'

'This is it lads,' said Martin Peters loudly, looking grim, doing his captain's bit. 'All out today lads!'

'We'll be in the semis after this,' shouted someone else, loudly.

'Let's really go!'

These shouts of self-encouragement had been sudden and now there was silence. The players couldn't think of what else to say or do, apart from looking round sternly and clenching their fists, showing how serious they were. Bill said

252

little else, waiting at the door to administer his final good wishes. This was a match whose importance didn't need to be rubbed in.

The Leeds team had gone out first, in fact a good ten minutes before three o'clock, and were apparently causing a sensation. Their whole squad, twelve players and trainer Les Cocker, were in gleaming white track suit tops with their names printed large in blue on the back. It was the first time such a thing had been seen in the English First Division. On the outside of each stocking top hung the player's number, another innovation. But the biggest gimmick was their exercises. They ran in formation to the far corner of the pitch and started dancing in unison, high kicking, bending and jumping, all perfectly together and in time. They went round the pitch and performed to each section of the crowd in turn. They radiated confidence and fitness and the crowd went wild with excitement.

When the Spurs came out the boos were equally tremendous. At least at Liverpool, the home of crowd excitement, they'd managed a cheer for the visiting side. But the Leeds crowd were now in a state of almost Nuremburg hysteria.

In the directors' box Mr Wale, was visibly upset. A big cup match in England is after all supposed to be partly a gala day. 'I remember when we came here for the first time after we'd won the double and the European title. We were booed onto the pitch, the only place we were booed. The crowd has never liked us here.'

Whether it was the excitement of their calisthetics or their innate skills, Leeds played the first twenty minutes as if they really were footballing gods. Their brilliance was frightening. Don Revie said later he'd never seen such twenty minutes of football in all his life. Spurs looked honest, solid journeymen, completely outclassed by the eleven artists of the Leeds team. It wouldn't have been unfair if Leeds had scored four goals in those first twenty minutes. They built up from the back, through the midfield and out to the wings in an intricate yet inevitable series of moves. Spurs defended stubbornly. They didn't become desperate or start fouling or obstructing. They simply didn't have a chance. Leeds hit the bar once, shot just wide three times and missed two open goals. Pat Jennings,

253

the only Spurs player to match their brilliance, saved at least three certain goals. It seemed impossible for Leeds not to score. Sometimes, when a team is unable to score, despite making all the running, they get over-excited, almost despairing, and start being frantic and eventually lose their cohesion. But Leeds didn't break rank or break spirit. They seemed to *know* they were the chosen team. Though Spurs were having miraculous escapes, nothing could stop Leeds, so why panic or worry.

After twenty minutes Spurs at last got a breathing space, not through Leeds letting up but through Spurs' indominatable spirit at last producing a few counter-moves. Peters narrowly missed with a side flick and Chivers had two good runs. Nevertheless the Spurs moves seemed gestures, sent only to underline the superiority of Leeds.

And then, just five minutes before half-time, as if to prove once again what a daft game football can be, Spurs scored. John Pratt sent a long hopeful lob towards the near post. Chivers jumped for it but didn't get it. Charlton and Hunter both jumped, with Sprake waiting behind. Unaccountably all three missed and the ball bounced into the net.

It was the sort of unfair piece of luck which teams hope for against Sprake, who is prone to such mistakes, but it had seemed impossible today with Leeds in such command and Spurs not once putting him in any real danger.

A couple of minutes later Leeds were even. A series of fierce shots, all luckily scrambled away, finally ended in the Spurs net. It wasn't a brilliant goal, considering all the brilliant moves Leeds had made, but it was well deserved.

Leeds started the second half like the first, forcing Spurs' defence back on its heels for twenty minutes of constant pressure. In this twenty-minute spell Leeds got their second goal. Again, it wasn't an inspired piece of football art, simply one of Leeds' best known dead ball situations. Charlton came up for a free kick, in full sight of everyone, rose in the air completely unimpeded and headed easily into the net.

Leeds could have scored several more but were stopped by Jennings' continued brilliance. Towards the end Spurs produced their best spell of the match. In the last twenty minutes they forced several corners and made a few breaks.

254

They'd scored one lucky goal. It wasn't impossible for them to do it again. With Sprake so patently insecure, Spurs just needed to get the ball in the Leeds penalty area to have a chance of forcing a draw. A draw would have been grossly unfair, but it was suddenly eminently possible. The crowd was becoming slightly impatient with Leeds' consummate passing and ball control, urging them to go forward, begging for another goal to sink Spurs once and for all. The game finished 2-1, a score line which flattered Spurs if anything. Four goals to nil would not have been unfair, yet Spurs had played well, keeping their heads and always trying. Admittedly Chivers and Gilzean had done very little, but they'd had little service, and Martin Peters had disappeared. He was finally brought off and Coates went on. Leeds were man for man superior to Spurs in every department, apart from Jennings, but though they had been humbled by Leeds, they'd not been humiliated.

While the exuberant Leeds players threw off their stocking tabs to the shrieking crowds, scattering flowers for the faithful, Spurs trooped into their dressing-room, saddened and dejected. Immediately they started arguing amongst themselves, which was even sadder. Bill demanded to know why Charlton had been allowed the header from the free kick, saying there had been no need for the defensive wall. Pat Jennings said he'd shouted that he hadn't wanted a wall, but they'd gone ahead and done it. The defence turned on each other, looking for someone to blame for not marking Charlton.

'I was marking two men,' shouted England. 'It wasn't my fault. I shouted to someone to go with him.'

'It wasn't me,' shouted Cyril Knowles.

'Who was at the back?' demanded Gilly.

'Roger Morgan was,' said England. 'But he couldn't have stopped Charlton. Somebody else should have been there.'

'Don't blame me,' said Knowles. 'It wasn't my bloody job.'

The voices got louder as they shouted. Bill kept silent, not joining in. Chivers and Peters sat very quietly, their heads bowed. It was mainly Gilly, Knowles and England doing all the shouting. I'd never heard the players raise their voices at each other before. Any post-match anger is usually subdued.

255

When Bill Nicholson criticises a player, the player goes all sullen, rarely shouting back. This time the post mortem fury was aimed at each other. After his first question Bill wasn't blaming anybody. But watching each of them, and their fury, it was obvious that it was themselves they were blaming. The argument continued in the bath, still going over who should have been marking Charlton. They were releasing their own emotions, the pent-up tension brought about by their own impotence.

When it had calmed down, Ray Evans said very quietly that Leeds were the better team. That was all there was to it. 'They're a different class.' Everybody nodded, agreeing they were a great team. 'No chance,' said Gilly sadly.

'We can have no complaints,' said Bill. The hot air had gone and the players were all humble and quietened. 'They ran and ran off the ball,' continued Bill. 'The man on the ball always had two choices. We didn't do that.'

'That Giles,' said Gilly. 'What a player. Fantastic. No chance.'

Bill didn't look too downhearted. He'd seemed fatalistic beforehand and now it had happened, perhaps not as badly as he'd feared. The score at least was respectable. He told everyone to hurry. The coach was going at five fifteen.

Elsewhere in the stand, Trevillion, modest as ever, was taking credit for the Leeds gimmicks. 'Jack Charlton wasn't very keen at first on the pre-match drill – he said he didn't want to look stupid. From now on we're going to do a different series of exercises before every match, home and away. It makes the other team feel inferior. I've got things planned which will blow your mind.'

There had already been enquiries about the stocking tabs, the ones with the numbers on. 'I've ordered a hundred dozen pairs to be made. Once the world sees them on TV tonight every team will go mad to have them. On each tab there was a little Beaver sign. That meant there were twenty-two Beavers out on the pitch playing for Leeds. No wonder they won.'

Next season, so he said, he wanted to change the Leeds strip, saying that all white was boring. He fancied a shirt with a blue cross on the front and back, then Leeds could be

256

called the Crusaders. 'I've not started yet. Just wait and watch Leeds!' I hadn't actually believed all his boastings the night before, convinced that no outsider could ever influence a football manager.

On the Spurs coach to the station Chivers was looking very fed-up. 'I know they think I could have done more. I never got a ball. I had no chance, yet all I get is stick for not scoring.' Nobody had actually said that, not even Bill, not as far as I'd noticed, but possibly a few felt it, though unfairly.

As we drew into the station one of the players said this is where we'll get the real stick. It wasn't clear if he expected Spurs' own fans to be furious, or the rivals. Just the opposite happened. The Spurs fans lined up outside the coach and cheered every player into the station. On the station hundreds of Leeds supporters going for their trains were almost as friendly, but then they had a good reason to feel pleased.

On the train four of the Spurs directors were deep in the menu when the carriage window was suddenly opened and two scruffy Leeds supporters stuck their heads through. The directors ignored the heads, expecting a string of obscenities but not wanting to try to force them out in case they turned violent.

'Go on,' said one of the lads, amused at the uptight features of the Spurs directors, manfully pretending nothing had happened, 'Order anything you like. It's on the house.'

'I suggest Yorkshire pud,' said the other lad, his head leaning right over the table. 'Just what you need. Put some lead in your pencil.'

'You must admit,' said the first lad, 'the better team won.'

The directors smiled, deciding at last to be friendly, knowing the train was about to leave.

'I'll tell you what,' said one of the lads. 'You've got a good goalie. We'll swap you Jennings for Sprake. What do you think?'

'No thanks,' said one of the directors.

The train suddenly moved, almost decapitating the two Leeds supporters, but they managed one final dig. 'See you at Wembley then . . . next year.'

It was a long boring and rather depressing ride home with

257

the train stopping at almost every station and the journey taking almost four hours, an hour longer than coming up on the Pullman. The dining-car service was very slow. There had been a fuse in the kitchen and they were cooking by candlelight. Everyone wanted to get home as quickly as possible.

'They weren't a team today,' said one of the directors, unable to get the match out of his head. 'They were just a collection of players.'

Phil Beal, further down the compartment, said he wasn't going out. A win or a draw would have called for celebrations, but not now.

Pat Jennings said he'd decided he would go up to Leeds again, not for the pleasure of seeing their team again but to see Trevillion. He too had been surprised that the Beaver's boasts about the Leeds team had come to pass. 'It's worth a try,' he said. 'But mind you, they'd have looked right silly buggers if we'd hammered them, after all that dancing.'

'No chance,' said Gilly. 'But you did well Pat.'

'I'd rather have played badly if only we could have won. I don't like playing well and losing.'

22

Pat Jennings

'If Jennings had been available on that memorable occasion when the Romans met the Etruscans, Horatius surely would have had to be satisfied with a seat on the substitutes' bench.' So said Eric Todd of the *Guardian* in his report of the Leeds match. Paul Trevillion is not the only football observer who can get carried away.

Of all the Spurs players, Pat Jennings is about the least likely to be carried away, even when the whole football Press is singing his praises, which they did that day. He's a genuine team man, quiet and retiring, with no signs of flash. His fans are always on at him to put a bit of show into his game, make it look a bit harder, just to work up the crowd excitement and draw attention to himself. Before that Leeds match Trevillion had told him that he must always pick up the ball with one hand. It's an easy thing to do, for any good goalie, but it's the sort of gimmick the crowd appreciates. Pat had said he would think about it, but come the game he never did it once, preferring to be dull but safe.

Several Spurs players had had a very consistent season, but of them all, Pat Jennings could be said to have had the *best* season. He'd risen to the occasion, turned on the magic, far more often than any of the others. Chivers had had several memorable, brilliant games, but he'd also had some dreadfully anonymous games which are best forgotten.

Looking back quickly over the fifty-three games which the team had played so far (only one of which Pat missed) I could remember only one game off hand where he'd made a major mistake. This was the very first game of the season, away to Wolves, right back in August. He'd failed to hold the ball and Wolves had scored. He hadn't been helped by a greasy surface or the fact that Mike England had banged

259

into him, but all the same it had been his mistake. It had ruined his weekend. He'd hardly spoken afterwards to his wife Eleanor.

'He never talks about the match. The only way I know how he's got on is by his face. If he's got a grin, I know it's been OK. If he says nothing, it's been bad. He's quiet enough at the best of times, God knows, but after Wolves he wouldn't say anything for two days.'

'Goals are always someone's mistake,' says Pat. 'It's impossible to have a goal without the manager being able to point at someone who should have stopped it. Very often the obvious one is the goalie.

'In the outfield, they can make mistakes all the time and get away with it. One mistake with a goalie and that's it. You can't redeem it, the way a forward can. He can miss five and then score one and everyone's pleased. Everybody sees a goalie's mistakes. That's the way it is.'

Knowles, Kinnear and Jennings each had a few years in other jobs before they came into football. But unlike the other two, Jennings was never turned down. His home situation was so remote from the world of professional soccer that it never occurred to him to want to be a footballer.

He comes from the small country town of Newry in County Down, Northern Ireland, the son of a labourer. His mother had ten children, eight of whom are living – seven boys and one girl. He was no good at school and hated every minute of it. 'I'm not exactly illiterate but I wouldn't say I was good at any school subjects.' He was good at running and jumping and enjoyed gaelic football, the only organised sport in his area. In gaelic football, which is a combination of catching and kicking, everyone is allowed to handle the ball. 'Professional soccer was only something I read about.'

He left school at fifteen and went to work as a factory hand and then as a labourer in a timber gang, felling trees up on a mountain side. 'I would have been quite happy to have stayed a labourer for ever. It would be hard to go back now, having been through what I've been through, but I'm sure I would have enjoyed it fine enough. It was a good, healthy, outdoor life. It was like being in Canada, being up in those mountains in the snow, dragging down the timber.

260

It was hard. At seventeen I was doing a man's job, being so big, but I loved it. I had no worries in them days.'

His arrival in football was sudden and meteoric. In just over eighteen months, from never having played in any sort of football team before, he was in the English First Division. He went along to watch a team in Newry one day, thought he could do just as well as their goalie, got a few games for them and was chosen for the Northern Ireland Youth team. This team played in an international youth tournament in Bognor Regis, being beaten by England in the finals. He was seen by Watford who signed him and then re-sold him the following season, 1964, to Spurs for £27,000.

'I've never had any coaching in my life. If I'd come up the normal way, I'd have had professional coaching from the age of eleven and been full-time on the ground staff at fifteen. When people get on to me, trying to make me do something a certain way, I might as well pack up. I can't do it. I was naturally good at it from the minute I tried it. So I'm just as likely to say bollocks if someone tries to tell me what to do. Bill was never a goalie, neither was Eddie, so what can they tell you.

'It might have been better if I had come up the hard way. I might be a better goalie today. Look at Bob Wilson at Arsenal. He had about five years in the reserves before he got a first team game. All the years of training and coaching he went through have probably helped to make him such a consistent goalie today.

'I'm sure in my first two years Spurs would have transferred me if they could have got their money back. I was still learning and I didn't have much confidence. I hated Saturday coming round. Since then, I've felt much better.'

Eleanor his wife used to be a professional singer with an Irish show band called the Hilton Show Band, which did one night stands all over Ireland. After they met she went on to even greater heights in England. She appeared at the London Palladium, sang on the David Frost show and toured all over the country. She brought out seven records, though none sold well. When she got married to Pat she decided to give up show business for good.

'I think I appreciate more than the other wives what it's

261

like to come out of the tunnel with the crowd roaring. I get more excited than Pat does. It's a fantastic feeling. You can understand why some footballers can do things better on the field than they can in training. It changes everything when you've got an audience. I'd love to have it back.'

Pat has no business interests and no investments, apart from the building society. Most of his money is tied up in a large new detached house he had recently moved into, worth about £20,000, in Broxbourne, Herts, just a few minutes away from Mike England.

He was looking forward to the end of the season – his latest contract would then be up and he was confident of negotiating some very good terms. When Bill came to ask him what he'd done for the club this year, he would have a lot to say.

Of all the players, Pat usually looks the most worried before a game, fussing and becoming irritable in the dressing-room. 'It's a great strain having to concentrate. Even in a game in which I've only touched the ball five times, I'm mentally shattered afterwards. I'm just as exhausted as the players who've been doing all the running.'

He says he probably enjoyed his football more when he was playing for Newry. 'I'm relieved today when every match is over. It's a great responsibility. So many other people depend on me doing well.'

When he plays for Northern Ireland, which he has done thirty-four times so far, he always rooms with Georgie Best. They couldn't be more different, as far as public images go. 'People expect George to be flash, but basically he's very quiet. In company he's not the one with the chat. He does live it up a lot and have a good time and he does make a lot of money, inside and out the game, but I think he deserves it all. He's done a lot for the game. He's a football genius. Think how much he'd get if he was a boxer. There's an expectation whenever he's playing. He's got the skill and he's always exciting. He's like Cassius Clay.'

When he goes home to Ulster he keeps well away from politics, though being a Catholic people are always after him for money or his signature, but he has never come out on either side. 'I'm really not interested in politics, here or in

Ireland, though I suppose if your house was being burned down you'd be forced to do something.'

During the season he had one threat on his life, though it was kept out of the papers. It came just after the threat to Georgie Best. Presumably some rival faction thought they'd even up the religious score by having a go at Pat. It was just before the Northern Ireland-Spain match. Pat wanted to go ahead and play but Bill Nicholson said he shouldn't risk it. He was very worried. Pat was offered police protection but he declined, saying that might make things worse, inciting somebody to do something stupid. (It's thought that the police did guard his house, keeping well hidden, unbeknown to Pat.) The problem of playing for Northern Ireland in Belfast was solved when the match itself was cancelled because of possible bomb incidents.

Although he's quiet and never pushes, he's surprisingly strong minded. He'd be very hard to con, even by a really eager beaver. A couple of weeks later, when Spurs were playing at Huddersfield, he went through to Leeds to have a look at the gloves Trevillion had designed. The idea was good, having a press stud at the wrist to keep them secure. Pat himself has an elastic band round the wrist of his gloves in matches because there's not a suitable glove on the market. 'They were like spacemen's gloves. Ridiculous. They'd tire your hands out just putting them on. I told him to try again.' So it was back to the drawing board for the Beaver.

While Pat was turning it on for Spurs, Mullery was getting more and more desperate. Despite his valiant efforts, proving once and for all that he was fit, it didn't look as if anyone could save Fulham.

It was now getting towards the end of the month's official loan, but there were no signs that Spurs wanted him back.

'Surely the end doesn't come like this?' said Mullery one Saturday evening just before Easter, after a match at Orient in which he'd been booed by the opposition crowd. Not for himself but because the crowd thought the system of a player being loaned was unfair to other clubs.

263

'I get an injury and suddenly wham, I'm an overnight failure. I'd like to be back at Spurs next season as captain, but I can't see it. What sickens me is that I bet seventy-five per cent of the Tottenham fans think of me as a cripple or something. I'm not. I'm playing as hard as I've ever done in my career. I've been really hurt by Tottenham's attitude. It's as though getting hurt while playing for them was some sort of crime.'

Alan finally gave a few interviews to the Press in which he sounded off about his disappointment at the way Spurs had treated him. Spurs said nothing in reply. Officially he was an injured player getting back to match fitness by playing with another club. Most people thought that by accusing the club he wasn't helping any future career very much. Not that Spurs had time to get involved in any row, over their handling of Mullery or the vexed question of loaning out players. Over Easter they were going to have their hardest sequence of games of the whole season, just at the time when they wanted a rest, to get fit and ready for the big one, the semi-final against AC Milan, their first European semi-final for nine years.

Over Easter they were due to play four games in six days – Friday, Saturday, Monday and then Milan on the Wednesday. Altogether, in a span of twelve days, they had to play six games. Despite a request to Milan they were unable to put back the Wednesday game.

Bill decided to permutate his players over the Easter games, resting some, bringing in others, in the hope of ending up on Wednesday with an eleven who weren't actually down on their knees. It didn't work. Not only did they get only two points out of the three Easter League games, they ended up with several serious injuries.

Joe Kinnear at last got a game, purely because of the congestion of fixtures. He played well, helping the team to beat Coventry 1-0. But at West Ham on Easter Saturday and Ipswich on Easter Monday, Ray Evans was back in.

At Ipswich the whole team played badly, particularly Ray Evans. Poor Tony Want, replacing Cyril for the first time for months, scored an own goal. But the most tragic incident of all concerned John Pratt who'd played well over the Easter period. His nose was broken in a collision and he had to go straight to hospital.

On Tuesday morning, the day before the home match against A.C. Milan, Bill made a momentous decision. He called back Mullery.

Alan Mullery has always believed in luck. He's one of the few players who puts it at the top of his list of elements which a footballer needs for success. (See Appendix 7.) In his early days as a boy at Fulham, he considers it was luck which got him into the first team so quickly, all because four players in his place were injured. Now, when everyone was sure his career was definitely finished, at least with Spurs, he was being recalled from the grave – all because John Pratt had broken his nose.

There was a crowd of forty-two thousand at White Hart Lane on Wednesday evening to welcome him back. Mullery didn't just come back as a player – he was back as captain, leading out his team as usual to the strains of McNamarra's Band, carrying a pennant to present to Milan's captain, Rivera, Italy's World Cup star. The Park Lane end, who'd kept up occasional shouts of Ra Ra Ra Mullery for months and months though he was miles away, went wild with delight.

It was almost as if Bill had gone back to square one. Through all the trials and tribulations of a long and hard season, with established players being dropped and youngsters tried out, he was now back to where he began. If only Phil Beal hadn't been injured, the team would have been exactly that which played at Wolverhampton on the first day of the season. It wasn't just Mullers who was back. Joe Kinnear was also in again. Ray's poor display at Ipswich, making it two defeats in a row, had told against him.

It turned out to be a disappointing game. Spurs continually pressurised the Milan penalty area, but their finishing was almost non-existent. High balls were constantly sent in by Knowles, Kinnear and Naylor for the head of Gilly or Chivers, but caused little danger. Gilly was being pulled up almost every time for pushing. The more Spurs pressed, the less likely they looked like scoring. Then the obvious happened. From a sudden breakaway, Milan split

265

the defence, helped by the run of the ball, and scored. It was unbelievable, considering Spurs' pressure, but by constantly bombarding the Milan penalty area Spurs had been wide open for a sudden attack.

Milan then started using all the old tactics, playing for time, body checking, but their defence held out well all the same. Spurs forwards still didn't look like scoring. Chivers seemed not to be in the game. He had an easy header when almost unmarked, but sent it wide. England and Gilly both headed over the bar. The woodwork was never in danger, far less the net. Then Steve Perryman, who'd played a first-class game, scored with a fine opportunist shot from the edge of the penalty area. At half-time it was 1-1. It looked now as if Spurs would pile on the goals, having found the way.

But the second half was just as dismal, with Milan frustrating Spurs even more in every way. Sogliano, the Milan number 7, was sent off for refusing to move ten yards away when Mullery was trying to take a free kick. Gilly and Schnellinger were both booked. It became a bad tempered match with the ref beginning to lose control. The more he blew, the more infringements there seemed to be.

Then Steve did it again, with an even better shot from even further out, this time about thirty-five yards. It came after a Mullery corner. The ball was cleared but Steve caught it on the bounce, volleying it into the far corner of the net for a spectacular goal the Spurs forwards had never looked like scoring, but Perryman had come to the rescue once again.

It ended 2-1 but Milan were nonetheless pleased. Away goals in Europe count double in the event of a draw. They'd done better than they'd hoped. They now felt confident of winning in Milan.

In the dressing-room Spurs sat silent and furious, annoyed with Milan and themselves. Chivers once again looked sullen and hollow eyed. Eddie Baily had worked himself into a state as usual with shouting at him, though being in the directors' box he'd been forced to keep his passions in control.

'Never mind,' said Mullery. 'We'll see who the big men are out there.' He was being hopeful and looked it, showing obvious signs of self-consciousness. He was back, but perhaps only on sufferance. He didn't know yet whether he was back for good.

'We can do it out there, you know,' said Bill. 'They'll be forced to come at us and it'll be our chance. I don't rate this lot any better than Torino. I think we'll do it.'

The players didn't look so confident. Propped up against the dressing-room wall was a large blackboard covered with the Milan team's names and numbers, the residue of Bill's afternoon two-hour team talk.

When the players were all dressed and ready, they slowly dragged themselves away. As Mullery was going out of the door Bill stopped him, standing in front of him, looking questioning.

'Feel OK?'

'I feel great,' said Mullery.

'Ten o'clock Friday then,' said Bill.

That was it. His month of playing and training at Fulham was over. Now he was back.

23

Milan

About a mile from the San Siro in Milan all roads were completely blocked, despite the efforts of the police car which was guiding the team coach. All seventy thousand supporters going to the match seemed to be going by car, each with his horn wailing. When the Spurs coach slowed down gangs of youths screamed and spat at the windows, banging so hard that the players took cover, convinced they were going to be broken. 'It'll be bricks on the way back,' said Gilly.

In Italy it's assumed that all British footballers are brutes, concentrating more on the physical side of football than on ball skills, tackling from behind, going in hard, charging the goalkeeper and other nasty tricks. In Britain it's assumed by the man on the terraces that Italian footballers are a bunch of hysterical fairies who throw tantrums, pull shirts, body check and other nasty tricks. It's not surprising, therefore, that Anglo-Italian matches have not got a reputation for their sweetness and light. Many matches have ended in brawls, on and off the pitch. Ralph Coates told the rest of the team about the time he played for Burnley in a match at Florence. They had to be locked in the dressing-room for two hours to stop the crowd lynching them.

The San Siro stadium is built like the Coliseum, with a high oval wall all the way round. We could see the thousands of supporters marching up it like ants on a treadmill, up and up and round and round, carrying their red and black banners and flags, screaming and chanting.

I went out with the team onto the pitch to inspect the turf and immediately ducked for cover. Fire crackers and smoke bombs were let off the minute the crowd caught sight of the

Spurs players. I'd never expected them and thought it was gun fire. I made a quick retreat back to the dressing-room, my ears blocked and my head reeling.

The dressing-room was long and enormous, with blue tiles half way up each wall. It seemed to swallow up the seventeen Spurs players as they got themselves undressed – except Gilly who was injured and not playing.

The drive through the dense crowds had taken so long that it was now eight thirty, just three quarters of an hour before kick-off. The players got ready very noisily, showing few signs of nerves or tension. They'd had the usual two days of waiting and hanging around, but for once it had left them relaxed. They'd used an Italian training camp up in the pine woods towards Como, lazing in the lounges, watching films, playing putting.

Joe Kinnear was looking for lavatory paper. Despite all the excellent amenities none had been left out. The substitutes, particularly Terry Naylor and Jimmy Pearce, were making up daft jokes. Eddie Baily was massaging Chivers' legs, telling him how brilliant he was, what a physique, while Chivers groaned, pretending to be annoyed with him.

'You better win this one lads,' said Gilzean, buttoning up a short raincoat he'd borrowed from someone. 'I need the bonus. I've got a wife, two kids and a budgie to keep.'

'And a pub,' shouted someone.

Ten minutes before time Alan Mullery started clapping his hands, trying to make everyone concentrate and in the right mood, but players were still chatting in little groups. Steve Perryman was worrying about his dad. He gave me some tickets and asked me to find him outside. He was coming on a day·trip from London for £3.50 (as he works at London airport) but hadn't got a match ticket. I rushed out and found him. I also saw Morris Keston. He and his wife had been staying for several days at one of Italy's poshest hotels beside Lake Como.

Back in the dressing-room Bill started his last minute rites. John Pratt, in place of Gilly, was going to play his first match since his broken nose. He and Steve were told to keep a tight hold of Rivera and Benetti. Peters wasn't to play his usual midfield role but to move up front and try to take

Gilzean's place, linking with Chivers and being ready to flick on free kicks or back head corners.

'You'll be Martin Gilzean tonight,' said Bill as he went over what he wanted him to do. Even Bill was still in surprisingly light-hearted mood. The corner kickers, Steve and Mullery, were told to try short corners when possible. This was Eddie's idea. He'd been to Italy to scout the Milan team and was convinced it would work. Their man marking system wasn't suited to short corners. If a man went out, then it still left Spurs with a two against one situation. And if Cyril and Joe were coming up on the flank, that would mean three to one.

Bill then went very serious and said on no account must anyone argue with the referee. 'I want you all to go back ten yards at every free kick. You don't have to rush back, but give the referee no chance to take your name. Everybody hear that? I want no dissent of any sort.'

'Bayonets out lads,' said Eddie once again. 'England expects every man this evening to do his duty.'

The buzzer went and they shouted the usual encouragements at each other. On the pitch they were met by a roar of fireworks, smoke bombs, streamers and a wall of screams. The noise was deafening but the chants were short and repetitive. There was no singing, just a continual roar of Mee-lan, Mee-lan. They could have been shouting any two syllables, any name you cared to imagine. I thought at first they were shouting Cee-ral. It's probably a help when playing in front of a foreign crowd not to understand a word of their shouts. All the same the noise was the loudest I'd heard all season, at home or abroad.

As usual Eddie kept up his constant screams from the bench, but this time I was half-deaf already. Even Eddie couldn't compete with a seventy thousand crowd.

The first five minutes were very worrying. Milan stormed forward and Spurs' defence looked very shaky, particularly Mike England. There were some wild clearances which might easily have failed. Then Spurs scored a goal, the goal they'd all been hoping for, the vital early goal which Milan dreaded above anything else. Milan's pressure had taken them up field, which gave Cyril his first chance to overlap.

270

He carried on unimpeded almost to their goal line, then pulled the ball back for Chivers to shoot. It was cleared, but only about forty yards to Steve Perryman. He picked it up and moved forward as the defence ran at him, expecting a block buster shot as he'd done at Tottenham. Instead he pushed it square to Mullery on his right who shot on the run first time, a brilliant shot, high and curving, scything through the defence and giving the goalkeeper no chance. Only seven minutes had elapsed. The goal was one of those which comes at the perfect psychological moment. And with the scorer being Mullery, the prodigal returned, it was indeed like a story straight out of the *Wizard* or *Hotspur*.

Milan now needed to score three goals to win. Judging by the low scoring standards of Italian football (Milan had scored only thirty goals in twenty-six League games), that was too much to expect.

Spurs steadied themselves after the goal, though it didn't stop Eddie screaming at Mike England for the rest of the first half, especially when he headed the ball against his own crossbar. But the midfield men were giving Milan few chances and the ones they did get were being wasted with bad finishing. Most important of all, Milan had no answer to Spurs overlapping full backs. Both Joe and Cyril were making tremendous runs down the wings. When the move did break down, they could be visibly seen to be on the point of collapse as they began their fifty or sixty yard haul, all the way back to the full back position. But when it worked and they got their final cross into the penalty area, causing panic amongst the Milan defence, then it was all worth it and success gave them the extra energy to rush back.

It was Milan's man marking system which was at fault. No one was prepared to move out of the defence to go and meet Cyril, scared to leave the man they were meant to mark, hoping someone else would do it.

It was 1-0 at half-time. In the Spurs dressing-room no one was smiling or boasting. They all looked intense and purposeful. Bill told them they were doing well but Benetti had to be picked up much quicker. He was their danger man and causing most trouble. Rivera was showing little determination in his finishing and Prati, Milan's leading scorer who'd

271

missed the Tottenham match, was playing out on the wing, not in the centre as Bill had expected, and was getting nowhere. Cyril complained that his leg was sore. Johnny Wallis treated him with a pain-killing spray. 'Just forty-five minutes to go,' said someone as they trooped back on again.

In the second half Eddie turned his invective from Mike England to Martin Chivers when he missed an open goal. He received the ball, alone and unmarked and only ten yards from goal. He took his time, not rushing the shot, and fired wide. Eddie and Bill both buried their heads in their hands. It might have been offside as the linesman's flag was up, but the referee appeared to let it go and pointed for a goal kick. All the same it was a terrible shot. If Spurs went on to lose Martin would be for it in the dressing-room.

Milan at last managed to score, thanks to Cyril making his only mistake of the game. He lost possession just outside his penalty area and let Bignon through. He was brought down by Philip Beal and Rivera scored from the penalty. Now, for the final twenty minutes of the match, Milan were being urged on by the crowd to score again and force extra time. Spurs were pushed back into their own half for long spells, but they held out and the game ended in a draw, 1-1. Spurs were now in the final, their first European final since 1963.

The crowd went silent, accepting the result without acrimony. Before the end they'd seemed irritated at times by some of Milan's passing movements. Spurs had won fairly and squarely and there could be little argument. It had been a well refereed match, played fairly by both sides. There had been few fouls and only one incident.

In the dressing-room Bill and Eddie were ecstatic, going round praising everyone. Bill said that Cyril had played an excellent game – apart from one mistake. He said Perryman had also been great. In fact everyone had done well. Eddie was personally praising Peters. 'You played a real team game, Martin,' said Eddie, shouting in Peters' ear. 'Do you hear me? Bloody great.' 'I hear you,' said Martin. 'Now I want to hear Bill say the same.'

Most of all, Mullery was being congratulated by everyone for his goal, a goal which had won the tie and got them into the final. 'I've scored a few good goals in my time,' said

Mullers. 'But that must be the most valuable ever.'

The only player not joining in the shouting and congratulating was Martin Chivers. He went to his place and sat silent and alone, looking sullen and morose. His natural expression tends to be rather grim, except when he's actually smiling, but this time there was no doubt he was feeling dissatisfied with himself. He knew he'd missed a great chance, one that he normally never misses. He knew that Bill and Eddie were displeased with him, thinking he should have tried harder and done more running. Once again, he had been left on his own up front. Peters had been forced for long spells to go back to midfield. It had been a game which had been won in the middle and on the flanks. The rest of the players left him alone with his thoughts, carefully walking round him.

The referee came in to congratulate Spurs, followed by the manager of Milan, Nereo Rocco. Through an interpreter he too congratulated Spurs on their good game, saying he had no complaints about the result. They were a fine team, worthy winners and he hoped they would do well in the final. Bill was equally profuse in his thanks, congratulating the Milan team. 'I know what it's like to be knocked out of a semi-final,' said Bill. 'It's like the end of the world. But I hope you do well in the League.'

The British Press were eventually allowed in. They rushed to Mullery, asking about his goal, then to Cyril Knowles for his view on his great game. The Spurs directors arrived, plus Brian Curtin, the team doctor, Geoffrey Jones, the club secretary and Bill Stevens, the assistant secretary, all three of whom had flown in that day from London. Mr Broderick of Cooks went into the bathroom to congratulate the players and emerged with his best suit soaked through. They'd shouted him over and then sprayed him with water. Brod, always a goer, stripped off naked and got in the bath with them. They roared when they saw his thin, weedy body. 'I thought Belsen had closed,' said John Pratt.

It took about an hour for the team coach to get clear of San Siro. Spurs were given strong police protection – a police car with a siren at the front followed by five camouflaged jeeps, full of extra policeman – but there were no incidents.

The team were going back to their hotel up in the woods near Lake Como, with no chance of any night life, but they were too excited to be worried by the lack of any celebrations to come. Winning was excitement enough. At the hotel, Bill ordered champagne all round for the players then most of them went straight to bed.

But on the plane next morning, going back to London, there was feasting and drinking all the way home. Nobody was sick. Nobody was drunk. Nobody made a fool of himself, but everyone was decidedly merry, players, directors, Press and officials. The drink that wasn't drunk was given to the players to take home. They staggered off the plane at Heathrow loaded down with big fluffy dolls they'd bought at Milan airport, with shoes they'd bought at Como, with the free bottles of champagne and miniature bottles of liqueur they'd got on the plane, and nicest of all, a free gold watch. Each player, including the substitutes, had been given a watch as a present by the Milan club. It was a gold, seventeen-rubies watch and must have cost around £15, according to an expert on the plane (Monty Fresco, the photographer).

On the plane they'd read the London newspapers which contained reports of the other semi-final. Wolves had beaten Ferencuaros of Hungary. They were all slightly disappointed, having hoped for another foreign trip. Playing Wolves in the final was going to be more than a slight disappointment for the wives. The club had promised to take all wives abroad if Spurs reached the final. A night in Wolverhampton wasn't exactly the wives' idea of a treat, not compared with Milan which they all would have loved.

But Spurs were at last in a final. They'd been knocked out of two other cups that season in the late stages but after nine months of trailing round Europe they'd made it. In the fourteen years since Bill had taken over as manager, he was now in line for his seventh major trophy.

The nicest news of all in the morning papers concerned Steve Perryman. He'd been chosen by Sir Alf Ramsey for the England Under 23 party. Most experts had said earlier in the season that Steve wasn't fulfilling the promise he'd shown the year before. Now he was going forward again, as those two goals against Milan had shown. Every player was genuinely pleased for Steve. Everyone is a Steve Perryman fan.

Things had come right for others as well, such as Joe Kinnear, but Mullery's was the most dramatic resurrection of all. There was no holding him on the plane. Looking at a photograph of his goal which showed the Milan keeper desperately throwing himself to the side, Mullery said he shouldn't have tried. 'Nobody could have stopped that goal.'

At the airport, Brian Curtin, the club doctor, let his carrier bag drop and there was a loud noise of glass breaking. Everyone cheered. 'I'm over twenty-seven,' said Mullery, 'but I don't let bottles drop!'

Mullery was referring to the doctor's theory that in future players would be retiring at twenty-seven. At the back of Alan's mind, throughout his months of injury, was the thought that Spurs had washed their hands of him, just because he was thirty.

'It's not true,' said the chairman as we went through Customs. 'All that was wrong was Alan's injury. Yet everybody thinks we treated him badly. We just wanted to get him fit again.'

The season had gone almost full circle. It had all begun at Wolverhampton, back in the sunny days of last August when Spurs had played their first game of the season. Now they were going to end the season as they'd begun, against the same opponents, with the same team captain and very probably with the same team.

24

The European Final

'The great fallacy is that the game is first and last about winning. It's nothing of the kind. The game is about glory. It's about doing things in style, with a flourish, about going out and beating the other lot, not waiting for them to die of boredom.' – Danny Blanchflower, ex-captain of Spurs.

It was a very festive party which left Tottenham for Wolverhampton for the first leg of the UEFA Cup Final. The club had booked three carriages on one of the five special trains from Euston. In the club party were a hundred members of the Spurs staff, from directors and players' wives down to catering officials and gatemen. The team itself had gone up to Wolverhampton the night before. The wives were still wishing they were going somewhere glamorous in Europe, but at least with it being so near, everyone had been included. It was a hot sunny day in London, with temperatures well up in the sixties, just as it had been in August when the season had begun with the same train ride to Wolverhampton. At Wolverhampton the sun had gone and it was cloudy and raining.

'After all these months dragging round Europe, I have to end up in the final against Waggy,' said Joe Kinnear in the dressing room. David Wagstaff, the Wolves winger, is one of the few wingers that Joe ever feels nervous about. Not scared. It's just that over the years he's become a bit superstitious about playing against him. Now that Joe was back in the side once again, he didn't want to make any mistakes.

'Don't worry, Joe,' said Alan Mullery, patting Joe's back. 'He won't get round you tonight.' Now that Mullers was back in the side once again, he didn't want anyone to mistake who was captain.

276

Mike England's bogey player is supposed to be the Wolves striker, Derek Dougan. Back in the days when Mike was a ground staff boy at Blackburn Rovers, Dougan was also there – as a first team player. One day Dougan threw his boots back at Mike, saying they hadn't been cleaned properly. The Doog has cooled down since those days (he can't actually remember the incident), as befits a TV star and a pillar of the Player's Union, but the rivalry still exists. At the beginning of the season Mike had felt nervous. Now he was back on top form and felt very confident.

'You could do it tonight lads,' shouted Eddie Baily. 'Win here and you've got the cup. Right. Over the top!' It was like an old and dusty record, one I'd heard echoing down the dressing-rooms of Europe all season.

It would be a shame for either team to lose. While Spurs had been triumphing in Iceland, France, Rumania and Italy, being unbeaten in ten matches and scoring 27 goals with only 4 against, Wolves had been equally successful in Portugal, Holland, East Germany, Italy and Hungary, scoring 25 goals with only 7 against. Both teams had been excellent adverts for English football. In the whole history of European cups, it was the first time two English teams had ended up in the same final.

It must have been rather strange for the referee and his two linesmen, all three of whom had trailed their way across Europe from Russia to spend a rainy, drizzly night in Wolverhampton for a match between two English teams. At least the teams would be able to swear at each other with impunity.

In the first half, there was nothing to swear or cheer about. Both sides, knowing each other too well, seemed to be holding back, stuck in their own lethargy, waiting for something to happen. The happening was Chivers. He didn't do it just once, but twice. After twelve minutes of the second half, he ran from the far post to meet a Mike England free kick and headed it straight into the net. It's one of the team's most successful free kick situations, one practised many times back in the pre-season training. Wolves came to life after this, managing to sneak in the equaliser from a quickly taken free kick.

Chivers' second goal was perhaps one of his best of the whole season. He got the ball from Mullery out on the left flank, after Cyril Knowles had overlapped up to the half-way line. Chivers was on his own, miles away from goal, and it seemed as if he would have to wait for reinforcements. But he didn't pause, turning simply on the ball and began racing for goal, shrugging off two defenders. While still a good thirty yards away, at full speed and without appearing to aim or break his stride, he shot with his right foot into the far corner of the net. The goalkeeper hardly moved, transfixed by the speed of the shot.

On his own, Chivers had won the match. Apart from the two goals, he hadn't actually done much. He'd simply risen to the occasion twice, turning on two moments of deadly accuracy, while all around him lesser players had been rushing, bustling and getting nowhere.

Eddie Baily was the first to rush on to the pitch, embracing Chivers as the whistle went. In the dressing-room, he said that if Martin liked he would lie down on the floor and let him walk all over him. 'What can I say? I can't say nuffink, can I? You've knocked me out, Martin. I'm out for the count. I'm on the floor bleeding for a count of three and you're saying 4-5-6-7- OUT! Martin, what can I say?'

'Thanks, Ed,' said Martin, grinning, his eyes narrowed, savouring Eddie's self-humiliation, but not really being fooled, knowing that if he didn't do it again in the return match, Eddie would be back to normal.

'It couldn't be better,' said Bill, all smiles. 'It just couldn't be better. We set our stall as best we could, and look what happened. There's no justice in football. If I was the Wolves manager now, I'd be in tears. That first goal came at the perfect time, just as we were going under.'

The chairman of Wolves came into the dressing-room, bringing with him a young boy who wanted the Spurs' autographs. 'Well done lads. Congratulations.'

'You don't mean that, do you,' said Joe Kinnear.

'I do,' said the Wolves chairman. 'No one could complain about those two goals. They were both beauties. I really do mean it. Well done.'

The return match at Tottenham was an even sadder night

for Wolves. They played better than they'd done at Wolverhampton, but could only draw 1-1. Spurs therefore won the final, 3-2 on aggregate.

From Spurs' point of view, it was a Glory Glory Helleluja evening. It was their biggest (54,303), most colourful, most excited home crowd of the whole year. As the last match of the season, it couldn't have been better stage managed. The crowd invaded the pitch afterwards and cheered the Spurs team as they triumphantly held aloft the enormous UEFA Cup. But most of all they cheered Alan Mullery. It seemed inevitable that he should be the star once again. He scored Spurs' only goal, a diving header from a Martin Peters' free kick. Yet again, one of the dead ball set pieces had come off. It was the one where Chivers and Gilzean are the decoy men, running to the near post and taking defenders with them.

It was champagne and hugs all round in the dressing-room afterwards, but somehow it was all slightly subdued. The team knew that they hadn't played as well as they can play. It would take some time for the full significance of their win to sink in.

'I'm going on the drink now,' said Gilly. 'And I'm not resting till Sunday.'

'We played rotten tonight and won,' said Martin Chivers. 'You can't do better than that.'

'Brilliant save, Pat,' said Bill, congratulating Jennings.

Eddie Baily was sitting very quietly in a corner. 'The nine months seemed long, but those last twenty minutes. Bloody hell. They were like an eternity.'

Upstairs the club had laid on a large banquet. All the players were there, from Wolves and Spurs. (None of the Spurs players nicked off this time to any rival party.) The Spurs background staff and players' wives were also invited. All in all, it was a splendid evening, a perfect climax to a long hard season.

'A season is only a good season if you win something,' said Philip Beal next day. 'It's no use being second in the League, or third or fourth. It's no use being beaten in a cup final. People don't look back to that. A season is only remembered by the trophies that's been won.'

279

Philip Beal is twenty-seven and has had twelve years at the club, far longer than any other player. His contract was up at the end of the season. He knew that with a big trophy behind them, he had a far better chance of getting some good terms out of the club. He was determined to ask this time for loyalty money.

Other players woke up to thoughts of new contracts, wondering how much they could get. Pat Jennings had had another fine game. One football manager had even been quoted as saying that he was now the best goalkeeper in Europe. His case was going to be very strong. The talk of contracts brought the season back to where it all began. The players might be making plans for their summer holidays, but Bill Nicholson knew that for him the worst part of the year was yet to come.

The club had made a good bit of money out of Europe, and of course so had the players. Their extra bonuses for winning in Europe came in all to about £1,000 each, quite modest by cup bonuses, but of course it was just the beginning. By winning, they were going to be in Europe for another year. Next season they would be the only London club with the honour of playing in Europe. The final match at Tottenham had brought in gate receipts of £45,000, a record for any match at White Hart Lane.

As Philip Beal said, it had been a good season, simply because of Europe. They'd flown 10,238 miles round Europe, but it had been worth it. In England they'd travelled 7,500 miles by train, but had ended up only sixth in the League. That would be quickly forgotten.

Perhaps the length of the season would be remembered. It had been the hardest ever in the number of matches played. Counting all their Cup and League games, and their two friendlies in Scotland, the team had played seventy games. In Bill and Eddie's day, a first division team averaged no more than forty-five matches.

Derby had won the League, by one point. Spurs at one stage hadn't been far behind them. If they could have been more consistent, they would have been well up with the leaders. But there seemed something in the team's character all season which made them fade in ordinary League matches against so-called lesser teams. They seemed to lack aggression, the killer instinct. However, to finish sixth in the League was respectable if not exciting.

But almost every big occasion had been a joy to watch, even on that momentous day when Leeds knocked them out of the FA Cup. Leeds, after all, went on to win the Cup and in that match they were unstoppable. During the season Spurs produced consistently high form in every cup match. Was their failure in ordinary matches a group weakness or a weakness of certain individuals in the group? It would take a psychologist to work out the reasons, but even then, unless he could come up with a positive way of solving the problem, Mr Nicholson would doubtless not want to know.

Of the personal stories of the year, Alan Mullery's was by far the most dramatic. His rise and fall and resurrection is a morality tale for all footballers. After he was called back from the dead for that first Milan match, Spurs had their best run of the season. Not one of their nine remaining matches was lost – and they included hard European matches and two London derby games, against Arsenal and Chelsea.

Not only did Alan come back for Spurs, he was back in the England party against West Germany. He withdrew from the second game, deciding that he'd already had a long and hard season, wanting instead to spend some time at home with his family. He reckoned that being an old man of thirty, he wouldn't make the England World Cup team for 1974, so he might as well let a younger player have his chance.

'As far as the team's concerned, it's been a fabulous season. They reached the quarter final of one cup, the semi-final of another and then won the European final. I think the UEFA cup is the hardest European trophy to win because there are so many matches to be played.

'As for me, at one stage I was sure I'd had it, but now I feel very much back in the fold. In the last two months, everything seems to have revolved round me.

'I don't feel bitter by what happened. It's all part of the game. You learn by it all. I know now that the club is bigger than the player. Far far bigger. I'd probably got complacent, thinking that as captain and an England player, I was sure of my place. It was a reminder to me and other players that you can't take your place for granted.'

It'll be interesting to see if Steve Perryman makes England's World Cup team. His fall from grace at the beginning of the season was undramatic, unnoticed by the general footballing public, but it gave him many sleepless nights. He was well aware that his play had become predictable, that he wasn't moving forward enough. But it all came right in the end. His two goals against Milan, which won Spurs their semi-final tie, couldn't have been more positive. And as the season ended, he was getting ready to tour Europe with England's Under 23 team.

Things also came right for Joe Kinnear, the full back who lost his place to the young reserve, Ray Evans. Joe had several long and miserable months, but he came back in the team with Mullery and never looked back.

'I'm on top of the world now,' said Joe the next day. 'Last night it didn't seem a very good match, for me or for anybody, but you've got to think about all the hard work that went into getting to the final. It was a long hard slog.

'It was like getting stabbed when I lost my place. You see the lads every day but you're not part of them any more. You don't get in the bath with them after the match, you don't chat with them or have any laughs together. You just walk around on your own. I had a long long wait to get back. Next season I've just got to fight to keep my place.'

Alas for Ray Evans. He finished the season as he began, back in the reserves. It was his best season ever, in the number of first team appearances, but it did him little good. As you would expect, he finished the season feeling sick, choked, diabolical.

Tony Want, the reserve who had the brain storm, deliberately giving up his chance that time of a first team game, was transferred on the day of the UEFA Cup Final. His years of hard, loyal service on the fringe of the first team had not gone unnoticed by other clubs. He was bought by Birmingham City, newly promoted to the First Division, for £50,000. As he hadn't asked for the move, he got his five per cent cut of the transfer. He was well pleased, if sad to leave Spurs.

During the year, that was the only sale, though there looked like being more during the close season. No one had been bought either, though it was thought by most people that a new forward would doubtless soon be bought as an eventual replacement for Alan Gilzean. It turned out to be the first and last season as a Spurs player for Bobby Scarth, the deaf and dumb boy. They decided at the end to let him go.

As for Ralph Coates, the season's new boy, he never seemed to be too depressed by his failure to produce the sort of brilliant form he'd displayed at Burnley. He took a long time to settle into the team's patterns and even at the end of the season, he still seemed slightly out of place. During the season, he was brought back into the midfield, after his lack of success as a forward. Surprisingly, it was from midfield he scored his only two League goals of the season, both of them beauties and worth waiting for – both the sort to endear him to the Tottenham fans. One was against Chelsea and one against Arsenal. His Arsenal goal was incredible – a run of eighty yards from his own penalty area, beating two men and scoring. He'd had similar, if shorter runs, all season, ending ignominiously, either running straight into a defender or losing control of the ball.

But in every game he'd shown great energy and hard work. If nothing else, it secured his place in the affection of the crowd. They always love a trier. Personally, he'd settled down very well, being accepted and liked by the team, finding himself a smart house and starting a second baby.

'The first half of the season was disappointing. I didn't really enjoy it. I wasn't happy with my performance. Then I had those injuries, the most I've had in my whole career. But I really enjoyed the last two months. I couldn't sleep last night for excitement. I got up at five and went to clean the cars. I never won anything at Burnley.'

Martin Chivers was the country's top marksman that season. In all, he scored forty-five goals for Spurs, plus two for England. If he seemed to come in for a lot of criticism it was only because he had set his own standards so high. Chivers is the player most likely. Chivers is the player England and Spurs expects.

He played sixty-seven games for Spurs and five for England, probably an all-time record for an English First Division player. 'All I feel now is knackered. It's definitely been my best season for goals, but I was disappointed with a lot of my games. I often got the vital goal, but deep down I knew I hadn't played well. I would like to be more consistent next season.'

Bill Nicholson was relieved but seemed far from ecstatic. Again his emotions were as much with Wolves, feeling for them in their hour of defeat, knowing that Spurs had achieved glory without being particularly glorious.

'As a European final, it was nothing like our 1963 win. That really was a wonderful occasion. I'd say that was the best cup victory I've known. Winning by five goals to one against Atletico Madrid was winning in style.'

The next day, he was early in his office as usual, interviewing parents, deciding on his youth players for the next season. In fourteen years as manager of Spurs, he'd now won seven major trophies. Spurs had still to be defeated in a Cup Final. They'd become the first British club to win twice in Europe.

'It's been a very full season and I've tried to look upon each match as being important. We wanted to keep a good position in the League all the time.

'I think the biggest disappointment was being knocked out of the League Cup by Chelsea. We gave away the goals. Being beaten by Leeds in the FA Cup was different. On the day, Leeds were the better team.

'We still have problems. For such experienced players, a lot of them are not consistent. I can't sit and watch them in comfort, not the way I've done with other teams I've had. But from the results' point of view it's been a very successful season. There's no argument about that.'

Mr Wale, also thought it had been a most successful season. 'It was a great culmination to a hard year's work. The most important thing is being in Europe again. There's something lacking for a top club today if it's not in Europe.'

During the year he changed his mind on one topic which has kept the Spurs board in discussions for generations. He started the season by saying he was against any advertising inside the Spurs ground. By the end, he no longer considered it a mortal sin. 'It's all a matter of money.' They'd taken soundings and discovered that a few selected advertisements placed discreetly around the side of the pitch, without desecrating the stands, could bring in at least £15,000 per season. 'It does seem silly not to allow it, if it can be done with taste. I think we'll try it next season.'

In the close season, they were going to spend £26,000 on installing new floodlights, so they needed all the money they could get.

During the year, the club opened a club shop for the first time, something most other top clubs have had for years. It was a great success, without taking away any business from the other shops around Tottenham which sell Spurs souvenirs. At the end of the season the shop's newest line was underpants for men and panties for women, in white with the Spurs' cockerel on the front. ('Very good quality,' said Ron Wick, the shop manager. 'Very tasteful.')

I started the season with the idea that being a footballer must be a good life. How lovely to be a hero. How wrong I was.

Footballers are worth every penny they can get. When it comes to the crunch, every player, however big a star, is disposable, as we have seen. There's an old joke in football about the manager of a Fourth Division club, pushing out his humble team for a Cup match against a big First Division club. 'Go out there lads and do your best,' he exhorts them. 'So I can get enough money to replace you.'

Footballers are the game's fodder, human sacrifices that are thrown without sentiment or apologies into the battlefield. The pressures only cause concern if they impair their powers. Physical injuries, like groin strains, have got to be endured. If they get too bad, out you go. Eddie Baily's continual stream of wartime metaphors made me think of the First World trenches, with the generals sending out miles of bodies, straight into the graveyards.

It's been interesting to see how the players react to all the pressures. They experience in extremis many of the pressures of the world today. Every occupation has its rat race, but football is one of the few where the race can end every week. From the minute they become full-time footballers at fifteen they're being tested, week in and week out. *No one* at any time is ever secure.

It's been interesting to see their group rituals, at home and at the club. Being accepted, being part of the gang, doing the right thing, being smart but not flash, is very important to them all. When you belong, you really belong. When you're out, you become a pariah.

I don't know how Mullery or Joe Kinnear or Tony Want or Ray Evans survived the season without a nervous breakdown. I don't know how Ralph Coates didn't go back on sleeping pills or come out in strange lumps the way he'd done at Burnley. Footballers are chosen for their character, as we've been told a hundred times, so perhaps the weakest are weeded out from the beginning. It's not just the best footballers who survive but the ones with the strongest nervous systems.

Yet who would be a manager? They nave complete power over their charges, but when it really matters they're helpless. Most players do forget, once they're out they're playing, but a manager has few releases, few safety valves. Their agony is constant.

· The public of course see it as a glamorous life. They're not interested in the fact that it's been a hard season. Only in the trophies. Clubs these days are always going on about the number of matches, but the public don't really care. I didn't either, not until I put in ten thousand hard miles, dragging round Europe. Altogether, Spurs spent five weeks of last season just hanging around strange hotels. My metabolism never got used to it. Putting in two days suspended in limbo in an Italian hotel was bad enough, but having to play before seventy-thousand screaming Italians at the end of it would have turned me into a jibbering wreck.

The public don't make allowances, naturally enough. They don't see all the tensions behind the scenes. Like the manager and his board, they want success, not excuses.

The glamour is there, on the outside anyway. The heroes are idolised. The fans thrill to their skills, there is big money to be earned. But inside the club, a player is only as good as his last game. Inside the club, they lead regimented lives, completely at the power of a manager who can ordain their every movement and trained by ex-players whose own playing lives were light years away from the conditions of today. Internally, they're despised more often than admired, criticised for being soft, accused of being spoiled.

At the same time, the old timers feel sorry for today's players' apparent lack of enjoyment. I've no doubt the dressing-room at Spurs is little different from any other big club. Joe Mercer of Manchester City says he often gets the feeling that his players are going off to Vietnam, not to play a game of football.

But each and every player comes willingly to the scaffold, pushing and fighting to be at the front. They know the rules and the pitfalls. They know they'll be sacrificed without a moment's hesitation. They know the physical strains, the disciplined life they'll have to lead and the arthritic middle age that lies ahead. To a man, they haven't the slightest regret. They're almost childlike in their gratitude for what football's done for them.

The alternative for most of them would have been the factory floor or the building site. Thanks to football, they're special.

'I'm glad the end didn't come for me last season,' says Alan Mullery. 'I wouldn't have liked to have gone out like that. In the end I was able to withdraw from the England party. They didn't chuck me out. I've been very very lucky. I've had thirteen good years. I've had all the good times. I've seen the world. I'd have been nobody, but for football.'

Appendices to 1972 Edition

NOTE All information was correct up to 1 June 1972. The players did not fill in the questionnaires themselves – they were each asked the questions verbally and I wrote down their answers. I am grateful to sociologist John Carrier for his help.

Appendix 1

DEAD BALL TACTICS: Free Kicks, corners, throw-ins
Drawings by Paul Trevillion

Spurs, like all professional teams, have a series of dead ball tactics which they work out in training at the beginning of each season. They don't always use the planned move – a quickly taken free kick, simply passed to the nearest player, or a direct shot at goal might be more effective. Some of the planned tactics are dropped as the season goes on, or modified when they've been found not to work, or added to when new players come into the team, but in most dead ball situations, they have several planned movements which they can use. From the arrangement of the team, or from the position of the ball, or sometimes by someone like Mullery or Peters calling out a number, each player knows what tactic is about to be tried and knows what position he must take up.

Dead ball tactics are worth practising. Spurs went on to score almost a quarter of their goals last season from dead ball situations. From free kicks alone they scored eleven goals.

Free-kick 1

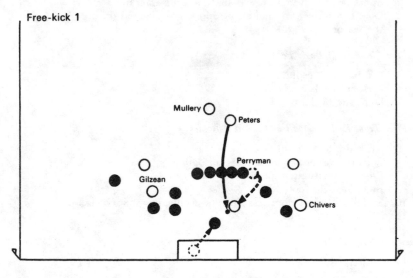

No 1 Free Kick: This is usually tried when the kick is directly in front of goal. The vital man is Perryman. He takes up his position at the end of the wall which the defence has lined up between the ball and their goalkeeper. The moment the ball is kicked – usually by Peters, with perhaps Mullery standing beside him to confuse the defence – Perryman whips round behind the wall. The defence is expecting to be blasted by a hard shot from Peters, but instead Peters chips the ball gently over the wall for the waiting Perryman to either head or shoot at goal. It's a hard manoeuvre to finish. The element of surprise is usually on Perryman's side – the

strikers, like Chivers and Gilzean are the ones being heavily marked – but the moment the goalkeeper realises what's happening, he comes charging out, going straight for Perryman. You have to be very brave to get in your shot. Which is why Perryman is chosen.

Free-kick 2

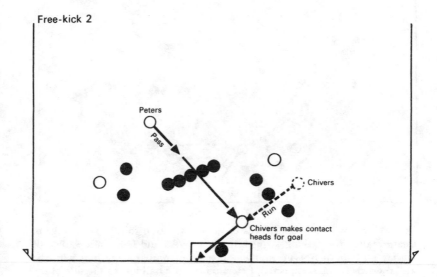

No 2 Free Kick: This is a quickly taken free kick, very simple and usually the most effective of all. Peters places the ball very quickly, before the opposition have arranged themselves, and kicks it straight away, without looking up. Chivers has taken up a position in front of the far post. But the second the ball is kicked, he is already moving, knowing that Peters will be chipping the ball to the empty space around the penalty spot. Chivers is meant to meet the ball with his head and score direct.

No 3 Free Kick: Chivers and Gilzean appear to be the obvious targets in this free kick but in fact they are decoys. They both stand towards the far post, heavily marked by defenders as usual. When the ball is kicked, they start running as fast as possible towards the near post, taking the defenders with them. The space they have left empty is where Peters has to land the ball, right in the path of Mullery (or Knowles or Kinnear) who has started running forward the moment the ball is hit. He either tries directly for goal, if it looks possible, or squares it for Chivers or Gilzean to flick in.

Free-kick 3

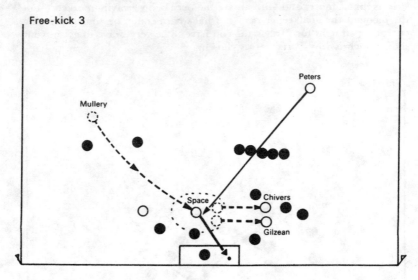

No 4 Free Kick: This free kick was created last season to take advantage of Coates' talent for making a quick burst. Chivers and Gilzean are towards the far post, both heavily marked. Instead of banging the ball over the wall towards them as expected, Peters pushes the ball low to the side of the wall, between the wall and their full back. Coates has to burst past the full back, race for the line and then cross the ball to Chivers and Gilzean at the far post.

Free-kick 4

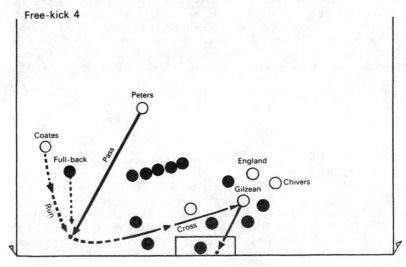

Corners

At the start of the season, there were two basic corners, but they were added to as the season progressed or dropped when players were out of the team.

Left hand corner: Perryman usually takes the left hand corners, or perhaps Neighbour or Pearce if they are playing. They are meant to be in-swinging lobs aimed at Gilzean's head who is standing in front of the defence at the

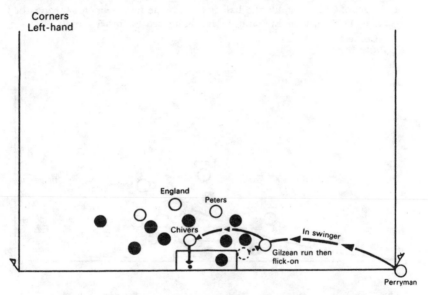

near post. Gilzean runs out to meet the ball the second it is kicked and back heads it either directly over his head for Chivers in the goal mouth or towards the penalty spot for Peters or England. English teams know only too well how Gilzean can flick the ball backwards with his head and he's always heavily marked, but it still works on many occasions.

Right hand corner: These are very hard, strong outswinging corners, usually taken by Mullery. They either go direct into the middle of the goal mouth, for Gilzean to head, or further over towards the far post for Peters or England.

For a spell during the second half of the season, when Mullery was out of the team injured, Chivers took several right hand corners. He'd taken one at Cheshunt, just by chance, which had caught everyone by surprise. He drives the ball, low and very hard, right across the goal mouth, for Peters or Gilzean to volley into the net. Defences always expect high corners, lobbed into the goal mouth, for the other team to head, so the Chivers' corners can be very effective.

Throw-ins

Chivers didn't know he had a long throw till one day at Cheshunt he found he could throw the ball with ease right into the goal mouth. Normally, a striker like Chivers is not expected to take throw-ins but to wait, lurking in the middle, to finish them off. But his long throw to the head of Gilzean has led directly to several goals and is always dangerous. Gilzean usually stands at the near post, to back head the ball into the goal. On other occasions, Chivers throws the ball further back and aims for England who has come up to try a header at goal. If it's going to be aimed at Gilzean, Chivers holds the ball first with the hand which is nearer the goal. If it's meant for England, he holds it with his other hand.

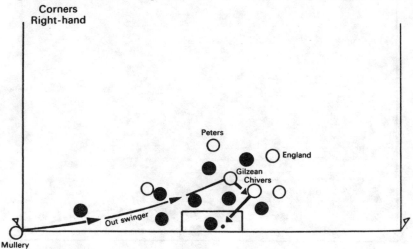

Appendix 2

Goal Categories

Categorising goals is always arbitrary, unless you simply list the goal scorer. The following system, based on how each goal was created, was devised at the beginning of the season and applied to all Spurs' goals.

1 Error: A goal which comes from a clear error by the defending side, made when a goal looked completely unlikely. It ranges from a bad pass back or the goalkeeper mishandling the ball, to an own-goal. The attacking side might still need to be quick off the mark to capitalise on the mistake, but the major factor has been the mistake itself.

2 Scramble: More skill is needed to score a Scramble goal. It's often a 50-50 situation, with the ball perhaps going either way, such as in a goal-mouth melée. There's still an element of mistake on the part of the defence but the attacking team has made an important contribution and seized the opportunity.

294

3 Dead Ball: This is a planned goal which comes from a re-start, such as a free kick, a corner or a throw-in.

4 Set Moves: Set moves are essentially *team* passing movements which to a major extent have been worked out in training, like overlapping, far post crosses, wall passes and others.

5 Individual: When a player on his own beats two men to score, or when someone scores with a brilliant shot from long range or from a difficult angle. An individual goal is the result of one player's effort as opposed to any of the other factors.

During the season, Spurs scored 119 goals – 63 in the League and 56 in all Cup games.
The type of goals were as follows:

	League	*Cup*	*Total*
Error	5	1	6
Scramble	8	7	15
Dead Ball	16	11	27
Set Moves	18	21	39
Individual	16	16	32

It's noticeable how few goals were actually given to Spurs, in the sense that they came directly from errors. It proves what most people already know. First Division defences are so well drilled and skilful these days that you rarely see defenders making mistakes.

Including the next category, Scramble goals, in which luck also plays a part, though not the major part, under twenty per cent of all Spurs goals could be said to have had an element of luck in them.

Of the 27 Dead Ball goals, 11 came from free kicks, 7 from corners, 5 from penalties and 4 from throw-ins. Spurs' most dangerous throw-in, Chivers' long throw for Gilzean to flick on with his head, became too well-known to work very often.

The majority of goals, around fifty-five per cent, were scored from either these Dead Ball tactics or Set Moves. Together they accounted for 66 goals out of the 119. Footballers might moan and groan about all the training they have to do, going over and over the same movements, but these figures leave no doubt that coaching pays dividends.

As for the goal scorers, Chivers was well ahead – scoring 44 Cup and League goals, the highest in his career, about half of them Individual goals. After Chivers came Gilzean with 22 goals (his highest for several seasons), Peters with 17, Pearce 8, Mullery 7, Perryman 5, Coates 4, England and Knowles 3, Pratt 2, Naylor, Neighbour, Morgan and Holder 1 each.

Appendix 3

First team pool: Football background

	Age	Birth date	Height	Weight	Previous Clubs	Joined Spurs	Cost	Caps
Mullery	30	23 November 1941	5' 9"	12st 10	Fulham	1964	£72,500	39 England
Jennings	26	12 June 1945	6'	13st	Watford	1964	£27,000	38 N. Ireland
Chivers	27	27 April 1945	6' 1½"	13st 9	Southampton	1968	£125,000	12 England
Perryman	20	21 December 1951	5' 8"	11st	—	1967	—	
England	29	2 December 1942	6' 2"	13st 3	Blackburn Rovers	1966	£95,000	35 Wales
Peters	28	8 November 1943	6'	12st	West Ham United	1970	£200,000	55 England
Gilzean	33	22 October 1938	6'	12st 7	Dundee	1964	£72,000	23 Scotland
Knowles	27	13 July 1944	6'	12st 2	Middlesbrough	1964	£45,000	4 England
Beal	27	1 January 1945	5' 10"	11st 11	—	1960	—	
Coates	26	26 April 1946	5' 7½"	11st 10	Burnley	1971	£190,000	4 England
Kinnear	25	27 December 1946	5' 8½"	11st 4	—	1964	—	11 Eire
Evans	22	20 September 1949	5' 9½"	12st 3	—	1965	—	
Pratt	23	26 June 1948	5' 8"	11st	—	1964	—	
Naylor	23	5 December 1948	5' 10½"	11st 3	—	1969	—	
Morgan	25	14 November 1946	5' 9"	11 st	Queens Park Rangers	1969	£100,000	
Pearce	24	27 November 1947	5' 9½"	12st	—	1963	—	
Want	23	13 December 1948	5' 8"	11st 2	—	1964	—	
Collins	23	29 November 1948	6' 1"	13st 8	Chelmsford City	1968	£5,500	

Appendix 4

Personal background

	Birthplace	Father's job	Brothers, Sisters	Education	Previous Job	Qualifications	Business Interests
Mullery	Notting Hill London	Electrician	1 brother 1 sister	St. John's Sec Mod Notting Hill	—	—	Sports shop
Jennings	Newry N. Ireland	Labourer	8 brothers 1 sister	St Joseph's Secondary Newry	Factory 1 yr Labourer 1 yr	—	—
Chivers	Southampton	Stevedore	1 brother 1 sister	Taunton's Grammar Southampton	Clerk 9 mths	5 GCE O	Garage Rep.
Perryman	Ealing London	Airport loader	2 brothers	Eliots Green Grammar Northolt	—	2 GCE O	Sports shop
England	Holywell Flintshire	Factory commissionaire	—	Basingwerk Sec Mod Holywell	—	—	Timber firm
Peters	Plaistow London	Thames lighterman	1 brother	Fanshawe Sec Mod Dagenham	—	FA Prelim coaching cert.	Martin Peters Promotions

Personal background *continued*

	Birthplace	Father's job	Brothers, Sisters	Education	Previous Job	Qualifi-cations	Business Interests
Gilzean	Perth	Painter and decorator	1 brother 1 sister	Couper Angus Junior Sec Perthshire	Book keeper 3 yrs	—	—
Knowles	Fitzwilliam Yorkshire	Miner	3 brothers 1 sister	Kinsley Sec Mod Fitzwilliam	Coal miner 3 yrs	—	Fish and Chip Shop
Beal	Godstone Surrey	Laboratory technician	1 sister	Bletchingley Sec Mod Surrey	—	—	—
Coates	Hetton-le-Hole Durham	Miner	1 brother 1 sister	Eppleton Clry. Sec Mod Durham	—	—	—
Kinnear	Dublin	Machine operator	4 sisters	Leggatt's Way Sec Mod Watford	Machine minder 1½ yrs	—	Property Co. Furniture Shop director
Evans	Edmonton London	Fitter's mate	3 brothers 2 sisters	Huxley Sec Mod Edmonton	—	—	—

Personal background continued

	Birthplace	Father's job	Brothers, Sisters	Education	Previous Job	Qualifications	Business Interests
Pratt	Hackney London	GPO Engineer	—	Clark's College Enfield	Clerk 2 mths	—	—
Naylor	Islington London	Smithfield porter	7 sisters 3 brothers	Rising Hill Sec Mod Islington	Shop 1 yr Smithfield porter 3 yrs	—	—
Morgan	Walthamstow London	Clerk	1 twin brother	Chingford Sec Mod Essex	—	2 GCE O FA Prelim coach cert.	—
Pearce	Tottenham London	Bricklayer	4 sisters 1 brother	Rowland Hill Sec Mod Tottenham	—	—	Builders merchants
Want	Shoreditch London	Warehouse foreman	2 sisters 1 brother	Parmiters Grammar Bethnal Green	—	FA Prelim coaching cert.	—
Collins	Chelmsford Essex	Sheet-metal worker	2 sisters 2 brothers	Moulshem Sec Mod Chelmsford	App. sheet metal 3 mths	—	Garage director

Appendix 5
Domestic background

	Wife	Children	House	Car	Last holiday	Interests
Mullery	June, ex-book-keeper	Samantha, 4	Large detached, Cheam, Surrey worth £19,000	1 Triumph 2 Austin 1300	Majorca	Golf
Jennings	Eleanor, ex-singer	Siobhan, 2	New detached, Herts, worth £20,000	Jaguar	Ireland	Golf, folk music
Chivers	Carol, ex-shorthand typist	Andrea, 5 Melanie, 2	Mock Georgian, Epping, worth £21,000	Zodiac	Majorca	Golf
Perryman	—	—	Parents' council house, Northolt	Cortina	Italy	—
England	Gwen, ex-hairdresser	Darren, 6 Wayne, 4 Gabrielle, 1	New detached, Herts, worth £22,000	1 Capri 2 Mini	Malta	Cricket, reading, gardening

Domestic background *continued*

	Wife	*Children*	*House*	*Car*	*Last holiday*	*Interests*
Peters	Kathy, ex-telephonist	Lee, 7 Grant, 2	Mock Georgian, Hornchurch, worth £25,000	Jaguar	Portugal	Golf, cricket
Gilzean	Irene, ex-policewoman	Kevin, 5 Ian, 3	Semi, Enfield, worth £12,000	Jaguar	Scotland	Golf
Knowles	Betty, ex-secretary	Jonathan, 4 Tracey, 1½	New detached, Cheshunt, worth £15,000	Volvo	Malta	Golf, cricket
Beal	Valerie, ex-hairdresser	Deiren, 4 Jason, 2	New detached, Surrey, worth £23,000	1 Rover 2000 2 MiniTraveller	Bournemouth	Pop music, watching football
Coates	Sandra, occupational therapist	Lisa, 3	New detached, Herts, £17,000	1 Rover 2000 2 MGC	Spain	Tennis, fishing
Kinnear	—	—	Parents' house Watford	MGB GT	Spain	Tennis, clothes, pop music
Evans	Sandra, comptometer operator	—	Rented flat, Edmonton	Vauxhall	Majorca	Golf, tennis

301

Domestic background continued

	Wife	Children	House	Car	Last holiday	Interests
Pratt	Marie, secretary	—	Semi, Ongar worth £9,000	Escort	Majorca	Cricket, table tennis
Naylor	Linda, ex-telephonist	Troy, 2 Keri Jo-Ann, 1	Rented house, Dulwich	—	Clacton	Tennis
Morgan	Marilyn, ex-hairdresser	Jason, 2	Semi, Waltham Abbey, £12,000	1 Lotus 2 Morris 1100	Cornwall	Tennis, cars, clothes
Pearce	Carole, ex-bank clerk	Leigh, 2	Semi, Ilford, £9,000	Cortina	Torquay	Tennis, golf, pop music
Want	—	—	Parents' council flat, Shoreditch	Cortina	Majorca	Golf
Collins	Sabina, ex-secretary	Matthew, 6 months	Bungalow, Chelmsford, £10,000	Capri	Ibiza	Swimming, tennis pop music

Appendix 6

Attitudes to football

How do you look upon being a professional footballer – is it a job of work or a career?

Mullery   *A job.* You go out at the same time every day. A professional man chooses his times. I'm given orders. A professional man gives orders. It's got to be a job.

Jennings   *A career.* It's my career, for the moment anyway, but it's really part of show business. When people ask me, I say I don't work, I'm a professional footballer.

Chivers   *A profession.* It sounds better if you say that. But I do see it as a specialist job, like a surgeon. You've got to be dedicated. Only one person in ten thousand does it.

Perryman   *A special job.* I talk about 'going to work' and people laugh. They think you just kick a ball about on a Saturday afternoon and that's your lot. It's special because you get attention from the public for doing it. You go to a party and they say, saw you on TV, or saw you play. I don't like the attention. If you could do it successfully without the attention, I'd prefer it, but you can't.

England   *A job.* I play it for a living as opposed to doing it just for sheer enjoyment. People depend on me to do a good job. It's not a relaxing thing. I never say I'm going to *play* football. It's work.

Attitudes to football continued

Peters *A career.* You entertain people, like show business. It gives you a lot of pride. An ordinary job doesn't do that. So it's got to be a career. My wife calls it work. If I'm going training, I say I'm going training. I never call it work.

Gilzean *A sport.* It's not a job or a career – you're meant to enjoy it. I've always enjoyed it so I've never called it work. People spend hundreds of pounds getting as fit as we are. I get paid to enjoy myself!

Knowles *A job.* It gives me a good income, at the time of going to press anyway. People pay to see me play. It's my job to make it worth it for them. It's how I get my living.

Beal *A job.* It's work, that's what I always call it. It's the job I do. What else can you call it?

Coates *A job.* I get paid for it, so it's a job. I can do without all the glamour that goes with it.

Kinnear *A career.* A career means you get on, you see things you'd never see in a factory. In a job, you don't get on. A job's a sort of routine thing.

Evans *A job.* But not an ordinary job. I *chose* it. You don't choose ordinary jobs. It's a job I like doing.

Naylor *A career.* It's a career because I have ambitions to do well in it, not like an ordinary job. I want to make the grade and be a regular first team player. I want to play for England. I want to get on.

Morgan *A job.* They pay me, don't they, so it's a job. But it's a bit like a career as well because it's entertainment. When you've a 9-5 job, you're only entertaining yourself. Being a pro footballer means earning as much money as you can in a short space of time and enjoying yourself at the same time.

Pearce *A career.* You don't get things like travel in an ordinary job. You don't have to do much grafting either. You get more spare time.

Attitudes to football continued

Want   *A profession.* I'm getting paid to do something I enjoy, so that can't be called work.

Collins   *A job.* I always call it work, so does my wife. When I come home, she says how did you get on at work. It's a job I try to do to the best of my ability. But it's a bit different from an ordinary job. When I come home from work I sit and think about all the things I did wrong. You don't do that in an ordinary job.

Pratt   *A job.* It can't be a career – you're not in it long enough. Five days a week I call it work, because I think of the money, but on the last day, Saturday, I call that play and I never think of the money.

Appendix 7

Qualities necessary for success in football

In order of importance, which of these are necessary for a successful professional footballer:
Confidence, Coaching, Luck, Perseverance, Personality, Physical toughness, Skill?

Mullery   *Luck*, skill, perseverance, coaching, confidence, toughness, personality.
I reckon I got my chance two years earlier than I would have done, just through luck. I got my chance because four people were injured in my position. I've been very lucky. Personality is definitely last. It's irrelevant. I know some great players I dislike very much.

Jennings *Skill*, confidence, luck, personality, perseverance, toughness, coaching.
You're no good without skill. I put coaching last because I've never had any. If anyone tried it now I'm as likely to say bollocks as to act on it.

Chivers   *Skill*, confidence, perseverance, luck, toughness, coaching, personality.
Personality means nothing – if you've got the rest, the crowd will still cheer you.

Perryman *Luck*, coaching, skill, confidence, perseverance, personality, toughness.
Lucky breaks make all the difference. I would never have got started but for luck.

England   *Skill*, perseverance, luck, coaching, personality, confidence, toughness.
They wouldn't look at you without skill and perseverance. The rest can be bred into you.

Qualities necessary to success in football continued

Peters

Coaching, personality, skill, confidence, perseverance, luck, toughness.

You've got to be able to listen and act on advice. I put personality high as well because you need the right character, to take 'stick when things are going wrong and the right moral character not to go off the rails when girls start chasing you when you're doing well.

Gilzean

Skill, perseverance, confidence, luck, personality, toughness, coaching.

Without skill, you haven't a chance. You could pick the best runner, the strongest athlete, but you couldn't turn him into a footballer unless he had the basic skill. I don't rate coaching very high. Any grade of manager or coach will give you that. That's what they're there for. I look upon training as getting fit to use the skills I've got naturally.

Knowles

Skill, coaching, personality, confidence, luck, perseverance, toughness.

It's like playing the piano. They can't teach you if it's not there. Skill is born into you. I think personality is important, so that people look up to you.

Beal

Luck, toughness, skill, confidence, personality, coaching, perseverance.

I was one of only two boys chosen out of thirty-three when I came for a trial – one of the ones turned down is now the captain of Chelsea. You need luck all the way along. I put perseverance last. If you get chopped from the first team and go into the reserves, it's hard to keep going and it doesn't do you any good anyway. You don't get back on reserve form but on the first team player losing his form.

Coates

Skill, confidence, coaching, luck, personality, perseverance, toughness.

If you've got no confidence in your skill, there's no point in going on the field.

Kinnear

Coaching, skill, perseverance, personality, luck, confidence, toughness.

My skill was never as great till I went to Spurs and they taught me, just simple things, like trapping the ball. You do get the naturals, the football geniuses, like Pele, Eusebio, Greaves, but everyone else needs a lot of help. How many are born being able to kick the ball with either foot?

307

Qualities necessary to success in football continued

Evans *Skill*, coaching, confidence, toughness, personality, perseverance, luck. I don't believe in luck. All the rest of these things are facts. Luck's not a fact. Footballers are always talking about luck but it's just an excuse. I'm waiting for a break, not for luck.

Naylor *Confidence*, coaching, toughness, skill, luck, perseverance, personality. You've got to go out there *thinking* you're a great player. You need coaching because they've been through the mill and can teach you a lot. Skill can come and go, but you must be tough all the time. If you're told to mark someone out of the game, you've got to do it.

Morgan *Coaching*, confidence, perseverance, skill, luck, personality, toughness. Skill isn't enough on its own. You've got to be able to use it. Toughness is last for me. I'm not tough.

Pearce *Luck*, perseverance, skill, personality, coaching, confidence, toughness. I've seen many good players go right out of the game through bad luck, such as an injury. You need perseverance to keep going when things are bad.

Want *Skill*, confidence, perseverance, luck, coaching, personality, toughness. Without skill, no one would ask you to be a player in the first place.

Collins *Skill*, luck, toughness, perseverance, coaching, personality, confidence. You do need skill to get in, but not *great* skill. I wouldn't call myself a skilful player. I owe a lot to my size and being tough. I think you can make someone a good defender but a forward has to be born.

Pratt *Luck*, skill, toughness, perseverance, coaching, confidence, personality. They're all on a par, except luck. Without luck, the rest wouldn't work. That's the vital element.

Comments

I expected every player would put skill at the top, but only half did – 9 out of the 18. But this can be misinterpreted. The ones who didn't put skill first weren't saying skill didn't matter, just that other factors went towards it being used successfully.

After skill, luck was considered the next important. Five players even put it top – Mullery, Perryman, Beal, Pratt and Pearce. Perryman was a surprise – all he's had in his career so far has been good luck whereas the other three have experienced bad luck of some sort.

Despite the fact that people on the coaching side of football are always going on about character and toughness, none of the players seemed to consider either very important. Toughness was generally placed near the end, apart from Terry Naylor who put it number 3 in his list. He's generally considered to be a tough character. Only Martin Peters talked about moral character. His reference to being chased by girls was interesting: is he secretly regretting his good character?

Appendix 8

Pre-match rituals, superstitions, anxieties.

Mullery   I always put my left pad on first. I always hang my towel on my peg with my clothes, not on the bench like the other lads. When I lead the lads out, I always bounce the ball twice on the ceiling in the corridor.

Jennings   I have no superstitions, but I get very irritable before a match. I hate any fuss. I always refuse to go shopping with the wife on a Saturday.

Chivers   I get a bit nervous away from home. When our fans shout my name, I never wave back, but at home, I always do. I feel at home that anything I do is right in their eyes. I don't have lucky signs, except my teeth. Sometimes I play with them in and sometimes out, but I can't decide which brings best luck. I worry about how I look with them out.

Perryman   I'm always third out on to the pitch. I did it once, years ago, and played a good game so I've done it ever since. I wear nothing under my shorts. I feel freer without anything. I don't worry about being injured but I worry about being dropped. Inside the club it would be OK, they'd understand, but outside, with friends and the Press, I wouldn't be able to bear the aggravation.

England   I start thinking about the game on a Friday night. I might be talking to Gwen, but I'm thinking about their centre forward's weak spot, going over his record in my mind. Every season I keep in my head a count of all the centre forwards who've scored against me. It's a little competition I have with myself. I like to be last in the

Prematch rituals, superstitions, anxieties continued

dressing-room. I stand in the car park, chatting, as long as possible. I never have a cup of tea in Mrs Wallace's office like the rest of the lads. I don't like her tea. Too strong. I worry about my ankles and always get them both strapped up.

Peters I never go through the main door to the dressing-room. I made a mistake the first time and went through the boot room so now I always do. I believe in lucky signs. I have lucky cuff links, ones I got in Brazil. I always put my shorts on last. I hate any larking around in the dressing-room, any music or noise. I think a dressing-room should always be quiet and tense. At Spurs, if we're playing a lower team in the League, there's usually a lot of noise. I think that's bad.

Gilzean I always have oils rubbed into my legs before a match. It's probably old age creeping up. But I haven't any superstitions. I never think about such things.

Knowles I've got no superstitions. I'm a terrible coward when it comes to pain, but I tend to worry more about losing form and being dropped than being injured.

Beal I'm always last out, even at half-time. I go round the toilets to make sure no one's left behind. I don't like wearing pads. I worry that they'll stop the circulation in my calf muscles.

Coates I oil my legs for good luck. If I have a bad game, I stop it for a week. I don't actually believe it makes any difference, but I always find myself doing it.

Kinnear I never put my shorts on till the buzzer goes. Until then I walk round in my jock strap, carrying my shorts. I worry about loss of form but I suppose every player does. I worry a bit about being right footed. I wish I'd started on my left years ago.

Evans I like to get changed as late as possible, that's all. I don't believe in lucky signs.

Prematch rituals, superstitions, anxieties *continued*

Naylor   At one time I always used to touch the ground before the match and after we'd scored. It's supposed to be a good luck sign, like touching something twice so your mother will live for ever. Then I just forgot to do it. I don't have any superstitions now. But I have little habits I like doing, such as splashing water on my face and legs. It makes me feel fresh.

Morgan   I always have chewing gum to go on the pitch, but I spit it out before the game starts. As I spit out, I try to kick it. If I hit it well, I'll have a good game. I've lots of superstitions. When they don't work, I change them.

Pearce   I always massage my legs before a match. I like playing top teams best. I don't play so well against not so good teams.

Want   I like getting changed very early, about forty minutes before the match. I always rub my thighs with Transvasin cream, all the season round, just out of habit.

Collins   I like to wear the same clothes to every match. I once wore the same suede jacket for two years. I always drive the same way to the ground. I always take my trousers off first and put my jock strap on before I take off my jacket. I like to go out on the field second from the end. I never carry a ball out.

Pratt   I always go to the kazzi in the dressing-room, save it up for the last thing. I feel better when I clear myself. Before big matches, I kiss my wedding ring for good luck. My only worry is whether I'm going to play – I rarely know till the day of the match and I worry about it all week.

Appendix 9

Enjoyment of football

Do you enjoy the act of playing football more today than you did at 15?

Mullery   *Today.* I was better than the others I played with as a kid. Now they're on a par with me, or better. We're playing the best all the time. I look upon that as a pleasure, not a worry.

Jennings   *At 15.* It was much more of a pleasure when I first began. Now I'm relieved when it's all over. So many people depend on me not to make mistakes. It's a big strain. I'm mentally exhausted after a game.

Chivers   *Today.* I enjoy it more now because of the tensions. I like having to concentrate, to use my brains. I never use them otherwise.

Perryman   *At 15.* At school I could take liberties, being better than the others. Now you've got a job to do and you have to stick to it.

England   *At 15.* Method outweighs skill today. You've got to be brilliant to shine.

Peters   *At 15.* I love football and always will, but I enjoyed it more at fifteen. There were no pressures then, no Press or public to worry about. It's much more difficult today.

Gilzean   *At 15.* Football's meant to be enjoyed and I still enjoy it, but I probably enjoyed it more at fifteen. The finer points disappeared when England won the World Cup in 1966. Now the object is not to get beat at all costs.

Knowles   *At 15.* Nothing was said if you made a mistake at school. Now it's your living. You can't make mistakes. I watch Sunday morning players do diabolical things and I think, I'd get a right roasting for that.

Enjoyment of football *continued*

Beal
At 15. There was less tension then. People think footballers have a cushy number, home during the week at two o'clock, but they don't know anything about the tensions.

Coates
At 15. The higher I've got in football the less I seem to have enjoyed it. The pressures of success spoil the fruits of success.

Kinnear
Today. It churns you up inside when it's places like Milan with all the firecrackers going off, but I love all the excitement and atmosphere of pro football. It's the place to be, being at the top.

Evans
The same. There wasn't much at risk at fifteen, but I enjoy my football now as much as I ever did.

Naylor
Today. It's more competitive now, which I like, and I'm playing with better players.

Morgan
At 15. I had no responsibilities then and much more enjoyment. Now the enjoyment's spoiled. I'd rather play for nothing and have an outside job, if I could get one. But there's nothing else I can do.

Pearce
At 15. Professionals are not allowed to play their natural game. There's too much system involved. I'm sure Sunday morning players get more pleasure than professionals. There's so much at stake. It's a shame. I don't look forward to playing as much as I did at fifteen.

Want
The same. If I train five days and then don't play on the Saturday, I'm heartbroken, just as much as ever I was. Perhaps being unmarried I don't feel the tensions as much. The first team married players seem to have more worries about doing well, about the money and security.

Collins
At 15. I had no worries then. Now you've got to go out there and be successful. That's all that matters.

Pratt
Today. I'm in the top bracket now. When I play for the first team on a Saturday, that's the ultimate. It must be better now.

314

Enjoyment of football continued

Comments

It's a sad reflection on modern football that the majority of this sample of top professionals should admit they don't enjoy the game as much as they did when they were younger. Over sixty per cent (eleven out of the eighteen) said they enjoyed it more at fifteen. It's not just the pressures of being in a top club, a club which has to have success, but perhaps the toughness of the English First Division and the prevailing methods of play which are to blame.

Appendix 10

Social attitudes

	Do you help in the house?	Do you follow current events?	Newspapers	Politics
Mullery	I can cook a steak and I'm learning to do omelettes. I dry the dishes when I'm at home. During Coronation Street I wash and dry. I bath Samantha and always have done. I used to change her nappies as a baby. I think it's only fair that I should take my turn in the house.	I would say I know roughly what's happening in the world.	Sun, Sunday Express, Sunday People, News of the World.	Tory (It seems obvious)
Jennings	I never help in the house. I couldn't change a nappy. I've never washed a dish. She's never asked me. I wouldn't expect her to, neither would she. In Ireland, men don't do any housework. If I'd married an English girl perhaps I'd be doing it now. They seem to accept it here. I just sit back in the house and I'm the boss, at least I like to think I am.	I've no interest in current events, except this year I've been reading about Ulster.	Sun, Sunday People, Sunday Mirror, News of the World.	None (I keep well out of it)

Social 'attitudes continued

	Do you help in the house?	Do you follow current events?	Newspapers	Politics
Chivers	I can't look after myself at all. I'm lost when she's away. I never do any housework. It's not nice to have to admit it, but Carol's accepted it so I never have to try.	No. I only read the sports pages. I've never read a book in my life. I haven't the time. I'm just not interested.	Sun, News of the World.	None (Not interested)
Perryman	I live at home. My Mum does everything.	I can't talk about what's happening. I'm no good at talking. But I watch the current affairs programmes on TV and I think I know what's going on.	Daily Mirror, Sunday Mirror, Sunday People, Sunday Express, News of the World.	Labour (Definitely. Aren't all the players Labour?)
England	I help with the kids, making up bedtime stories for them. I dry the dishes sometimes and generally help out. My wife is an equal partner – in fact she's the boss if anything.	I think I keep well in touch. I know what's happening in Vietnam.	Daily Telegraph, Sunday Telegraph.	Tory.
Peters	I do my share, putting the baby to bed if it's my turn, washing up the dishes, put the baby's nappy on. Kathy does most of course. She pays the bills and if there's any complaints to be made, she does it. I don't like telling people off.	No. I don't know much about what's happening. I never read books.	Sun, Sunday People, News of the World.	Tory. (But I'm not interested)

317

Social attitudes *continued*

	Do you help in the house?	Do you follow current events?	Newspapers	Politics
Gilzean	I don't do much, just look after the kids now and again.	I'm not interested.	Daily Express, Sunday Express.	Tory (But there's nothing between them)
Knowles	If I'm sat doing nothing I might dry the pots. With young kids in the house I think you should help out.	I'm not that way minded.	Sun, Sunday Mirror, News of the World.	Labour (It's my background)
Beal	I help a bit in the house, get the kids' breakfast of a Saturday morning. I wash the dishes now and again. But the wife chooses everything for the house. I'm colour blind.	I'm not really interested.	Sun, Sunday Express, Sunday People, News of the World.	Tory
Coates	I help a bit, but not much. My wife decides most things in the house. She's got the intelligence.	News at Ten is my favourite TV programme. I like to know what's happening.	Daily Express, Sunday Express, Observer.	Labour (I liked the candidate)

Social attitudes · continued

	Do you help in the house?	Do you follow current events?	Newspapers	Politics
Kinnear	I live at home so my Mum does everything. When I get married, I just want my wife to be a woman, you know, bring up the kids. I'd be the boss, but I'd ask her opinions. I'd want someone intelligent.	Outside football, I don't know anything. The world could be coming to an end and I wouldn't know, unless it was on the sports pages.	Sun, Sunday Mirror, Sunday People, News of the World.	Tory
Evans	I help out, if I'm asked, like washing up, but she doesn't often ask me.	Not interested.	Sun, Sunday People, Sunday Express, News of the World.	Tory
Naylor	I help with the baby, change nappies, give bottles. I want to give my wife all the help I can. She works hard in the house. I take her advice, but I make all the big decisions.	Not interested.	Sun, Sunday People, Sunday Mirror.	Tory
Morgan	I dry after a meal and play with the kid, fighting on the floor with him. She can have anything she wants in the house. I feel sorry for her having to stay at home while I'm off enjoying myself.	I watch the news and I like the debates, but I don't know much. I'm not a racialist like some of them.	Sun, Sunday People.	Tory (But not interested)

319

Social attitudes continued

	Do you help in the house?	Do you follow current events?	Newspapers	Politics
Pearce	The bloke has to be in charge. A wife shouldn't be equal. I do the decorating but the baby's hers. She looks after it.	It doesn't mean anything to me.	Sun, Sunday Mirror, Sunday People, News of the World.	None
Want	I live at home. My Mum does everything.	Not interested.		None
Collins	I occasionally help with the dishes. I did more when she was pregnant.	It's not one of the things I think about. I just accept whichever Government is in and moan about it, like everyone else.	Sun, Sunday Express, Sunday People, News of the World.	None
Pratt	I might wash up now and again. She says I don't do enough.	I'm interested in the news. In company I can talk about it..	Sun, Sunday Express, Sunday People, News of the World.	None

Comments

Of all the players, the only one with any real political feeling was Steve Perryman. Three altogether said they voted Labour, but Coates and Knowles, the other two, did it simply because of their background, without thinking about it either way. But Perryman has very strong views on tax ('It's got to be paid') which are different from the other players, and is against private schools. He couldn't believe that so many of the other players were Tory and were planning to send their kids to fee paying schools.   Several of the players were decidedly racist in their views. Most were apathetic Tories.

Despite the affluence of their houses, the majority still reflect their working class upbringing in their normal domestic life.

320

Appendix 11

Plans for the future

	Would you like to stay in football when your playing days are over?	*What plans or preparations have you made?*
Mullery	When I finish at Spurs, I would like another club, if I wasn't too old. I hope to carry on till I'm thirty-five. But once that's over, that's it. I don't want to become a manager. I couldn't do what Bill Nick does. I'd end up in the loony bin.	It's a big problem. I want my standard of living to continue, but where do I get a job with £5,000 a year for the rest of my life? My shop only gives me a small income and anyway I don't want to work in that. I don't know what I'll do.
Jennings	If some other team wanted me, I'd keep going as long as possible. I would like to stay in football, but I'd be no good. I know the game well but I can't talk it. I'll have to look for an ordinary job.	I've got no plans. All I hope is that I'll end up with enough money saved to start a little business. It doesn't worry me really. I've got a nice house. I've seen the world. I'm grateful to football for what I've had.
Chivers	I dread the day I won't be able to play any more. I want to stay in the game, not as a manager but perhaps as a coach.	I've made no plans. I don't see why you need to pass these FA badges to be a coach. As a player you know all that. And I've been educated. I think I'll get some sort of coaching job when the time comes.
Perryman	I've never thought about it.	I've got my sports shop, which is a bit of security, but I've no idea what I'll end up doing.

Plans for the future continued

	Would you like to stay in football when your playing days are over?	What plans or preparations have you made?
England	No. I don't think I'd be good at it.	Being injured for seven months really brought the future home to me. I realised I'd never thought about it properly before. Now I've got my timber business and a new venture I've just planned which could be very big.
Peters	I'd love to stay in football. I love the game so much. I'll start at the bottom, as some sort of coach. I know there are a lot more worries, being a manager than a player, but I'd still be part of the game, living it with the players.	I've got my FA prelim badge, which is a start. Outside football, I've got no plans. I don't want the worries of a business while I'm still playing.
Gilzean	You must be joking. When I've finished playing, that's it. I couldn't stand the aggravation of being a manager, having fans, directors, Press, everyone after you. No thanks.	I fancy going to South Africa for a year or so, play with some club and get a bit of sun. After that, I don't know. I never plan. I never worry. I've got no business interests at all. I admire wee Joe with his property, but I couldn't do it. Today, I'm playing for Tottenham. Tomorrow, we'll have to wait and see.
Knowles	When you've seen Bill before a match, that really puts you off.	The chip shop I'm involved in is up in Leeds and I'm selling it soon. I don't know whether I'll go back there or not. I've got no plans.
Beal	I'd be no good as a coach. I haven't the authority to put it across. But I like watching football, at any level, so I wouldn't mind being a scout.	I fancy South Africa for a year or so, then I'll come back and buy a little business. Perhaps a baby boutique. I've got an insurance policy which matures when I'm thirty-five and gives me £9,000, so that's a start. I couldn't do anything now, not when I'm playing, I've enough worries.

Plans for the future continued

	Would you like to stay in football when your playing days are over?	*What plans or preparations have you made?*
Coates	I wouldn't like to be a coach or a manager. There are too many pressures. As a spare time interest, I might coach amateurs. I like winning. I don't like *having* to win.	It's sufficient playing without having any business worries. When I finish, I might buy a little business. I've got a few investments. I should manage something.
Kinnear	I can't imagine a life outside football. It'll be very sad when it comes. I wouldn't go and ponce at a lower club, just for the sake of a living. I'd like to stay in football somehow, perhaps as a coach.	Financially, I expect to be completely secure when I retire from football. I've got several houses now and I plan to buy one every season. I don't know what my actual job will be, perhaps something in fashion. To get experience I do odd afternoons in a furniture showroom.
Evans	I wouldn't like football to be suddenly cut off. I can't imagine a life without it. I'd like to stay in it, but I don't know what as.	I haven't thought about it. It's too early. I couldn't go into a business because I don't know from week to week what sort of money I'll be making. One day I probably will think about it properly, but I haven't yet.
Naylor	I'd like to stay in football perhaps as a coach. I don't know if I'd be up to being a manager. Perhaps as I mature I might think more on those lines.	I plan to do the FA coaching badge some time, but apart from that, I've no plans. If it ended tomorrow, I'd still be pleased — I've done something, which is better than those who've done nothing.
Morgan	When I finish, I want to get right away from football. It's bloody football wherever you go these days. Every pub you go into is the same, even in the summer. Having it drummed into you all season is bad enough.	No plans. If I got enough money together, I'd like a little business. I wouldn't mind working in a holiday camp, organising the sports side.

Plans for the future continued

	Would you like to stay in football when your playing days are over?	What plans on preparations have you made?
Pearce	I'd never stay in football on the management side. That's a rotten job. Just a load of worries, looking after forty blokes. Never.	My only plan is to go into my father-in-law's central heating business, perhaps looking after the shop. I've no qualifications. What else can I do?
Want	I want to stay in football, as a coach. I don't think I'm cut out to be a manager. You've got to eat, drink and sleep football to be a manager. I don't think any of our first team squad could be a manager. None of them are as dedicated as Bill or Eddie.	I've got my FA prelim badge and I'm going to do the full badge soon. I coach the schoolboys twice a week. Football's the only thing I want to do.
Collins	I could never be a manager, even if I wanted to. I've seen Bill too many times with the blinking shakes to want his sort of job.	I've got a share in a garage but it hasn't made money yet. I don't know what I'll do for a job. But I'll have a roof over my head, that's the main thing.
Pratt	I want to stay in, to help the young boys. I've enjoyed the life I've led and I want them to do the same.	I coach the schoolboys at Spurs twice a week. I failed the theory part of my FA prelim badge but I plan to do it again. Outside football, I've no plans.

324

Appendix 12

Spurs management

	Position	Born	Jobs	Playing career	Honours	Management Career
Bill Nicholson	Manager	1919 Scarborough	Laundry, 6 months	Spurs, 1936-56	1 Cap for England	Spurs Coach, 1956-8. Spurs manager, 1958-
Eddie Baily	Assistant Manager	1926 Clapton	Factory, 6 months. Clerk, 2 years	Spurs, 1947-54 Port Vale, 1954-7 Notts. For. 1957-9 Orient, 1959-60	11 Caps for England	Orient trainer, 1960-2. Spurs Ass. Man. 1962-
Pat Welton	Youth Team Manager	1928 Eltham	Shop Assistant, 3 years	Orient, 1948-58 Q.P.R., 1958-9	—	Amateur League manager, 1959-62. FA staff coach, 1962. England Youth Team manager, 1963-9. Spurs, 1969-
Cecil Poynton	Trainer	1901 Brownhills, Staffs.	Colliery worker, 5 years	Spurs, 1921-35 Ramsgate, 1935-6	England tour of Australia, 1925	Player-manager Ramsgate, 1935-6. Spurs training staff, 1936-
Johnny Wallis	Trainer	1923 Finchley	None	Spurs, 1937-47	—	Spurs training staff, 1947-

Appendix 13

Spurs Board of Directors.

	Born	Educated	Profession	Job	Married	House	Joined Spurs
Sidney Wale (Chairman)	1913 Stoke Newington	Tottenham Grammar School	Chartered accountant	Retired. (Formerly M.D. of bolt and nut firm)	Wife, Cynthia, 2 daughters	Detached, Hadley Wood, worth £30,000.	Director 1957 Chairman 1969
Charles Cox (Vice-chairman)	1899 Holloway	Cambridge House School	Salesman	Retired. (Formerly sales promotion manager of car sales firm)	Widower, 1 daughter	Semi-detached, Finchley, worth £12,000	Director 1962
Arthur Richardson	1905 Islington	Barnsbury Park Secondary	Company director	M.D. of family wastepaper firm	Widower, 2 daughters, 1 son	Detached, Potters Bar, worth £30,000	Director 1961
Godfrey Groves	1908 Tottenham	Tottenham Grammar School	Quantity Surveyor	Senior Partner in own surveying firm	Bachelor	Elizabethan mansion, Enfield worth £100,000	Director 1969
Geoffrey Richardson (son of Arthur)	1940 Stoke Newington	Highgate School	Company director	Director of family wastepaper firm	Wife, Vivien	Flat, Potters Bar, worth £12,000.	Director 1970

Appendices to 1985 Edition

327

Appendix 1 *SPURS, 1971-72: Where are they now?*

Mullery   Ex-manager. Was at Brighton, Crystal Palace, QPR. Now out of work . . .

Jennings   Still playing, for Arsenal, in 1984-85 season — then retired.

Chivers   Publican. Went to Servette (Switzerland), then Norwich, Brighton, Barnet, then retired. Occasional radio work on football.

Perryman   Still playing — Captain of Spurs

England   Manager of Wales

Peters   Business Executive in Essex. Was player-manager at Sheffield Utd, then non-league, then retired.

Gilzean   Transport manager for a lorry firm. Played in South Africa, player-manager Stevenage, then retired.

Knowles   Manager of Darlington

Beal   Sports teacher. Played for Brighton, Crewe, then retired.

Coates   Manager Ware Town. Played for Orient, then in Australia.

Kinnear   Leisure Centre Manager. Played for Brighton, then player-manager non-league, then retired. Part-time BBC work.

Evans   Still playing — indoor football in USA. Played with Millwall, Stoke and Fulham, before going to USA.

Pratt   Assistant First Team Coach, Spurs.

Naylor   Player-coach, Gravesend. Played for Charlton.

Morgan   Sports teacher. Retired injured from Spurs.

Pearce   Working in rag trade. Retired injured from Spurs.

Want   Warehouse manager in Birmingham. Played for Birmingham, then in USA, then retired.

Collins   Market stall holder, Chelmsford.

SPURS, 1971-72: Where are they now?

Management

Bill Nicholson	Consultant to Spurs
Eddie Baily	Chief Scout, West Ham
Pat Welton	Publican
Cecil Poynton	Dead
Johnny Wallis	Trainer/Kit man

Appendix 2 *Spurs Board of Directors: 1985*

Name	Age	Profession	Joined Spurs
Irving Scholar (Chairman)	37	Company Director	1983
Douglas Alexiou (Vice Chairman)	43	Solicitor	1980
Paul Bobroff	34	Chairman of Markheath Securities	1982
Frank Sinclair	69	Joint MD of Mountview Estates	1982

329

Appendix 3 *Spurs Management: 1985*

Name	Position	Born (Place & Year)	Outside Jobs	Playing Career	Management Career
PETER SHREEVES	Manager	Neath S. Wales 1940	Taxi driver	Reading FC, Wimbledon, Chelmsford City	Youth Team Manager, 1974. Asst. Man., 1981.
JOHN PRATT	Asst First Team Coach	Hackney 1948.	Clerk 2 months.	Spurs, 1956-80. Portland Timbers, US	Youth team Manager, 1983.
DOUG LIVERMORE	Reserve Team Manager	Liverpool 1947	Apprentice Electrician	Liverpool, Norwich, Chester, Cardiff, Swansea.	Coach, Swansea. Spurs, 1984.
KEITH BLUNT	Youth Team Manager	Hull 1947	Teacher (Law Degree Sheffield Univ)	Sutton	Manager, Malmo, Sweden. Manager, Sutton.
MIKE VARNEY	Physio-therapist	Leeds 1945	Army PE Sergeant, 10 years Physiotherapist	None	Spurs physiotherapist, 1975-
JOHNNY WALLIS	Trainer/ Kit man	Finchley, 1923	None	Spurs, 1937-47	Spurs training staff, 1947-

Appendix 4A – Players: *Basic Facts*

Spurs 1984-85	Age	Birth Date	Birth Place	Height	Weight
PERRYMAN, Steve	34	21 December, 1951	Ealing	5.8	11.7
CLEMENCE, Ray	37	5 August, 1948	Skegness	5.11½	12.9
HODDLE, Glenn	28	27 October, 1957	Hayes, Middlesex	6.1	12.7
ROBERTS, Graham	26	3 July, 1959	Southampton	6.0	13.0
MABBUTT, Gary	24	23 August, 1961	Bristol	5.9	11.7
ARDILES, Ossie	33	3 August, 1952	Cordoba, Argentina	5.6	9.10
STEVENS, Gary	23	30 March, 1962	Hillingdon	6.0	12.0
ALLEN, Clive	24	20 May, 1961	London	5.10	12.3
CROOKS, Garth	27	10 March, 1958	Stoke	5.8	11.6
MILLER, Paul	26	11 October, 1959	Stepney	6.1	12.12
GALVIN, Tony	29	12 July, 1956	Huddersfield	5.9	11.0
HAZARD, Mike	25	5 February, 1960	Sunderland	5.7	10.5
CHIEDOZIE, John	25	18 April, 1960	Nigeria	5.7	10.10
THOMAS, Danny	24	12 November, 1961	Worksop	5.7	10.2
HUGHTON, Chris	27	11 December, 1958	Forestgate	5.7¾	11.0
FALCO, Mark	25	22 October, 1960	Hackney	6.0	12.0
BROOKE, Garry	25	24 November, 1960	Bethnal Green	5.6	10.5
LEWORTHY, Dave	23	22 October, 1962	Portsmouth	5.8½	12.0
WADDLE, Chris	25	14 December, 1960	Hepworth, Co. Durham	6.0	11.5

Appendix 4B – Players: *Football Career*

Spurs 1985	Joined Spurs	Previous Clubs	Cost	Caps
PERRYMAN	1967	None	Nil	1 (England)
CLEMENCE	1981	Scunthorpe, Liverpool	£300,000	61 (England)
HODDLE	1974	None	Nil	22 (England)
ROBERTS	1980	Portsmouth, Bournemouth, Weymouth	£35,000	6 (England)
MABBUTT	1982	Bristol Rovers	£115,000	9 (England)
ARDILES	1978	Huracan, Instituto, Cordoba	£325,000	42 (Argentina)
STEVENS	1983	Brighton	£300,000	3 (England)
ALLEN	1984	QPR, Arsenal, Crystal Palace, QPR	£700,000	3 (England)
CROOKS	1980	Stoke	£600,000	None
MILLER	1976	None	Nil	None
GALVIN	1978	Goole Town	£5,000	10 (Eire)
HAZARD	1977	None	Nil	None
CHIEDOZIE	1984	Orient, Notts Co.	£370,000	8 (Nigeria)
THOMAS	1983	Coventry	£230,000	2 (England)
HUGHTON	1977	None	Nil	25 (Eire)
FALCO	1978	None	Nil	None
BROOKE	1977	None	Nil	None
LEWORTHY	1984	Portsmouth, Fareham Town	£5,000	None
WADDLE	1985	Tow Law Town, Newcastle Utd.	?	3 (England)

Note: The surveys include the 18 who played in the first team 1984-85; plus Chris Waddle, due to arrive in the summer of 1985, who kindly agreed to answer the same questionnaire.

Appendix 4C – Personal Background

Spurs 1985	Father's Job	Educ. Qualifications	Non-football jobs	Business Interests
PERRYMAN	Airport loader	2 O levels	None	4 Sports Shops (3 London, 1 Norway)
CLEMENCE	–	1 O level	Bank Clerk	Building Contractor
HODDLE	Printer	Nil	None	Sports Shop
ROBERTS	Fruit Stall holder	–	Fruit Stall, fitter's mate	–
MABBUTT	Financial Consultant	4 O levels	None	None so far
ARDILES	Solicitor	Almost completed law degree	None	None
STEVENS	Quality Controller	9 O levels	None	Sports Firm, Children Sports Holidays
ALLEN	Ex-Pro Footballer, now a Carpenter	6 O levels	None	None Yet
CROOKS	–	5 O levels	–	Broadcasting
MILLER	Security Officer	Nil	None	Finance Consultant
GALVIN	Bus driver	B.A. (Russian Studies – Hull University)	Teacher Training	None
HAZARD	Out of work	3 O levels	None	None
CHIEDOZIE	–	–	None	None
THOMAS	Retired Miner	6 O levels	None	None as of this moment
HUGHTON	–	None	Lift engineer (Qualified)	None at present
FALCO	–	–	None	–
BROOKE	–	–	None	–
LEWORTHY	Ex-Pro Footballer, now plumber	None	Unemployed	None
WADDLE	Retired NCB worker	None	Job in seasoning factory	None

Appendix 4D – Domestic

Spurs 1985	Wife — Previous Job?	Children	House – Value?	Car	Do you help in house?
PERRYMAN	Cherrill — NCR operator	Loren (10) Glenn (7)	4 bed, modern, £100,000	Renault	No
CLEMENCE	Vee	Sarah Jane (12) Julie (11) Stephen (7)	—	Sierra	—
HODDLE	Anne — teacher	Zoë (1)	4 bed, modern, £120,000	Mercedes	—
ROBERTS	Ann	Hollie-Ann (2)	—	Porsche 944	—
MABBUTT	Not married		4 bed, modern, det.	Ford XR3i	I live alone
ARDILES	Silvia — secretary	Pablo (10) Federico (7)	4 bed, det.	Jaguar	Not at all
STEVENS	Not married		4 bed, det. neo Georgian	Sierra	Run it totally — single lad
ALLEN	Lisa — physiotherapist	—	—	Ford XR3i	As much as I can
CROOKS	Not married	—	Modern House	—	
MILLER	Shelley — travel agent	Charlotte (1)	4 bed, Old, £150,000	BMW 735	No
GALVIN	Julie — French teacher	Lucy (3) Thomas (1)	New house	Sierra XR4	Yes — especially with children
HAZARD	Yvonne — travel agent	—	3 bed, modern	Ford Escort	Yes, a lot
CHIEDOZIE	Not married	—	—	Austin Montego	Yes — washing up, cooking
THOMAS	Angie — Secretary		3 bed, new £90,000	Austin Montego	A little
HUGHTON	Cheryl — acounts admin.	Leon (9) Carleen (5)	3 bed, 1965 £95,000	Mazda 323	Yes
FALCO	Not married	None	—	Rover	—
BROOKE	Tracey — secretary	None	—		
LEWORTHY	Helen — secretary	Kelly (2) Craig (1 month)	2 Bed Flat £28,000	Ford Capri	When I can
WADDLE	Lorna — Printing works	None	3 bed, Link house 15 years, £27,500	Ford XR3i	Yes

Appendix 4E– *Interests*

Spurs 1985	Hobbies, Interests	Newspapers	Last Holiday	Politics
PERRYMAN	Football, family	D Ex/Sun Mirror, Sun People, NoW	Algarve	I said Labour last time, but I didn't vote at last election.
CLEMENCE	Golf, badminton, squash	D Mirror/Sun Ex	Portugal	— ,
HODDLE	Golf, tennis, snooker	D Mirror	Florida	Liberal
ROBERTS	Golf, tennis, horse racing	Sporting Life	Tenerife	—
MABBUTT	Walking the dog, golf, tennis, driving	D Ex/Sun Times, Sun Mail, Sun Mirror	Florida	None
ARDILES	Chess, tennis, snooker, reading	Times/Sun Times	Bahamas	—
STEVENS	Golf, gardening, building a career for after football	D Ex/Sun Ex	Tenerife	—
ALLEN	Tennis, squash, golf	D Ex/Sun Mirror, Mail	Portugal	Not really
CROOKS	Pop Music	—	—	—
MILLER	Golf	D Ex, Sun/NoW, Sun Ex	Rhodes	Conservative
GALVIN	Coaching kids; my children; newspapers; politics; quiz games	Guardian, Mirror/Observer	Cornwall	Labour — fan of Neil Kinnock
HAZARD	Beating Ossie at golf, tennis, cricket, snooker	Sun; Mirror/Sun People, Sun Mirror	Crete	Labour
CHIEDOZIE	Golf, snooker, tennis	Sun/NoW	Portugal	—
THOMAS	Most other Sports	D Mail/Sun Ex	Barbados	—
HUGHTON	Reading, soul music, clothes, friends	D Mirror D Ex /Sun Mirror, Sun People, Sun Telegraph	Portugal	—
FALCO	Clay pigeon shooting, driving, all sports	Spurs News	Florida	—
BROOKE	—	—	—	—
LEWORTHY	Tennis, playing with my children	Sun, Star/Sun Mirror	Dawlish, Devon	—
WADDLE	TV	Mirror/Sun People	Cyprus	—

Appendix 4F – Spurs 1985

Spurs 1985	Pre-match rituals	Future plans – would you like to stay in football?
PERRYMAN	Always first out. Now I do wear a jock strap under shorts	I would like to, and pass on what I've learned. I could work in my shops, but I'd find that a bit static. If I can't get into management, I have an idea for coaching kids.
CLEMENCE	Always same warm-up routines	Running my building business — or like to try my hand at public relations
HODDLE	Like to wear no 10 shirt	At the moment — I just want to stay in football
ROBERTS	Always go out last	—
MABBUTT	I drink Lucozade	I am undecided at this moment in time
ARDILES	None	I would like to stay in football
STEVENS	None	After playing, I want to run my own business which will be established during my playing days
ALLEN	Never score in kick-in	Not sure. Would like to run my own business
CROOKS	—	—
MILLER	None really	No plans really, but I would like to have a choice
GALVIN	Never wear shin pads	Perhaps — maybe on youth or schoolboy side. Have done a couple of courses in Sports Centre Management which interests me
HAZARD	None	No. Not stay in football. I'd like to start a business
CHIEDOZIE	—	—
THOMAS	No set pattern	No, I'm going to be a businessman
HUGHTON	None	I would like to stay in the game in some coaching capacity
FALCO	Bad luck to discuss superstitions — too many to mention	—
BROOKE	—	—
LEWORTHY	None	To stay in the game as long as I can
WADDLE	Go out third if possible	It's all a question mark

Appendix 5

Comments on 1985 players

The questionnaire I gave the players in 1972 was much more detailed than in 1985. I had got to know each one personally and sat with them at home and talked them through their answers. This time, I kept the questions much simpler and relied on each one to fill in their own answers and post them to me. I had to chase many of them for their replies, or get Steve Perryman to help, but even so I ended up with quite a few blanks. Sometimes, as with the question about politics, there was indeed no answer, as many of them have no views on politics. On some other topics some of them preferred to keep certain things private.

It is therefore a bit difficult in some respects to compare the eighteen Spurs players of 1972 with the eighteen players of today, but I intend to do so all the same. That's the fun of surveys. Looking for changes and trends.

Firstly, the proportion of bought as opposed to home grown players is almost exactly the same. In 1972, ten of the eighteen had been bought from other clubs, while eight came up through the ranks of the apprentices. In the 1984-85 season, eleven were bought and seven were home grown. There are slightly more internationals in the team today, eleven in all, compared with nine in the 1972 squad.

Ralph Coates was the most expensive player in 1972, having cost £190,000, while Clive Allen was the most expensive in 1985, at £700,000. Not much can be read into these sums, nor would any fan of either generation consider either of these the 'best' player. That is simply the money that had to be paid at a certain time to get them. Values generally appeared to have

337

risen about five times. In those days, the established players lived in £20,000 houses — today it is nearer £100,000. In each case, they have tended to go for four-bedroom, new, detached neo-Georgian houses on new estates.

Their wages are of course utterly secret, but they too appeared to have risen five times. In 1972, the established first team players were earning about £5,000 a year. In 1985, they were getting around £25,000-£30,000, with presumably senior or star people like Hoddle, Clemence and Perrymen getting more. (In the club's 1984 Annual Report, one employee only was stated to be in the £35,000-£40,000 wage bracket. Now who could that have been?) Senior players also have a high income apart from their playing salary, much more than in 1972, from advertising, sponsorship and other commercial activities.

From an educational and social point of view, there have been some marked changes. It would appear that the players, on the whole, are becoming better educated and more middle class. At least nine of them today have got O levels, including one who is a graduate, Tony Galvin. There is also Ardiles, who has almost completed his law degree. In 1972, only three could boast any O levels. People like Galvin and Ardiles do raise the tone when it comes to personal interests (not many footballers anywhere would list their interests as chess or politics), but even discounting these two graduate minds, it is noticeable that in 1972 the average player put some form of pop music as a main interest. In 1985, only two of the 18 mentioned popular music.

In 1972, the Sun was overwhelmingly the most popular daily paper — being mentioned 13 times, followed by the Daily Express 2, the Mirror 1, and the Telegraph 1. This time, the Sun has been eclipsed, being mentioned only 4 times. The two most popular daily papers are the Express 6 and the Mirror 5, then comes the Sun 4, Star 1, Guardian 1, Times 1, Mail 1.

Amongst the Sunday papers in 1972, the People and the News of the World were most popular, with 12 each, followed by the Sunday Express 8, Mirror 7, Telegraph 1, Observer 1. There were fewer totals mentioned today, but the Sunday Mirror now appears marginally the most popular, with 6 mentions, followed by the Sunday Express 4, the People 4, and the News of the World 3, Mail on Sunday 2, Telegraph 1, Observer 1 and Sunday Times 1.

Domestically, it is interesting to see a scattering of players who are buying and running their own houses, and living there (as far as they are prepared to tell us) on their own. Their holidays these days are more exotic, which is the general pattern anyway, with only two staying in Britain for their last holiday, as opposed to six in 1972 who did not go abroad.

As for their future plans, they are interesting if not very informative. In 1972, Cyril Knowles was definite that he did not fancy a career in management, which is what he is doing today, at the last count. Who knows if he will continue, or whether those with management ambitions today will ever make it? We shall see. Steve Perryman to me has also *looked* management material, but will he make it? Perhaps in 1999 someone will do another book about Spurs and tell us all what happened to today's stars . . .

P.S. As the 1984-85 season ended, a new player arrived from Newcastle United, yet another exciting and expensive newcomer to keep all the fans interested — Chris Waddle. He won't be playing, till the 1985-86 season, but he kindly agreed to fill in my little questionnaire and so has been included in the various tables.

Index

341